New York Common Council

A Compilation of the Ferry Leases and Railroad Grants

Made by the Corporation of the City of New York, from July 1, 1849

New York Common Council

A Compilation of the Ferry Leases and Railroad Grants
Made by the Corporation of the City of New York, from July 1, 1849

ISBN/EAN: 9783744729420

Printed in Europe, USA, Canada, Australia, Japan

Cover: Foto ©ninafisch / pixelio.de

More available books at **www.hansebooks.com**

A COMPILATION

OF THE

Ferry Leases and Railroad Grants

MADE BY THE

CORPORATION OF THE CITY OF NEW YORK,

From July 1, 1849, to July 1, 1860;

TOGETHER WITH THE

VARIOUS ORDINANCES, RESOLUTIONS, &c., PASSED BY THE COMMON COUNCIL,

RELATIVE TO OR AFFECTING THE SAME

Published by Order of the Common Council.

BY THE CLERK OF THE BOARD OF COUNCILMEN.

DOCUMENT No. **13.**

NEW YORK:
EDMUND JONES & CO., PRINTERS TO BOARD OF COUNCILMEN,
No. 26 JOHN STREET.
1860.

PREFACE.

In the compiling of this work, under the authority and by the direction of the Common Council, the undersigned has taken extraordinary pains, and devoted much time and labor for the purpose of furnishing a *text-book*, in relation to all matters concerning the FERRIES AND RAILROADS around and in the city, that may be depended upon for its accuracy and be complete in its details.

The undoubted right of the Corporation of the city of New York to the exclusive power of granting privileges for ferries to be run from the shores of this island to those opposite thereto, seems to be so little understood, that many, even well-informed persons, have been inclined to doubt it, and some parties have gone so far as to contest it. The various charters of the city have, however, placed that fact beyond dispute, for in that known as the "Montgomerie Charter," of 1730, we find the 15th section containing a very specific and emphatic grant of the power to control all ferries that may be established "from the said Island of Manhattan's to any of the opposite shores all around the same Island," to "the Mayor, Aldermen and Commonalty of the said City of New York;" and we further find therein the express declaration, that "*No other person or persons whomsoever*, without the consent, grant, or license of the said Common Council of the said City," shall have any control over the Ferries, or possess any power in regard to them.

The portion of section 15 of the Montgomerie Charter, referred to, reads as follows :

* * * * * * * * * * *

"*And we do further*, for us, our heirs and successors, give
"grant, and confirm, unto the Mayor, Aldermen, and Common-
"alty of the said City of New York, and their successors, for-
"ever, that the Common Council of the said city, for the time
"being, or the major part of them (but no other person or
"persons whomsoever, without the consent, grant or license of
"the said Common Council of the said city, for the time being,
"or the major part of them), from time to time, and at all times
"hereafter, shall, and may have the sole, full and whole power
"and authority of settling, appointing, establishing, ordering
"and directing, and shall and may settle, appoint, establish
"and direct, such and so many ferries, around Manhattan's
"Island, alias New York Island, for the carrying and trans-
"porting people, horses, cattle, goods and chattels from the
"said Island of Manhattan's to Nassau Island, and from thence
"back to Manhattan's ; and also from the said Island of Man-
"hattan's to any of the opposite shores all around the same
"Island, in such and so many places as the said Common
"Council, or the major part of them, shall think fit ; who have
"hereby, likewise, full power to let, set or otherwise dispose
"of, all or any of such ferries, to any person or persons whom-
"soever ; and the rents, issues, profits, ferriages, fees and
"other advantages arising and accruing from all and every
"such ferries ; we do hereby fully and freely, for us, our heirs
"and successors, give and grant unto the Mayor, Aldermen
"and Commonalty of the City of New York, aforesaid, and
"their successors forever, to have, take, hold, and enjoy the
"same to their own use, without being accountable to us, our
"heirs or successors, for the same or any part thereof."

And again, in section 37 of the same charter, we find these

powers and grants referred to and confirmed in the following language :

"§ 37. *And we do,* by these presents, * * * grant, ratify, " and confirm unto the said Mayor, Aldermen, and Commonalty " of the city of New York, and their successors forever, * * " * * and the ferry and ferries on both sides of the East River, " and all other ferries now and hereafter to be erected and " established all around the Island of Manhattan's ; and the " management and rule of, and all fees, ferriages, and perqui- " sites to the same, or any part thereof, belonging or to belong; " and also the ferry-houses on Nassau Island, with the barns, " stables, pens or pounds, and lot of ground thereto belonging; " and also all the ground, soil, or land between high-water and " low-water mark, on the said Island of Nassau, from the east " side of the place called Wallabout to the west side of Red " Hook ; and also to make laws and rules for the governing " and well ordering of all the ferries now erected or estab- " lished, or hereafter to be erected or established, around the " said Island Manhattan's, and all the waste, vacant, unpat- " ented, and unappropriated land lying and being within the " said city of New York, and on Manhattan's Island aforesaid, " extending to low-water mark * * *."

Nothing could be more explicit than the grant now quoted; and all subsequent charters, whenever reference has been made therein to this subject, so far from lessening the powers thus conferred upon the corporate authority of New York city, have universally confirmed and strengthened them.

In the exercise of these powers in regard to the ferries, more general satisfaction has been given than in any other branch of legislation, and those who are ever seeking cause to cavil at the action of our City Legislature have but seldom been able to avail themselves of any apparent neglect of the city's interest in this direction.

The subject of various charters for projected railroads, to be constructed in the city, granted by the last Legislature, has given rise to much discussion as to the respective powers of the Common Council and of the State Legislature in matters affecting our city property and improvements.

That the public streets of the city are under the sole control of the Common Council, is beyond dispute, and no interference with them, without the consent of that body, can be legalized, under the present charter, by any action of the State Legislature ; the charters granted for the purposes of constructing railroads through the streets of New York (copies of which are inserted in this work) can, therefore, have no legal force or value until confirmed by the Common Council.

All which is respectfully submitted.

CHAS. T. McCLENACHAN.

NEW YORK, August 1, 1860

FERRIES
RUNNING FROM THE CITY OF NEW YORK
ON THE EAST RIVER.

FROM	TO	LEASED FROM	LEASE EXPIRES
Whitehall street	Staten Island	May 1, 1855.	May 1, 1865.
do	Hamilton avenue, Brooklyn	May 1, 1851.	May 1, 1861.
do	Atlantic street, Brooklyn	May 1, 1851.	May 1, 1861.
Wall street	Montague street, Brooklyn	July 1, 1852.	July 1, 1862.
Fulton street	Fulton street, Brooklyn	May 1, 1851.	May 1, 1861.
Peck slip	South Eighth street, Williamsburgh	May 1, 1859.	May 1, 1869.
Roosevelt street	South Seventh street, Williamsburgh	Oct. 1, 1852.	Oct. 1, 1867.
*James slip	Hunter's Point, L. I.	May 1, 1853.	May 1, 1863.
Catharine street	Main street, Brooklyn	May 1, 1853.	May 1, 1863.
Jackson street	Bridge street, Brooklyn	Feb. 1, 1858.	Feb. 1, 1868.
Grand street	Grand street, Williamsburgh	May 1, 1859.	May 1, 1869.
do	South Seventh street, Williamsburgh	No lease—	in litigation.
Houston street	Grand street, Williamsburgh	May 1, 1853.	May 1, 1863.
Tenth street	Greenpoint, L. I	No lease.	
Fourteenth street	Greenpoint, L. I	May 1, 1851.	May 1, 1865.
†Sixteenth street	Greenpoint, L. I	May 1, 1850.	May 1, 1860.
Twenty-third street	Greenpoint, L. I	Dec. 27, 1853.	Dec. 27, 1863.

* This Ferry has been created by changing the terminī of the Ferry leased to Hicks & Berry, from Pier No. 35, East River, to Williamsburgh.

† This Ferry has been discontinued; its New York terminus having been, by consent, transferred to the foot of Fourteenth street, East River.

FROM	TO	LEASED FROM	LEASE EXPIRES
Thirty-fourth street	Hunter's Point, L. I.	Aug. 1, 1857.	Aug. 1, 1867.
Horne's Hook (Eighty-sixth street)	Astoria	No writ'n lease.	

NORTH RIVER.

FROM	TO	LEASED FROM	LEASE EXPIRES
Cortlandt street	Jersey City	May 1, 1856.	May 1, 1866.
Barclay street	Hoboken	May 1, 1855.	May 1, 1865.
a Chambers street	Pavonia, N. J.	May 1, 1854.	May 1, 1864.
Hoboken street	Hoboken	May 1, 1852.	May 1, 1860.
Christopher street	Hoboken	May 1, 1852.	May 1, 1862.
Thirty-ninth street	Bull's Ferry	Aug. 1, 1852.	Aug. 1, 1862.
Forty-second street	Weehawken	Nov. 1, 1856.	Nov. 1, 1866.
Eighty-sixth street	Bull's Ferry	Completion of grade of 86th st	Ten years after establishment.

*There is no Ferry running to Pavonia, but the rent is regularly paid by the Erie Railroad Company.

FERRY FROM
WHITEHALL TO STATEN ISLAND.

THIS INDENTURE, made the 15th day of May, 1856, between the Mayor, Aldermen, and Commonalty of the city of New York, of the first part, and Jacob L. Smith, of the second part—witnesseth: Whereas, under and in pursuance of the 7th section of the act entitled "An act further to amend the Charter of the City of New York," passed April 12, 1853, the Comptroller of the city of New York caused previous notice to be given in the Corporation newspapers, printed and published in the city of New York, for thirty days preceding the day of sale, of his intention to sell, by public auction, all that certain ferry lease, from the slip at the foot of Whitehall street, East river, to Staten Island, for ten years, from the first day of May, 1855: and whereas, in pursuance of said last-mentioned notice, a ferry lease, from the slip at the foot of Whitehall street, East river, to Staten Island, was duly advertised to be sold to the highest bidder; and same having been, on the 15th day of May, 1855, set up to be sold by public auction in the city of New York, subject to certain conditions expressed in the terms of sale, and hereinafter particularly mentioned; and the said Jacob L. Smith, having bid the yearly rent of $5,100 for said premises, and no other person having bid so much, the said Jacob L. Smith was thereupon declared the highest bidder, and the the lessee of said premises, at said annual rent of $5,100, which said conditions are in the words and figures following, viz.:

This sale will embrace only the ferry slip between Pier No. 1, East river, now occupied by the United States, and the pier west of Pier No. 1, built for the purpose of a ferry to Staten Island, including the latter pier, except such portions of the surface of the pier on the west side thereof as may be required for the accommodation of a boat-house and landing-place for small boats from Governor's Island, and from public vessels of the United States and of foreign governments, according to a plan now under consideration in the Common Council; it being distinctly understood that this ferry grant is to confer no privilege to occupy any portion of the water on the west side of said pier, but that the same is reserved to be rented or used temporarily by the Corporation of the city of New York, until the same is otherwise disposed of by the Common Council in altering the line of the Battery wall, establishing a second ferry slip, or, until interfered with by the operations of the contractor in completing the wall of the Battery enlargement.

It is also to be understood that the ferry grant is not to interfere with Pier No. 1, by landing on it, but that the United States Government is to have the sole use of that pier according to the terms of their lease, and as the same has been occupied by them.

The lease to contain covenants for the usual ferry franchise from the foot of Whitehall street to the Quarantine Dock on Staten Island, or such convenient place as may be selected by the lessee, to be approved of by the Mayor and Common Council.

Also that the lessee will provide safe and convenient steam ferry-boats, adapted to the navigation between the city and island ; that suitable, convenient, and comfortable ferry-houses shall be erected and maintained during the term of the lease at the several ferry landings, for the shelter and accommodation of passengers ; that the docks and slips occupied by the lessee shall be kept in good repair and secure condition for the protection of passengers and property, with such other covenants as may be required by any act of the Common Council, provided the same be passed in time to have notice given at the auction sale.

Also, covenants on the part of the lessee that he will conduct and manage the said ferry agreeably to such rules, regulations, ordinances, or by-laws, as now are or may hereafter from time to time be made or passed by the Common Council or State Legislature.

The grant of this ferry is not to interfere with the right of the Corporation to grant other ferries to and from Staten Island, or to and from any other place.

Security for the faithful performance of all the covenants will be required, to be approved of by the Mayor and Comptroller.

Now, therefore, this indenture witnesseth, that the said parties of the first part, for and in consideration of the rents, covenants, premises, articles, and agreements hereinafter mentioned, reserved, and contained, on the part and behalf of the said party of the second part, his executors, administrators and assigns, to be paid, performed, observed, fulfilled, and kept, have granted, demised, and to farm let, and by these presents do grant, demise, and to farm let, unto the said party of the second part, his executors, administrators, and assigns, all that certain ferry, ferry-houses, pier, slip, and bulkhead west of Pier No. 1,

East river, with the appurtenances, situate, lying, and being in the first ward of the city of New York, at the foot of Whitehall street, lying westerly of Pier No. 1 : the said premises and bulkhead to be used for the accommodation of the ferry hereinafter mentioned; together with the right of ferrying and transporting passengers, horses, carriages, and freights to and from the same premises, and, by means thereof, to and from the dock on Staten Island now used as a landing-place for such purposes by the Staten Island Ferry Co., or such other convenient place as may be selected by the lessee, to be approved of by the Mayor and Common Council of the city of New York, and from thence back again to the said premises herein and hereby demised : and all that certain pier now used by the Staten Island Ferry Co. (except such portions of the surface of the pier on the west side thereof as may be required for the accommodation of a boat-house and landing-place for small boats from Governor's Island, and from public vessels of the United States and of foreign governments, according to a plan now under consideration in the Common Council : it being distinctly understood that this ferry grant is to confer no privilege to occupy any portion of the water on the west side of said pier, but that the same is reserved to be rented or used temporarily by the Corporation of the city of New York, or until the same is otherwise disposed of by the Common Council in altering the line of the Battery wall, establishing a second ferry slip, or until interfered with by the operations of the contractors in completing the wall of the Battery enlargement.

It is also expressly understood and agreed, that this ferry grant is not in any manner to interfere with Pier No. 1, by landing on it, but that the United States Government is to have the sole use of that pier, according to the terms of their lease, and as the same has been occupied by them ; to have and to hold the said above mentioned and described premises, with the appurtenances, unto the said party of the second part, his executors, administrators and assigns, from the 1st day of May, A. D. 1855, for and during and until the full end and term of ten years from thence next ensuing, and fully to be completed and ended, yielding and paying therefor, unto the said parties of the first part, their successors and assigns, yearly, and every year during the said term hereby granted, the annual rent or sum of $5,100, lawful money of the United States of America, payable quarterly on the usual days for the payment of rent in the city of New York, that is to say, one-fourth part on the first day of August, November, February, and May, in each and every year during said term.

Provided, and these presents and the premises hereby demised are upon this express condition, that if it should so happen that the said yearly rent above reserved, or any part thereof, should be behind or unpaid for the space of ten days after any of the days of payment on which the same, or any part thereof, ought to be paid, as aforesaid, or if default shall be made in the performance of any covenant herein contained, on the part and behalf of the said party of the second part, his executors, administrators and assigns, to be paid, kept, or performed, thence and from thenceforth, it shall and may be lawful for the said parties of the first part, their successors or assigns, into and upon the said demised premises, and every part thereof, wholly to re-enter, and the same to have again, repossess and enjoy, as in their first and former estate, in the manner prescribed by law, any thing hereinbefore contained to the contrary, in any wise, notwithstanding.

And the said party of the second part, for himself, his heirs, executors, administrators and assigns, doth covenant and agree to and with the said parties of the first part, their successors and assigns, by these presents, that he, the said party of the second part, his executors, administrators or assigns, shall and will, yearly, and every year during the said term hereby granted, well and truly pay, or cause to be paid, unto the said parties of the first part, their successors or assigns, the said yearly rent or sum of money hereinbefore mentioned, on the days and times above specified for the payment thereof, without any deduction, fraud, or delay, according to the true intent and meaning of these presents.

And the said party of the second part, for himself, his heirs, executors, administrators and assigns, doth covenant, promise and agree to and with the said parties of the first part, their successors and assigns, by these presents, that the said party of the second part, and his assigns, shall and will, during the said term hereby demised, at his and their own proper costs, charges and expenses, erect, keep and maintain, or cause to be erected, kept and maintained, suitable, comfortable and convenient ferry-houses during the term of this demise, at the several ferry landings, for the shelter and accommodation of passengers; and, also, that the said party of the second part shall and will keep in good repair and secure condition, for the protection of passengers and property, all the docks and slips occupied by the said party of the second part, during the term hereby granted; and, also, that the said party of the second part, for himself, his heirs, executors, administrators and assigns, doth covenant, promise and agree, to and with the said parties of the first part, their successors and assigns, by these presents, that he, the said party of the second part, and his assigns, shall and will, during the said term hereby demised, at his own proper costs, charges and expenses, find, furnish, provide and maintain, keep and navigate, upon the said ferry, from the foot of Whitehall street to Staten Island as aforesaid, such number of safe and comfortable steam ferry-boats, adapted to the navigation between the said city of New York and Staten Island, as the public convenience may require, and to be approved of by the Commissioners of the Sinking Fund, and keep the said steam ferry-boats, at all reasonable times, continually employed on the said ferry during the time hereby demised, and will run the same as frequently, on every day, as the public convenience may require.

And also, that the said party of the second part, and his assigns, shall and will, from time to time, and all times hereafter, during the said term, at his and their proper costs and charges, well and sufficiently repair, support, uphold, sustain, maintain, amend, and keep the premises herein and hereby demised, and shall furnish and keep furnished said steamboats, with all necessary and proper implements and machinery adapted to their respective kind, and be manned with a sufficient number of able-bodied men, skilled in water service, to manage the same ; and that the said men, so to be employed in all and each of the said boats, shall and will, at all times, be ready and willing to give their constant attendance at said ferry for the prompt, safe, expeditious, and convenient transportation of passengers and effects, horses and carriages, across the said ferry ; and further, that the said party of the second part, and his assigns, the said premises herein and hereby demised, and the pier, wharf, and bulkhead thereunto belonging, or in any wise appertaining to, being well and sufficiently repaired, supported or upheld, maintained, sustained, amended and kept, and every thing herein and hereby demised, with the appurtenances, at the end of the said term, or other sooner determination of these presents, shall and will peaceably and quietly leave, surrender, and yield up the said hereby demised premises, with the rights, privileges, and appurtenances thereunto belonging, in good order and condition, into the hands and possession of the said parties of the first part, their successors or assigns, without any compensation therefor, to the said party of the second part, or his assigns, without fraud or delay.

Provided always, and the premises hereby demised are upon this express condition, any thing hereinbefore contained to the contrary notwithstanding, that the said party of the second part, or his assigns, shall conduct and manage the said ferry agreeable to such rules, regulations, ordinances, or by-laws, as now are, or may hereafter, from time to time during the said term, by any by-law, ordinance, or resolution of the said parties of the first part, or their successors; or by any statute of this State, be made or passed in relation thereto.

And it is hereby further mutually covenanted and agreed by and between the parties to these presents, and these presents are upon the express condition, that nothing herein contained shall be taken or construed to operate as a covenant by the said parties of the first part, or their successors, for possession or quiet enjoyment by the party of the second part, or his successor or assigns, of the said ferry and right of ferriage, nor shall the same be taken or construed to interfere, in any manner, with any provisions, grants, or rights made by the said parties of the first part, of other premises, nor with the right to grant any future ferries to and from Staten Island, or to and from elsewhere wheresoever, nor, so far as regards the said ferry and demised premises, to operate further than to grant the possession of the estate, right, title, or interest, which the said parties of the first part may have or lawfully claim in the said ferry and right of ferriage, and the premises hereby demised, by virtue of their several charters, and the various acts of the Legislature of the people of the State of New York.

In witness, the said the Mayor and Clerk of the parties of the first part have, by virtue of a resolution of the said Corporation, hereunto set their hands and caused their corporate seal to be hereto affixed, and the party of the second part hath hereunto set his hand and seal, the day and year first above written.

JACOB L. SMITH. [L. S.]

Sealed and delivered in the presence of
 H. W. ROBINSON.

In consideration of one dollar to us in hand paid, we do hereby covenant and agree to and with the Mayor, Aldermen, and Commonalty of the city of New York, within named, and their successors, that if default shall at any time be made by the said Jacob L. Smith, in the payment of the rent and performance of the covenants and conditions in the foregoing lease, that we will pay the said rent, or any arrears thereof, that may remain due unto the said the Mayor, Aldermen, and Commonalty of the city of New York, and also, all damages arising from the nonperformance of any or all of the said covenants and conditions without notice of any such default.

Witness our hands and seals this 6th day of May, 1857.

VOR. D. LAUNAY. [L. S.]
J. C. THOMPSON. [L. S.]
W. J. STAPLEY. [L. S.]
F. E. GILBERT. [L. S.]

In presence of, as to all of sureties,

JAS. J. THOMSON.

HAMILTON AVENUE, SOUTH, AND FULTON FERRIES.

THIS INDENTURE, made the twenty-seventh day of December, in the year of our Lord one thousand eight hundred and fifty, between the Mayor, Aldermen, and Commonalty of the City of New York, of the first part, and Jacob R. Leroy and Henry E. Pierrepoint, of the City of Brooklyn, of the second part—

Witnesseth, That the said parties of the first part, for and in consideration of the rents, covenants and agreements hereinafter contained, on the part and behalf of the said parties of the second part, their executors, administrators and assigns, well and truly to be paid, observed, performed and kept, according to the true intent and meaning of these presents, have granted, demised and to farm letten, and by these presents, do grant, demise, and to farm let, unto the said parties of the second part, their executors, administrators and assigns, all those three certain ferries ; the one thereof established from the foot of Fulton street, in the city of New York, across the East River, to the foot of Fulton street, in the city of Brooklyn, and commonly called or known by the name of " The Fulton Ferry ;" the other thereof established from the foot of Whitehall street, in the said city of New York, across the said river, to the foot of Atlantic street, in the said city of Brooklyn, and commmnonly called and known by the name of " The South Ferry ;" and the other thereof, established from the foot of Whitehall street, in the said city of New York, across the said river, to the foot of Hamilton avenue, in the said city of Brooklyn, and commonly called and known as " The Hamilton Avenue Ferry;" together with all and singular the ferriage and right of ferriage, fees, perquisites, benefits, profits and advantages whatsoever, to the said ferries respectively belonging, or to arise or accrue from the same, and all and singular the bulkheads, wharves, premises, piers and slips, now used and occupied by the said ferries respectively, in the cities of New York and Brooklyn, together with all the fixtures connected with the slips and ferry houses.

To have and to hold, the said ferries respectively, with all and singular the floats, bridges, fixtures, and appurtenances whatsoever, thereunto in any manner belonging, or which now are appropriated to or used by the said ferries respectively, so far as the said parties of the first part have or shall have at the commencement of the term hereby demised, any right or interest in and to the same, unto the the said parties of the second part, their executors, administrators, and assigns, from the first day of May, one thousand eight hundred and fifty-one, for and during, and until the full end and term of ten years, thence next ensuing, and fully to be complete and ended. Yielding and paying therefor, unto the said parties of the first part, their successors or assigns, yearly and every year during the said term, the yearly rent or sum of thirty-five thousand dollars, lawful money of the United States of America, in equal quarter-yearly payments; to wit, on the first days of August, November, February, and May, in each and every of the said years.

Provided always, and these presents are upon this express condition, that if it should so happen that the said yearly rent above reserved, or any part thereof, shall be behind or unpaid for the space of ten days after any day of payment, on which the same or any part thereof ought to be paid as aforesaid; or if the said parties of the second part, their executors, administrators, or assigns, shall neglect to pay, fulfill, perform and keep, any or either of the payments, articles, covenants, claims, agreements, matters and things herein contained, which on their part are to be paid, performed, fulfilled and kept, during the said term, according to the true intent and meaning of these presents; then and in every such case it shall and may be lawful to and for the said parties of the first part, their successors and assigns, to enter into and upon the premises hereby demised, and to have, possess and enjoy the same, as fully as though these presents had not been made, anything herein contained to the contrary notwithstanding.

And the said parties of the second part, for themselves, their heirs, executors, administrators, and assigns, do covenant, promise and agree, to and with the said parties of the first part, their successors, and assigns, in manner following: that is to say, that the said parties of the second part, their executors and assigns, shall and will, yearly and every year during the said term hereby demised, well and truly pay unto the said parties of the first part, their successors or assigns, the said yearly rent above reserved, on the days and in the manner limited and prescribed as aforesaid. And also that the said parties of the second part, their executors, administrators or assigns, shall and will, for and during the term for which the said premises are hereby granted, at their own proper cost and expense, provide, furnish, navigate, and use, three good substantial steam ferry boats on the said Fulton Ferry, two good substantial steam ferry boats on the said South Ferry, and two good substantial steam ferry boats on the said Hamilton Avenue Ferry, to be approved by the Committees on Ferries of the said parties of the first part, and the Mayor of the city of New York; and that the said boats shall, at all times thereafter, be exclusively employed upon the said ferries respectively, during the said term, to carry, transport and convey carriages, horses, passengers, and effects, across the same with safety, convenience and expedition.

And, that the said boats shall always, during the said term, be kept in good repair, and furnished with all necessary and proper implements and machinery, and be manned with a sufficient number of able-bodied and skillful men, to manage the same; and who shall and will, at all times, be ready and willing to give their constant and ready attendance at the said ferries respectively, for the prompt and convenient transportation of passengers, horses, carriages, and effects, across the same, and shall and will, in all things, conduct and manage the said ferries respectively, in conformity with all acts of the Legislature of the State of New York, and agreeably to such rules, regulations and restrictions, whether as to the time of departure of said boats, from each end of said ferries respectively, the time of starting the same on the morning of each day, or of laying up the same at night, or of running the same during the night, or otherwise, as from time to time during the said term shall, by the said Committees on Ferries, with the Mayor, or by any ordinance or resolution of the said parties of the first part, or their successors, be made or passed in relation thereto, and shall and will, under the direction of the said Ferry Committees and Mayor, build, erect, make and furnish, all the fixtures and other improvements necessary for the well conducting of the said ferries, during the said term, and will well and sufficiently maintain, uphold, and keep the same, and the present bulkheads and fixtures now used for the said ferries, in good repair, at their own proper costs and charges; and shall and will purchase, receive, and take, from the late lessees of said three ferries respectively, all the boats and other property which the said parties of the first part are bound to purchase, take, and receive, at the expiration of their lease, and to pay therefor, in the same manner as the said parties of the first part are required to do, and shall not, and will not, during the said term, raise the rates of commutation above the present prices, as appears by the schedule thereof hereunto annexed, and shall not and will not assign, or transfer this present lease, or any term therein, or the said demised premises, or any part thereof, without the consent in writing of the said parties of the first part first had and obtained.

And, it is hereby expressly understood and agreed, that nothing contained in these presents shall prevent the establishing of any other ferry or ferries across the said East River, previous to the expiration of the said term hereby granted. *And also*, that at the expiration of the said term hereby demised, the said parties of the second part, their executors, administrators or assigns, shall and will (in case the said ferries be not re-demised, or this lease renewed or extended to the said parties of the second part, their executors, administrators, or assigns), peaceably and quietly leave, surrender and yield up the said ferries, and everything hereby demised, in good order and condition, into the hands and possession of the said parties of the first part, their successors and assigns; *And*, that at the expiration of the said term, the parties of the first part, or their successors, shall purchase and take from the said parties of the second part, their executors, administrators, or assigns, all the steam ferry boats, to be furnished and procured for the said ferries respectively, by the said parties of the second part, as hereinbefore mentioned, and actually in use thereon, not exceeding the number in possession of the late lessees at the expiration of their lease, at such price or value as may be fixed by two indifferent appraisers, to be chosen by the parties mutually, or by an umpire to be appointed by such appraisers, to decide between them, in case of their disagreement.

And the said parties of the second part, for themselves, their executors, and administrators, do hereby covenant and agree, to and with the said parties of the first part, and their successors: *First*, That the Mayor of the City of New York, and the Chairman of the Committee on Ferries, of each Board of the Common Council of the said city shall be, *ex-officio*, members of the Board of Managers, and shall be notified of the meetings of said Board, and be entitled to vote at such meetings. *Second*, That the said lessees shall, whenever required by resolution of the Common Council of the city of New York, remove, at their own expense, said ferry, ferry-house and fixtures, from *Fulton street*, its present landing, to *Burling slip*, in said city. *Third*, That said lessees, if required by resolution of the Common Council of the city of New York, shall remove or extend into the slips or basins occupied by them in the city of New York, their ferry-houses and fixtures, to such extent as may be required by said Common Council. *Fourth*, That should said parties of the second part, at any time hereafter, or during the tenure of this lease, attempt to establish, or establish or run any ferry or ferries between said city of New York and Brooklyn, under any state law, or under any license granted by any commissioners appointed, or by virtue of such law, in violation of the chartered ferry franchise of the city of New York; then, and in such case, said parties of the second part shall forfeit this lease, and it shall be competent for the parties of the first part to take possession of and lease the same to other parties.

IN WITNESS WHEREOF, to one part of these presents, remaining with the said parties of the first part, the said parties of the second part have set their hands and seals; and to the other part thereof, remaining with the said parties of the second part, the said parties of the first part have caused the common seal of the said city to be affixed, the day and year first above written.

Sealed and delivered in the presence of
    GEO. L. TAYLOR.

                JACOB R. LE ROY,   [L. S.]
                HENRY E. PIERREPONT. [L. S.]

City and County of New York, ss.:

On the 13th day of February, in the year one thousand eight hundred and fifty-one, before me personally came

Jacob R. Le Roy and Henry E. Pierrepont, known to me to be the individuals described in, and who executed the within conveyance, and severally acknowledged to me that they executed the same for the purposes therein mentioned.

GEO. L. TAYLOR,
Commissioner of Deeds.

The Mayor, Aldermen, and Commonalty hereby give permission for the transfer of this lease to the Union Ferry Company of Brooklyn.

COMPTROLLER'S OFFICE, }   A. C. FLAGG,
New York, Nov. 14, 1854. }   *Comptroller.*

Resolved, That the Union Ferry Company be, and they are hereby, directed to commute with passengers, as heretofore; and in case of the refusal of said company so to do, the Counsel to the Corporation be, and he is, authorized and directed, within ten days after the passage of this resolution, to take the necessary legal measures to carry the same into effect, if, in his opinion, the conditions of their lease have been violated.

Adopted by the Board of Aldermen, December 29, 1856.

Adopted by the Board of Councilmen, December 31, 1856.

Received from his Honor, the Mayor, January 5, 1857, without his approval or objections thereto; therefore under the provisions of the amended Charter, the same became adopted.

SCHEDULE.

RATES OF COMMUTATION.

Foot passengers,   Gentlemen........$10 00 per annum.
Foot passengers,   Ladies .... 5 00 per annum.
Foot passengers,   Boys, 15 years old.. 6 00 per annum.
Foot passengers,   Boys, 12 years old
                   and under...... 5 00 per annum.
Foot passengers,   Girls, 12 years old
                   and under...... 4 00 per annum.
Carriages,   A two-horse carriage 20 00 per annum.
Carriages   A one-horse carriage 15 00 per annum.
Carts,   Commutation tickets 10 00 pr hundred.
If any person shall purchase 500 tickets, they shall be $8 00.
Milk wagons......................$40 00 per annum.

FERRY FROM

WALL STREET TO BROOKLYN.

THIS INDENTURE, made the 1st day of July, 1852, between the Mayor, Aldermen, and Commonalty of the city of New York, parties of the first part, and Jacob Sharp, party of the second part—

Whereas, on the 16th day of June, in the year of our Lord one thousand eight hundred and fifty-two, a certain resolution was adopted by the Common Council of the city of New York, which said resolution was in the words and figures following, to wit: "*Resolved*, That a lease of the slip at the foot of Wall street, in the city of New York, or so much thereof as belongs to the Corporation, together with the northerly side of Pier (15) fifteen, and also, a ferry lease with the privilege to establish and run a ferry from the foot of Joralemon street, or some convenient point adjacent thereto, in the city of Brooklyn, be granted to Jacob Sharp, for the term of ten years, at an annual rent of $20,000, with power to regulate the same from time to time by the Common Council, said rent to be paid quarterly, on the usual quarter days, and to commence fifteen months after the execution of the lease, the said lease to contain the usual covenants contained in ferry leases; and, unless said ferry shall be put in operation within fifteen months from its execution, the said lease shall be cancelled, and further, that said lessee shall only be required to pay the rent for said slip at the rate now received therefor by the Corporation, until the said fifteen months expire."

Now, this indenture witnesseth, that the said parties of the first part, for and in consideration of the rents, covenants, provisions, articles and agreements, hereinafter mentioned, on the part and behalf of the said party of the second part, his executors, administrators and assigns, to be had, performed, observed, fulfilled and kept, have granted, demised, and to farm letten, and by these presents do grant, demise, and to farm let, unto the said party of the second part, his executors, administrators and assigns, the slip at the foot of Wall street, in the city of New York, or so much thereof as belongs to the said parties of the first part, together with the northerly side of the pier known as number fifteen (15) East river, and also all that certain ferry to be established and located as hereinafter provided, at and from the foot of Wall street, aforesaid, to the foot of Joralemon street, or some convenient point adjacent thereto, in the city of Brooklyn, with the privilege of running steamboats thereon, and with all and singular the ferriage fees, perquisites, rents, issues, profits, benefits and advantages whatsoever, which may arise or accrue from the said ferry.

To have and to hold the said part of pier number fifteen (15), and the said slip, or so much thereof, as belongs to the said parties of the first part, and also the said ferry, with the appurtenance, unto the said party of the second part, his executors, administrators and assigns, as hereinafter covenanted and agreed, for and during and until the full end and term of ten years from thence next ensuing, and fully to be complete and ended, yielding and paying therefor yearly, and every year during the said term, the annual rent or sum of twenty thousand dollars ($20,000), lawful money of the United States of America, in quarter-yearly payments, on the usual quarter days for the payment of rent in the said city of New York, that is to say: one-fourth part thereof on the first days of August, November, February and May, in each and every year during the said term ; the first payment to be made on the first quarter day after the establishment of said ferry: provided always, that if it should so happen that the said yearly rent, or any part thereof, shall be behind and unpaid for the space of ten days after any day of payment on which the same ought to be paid as aforesaid, or if the said party of the second part, his executors, administrators or assigns, shall neglect, or omit to pay, perform, fulfill, observe and keep any or either of the payments, articles, covenants, clauses, agreements, provisions, matters or things herein contained, which, on the part and behalf of the said party of the second part, his executors, administrators or assigns, are to be paid, performed, observed, fulfilled and kept, during the said term of ten years, according to the true intent and meaning of these presents, that then, and in every and in all such case or cases, it shall and may be lawful for the said parties of the first part, their successors or assigns, to enter into and upon the premises hereby demised, and to have, possess and enjoy the same again as fully as though these presents had never been made, anything herein contained to the contrary notwithstanding.

And the said party of the second part, for himself, his heirs, executors, administrators and assigns, doth covenant and agree to and with the said parties of the first part, their successors and assigns, by these presents, in manner following, that is to say :

That the said party of the second part, his executors, administrators and assigns, shall and will, yearly and every year during the said term hereby demised, well and truly pay unto the said parties of the first part, their successors or assigns, the said yearly rent sum of money hereinbefore mentioned, at the days and times above specified for the payment thereof, without fraud or delay, except that, during the period of fifteen months from the execution of this indenture, within which time the said party of the second part is required to have said ferry in operation, as herein after particularly stipulated, covenanted and agreed, the said party of the second part shall only be required to pay the rent for said slip at the rate now received therefor by the parties of the first part, which the said party of the second part hereby covenants and agrees well and truly to pay to the said parties of the first part; and the said party of the second part, for himself, his heirs, executors. administrators and assigns, doth covenant and agree to and with the said parties of the first part, their successors and assigns, that he, the said party of the second part, shall and will, at his own proper costs, charges and expenses, furnish, provide and navigate upon the said ferry to and from the foot of Wall street to Joralemon street, or a point near thereto, aforesaid, good and substantial steam ferry-boats, and keep the said steam ferry-boats at all reasonable times continually employed in the said ferry during the term hereby granted; and, also, that he will, whenever thereunto required by the said parties of the first part, at his own proper costs, charges and expenses, provide and navigate upon the said ferry such and so many additional good and substantial steam ferry-boats as may be required by the said parties of the first part, which said ferry-boats shall be approved by the Street Commissioner of the city of New York, and shall be used to carry, transport and convey carriages, horses, passengers and effects upon the said ferry, and that the said steamboats shall always during the said term be kept in good repair and furnished with all necessary and proper implements and machinery adapted to their respective kind, and be manned with a sufficient number of able-bodied men, skilled in water service, to manage the same, and that the said men so to be employed on all and each of the said boats shall and will at all times be ready and willing to give their constant attendance at the said ferry, for the prompt and convenient transportation of passengers and effects, horses and carriages, across the said ferry; and, also, that he, the said party of the second part, his executors, administrators and assigns, shall conduct and manage the said ferry agreeably to such rules, regulations, rates of ferriage, times of running, and restrictions, as from time to time during the said term shall, by any by-law, ordinance, order, or resolution of the said parties of the first part, or their successors, in Common Council convened, be made or passed in relation to the said ferry.

And, also, that he, the said party of the second part, his executors, administrators, or assigns, shall and will, at his or their own proper costs, charges, and expenses, build, erect, make, and finish, or cause to be built, erected, made, and finished, such improvements as may be necessary for the accommodation of such ferry, and at all times during the said term, hereby demised, well and sufficiently repair, uphold, sustain, amend, maintain, and keep, all and singular the floats, racks, fenders, bridges, and other ferry fixtures, at each landing place of the said ferry, and shall and will, also, keep in repair the piers adjoining, or which may be made or built adjoining both slips used for the said ferry, both at Brooklyn and New York, or such parts or proportions of said piers as may belong to the said parties of the first part.

And, also, that the said party of the second part, his executors, administrators or assigns, shall and will, at the expiration of the said term, hereby demised, peaceably and quietly leave, surrender and yield up the said ferry and other hereby demised premises, and the piers, in good order and condition, into the hands and possession of the said parties of the first part, their successors or assigns.

And, also, that the said party of the second part, his executors, administrators and assigns, shall not nor will, during the said term, transfer, assign or set over, let or underlet, or in any other manner convey, during this present lease, or any part thereof, or their estate or interest therein, or in or to the above demised premises, or any part of the same, without the leave or consent of the said parties of the first part, their successors or assigns, in writing, first had and obtained.

And it is hereby mutually agreed and understood, by and between the parties to these presents, that unless the said ferry shall be put into operation, according to the terms and requirements of this indenture, within fifteen months after the execution hereof, then and in that case this said indenture, and every article, clause and thing herein contained, shall be and become, from that date, of no effect.

And it is hereby mutually covenanted and agreed by and between the parties to these presents, and these presents are upon the express understanding, that nothing herein contained shall be taken or construed to operate as a covenant, by the said parties of the first part, or their successors, for possession or quiet enjoyment by the said parties of the second part, his executor, administrator or assigns, of the said ferry, or right of ferriage, nor shall the same be taken or construed to interfere in any manner with any previous grants or rights made by the said parties of the first part, nor with the right to grant any future ferries to and from the city of Brooklyn, or to and from elsewhere wheresoever, nor to operate further than to grant the possession of the estate, right, title, or interest, which the said parties of the first part may have or lawfully claim in the said ferry and right of ferriage hereby demised, by virtue of their several charters, and the various acts of the Legislature of the people of the State of New York.

In witness whereof, to one part of these presents, remaining with the said parties of the first part, the said party of the second part hath set his hand and seal; and to the other part thereof, remaining with the said party of the second part, the said parties of the first part have caused the common seal of the city of New York to be affixed, this day and year first above written.

JACOB SHARP, [L. S.]

In the presence of
  GEO. L. TAYLOR.

City and County of New York, ss.:

On this 28th day of August, one thousand eight hundred and fifty-two, before me came Jacob Sharp, to me known to be the same person described in, and who executed the foregoing indenture of ferry lease, and acknowledged that he executed the same for the purposes therein mentioned.

GEO. L. TAYLOR,
Com'r of Deeds.

COMPTROLLER'S OFFICE,
New York, Sept. 16, 1852.

The Mayor, Aldermen, and Commonalty of the city of New York hereby give permission to the transfer of one undivided half of this lease to Freeman Campbell and Rutherford Moody.

JOS. R. TAYLOR,
Comptroller.

Resolved, That the rent of the Wall street Ferry be, and the same is hereby, reduced to five thousand dollars a year, and that an instrument to that effect be executed by the proper officers.

Adopted by the Board of Assistants, Oct. 5, 1853.

Adopted by the Board of Aldermen, Oct. 21, 1853.

Received from his Honor the Mayor, Nov. 15, 1853, without his approval or objections thereto; therefore, under the provisions of the amended charter, the same became adopted.

NOTE.—It was mutually agreed that the lease should terminate on May 1st, 1861, and the lease was sold in connection with those of the Hamilton avenue, South, Fulton, and Catharine street Ferries, as will appear on reference to page 61.

FERRY FROM

PECK SLIP TO WILLIAMSBURGH.

THIS INDENTURE, made the 20th day of April, A.D. 1859, between the Mayor, Aldermen, and Commonalty of the city of New York, of the first part, and Jeremiah V. Meserole, Fleming Duncan, Gerrit Smith, Wm. R. Painter, John O'Donohue, Francis Dubois, and Loftus Wood (of the counties of New York and Kings), in the State of New York, parties of the second part—

Witnesseth, That the said parties of the first part, for and in consideration of the rents, covenants, and agreements hereinafter mentioned and contained, on the part of the said parties of the second part, their executors, administrators and assigns, well and truly to be paid, observed and performed, fulfilled and kept, according to the true intent and meaning of these presents, have granted, demised and to farm let, and by these presents do grant, demise and farm to let, unto the said parties of the second part, and their executors, administrators and assigns, all that ferry established from the northerly basin at Peck slip, in the city of New York, now used for a ferry over and across the said East river, to the foot of South Seventh street, in the city of Brooklyn (E. D.), late town of Wiliamsburgh, or to some landing or place in said city of Brooklyn (E. D.) aforesaid, adjacent to the foot of said South Seventh street; with all and singular the rights, privileges and advantages thereof, belonging to the said parties of the first part.

To have and to hold the same unto the said parties of the second part, their executors, administrators and assigns, for and during, and until the full end and term of ten years from and after the first day of May, in the year of our Lord one thousand eight hundred and fifty-nine, yielding and paying therefor yearly, and every year, during the said term, the yearly rent of twenty-one thousand dollars, in quarter-yearly payments, on the usual days of payment, to wit: on the first days of August, November, February and May, in each and every year, during the term hereby demised.

And the said parties of the second part, for themselves, their executors, administrators and assigns, do covenant and agree to and with the said parties of the first part, their successors and assigns, that they, the said parties of the second part, their executors, administrators and assigns, shall and will well and truly pay, or cause to be paid, unto the said parties of the first part, their successors and assigns, the said yearly rent above reserved, at the several times above limited and appointed for the payment thereof; and also, that they, the said parties of the second part, their executors, administrators or assigns, shall and will from the first day of May next, at their own proper costs and expenses, furnish, provide, and navigate on said ferry from Peck slip aforesaid, to the foot of South Seventh street, or some point adjacent thereto, as aforesaid, three good, swift, and substantial single-keeled steamboats; that the said steam ferry-boats shall not be less than one hundred and thirty feet in length, and of corresponding dimensions.

And, also, that they, the said parties of the second part, shall and will, on or before the first day of August, one thousand eight hundred and fifty-nine, furnish, provide and navigate upon the said ferry from Peck slip aforesaid, to the foot of South Seventh street aforesaid, or some point adjacent thereto, three new, swift, good, and substantial single-keeled steamboats, which shall be provided and furnished in a style equal to that of the boat called the "Exchange," now employed upon the Wall Street Ferry.

And each of said boats so to be provided and navigated on and after the first of May, one thousand eight hundred and fifty-nine, and each of said new boats to be provided and navigated on and after the first of August, one thousand eight hundred and fifty-nine, shall have attached to the engine a fire apparatus or force-pump, with not less than four hundred feet of hose, of the same quality and dimensions as that used by the Fire Department of the city of New York, which fire apparatus or force-pump shall be used for the extinguishment of fires whenever required by the Chief Engineer of the Fire Department of the city of New York, or his Assistants, for which services the parties of the second part shall be entitled to, and shall receive from the parties of the first part, the sum of twenty dollars per hour for each hour engaged, but no time shall be counted less than one hour.

And said ferry-boats shall, in all respects, be such as

shall be approved by the Comptroller of the said parties of the first part.

And the said parties of the second part shall and will further keep the said steam ferry-boats employed on said ferry in such manner and at such times as the public accommodation shall require, and as shall be directed by the said Comptroller of the said parties of the first part, and shall and will, at all times, cause one or other of said boats to leave each of the said landings as often as is hereinafter mentioned, viz.: once in every ten minutes, beginning one hour before sunrise and continuing until one hour after sunset, and once in every half-hour from one hour after sunset until one hour before sunrise, or as fast as the passengers and freights can be discharged from the said steam ferry boats.

And the said steamboats shall always, during the said term, be furnished and manned with a sufficient number of able-bodied men, skilled in water service, to sail and manage the same; and that the men so to be employed, in all and every of said boats, shall, at all reasonable times, be ready and willing to give their ready and constant attendance at the said ferry, for the prompt and convenient transportation of horses, carriages, passengers, and effects across the said river; and that the said parties of the second part, their executors, administrators, and assigns, shall not ask demand, or receive any higher or greater toll, fare, or rate of ferriage, or any higher or greater commutation for passengers, carriages, horses, or effects, than such as is specified in the schedule of rates of ferriage which is hereunto annexed.

And that the said parties of the second part, their executors, administrators, or assigns, shall and will, at their own proper costs and charges, provide good and sufficient bridges, floats, ferry accommodations, and fixtures at each landing-place of the said ferry, to the extent the same may be required or necessary; and that the said parties of the second part, their executors, administrators, or assigns, shall and will, at their own proper costs and charges, at all times during the term hereby demised, well and sufficiently uphold, maintain, and keep in good and substantial repair, all such necessary bridges, floats, ferry accommodations, and fixtures as aforesaid.

And it is hereby further understood that the parties of the first part furnish only for the use of the Peck slip ferry the northerly basin at Peck slip, now in use for said ferry, and that the parties of the second part are to provide themselves with the necessary landing-place at or near South Seventh street, Brooklyn (E. D.), and with all the docks, ferry-houses, floats, fixtures, and other appurtenances for the faithful and proper conducting of said ferry; and also that, at the expiration or sooner determination of the said terms hereby demised, the said parties of the second part, their executors, administrators, or assigns, shall and will peaceably and quietly leave, surrender, and yield up the said ferries, and every thing hereby demised, together with the bulkheads, piers, floats, bridges, and other fixtures, ferry accommodations, and improvements which may have been erected, made, or furnished by either of said parties for the use of the said ferries, in good order and condition, into the possession of the said parties of the first part, their successors or assigns, without fraud or delay; and nothing herein contained shall be construed to impair the right of them, the said parties of the second part, their executors, administrators, or assigns, of, in and to the docks, floats, ferry-houses, and other appurtenances erected or to be erected by the parties of the second part at the foot of South Seventh street, Brooklyn (E. D.), or other place of landing adjacent thereto in Brooklyn (E. D.) aforesaid; or of, in or to the floats, ferry-houses, and appurtenances built or to be built, by the parties of the second part, at, upon, or in the northerly basin of Peck slip aforesaid; but it is expressly understood and agreed that, at the determination of this lease, the said parties of the second part, their executors, administrators, or assigns, are to have the right, within ten days thereafter, to remove and take away said ferry-houses, floats, and appurtenances so to be erected upon or in the northerly basin of Peck slip aforesaid, and to have, possess, and enjoy, in their own right and as their own property, all the floats, bridges, docks, and ferry-houses which may be provided or erected by them, the said parties of the second part, at the foot of South Seventh street, or other point of landing adjacent thereto.

And also, that the said parties of the second part, their executors, administrators, and assigns, shall not, nor will, during the said term, assign, transfer, set over, mortgage, encumber, underlet, or in any other manner, convey this present lease, or any part of the same, without the leave or consent of the said parties of the first part, their successors or assigns, in writing, first had and obtained.

And also, that the said parties of the second part, their executors, administrators, and assigns, shall, at all times during the said term, conduct and manage the said ferry agreeably to such rules, regulations, rates of ferriage, times of running, and restrictions, as now are, or may, from time to time, hereafter, during the said term, by any by-law, ordinance, or resolution of the said parties of the first part, or their successors, be made or passed in relation thereto.

Provided always, nevertheless, and these presents are upon this express condition, that if the said yearly rent, or any part thereof, shall be behind and unpaid, for the space of ten days after any day of payment, on which the same ought to be paid, as aforesaid, or if the said parties of the second part, their executors, administrators or assigns, shall neglect to perform, fulfill, and keep any or either of the articles, clauses, or agreements herein contained, which are, on their part, to be performed, fulfilled, and kept, according to the true intent and meaning of these presents, then, and in such case, it shall be lawful for the said parties of the first part, their successors or assigns, to declare, in writing, to the said parties of the second part, their executors, administrators, and assigns, that these presents, and the estate hereby created, shall be null and void; in which case, every clause, article, or thing herein contained, shall be thenceforth null and void.

In witness whereof, to one part of these presents, remaining with the said parties of the first part, the said parties of the second part have set their several hands and seals; and to the other part of these presents, remaining with the said parties of the second part, the said parties of the first part have caused their common seal to be affixed, the day and year first above written.

J. V. MESEROLE. [L. S.]
F. DUNCAN. [L. S.]
GERRIT SMITH. [L. S.]
W. R. PAINTER. [L. S.]
JOHN O'DONOHUE. [L. S.]
FRANCIS DUBOIS. [L. S.]
LOFTUS WOOD. [L. S.]

Sealed and delivered in presence of
  JAMES SANDFORD.

City and County of New York, ss.:

On the 20th day of April, A. D. 1859, before me personally came J. V. Meserole, F. Duncan, W. R. Painter, J. O'Donohue, and F. Dubois, and on the 21st day of April, A. D. 1859, before me personally came Gerrit Smith and Loftus Wood, all of whom were known to me to be the individuals described in, and who executed the foregoing lease, and severally acknowledged to me that they executed the same.

JAMES SANDFORD,
Commissioner of Deeds.

ABM. MESEROLE,
JOHN O'DONOHUE, } *Securities.*   ($42,000.)

SCHEDULE *of the rates of ferriage referred to in the foregoing lease:*

For foot passengers	04
Commutation of foot passengers per year	$10 00
For man and horse	12
One-horse pleasure carriage and two persons	25
Gig or sulky	25
Two-horse pleasure carriage with four persons	37
One-horse wagon, loaded	25
One-horse wagon, light	18
Two-horse wagon, loaded	37
Two-horse wagon, light	25
Two-horse wagon, hay or straw	50
Every steer, ox, or cow	12
Every score of sheep or hogs	75
Every calf	03
Every dead hog, weighing 100 lbs. or under	06

Every dead hog, weighing over 100 lbs.	08
Every 100 lbs. iron, butter, cheese, &c.	04
Every barrel cider, liquors, or pork	06
Every milk wagon, one horse, commutation pr. month	4 00
Every barrel of flour	04
Commutation for foot passengers for six months	5 00

All other articles not enumerated, in proportion, at the above rates.

NEW YORK, April 20, 1859.

The following preamble and resolutions passed the Common Council in reference to the sale of leases of the ferries from Grand street and Peck slip to Williamsburgh;

Whereas, The 15th section of the Montgomery Charter gives, grants, and confirms unto the Mayor, Aldermen, and Commonalty of the City of New York and their successors forever, that the Common Council of the said city (but no other person or persons whomsoever, without the consent of the Common Council), from time to time, and at all times thereafter, shall and may have the sole, full, and whole power and authority of establishing, directing, &c., such and so many ferries from Manhattan Island to any of the opposite shores, as the Common Council shall think fit, and likewise full power to let, set, or dispose of all or any of such ferries, and

Whereas, The said 15th section of the Montgomery Charter is the basis upon which all ferries are leased, and never has been repealed or amended so as to deprive the Common Council of the aforesaid authority and right, but on the contrary is continued and remains in full force; and inasmuch as no authority exists in the Commissioners of the

Sinking Fund, or any officer or body other than the Common Council, of their own motion to order or execute any ferry lease, but that the authority, sanction, and approval of the Common Council is required, to order such lease, the execution of which must be by the Mayor and Clerk of the Common Council, under their hands and the seal of the city; and

Whereas The ferry from the foot of Grand street, New York, to the foot of Grand street, Brooklyn, East District, as also the ferry from the northerly basin at Peck slip, New York, to the foot of South Seventh street, Brooklyn, East District, were let by the Comptroller under the sanction or authority of the Commissioners of the Sinking Fund, and not by the sanction of the Common Council, neither were the same confirmed by the latter named body; and inasmuch as the inherent right of the Common Council should be maintained, and no precedent of this nature allowed to transpire: therefore be it

Resolved, That the unauthorized leases granted to J. V. Meserole, and others, to run ferries from the foot of Grand street, New York, to the foot of Grand street, Brooklyn, East District, and from Peck slip, New York, to South Seventh street, Brooklyn, East District, or adjacent thereto, for a period of ten years from the 1st of May, 1859, are hereby declared to be null and void. And be it further

Resolved, That the Corporation Counsel immediately take such proceedings as shall be necessary and proper to prevent the unauthorized use of, and interference with, such ferries. And be it further

Resolved, That the Comptroller forthwith proceed to advertise, and sell at public auction, leases of the ferry from the foot of Grand street, East River, New York, to the foot of Grand street, Brooklyn, East District, or to some landing adjacent thereto; and also a lease of a ferry from the northerly basin at Peck slip, New York, to the foot of South Seventh street, Brooklyn, East District, for the term of ten years from the 1st day of January next, and that such leases be submitted to the Common Council for their approval.

Adopted by the Board of Councilmen, Sept. 19, 1859.

Adopted by the Board of Aldermen, Sept. 19, 1859.

Board of Councilmen, Oct. 3, 1859, received from his Honor the Mayor, with his objections thereto.

Board of Councilmen, Oct. 24, 1859, adopted, notwithstanding the objections of his Honor the Mayor, two-thirds of all the members elected having voted therefor.

Board of Aldermen, Oct. 27, 1859, taken up, and the above action of the Board of Councilmen concurred in, two-thirds of all the members elected having voted therefor; therefore, under the provisions of the amended charter, the same became adopted.

Resolved, That the Brooklyn Ferry Co. be, and hereby is, authorized to agree with the owners of the lease of the ferry known as the Peck slip Ferry, for the purchase of the lease of said ferry for the unexpired term thereof, and to run said ferry to and from the foot of Fulton street, in the city of Brooklyn, or near thereto.

Adopted by Board of Aldermen, May 28, 1860.

Adopted by Board of Councilmen, May 28, 1860.

Approved by the Mayor, May 31, 1860.

FERRY FROM

ROOSEVELT STREET TO BROOKLYN.

THIS INDENTURE, made this 28th day of June, in the year of our Lord one thousand eight hundred and fifty-two, between the Mayor, Aldermen, and Commonalty of the city of New York, of the first part, and John H. Martine, of the said city of New York, of the second part—

Witnesseth, that the said parties of the first part, for and in consideration of the rents, covenants, payments, agreements, and articles, hereinafter mentioned and contained, on the part and behalf of the said party of the second part, his several respective executors, administrators, and assigns, to be paid, done and performed, and kept, have demised, granted, and to farm letten, and by these presents do demise, grant, and to farm let, unto the said party of the second part, his executors, administrators and assigns, all that ferry from the foot of Roosevelt street, in the city of New York, over and across the East river, to a point at or near the foot of Bridge street, in the city of Brooklyn, in the county of Kings, and from thence to the foot of Roosevelt street as aforesaid, and one hundred feet of the bulkhead, at the foot of Roosevelt street, East river, in the city of New York, together with all and singular the ferriage fees, perquisites, issues, profits, benefits, and emoluments thereof; to have and to hold the said ferry and the premises aforesaid, with the appurtenances, unto the said party of the second part, his executors, administrators and assigns, for and during the full end and term of fifteen years, from the first day of October, in the year of our Lord one thousand eight hundred and fifty-two, yielding and paying therefor, unto the said parties of the first part, their successors and assigns, yearly, and every year during the said term, the sum of three thousand dollars, to be paid in quarter-yearly payments, to wit: on the first days of August, November, February, and May, in each and every year during the said term hereby demised.

Provided, always, and these presents and the premises hereby demised are upon this express condition, that if the said quarterly rent, or any part thereof, should be behind and unpaid, for the space of ten days after any day of payment on which the same, or any part thereof, ought to be paid as aforesaid, or if the said party of the second part, his executors, administrators or assigns, shall neglect to pay, perform, fulfill, and keep any or either of the payments, articles, covenants, clauses, agreements, matters and things herein contained, which, on his part, is to be paid, performed, fulfilled, and kept during the term aforesaid, according to the true intent and meaning of these presents, that then, and in every such case, it shall and may be lawful for the said parties of the first part, their executors and assigns, to enter into and upon the premises hereby demised, and to have, possess and enjoy the same as fully as though these presents had not been made, any thing herein contained to the contrary notwithstanding. And the said party of the second part, for himself, his executors, administrators and assigns, doth covenant and agree to and with the said parties of the first part, their successors and assigns, by these presents, that he, the said party of the second part, his executors, administrators and assigns, shall and will yearly, and every year during the said term, well and truly pay unto the said parties of the first part, their successors and assigns, the said yearly rent and sum of money hereinbefore mentioned, at the days and times above specified for the payment thereof, without fraud or delay; and, also, that he, the said party of the second part, his executors, administrators and assigns, shall and will, on or before the first day of May, in the year of our Lord one thousand eight hundred and fifty-three, and thenceforth during the continuance of the said term hereby demised, at his own proper cost and expense, forthwith provide and navigate upon the said ferry one good and substantial steam ferry-boat, to be approved of by the said parties of the first part, or their successors, to carry, transport, and convey passengers, horses, cattle, carts, carriages, and wagons, goods, merchandise, and other things whatsoever on the said ferry between Roosevelt street and Brooklyn, as aforesaid, with safety, convenience, and expedition, in such manner as that the said steam ferry-boat shall leave the landing place of said ferry at the foot of Roosevelt street at least once in every half-hour, unless prevented by the elements, from sunrise to eight o'clock in the evening of each day; and also that he shall and will, when required by any resolution of the said parties of the first part, or their successors, passed in Common Council at any time during the said term hereby demised, place and navigate one or more additional steam ferry-boats, to be approved of as aforesaid, upon the said ferry, and that the said boat or boats shall at all times during the said term be kept in good repair, and properly furnished and provided with the necessary implements and tackle, and with a sufficient number of sober, skillful, and able-bodied men, who shall be competent to manage the same, and who shall, at all reasonable times, give their constant and ready attendance at the said ferry for the prompt and expeditious transportation of passengers, horses, cattle, carts, carriages, wagons, goods, merchandise, and other things whatsoever across the said river;

and, also, that he shall conduct and manage the said ferry agreeably to such rules, regulations, rates of ferriage, times of running, and restrictions, as are now or may be from time to time hereafter, during said term, by any by-law, ordinance, or resolution of the said parties of the first part, or their successors, or by any statute of this State, be made or passed in relation to the same; also, that he, the said party of the second part, his executors, administrators, and assigns, shall and will at his own proper cost, charges, and expenses, build, erect, make, and furnish, and at all times during the term hereby demised will well and sufficiently uphold, maintain, and keep in good and substantial repair, the necessary bridges and boats and other fixtures at each landing place of the said ferry, and the necessary docks and piers on Long Island shore, and that he will likewise keep in like good repair, during the term hereby demised, the bulkhead hereby demised by the said parties of the first part, for the accommodation of said ferry at the foot of Roosevelt street as aforesaid, and the street in front of the bulkhead at the foot of Roosevelt street, to the extent of twenty-five feet back from the said bulkhead, and to the full width thereof, and that, at the expiration or sooner determination of the said term hereby demised, he, the said party of the second part, his executors, administrators, or assigns, shall and will peaceably and quietly leave, surrender, and yield up the said ferry and every thing hereby demised, together with the bulkhead, piers, docks, floats, bridges, and other fixtures and improvements which may have been erected or made by either of the parties for the use of the said ferry at the foot of Roosevelt street, in good order and condition, into the possession of the said parties of the first part, their successors or assigns, without fraud or delay.

And, also, that the said party of the second part, his executors, administrators, and assigns shall not, nor will, during the said term, assign, transfer, set over, mortgage, encumber, underlet, or in any other manner convey this present lease, or any part thereof, or the above demised premises, or any part of the same, without the leave and consent of the said parties of the first part, their successors, or assigns, in writing first had and obtained ; and it is hereby expressly understood and agreed that nothing contained in these presents shall prevent the establishment of any other ferry or ferries across the East river, at any place or at any time previous to the expiration of the said term hereby granted by the said parties of the first part, and the said party of the second part, for himself, and his executors, administrators, and assigns, doth covenant and agree to and with the said parties of the first part, their successors and assigns, in manner and form following, that is to say: That unless the said ferry shall, on or before the first day of May, 1853, be put in operation according to the terms and conditions of this indenture, then and in that case, and immediately after the said first day of May, 1853, this lease and every article, clause, and thing herein contained, except as to the payment of the rent to be or become due upon that day, shall be and become null and void and of no effect.

In witness whereof, to one part of these presents, remaining with the said party of the second part, the said parties of the first part have caused the common seal of the said city of New York to be affixed, and to the other part thereof, remaining with the said parties of the first part, the said party of the second part hath affixed his seal the day and year first in these presents written.

J. H. MARTINE.

Sealed and delivered in the presence of
GEO. L. TAYLOR.

City and County of New York, ss.:

On the 21st day of September, 1852, before me came John H. Martine, to me personally known to be the person described in, and who executed the foregoing lease, and acknowledged that he executed the same for the purposes therein mentioned.

GEO. L. TAYLOR,
Commissioner of Deeds.

COMPTROLLER'S OFFICE,
New York, December 30, 1852.

Rent on this lease to commence on January 1st, 1853, the said bulkhead, foot of Roosevelt street, having been used for manure up to that date.

JOS. R. TAYLOR,
Comptroller.

Consent given to transfer the Roosevelt street ferry to Jacob R. Leroy and Henry E. Pierpont.

December 14, 1853.

Resolved, That the Brooklyn Ferry Company be permitted to occupy the slip between piers Nos. 31 and 32, East river, and run their ferry-boats to such slip, provided they shall procure, at their own cost and expense, the possession from the present lessee, and erect, at their own expense, such ferry fixtures as they may require for ferry purposes.

Adopted by the Board of Councilmen, July 11, 1856.
Adopted by the Board of Aldermen, October 13, 1856.

Received from his Honor the Mayor, October 22, 1856, without his approval or objections thereto; therefore, under the provisions of the amended charter, the same became adopted.

Resolved, That the Brooklyn Ferry Company be, and is hereby, authorized to agree with the Union Ferry Company, for the use of the ferry slip and purchase of the ferry fixtures at the foot of Roosevelt street, East river, in the city of New York, and the purchase of the ferry lease under which a ferry is now run from Roosevelt street, New York, to Bridge street, Brooklyn, and to run said ferry from Roosevelt street to South 7th street, Brooklyn (E. D.), for the unexpired term of said lease, provided the Brooklyn Ferry Company pay to the Corporation of the city of New York the same rent as is now paid by the Union Ferry Company for the said lease, which lease is dated the 28th day of June, 1852; and be it further

Resolved, That the Brooklyn Ferry Company be, and is hereby, authorized to change the Brooklyn terminus of the ferry, as now run from James slip, New York, to South 7th street, Brooklyn (E. D.), to, or near Hunter's Point, L. I., and run the same ferry from James slip, New York, to, or near Hunter's Point, L. I., for the unexpired term of the lease, dated the 14th day of December, 1852, or dispose of the same lease and ferry fixtures, at James slip, for a ferry to be run for the unexpired term of said lease, between James slip, New York, and Hunter's Point, L. I.; provided, in either case, the same rent be paid to the Corporation of the City of New York as is now paid by the Brooklyn Ferry Company.

Adopted by the Board of Councilmen, July 11, 1859.
Adopted by the Board of Aldermen, July 14, 1859.
Approved by the Mayor, July 23, 1859.

FERRY FROM
CATHARINE STREET TO BROOKLYN.

THIS INDENTURE, made the fourteenth day of October, in the year of our Lord one thousand eight hundred and fifty-one, between the Mayor, Aldermen, and Commonalty of the City of New York, of the first part, and William Cockroft and George G. Taylor, of the City of New York, parties of the second part:

Whereas, on the ninth day of June, in the year one thousand eight hundred and fifty-one, certain resolutions, passed by the Common Council of the City of New York, were approved by the Mayor of said City, which resolutions were in the words and figures following, to wit:

Resolved, that a lease for the right to run a ferry from the foot of Catharine street, in this city, to the foot of Main street, Brooklyn, be granted to William Cockroft and George G. Taylor, for *ten years* from the first day of May, one thousand eight hundred and fifty-three, for the annual rent of *Sixteen Thousand Dollars*, payable quarterly; said lease to contain, in addition to the stipulations and conditions in the present lease of said ferry, those mentioned in the foregoing report.

Resolved, That the Counsel to the Corporation be directed to prepare a lease in conformity with the preceding report and resolution, and the same be submitted to the Common Council for approval before execution.

Now, this indenture witnesseth, that the said parties of the first part, for, and in consideration of the rents, covenants, promises, articles and agreements hereinafter mentioned, on the part and behalf of the said parties of the second part, their executors, administrators, and assigns, to be paid, performed, observed, fulfilled, and kept, have granted, demised, and to farm let, and by these presents do grant, demise, and to farm let, unto the said parties of the second part, their executors, administrators and assigns, all that certain ferry established from the new or Catharine market slip, in the city of New York, over the East river to the foot of Main street in Brooklyn, and from the foot of Main street, in Brooklyn aforesaid, back to Catharine market slip aforesaid, with all and singular the usual accustomed ferriage fees, perquisites, rents, issues, benefits, profits, and advantages whatsoever, to the said ferry belonging, or therewith used, or thereout arising; and also the ferry house and lot in Brooklyn, appertaining to the said ferry.

To have and to hold the said ferry with the appurtenances, and house and lot aforesaid, unto the said parties of the second part, their executors, administrators, and assigns, for and during the full end and term of ten years, from the first day of May, in the year of our Lord one thousand eight hundred and fifty-three. Yielding and paying therefor, yearly and every year during the said term, unto the said parties of the first part, their successors or assigns, the annual rent or sum of sixteen thousand dollars, payable quarterly on the usual days for the payment of rent in the city of New York; that is to say, one-fourth part on the first days of August, November, February, and May, in each and every year during the said term.

Provided always, and these presents and the premises hereby demised are upon this express condition, that if it should so happen that the said yearly rent, or any part thereof, should be behind and unpaid for the space of ten days after any day of payment, on which the same or any part thereof ought to be paid as aforesaid ; or if the said parties of the second part, their executors, administrators or assigns, shall neglect to pay, perform, fulfill, and keep, any or either of the payments, articles, covenants, clauses, provisions, agreements, matters, and things herein contained, which on their part are to be paid, performed, fulfilled, observed, and kept, during the term aforesaid, according to the true intent and meaning of these presents, that then, and in every such case or cases, it shall and may be lawful to and for the said parties of the first part, their successors and assigns, to enter into and upon the premises hereby demised, and to have, possess, and enjoy the same, as fully as though these presents had not been made, anything herein contained to the contrary notwithstanding.

And the said parties of the first part, for themselves and their successors, do covenant and agree to and with the said parties of the second part, their executors, administrators, and assigns, to keep the chain used on the easterly side of the said ferry, at the foot of Catharine slip, in good order and repair during the continuance of this lease ; and the said parties of the second part, for themselves, their heirs, executors, administrators, and assigns, do covenant and agree to and with the said parties of the first part, their successors and assigns, by these presents, that they, the said parties of the second part, their heirs, executors, administrators, and assigns, shall and will, yearly and every year during the said term, well and truly pay unto the said parties of the first part, their successors or assigns, the said yearly rent or sum of money hereinbefore mentioned, at the days and times above specified for the payment thereof, without fraud or delay; and also that they, the said parties of the second part, their heirs, executors, administrators, or assigns, shall and will, during the whole of the said term, at their own proper cost and expense, furnish, provide, and navigate upon the said ferry, from Catharine street to Brooklyn aforesaid, three good and substantial steam ferry-boats, of the same size and power, and equal in all respects to those now used upon the Fulton ferry, and keep at least two of the said steam ferry-boats, at all reasonable times, continually employed on the said ferry, during the term hereby granted, and will run the same as frequently on every day, from six o'clock A. M. to nine o'clock P. M., as the loading and unloading of vehicles and freight will permit; and from nine o'clock P. M. to six o'clock A. M., at such times as the Common Council may require; and also that they, the said parties of the second part, their heirs, executors, administrators, or assigns, shall not, during the term of this lease, charge or receive as rates of ferriage, for each foot passenger, a sum exceeding two cents; and for vehicles, the rate shall not exceed that now charged by the Union ferry company.

And also that they, the said parties of the second part, their heirs, executors, administrators, or assigns, shall and will keep the frames, ferry stairs, and bridges used at the said ferry, on each side of the same, and the whole of the old part of the pier on the easterly side of the slip occupied for the use of the said ferry at Brooklyn, and one-half of the new part of said pier, in good order and repair, at their own expense, during the continuance of this lease.

And also that the said parties of the second part, their heirs, executors, or administrators, shall not nor will, at any time during the said term, in any manner grant, assign, transfer, let, underlet, or set over this present lease or any part thereof, or their or either of their estate or interest therein, or in or to the above-described and demised premises or any part of the same, without the leave or consent of the said parties of the first part, or their successors, in writing, under their common seal, first had and obtained; nor shall nor will do, commit, or suffer any act or acts, thing or things, either by commission or omission, which shall create a forfeiture of these presents, or the premises hereby demised, or in any wise lessen, injure, or encumber the same, or the rents or revenues thereof; but that they, the said parties of the second part, their heirs, executors, administrators, or assigns, shall and will conduct and manage the said ferry agreeably to such rules, regulations, and restrictions as now are, or from time to time hereafter during the said term shall, by any by-law, ordinance, order, or resolution of the said parties of the first part, or their successors, be made or passed in relation thereto.

And also, that they, the said parties of the second part, their heirs, executors, administrators, or assigns, shall and will, on the last day of the term hereby granted, or other sooner determination of these presents, well and truly deliver up the said hereby demised premises, with the rights, privileges, and appurtenances thereunto belonging, into the hands and possession of the said parties of the first part, their successors or assigns, without fraud or delay.

And the said parties of the second part, for themselves, their heirs, executors, administrators and assigns, and the said parties of the first part, for themselves and their successors, do mutually covenant, grant and agree to and with each other respectively in manner following; *that is to say,* That the steamboats and all other boats and furniture, of what description soever, as shall be actually employed on the said ferry, at the expiration of the said term, shall be valued by three different persons or appraisers, one to be chosen by the said parties of the first part, or their successors, one by the parties of the second part, their heirs, executors, administrators or assigns, and the third by the persons or appraisers so chosen by the said parties to these presents, and before they proceed to make the said valuation; the decision of two of which said persons or appraisers, given in writing under their hands and seals, shall be final and conclusive, provided that the said parties of the first part shall not be bound to pay for any number of boats, commonly denominated steam ferry-boats, exceeding three, unless they, the said parties of the first part, or their successors, shall, during the said term, request the said party of the second part, his heirs, executors, administrators or assigns, to build a greater number of boats of that description.

And it is hereby further agreed by and between the said parties, that such decision shall be made and given within twenty days after the expiration of the said term, or other sooner determination of these presents as aforesaid; and that the said parties of the first part, their successors or assigns, shall and will, within ten days thereafter, pay to the said parties of the second part, their heirs, executors, administrators or assigns, the sum awarded to be due to him or them, provided the said boats and furniture shall be assigned and delivered over within the said time, by the said parties of the second part, their heirs, executors, administrators or assigns, to the said parties of the first part, their successors or assigns, free and clear from any claim or demands from any person or persons whomsoever.

And it is hereby further mutually agreed, that in case any of the persons to be employed upon the said ferry by the said parties of the second part, their heirs, executors, administrators or assigns, shall at any time conduct himself improperly while in the discharge of his duties, or shall conduct himself in such manner as to give offense to the public, for whose convenience these presents have been made, and this lease granted by the said parties of the first part, that then, and in such case, the said parties of the second part, their heirs, executors, administrators or assigns, shall and will, upon being requested so to do by the Committees on Ferries for the time being, of the said Common Council of the city of New York, discharge such person from their employment at such ferry.

And it is hereby further mutually covenanted and agreed by and between the parties to these presents, and these presents are upon the express understanding that nothing herein contained shall be taken or construed to operate as a covenant, by the said parties of the first part, or their successors, for possession or quiet enjoyment by the said parties of the second part, or their executors, administrators or assigns, of the said ferry or right of ferriage ; nor shall the same be taken or construed to interfere, in any manner, with any provisions, grants or rights made by the said parties of the first part, nor with the right to grant any future ferries, to and from Brooklyn, or to and from elsewhere wheresoever ; nor to operate further than to grant the possession of the estate, right, title or interest, which the said parties of the first part may have or lawfully claim, in the said ferry and right of ferriage hereby demised, by virtue of their several charters, and the various acts of the Legislature of the people of the State of New York.

In witness whereof, to one part of these presents, remaining with the said parties of the first part, the said parties of the second part have set their hands and seals; and to the other part thereof, remaining with the said parties of the second part, the said parties of the first part have caused the common seal of the City of New York to be affixed, the day and year first above written.

Sealed and delivered in the presence of
  GEORGE L. TAYLOR.
            WILLIAM COCKROFT. [L. S.]
            GEORGE G. TAYLOR. [L. S.]

     NEW YORK, COMPTROLLER'S OFFICE,
         February 19th, 1852.

The Mayor, Aldermen, and Commonalty of the city of New York hereby give permission for the transfer of this lease to CALEB S. WOODHULL.

            JOS. R. TAYLOR,
                Comptroller.

     NEW YORK, COMPTROLLER'S OFFICE,
         February 19th, 1852.

The Mayor, Aldermen, and Commonalty of the city of New York hereby give permission for the transfer of this lease to CYRUS P. SMITH and WILLIAM F. BULKLEY, *of the city of Brooklyn.*

            JOS. R. TAYLOR,
                Comptroller.

Resolved, That a bulkhead be sunk in the East River, between piers No. 34 and 35, at least one hundred feet from the line of the present bulkhead, and that the intermediate space be filled in with good and wholesome earth, under the direction of the Street Commissioner, the expense thereof to be charged to Docks and Slips—new work.

Resolved, That the whole of the slip be appropriated to ferry purposes, reserving so much of the new-made premises as may be necessary for the fish market, as proposed to be turned round, and reserving so much of the water on the side of the upper pier, as may be necessary for the free ingress and egress of fishing smacks and boats only, and at least forty feet of the front of the new bulkhead for fishing smacks and boats to be laid to.

Resolved, That the proprietors of the ferry erect new and suitable ferry houses of the new bulkhead, reconstruct and build the racks, bridges and floats, at their own cost and expense, under the direction and approval of the Street Commissioner, the same to become the property of the city at the expiration of their lease.

Adopted by the Board of Assistants, Oct. 6, 1852.
Adopted by the Board of Aldermen, Nov. 4, 1852.
Approved by the Mayor, Nov. 9, 1852.

Resolved, That the Union Ferry Company be, and they are hereby, directed to run a boat on the Catharine Street Ferry every ten minutes, from 9 o'clock, P. M., until 12 o'clock, P. M., and every hour from that time until 4 o'clock, A. M.

Adopted by the Board of Aldermen, June 5, 1855.
Adopted by the Board of Councilmen, Sept. 5, 1855.

Approved by the Mayor, Sept. 6, 1855.

NOTE.—It was mutually agreed that this lease should terminate on the 1st May, 1861, and the lease was sold in connection with those of the Hamilton avenue, South, Wall street, and Fulton Ferries, as will appear upon reference to page 61,—Vide *below*.

HAMILTON AVENUE, SOUTH, WALL STREET, FULTON STREET, AND CATHARINE STREET FERRIES.

These ferries were all leased in a body, pursuant to the resolutions following, which, together with the preamble attached, fully explain the reasons why such action was considered desirable.

Whereas, The ferries known as the Fulton, South, and Hamilton avenue ferries have been heretofore leased under one lease, and the lease of the same will expire on the first of May, 1861, and the lease of the Catharine ferry will expire on the first of May, 1863, and the lease of the Wall street ferry will expire on the first of July, 1863, and

Whereas, The said ferries are now all run at a uniform rate of fare, and the running of said ferries together, at the same rates, and affording equal facilities at all the points on both sides of the river, is advantageous to the city of New York and Brooklyn, therefore,

Resolved, That the leases of the Catharine and Wall street ferries shall, by the consent of the lessees thereof, filed with the Comptroller, be deemed to expire on the first of May, 1861.

Resolved, That all the above-named ferries be sold at public auction, in accordance with the act of the Legislature, passed April 14th, 1857, together, under one lease, to the party bidding the highest price therefor, for the term of ten years, from the first of May, 1861, rent payable quarterly, and the lease be made in the usual form of ferry leases, to run to and from the slips, landings, and premises, to and from which they are now run, so far as such slips, landings, and premises are owned by the Corporation of New York, or are, or have been reserved and appropriated for ferry purposes, except that the landing at the foot of Hamilton avenue, Brooklyn, may be at the foot of said avenue, or in the vicinity thereof, with the express stipulation therein, that the party purchasing the same shall run the said several ferries at a uniform rate of fare, not exceeding the present rates, and the discontinuance of any one of the said ferries during the term of said lease shall be deemed and held to be a forfeiture of the lease of said ferries, and the said lease thereby become absolutely null and void.

Resolved, That the Comptroller be, and he is hereby, directed to advertise and sell at public auction, according to the act of the Legislature, passed April 14th, 1857, the several ferries mentioned in the foregoing recital and resolutions, in one lease, and the sale to be made on or before the first day of January next, and that he deliver to the lessee the proper lease therefor. Provided, always, that in the notice and terms of sale and in the lease made in accordance therewith, it shall be stipulated, that so far as relates to the landings and slips not owned by the Mayor, Aldermen, and Commonalty of the city of New York, the landings or termination may be made at some point in the vicinity of the present landings or terminations, if the lessee shall so elect, and provide further that the Comptroller be, and is hereby, directed not to sell the said several ferries as above provided, for an annual rent less than the aggregate amount of annual rent now received for the said ferries, and in case no sale is made, that the term of the leases of the Catharine and Wall street ferries shall not be shortened as above provided.

Adopted by the Board of Councilmen, Oct. 27, 1859.

Adopted by the Board of Aldermen, Oct. 31, 1859.

Approved by the Mayor, Nov. 11, 1859.

THIS INDENTURE, made the 29th day of May, in the year 1860, between the Mayor, Aldermen, and Commonalty of the city of New York, parties of the first part, and the Union Ferry Company, of Brooklyn, parties of the second part, made pursuant to certain resolutions of the Common Court, of said parties of the first part, adopted and approved Nov. 10, 1859, witnesseth, that the said parties of the first part, for and in consideration of the rents, covenants, and agreements hereinafter contained, on the part and behalf of the said parties of the second part, their successors and assigns, well and truly to be paid, observed, performed, and kept according to the true intent and meaning of these presents, have granted, demised, and to farm let unto the said parties of the second part, their successors and assigns, all those five certain ferries, commonly called and known as the Fulton Ferry, the South Ferry, the Hamilton Avenue Ferry, the Catharine Ferry, and the Wall street Ferry, together with all and singular the ferriage and right of ferriage, fees, perquisites, benefits, profits, and advantages whatsoever to the said ferries respectively belonging, or to arise or accrue from the same, and all and singular the bulkheads, wharves, premises, piers and slips, now used and occupied by the said ferries respectively in the cities of New York and Brooklyn, so far as such slips, landings and premises, and owned by the said parties of the first part, and have been reserved and appropriated for ferry purposes, together with all the fixtures connected with the slips and ferry houses, and all the floats, bridges, fixtures and appurtenances whatsoever thereunto in any manner belonging, or which, at the commencement of the term hereby demised, shall be appropriated to, or used by the said ferries respectively, so far as the said parties of the first part shall have, at the commencement of said term, hereby demised any right or interest in and to the same, including in the premises hereby demised, the whole of the bulkhead or wharf at the foot of Fulton street, in the city of Brooklyn; also, lots known as Nos. 16 and 17, on map of corporation property, on file in office of the Comptroller of the city of New York, and situated between Water street and the East river, near Fulton ferry. *To have and to hold* the said ferries and appurtenances, unto the said parties of the second part, their successors and assigns, from the first day of May, in the year 1861, for and during and until the full end and term of ten years then next ensuing, and fully to be completed and ended, yielding and paying therefor unto the said parties of the first part, their successors or assigns, yearly, and every year during the said term, the rent or sum of ONE HUNDRED AND THREE THOUSAND DOLLARS, in quarter-yearly payments, on the usual days of payment, to wit: on the first day of August, November, February, and May, in each and every year during the term hereby demised.

Provided always, and these presents and everything herein contained, on the part of the parties of the first part to be performed and done, are upon the express condition that, if and whenever it should happen that the said yearly rent, above reserved, shall be behind or unpaid, for the space of ten days after any day of payment on which the same, or any part thereof, ought to be paid as aforesaid, or if the said parties of the second part, their successors or assigns, shall discontinue either of said ferries, or suffer either of them to be discontinued, or shall neglect or omit to pay, fulfill, perform, or keep any or either of the payments, articles, covenants, clauses, conditions, or agreements herein contained, which, on their part, are to be paid, performed, fulfilled, and kept, during the said term, according to the true intent and meaning of these presents, then and in every such case, this lease and everything herein contained to be performed or done by said parties of the first part shall cease and determine, and it shall and may be lawful for the said parties of the first part, their successors and assigns, to enter into and upon the premises hereby demised, and to have, possess, and enjoy the same as fully as though these presents had not been made, anything herein contained to the contrary notwithstanding.

And the said parties of the second part, for themselves, their successors and assigns, do covenant, promise, and agree with the said parties of first part, their successors and assigns, in manner following: that is to say, that the said parties of the second part, their successors and assigns, shall and will, yearly, during the said term hereby demised, well and truly pay unto the said parties of the first part, their successors or assigns, the said yearly rent, above reserved, on the days and times, and in the manner above specified, without fraud or delay, and also that the said parties of the second part, their successors and assigns, shall and will, for and during the term for which said premises are hereby demised, at their own proper cost and expense, provide, furnish, navigate, and use, at each of said ferries, as many good and substantial steam ferry-boats as may be necessary to transport and convey, with safety, convenience, and expedition, all persons who may desire to cross said ferries, respectively, and that they will so provide, furnish, navigate, and use, at least, three of such good and substantial steam ferry-boats on the said Fulton Ferry, two on the said South Ferry, two on the said Hamilton avenue Ferry, two on the said Wall street Ferry, and two on the said Catharine Ferry; and they shall keep on hand, ready for use, such and so many extra or spare boats as may be necessary to keep up the supply of boats at the several ferries, in case of damage to, or requiring repairs of, the boats regularly employed on said several ferries, each and all of such boats to be approved by the Comptroller of the city of New York, and that said boats shall, at all times, be exclusively employed upon said ferries, respectively, during said term, to carry, transport, and convey carriages, horses, cattle, passengers, and other property and effects, across the same with safety, convenience and expedition, and that the said boats shall always, during the said term, be kept in good repair, and furnished with all necessary and proper implements and machinery, and be manned, while running, with a sufficient number of able-bodied and skillful men to manage the same, and who shall and will, at all times, be ready and willing to, and who shall, give their constant and ready attendance at the said ferries respectively, for the prompt and convenient transportation of passengers, horses, cattle, and other property across the same, and that the said parties of the second part shall and will, in all things, conduct and manage the said ferries respectively in conformity with, and will obey in respect thereof, all laws and ordinances of the Common Council of the city of New York, and agreeably to such rules and regulations, and resolutions, whether as to the time of departure of said boats from each end of said ferries respectively, the time of starting the same on the morning of each day, or of running the same during the night, or otherwise, and as to all matters pertaining to the good management of said ferries, and the sufficient accommodation of the public thereat, during the said term, as shall, from time to time, be required by the said Comptroller, or by any ordinance or resolution of the said parties of the first part, or their successors, made or passed, or which may hereafter be made or passed, in relation thereto, and shall and will, under the direction of the said Comptroller, build, erect, make, and furnish all the fixtures and other improvements necessary for the well conducting of the said several ferries during the said term, and that they will well and sufficiently maintain, uphold, and keep the same, and the bulkheads and fixtures in use for the said ferries, in good repair, at their own proper cost and charges; and that, in the event of any damage to the bulkheads or piers adjoining either of said ferries, from collision by the ferry boats, or otherwise, from any action or negligence of said parties of second part, their successors, servants, agents, or assigns, that said parties of the second part will immediately repair and restore said bulkheads and piers to their former good condition, at their own cost and expense; and said parties of the second part, being now the assignees or owners of the lease or leases under which some or all of said ferries are now used, do, by these presents, release and acquit the said parties of the first part of and from all obligation which they may be under, by virtue of said lease or leases, to purchase, at the expiration of said lease or leases, the boats or other property used on said ferries, or any of them ; and as to such lease or leases of any of said ferries as are not now owned by said parties of the second part, if any such there be, they do hereby covenant and agree that they will purchase, receive. and take, from the present lessees of the said ferries respectively, all the boats and other property which the said parties of the first part are bound to purchase, take, and receive at the expiration of any of the existing leases thereof, and will pay therefor in the same manner as the said parties of the first part are required to do, and will indemnify and save harmless said parties of the first part, and their successors, of and from all liability, of every name and kind, arising or to arise upon or by reason of any covenants or agreements in such leases contained, respecting the purchase of the boats and other property of the lessees named in the said leases respectively.

And said parties of the second part do, for themselves, their successors and assigns, further covenant and agree that they will run said ferries at a uniform rate of fare, not exceeding the rates established and charged on the tenth of November, 1859, when the said resolutions of the Common Council were adopted, and that they will not, during the said term, raise the rates above the rates or prices established and charged on said tenth day of November, 1859; and that they will not assign, transfer, or set over. underlet, or in any manner convey this present lease, or any part thereof, or any term therein, or the said demised premises or ferries, or any one, or part thereof, without leave and consent first had and obtained, in writing, signed by the Comptroller of said city. And said parties of the second part, for themselves, their successors, and assigns, do hereby further covenant and agree that said ferries shall be run to and from the slips, landings, and premises, to and from which they are now run, so far as such slips, landings, and premises are owned by said parties of the first part, or are, or have been reserved by them for ferry purposes, except that the landing at the foot of Hamilton avenue, Brooklyn, may be at the foot of said avenue, or in the vicinity thereof; and, further, that so far as relates to the landings and slips not owned by said parties of the first part, the landings or terminations of said respective ferries may be made at some point in the vicinity of the present terminations, but at the cost and expense of said parties of the second part. And it is further expressly understood and agreed by the parties to these presents, that no expense whatever is to be incurred by said parties of the first part on or in connection with the piers, slips, bulkheads, or premises, proposed to be leased, during the term hereby demised, and that no abatement of rent whatever shall be claimed or made by reason of any recovery that may be had against the said parties of the second part, in or by reason of any suits commenced, or which may be hereafter commenced, in relation to the rights of the said parties of the first part to any of the property or rights hereby demised, and especially in relation to the landing-place or slip at the foot of Hamilton avenue, in the city of Brooklyn, or in relation to the slip between piers numbered 15 and 16, at the foot of Wall street, in the city of New York; and that no claim for damage shall be made or maintained by said parties of the second part, their successors or assigns, against said parties of the first part, by reason of any determination that may hereafter be made adverse to the rights claimed by the said parties of the first part to any of the said property or rights hereby demised, or intended so to be; and it is further understood and agreed by the parties to these presents, that the lot on the southwest side of Main street, between Water street and Plymouth street, in the city of Brooklyn, at present leased unto the Catharine ferry, is not to be included in this lease, but is reserved without and therefrom to the use of the said parties of the first part, their successors and assigns, for other purposes, and said parties of the second part, for themselves, their successors and assigns, hereby covenant and agree, to and with said parties of the first part, their successors and assigns, that said parties of the second part, their successors and assigns, shall and will, on the last day of the term hereby granted, or at the soonest determination of the term hereby demised, peaceably and quietly leave, surrender and yield up the said ferries, and the premises and property hereby demised, with the rights, privileges and appurtenances thereunto belonging, with the bulkheads, piers, docks, floats, bridges, and other fixtures and improvements, which may have been erected by either of said parties, for the use of either of said ferries, in good order and condition, into the possession of said parties of the first part, their successors or assigns, without fraud or delay, and said parties of the first part do, for themselves, successors and assigns, covenant and agree, to and with said parties of the second part, their successors and assigns, that upon the surrender and yielding up of said premises, by said parties of the second part, as hereinbefore provided, said parties of the first part shall purchase, or cause to be purchased, of said parties of the second part, their successors or assigns, at a fair appraised valuation, the boats, buildings and other property of said parties of the second part, their successors or assigns, used upon said ferries, respectively and actually necessary for the purposes of said ferries, and said parties of the second part, for themselves, their successors and assigns, do covenant and agree, to and with said parties of the first part, their successors and assigns, that each ferry boat employed upon the said ferries shall have attached to the engine thereof a fire apparatus, or force pump, with not less than 400 feet of hose, of the quality and dimensions as used by the Fire Department of the City of New York, to be used in the extinguishment of fires, whenever required, by the Chief Engineer of the Fire Department of the City of New York, or his assistants, and said parties of the first part agree to allow to said parties of the second part $20 per hour, for each hour so engaged.

In witness whereof, to the part of these presents remaining with said parties of the first part, the parties of the second part have caused their corporate seal to be affixed, duly attested by their President, and to the part thereof remaining with said parties of the second part, the said parties of the first part have set their common seal, the day and year first above written.

N. B. MORSE, [L. S.]
President of the Union Ferry Co. of Brooklyn.

In presence of
H. J. STORRS.

City and County of New York, ss.:

On this 4th day of September, 1860, before me came N. B. Morse, to me known to be the individual who executed the foregoing Indenture, who, being by me duly sworn, did depose and say, that he is the President of the Union Ferry Company of Brooklyn, that the seal above affixed is the seal of said company, and is so affixed by their authority.

WM. ALLEN,
Com. of Deeds.

The following preamble and resolution were passed by the Board of Directors of the Union Ferry Company of Brooklyn:

The lease of the Fulton, South, Hamilton avenue, Wall, and Catharine ferries having been sold at public auction, by the Comptroller of the city of New York, on the 29th of May last, and the same was purchased by this Company,

Resolved, That the President of this Board be, and is hereby, authorized to execute such lease, and affix the corporate seal of the company thereto, when said lease shall be ready for execution.

(A true copy of the minutes.)

J. A. PERRY,
Secretary.

Know all men by these presents, that we, James S. T. Stranahan and Cyrus P. Smith, both of the city of Brooklyn, State of New York, are held and firmly bound unto the Mayor, Aldermen, and Commonalty of the city of New York, in the sum of $100,000, lawful money of the United States of America, to be paid to the said the Mayor, Aldermen, and Commonalty of the City of New York, their successors or assigns, for which payment, well and truly to be made, we bind ourselves, our heirs, executors, and administrators, firmly by these presents. Sealed with our seals, dated the 29th day of May, 1860.

A lease having been made by indenture of even date with these presents, by the said the Mayor, Aldermen, and Commonalty of the city of New York, to the Union Ferry Company of Brooklyn, of the Fulton, South, Hamilton avenue, Catharine, and Wall street ferries, for the term of 10 years, from the 1st day of May, 1861, at the yearly rent of 103,000 dollars, and the said Union Ferry Company having thereby entered into certain covenants and agreements therein fully set forth,

Now, the condition of the above obligation is such, that if the said Union Ferry Company of Brooklyn, their successors or assigns, shall well and truly pay, or cause to be paid, unto the above named Mayor, Aldermen, and Commonalty, their successors or assigns all the rent in and by said lease agreed to be paid, as the same shall become due and payable, and upon the several days and in the manner expressed in said lease, and shall well and faithfully observe, perform, and keep all the covenants and agreements in said lease contained, on the part of said Company to be observed and kept, according to the true intent and meaning thereof, then the above obligation to be void, otherwise to remain in full force and virtue.

       J. S. T. STRANAHAN. [L. S.]
       C. P. SMITH.   [L. S.]

Sealed and delivered in presence of
    WM. ALLEN.

City and County of New York, ss.:

On this 4th day of September, 1860, before me came James J. S. T. Stranahan and Cyrus P. Smith, to me personally known to be the persons described in, and who executed the foregoing instrument, and severally acknowledged to me that they executed the same.

WM. ALLEN,
Comm'r of Deeds.

FERRY FROM
PIER No. 35, EAST RIVER, TO WILLIAMSBURGH.

THIS INDENTURE, made the 14th day of December, in the year of our Lord 1852, between the Mayor, Aldermen, and Commonalty of the city of New York, of the first part, and Abraham J. Berry and John J. Hicks, parties of the second part:

Whereas, On the 10th day of December, in the year 1852, certain resolutions, passed by the Common Council of the city of New York, were approved by the Mayor of said city, which resolutions were in the words and figures following: to wit,

Resolved, That a lease be granted to Abraham J. Berry and John J. Hicks, for permission to run a ferry from the property of the said John J. Hicks, at the easterly side of Pier No. 35, East river, to, or near the property of the said Abraham J. Berry, in the city of Williamsburgh, near the boundary line of the city of Brooklyn, for the term of fifteen years, from the 1st day of May, 1853, at the annual rent

$3,000, payable quarterly; the rates for passage and the transportation of goods not to exceed those of the Peck slip ferry. That the said Abraham J. Berry and John J. Hicks shall, at their own proper costs and charges, sink a block, on the southeasterly side of Pier No. 35, East river, for the purpose of erecting bridges and such fixtures, and further, to provide good and sufficient bridges, floats, ferry accommodations and fixtures, at each landing of said ferry, to the extent the same may be required or necessary, and that said parties will place upon such ferry good and substantial boats, in all respects as commodious as those now running and in use on the Fulton and South ferries, and to run the same at such times and under such regulations as may be approved by the Comptroller and the Counsel to the Corporation; and further, that at the expiration of said lease said parties will quietly leave, surrender, and yield up the said ferry, and every thing hereby granted.

Resolved, That the Counsel to the Corporation be, and he is hereby, instructed to prepare a lease, in conformity with the foregoing resolution, and that the Comptroller cause said lease to be executed, within thirty days after the approval of these resolutions.

Now, this indenture witnesseth, that the said parties of the first part, for and in consideration of the rents, covenants, provisions, articles, and agreements hereinafter mentioned, on the part and in behalf of the said parties of the second part, their executors, administrators, and assigns, to be paid, performed, observed, fulfilled, and kept, have granted, demised, and to farm let, and by these presents do grant, demise, and to farm let, unto the said parties of the second part, their executors, administrators, and assigns, all that certain ferry, established from the property of the said John J. Hicks, at the easterly side of Pier No. 35, East river, to, or near the property of the said Abraham J. Berry, in the city of Williamsburgh, near the boundary line of the city of Brooklyn, and from the property of said Berry, in Williamsburgh, aforesaid, back to the easterly side of Pier No. 35, at the property of said Hicks, aforesaid, with all and singular the usual accustomed ferriage fees, perquisites, rents, issues, benefits, profits, and advantages, whatsoever, to the said ferry belonging, or therewith used, or thereout arising.

To have and to hold the said ferry with the appurtenances unto the said parties of the second part, with their executors, administrators and assigns, for and during the full end and term of fifteen years, from the first day of May, in the year of our Lord 1853, yielding and paying therefor yearly, and every year during the said term, unto the said parties of the first part, their successors or assigns, the annual rent or sum of three thousand dollars, payable quarterly, on the usual days for the payment of rent in the city of New York, that is to say: one-fourth part on the first days of August, November, February, and May, in each and every year during the said term. Provided always, and these presents and the premises hereby demised are upon this express condition, that if it should so happen that the said yearly rent, or any part thereof, should be behind and unpaid, for the space of ten days after any day of payment, on which the same, or any part thereof, ought to be paid as aforesaid; or if the said parties of the second part, their executors, administrators or assigns, shall neglect to pay, perform, fulfill, and keep any or either of the payments, articles, covenants, clauses, provisions, agreements, matters and things herein contained, which on their part are to be paid, performed, fulfilled, observed and kept during the term aforesaid, according to the true intent and meaning of these presents, that then, and in every such case and cases, it shall and may be lawful to and for the said parties of the first part, their successors and assigns, to enter into and upon the premises hereby demised, and to have, possess and hold the same as fully as though these presents had not been made, anything herein contained to the contrary notwithstanding.

And the said parties of the second part, for themselves and their heirs and assigns, do covenant and agree to and with the said parties of the first part, their successors and assigns, by these presents, that they, the said parties of the second part, their heirs, executors, administrators and assigns, shall and will yearly, and every year during the said term, well and truly pay unto the said parties of the first part, their successors or assigns, the said yearly rent or sum of money hereinbefore mentioned, at the days and times above specified for the payment thereof, without fraud or delay; and also, that they, the said parties of the second part, their heirs, executors, administrators or assigns, shall and will, during the whole of the said term, at their own proper cost and expense, furnish, provide and navigate upon the said ferry, from the property of the said Hicks, in the city of New York, to the property of the said Berry, in Williamsburgh, aforesaid, three good and substantial steam ferry-boats, of the same size and power, and as commodious, and equal in all respects to those now used upon the Fulton and South ferries, and keep at least two of the said steam ferry-boats at all reasonable times continually employed on the said ferry, during the term hereby granted, and will run the same as frequently, on every day from six o'clock A. M. to nine o'clock P. M., as the loading and unloading of vehicles and freights will permit, and from nine o'clock P. M. to twelve o'clock at night, every half-hour, and from twelve o'clock at night to six o'clock A. M., every hour, as the Common Council may require.

And also, that they, the said parties of the second part, their heirs, executors, administrators, or assigns, shall not, during the term of this lease, charge or receive, as rates of ferriage for passage and for vehicles and the transportation of goods, a sum to exceed that of the Peck Slip ferry.

And also, that they, the said parties of the second part, their heirs, executors, administrators, or assigns, shall and will keep the frames, ferry stairs, and bridges used at the said ferry, on each side of the same, in good order and repair, at their own expense, during the continuance of this lease, and that they will, at their own proper costs and charges, sink a block on the southeasterly side of Pier No. 35, East river, for the purpose of erecting bridges, floats, ferry accommodations, and fixtures at each landing of said ferry, to the extent the same may be required or necessary.

And also, that said parties of the second part, their heirs, executors, or administrators, shall not nor will, at any time during the said term, in any manner grant, assign, transfer, let, underlet, or set over this present lease, or any part thereof, or their or either of their estate or interest therein, or in or to the above described and demised premises, or any part of the same, without the leave or consent of the said parties of the first part, or their successors, in writing, under their common seal, first had and obtained, nor shall nor will do, commit, or suffer any act or acts, thing or things, either by commission or omission, which shall create a forfeiture of these presents or the premises hereby demised, or in anywise lessen, injure, or encumber the same or the rents or revenues thereof; but that they, the said parties of the second part, their heirs, executors, administrators, or assigns, shall and will conduct and manage the said ferry agreeably to such rules, regulations, and restrictions as are now, or from time to time hereafter during the said term shall, by any by-law, ordinance, order, or resolution of the said parties of the first part, or their successors, be made or passed in relation thereto.

And also, that they, the said parties of the second part, their heirs, executors, administrators, or assigns, shall and will, on the last day of the term hereby granted or other sooner determination of these presents, well and truly deliver up the said hereby demised premises, with the rights, privileges, and appurtenances thereunto belonging, into the hands and possession of the said parties of the first part, their successors or assigns, without fraud or delay, and the said parties of the second part, for themselves, their heirs, executors, administrators and assigns, and the said parties of the first part, for themselves and their successors, do mutually covenant, grant, and agree to and with each other, respectively, in manner following, that is to say:

That the steamboats and all other boats and furniture of what description soever as shall be actually employed on the said ferry, at the expiration of the said term, shall be valued by three indifferent persons or appraisers, one to be chosen by the said parties of the first part, or their successors, one by the parties of the second part, their heirs, executors, administrators, or assigns, and the third by the persons or appraisers so chosen by the said parties to these presents, and before they proceed to make the said valuation; the decision of two of which of said persons or appraisers, given in writing under their hands and seals, shall be final and conclusive, provided that the said parties of the first part shall not be bound to pay for any number of boats, commonly denominated steam ferry-boats, exceeding three, unless they, the said parties of the first part, or their successors, shall, during the said term, request the said party of the second part, his heirs, executors, administrators, or assigns, to build a greater number of boats of that description.

And it is hereby further agreed, by and between the said parties, that such decision shall be made and given within twenty days after the expiration of the said term or other sooner determination of these presents as aforesaid, and that the said parties of the first part, their successors, or assigns, shall and will, within ten days thereafter, pay to the said parties of the second part, their heirs, executors, administrators, or assigns, the sum awarded to be due to him or them, provided the said boats and furniture shall be assigned and delivered over within the said time by the said parties of the second part, their heirs, executors, administrators, or assigns, to the said parties of the first part, their successors, or assigns, free and clear of any claim or demand from any person or persons whomsoever.

And it is hereby further mutually agreed, that in case any of the persons to be employed upon the said ferry by the said parties of the second part, their heirs, executors, administrators, or assigns, shall at any time conduct himself improperly while in the discharge of his duties, or shall conduct himself in such manner as to give offense to the public, for whose convenience these presents have been made, and this lease granted by the said parties of the first part, that then and in such case the said parties of the second part, their heirs, executors, administrators, or assigns, shall and will, upon being requested so to do by the Street Commissioner for the time being of the said Common Council of the City of New York, discharge such person from their employment at such ferry.

And it is hereby further mutually covenanted and agreed, by and between the parties to these presents, and these presents are upon this express understanding, that nothing herein contained shall be taken or construed to operate as a covenant by the said parties of the first part, or their successors, for possession or quiet enjoyment by the said parties of the second part, or their executors, administrators, or assigns, of the said ferry or right of ferriage, nor shall the same be taken or construed to interfere in any manner with any provisions, grants, or rights made by the said parties of the first part, nor with the right to grant any future ferries to and from Williamsburgh, or to and from elsewhere wheresoever, nor to operate further than to grant the possession of the estate, right, title, or interest, which the said parties of the first part may have or lawfully claim in the said ferry and right of ferriage hereby demised, by virtue of their several charters and the various acts of the Legislature of the people of the State of New York.

In witness whereof, to one part of these presents, remaining with the said parties of the first part, the said parties of the second part have set their hands and seals; and to the other part thereof, remaining with the said parties of the second part, the said parties of the first part have caused the common seal of the city of New York to be affixed, the day and year first above written.

      ABRAHAM J. BERRY. [L. S.]
      JOHN J. HICKS.   [L. S.]

Sealed and delivered in presence of
  HENRY E. DAVIES.

The termini of this Ferry were afterwards changed to the slip between piers Nos. 31 and 32, East River, on the New York and to the foot of South Seventh street, on the Williamsburgh side, and the lease of the same subsequently transferred to the Brooklyn Ferry Company.

By the following resolution it will appear that the Long Island terminus was again changed to Hunter's Point, to which place the boats now run, constituting what is called the "JAMES SLIP AND HUNTER'S POINT FERRY," and the rent in the original lease mentioned (viz.: $3,000) is paid therefor.

Resolved, That the Brooklyn Ferry Company be, and is hereby, authorized to change the Brooklyn terminus of the ferry, as now run from James slip, New York, to South Seventh street, Brooklyn, E. D., to or near Hunter's Point, Long Island, and run the same from James slip, New York, to or near Hunter's Point, Long Island, for the unexpired term of the lease, dated the 14th of December, 1852; or dispose of the said lease and ferry fixtures at James slip, for a ferry to be run, for the unexpired term of said lease, between James slip, New York, and Hunter's Point, Long Island, provided, in either case, the same rent be paid to the Corporation of the city of New York as is now paid by the Brooklyn Ferry Company.

Adopted by the Board of Councilmen, July 11, 1859.
Adopted by the Board of Aldermen, July 14, 1859.
Approved by the Mayor, July 23, 1859.

FERRY FROM

JACKSON STREET TO BROOKLYN.

THIS INDENTURE, made this first day of February, in the year of our Lord one thousand eight hundred and fifty-eight, between the Mayor, Aldermen, and Commonalty of the city of New York, parties of the first part, and James Wilson, of said city, party of the second part—

Whereas, on the twelfth day of October, A. D. one thousand eight hundred and fifty-seven, a certain resolution, passed by the Common Council of the city of New York, was approved of by the Mayor of said city, which resolution was in the words and figures following, to wit:

Resolved, That the Comptroller be, and he is hereby, directed to advertise for sale, forthwith, the ferry franchise from the foot of Jackson street, East river, to Hudson avenue, Brooklyn, or some other point adjacent thereto, at public auction, for a term of ten years, under the same conditions as the Union Ferry Company, as far as applicable, and return the lease to the Common Council for confirmation;

And whereas, the Comptroller of the city of New York,

in pursuance of the authority in him vested by the foregoing resolution of the Common Council of the city of New York, and by the laws of the State of New York, did sell at public auction, on the 26th day of January, 1858, at the City Hall, in the city of New York, the ferry franchise from the foot of Jackson street, East river, to Hudson avenue, Brooklyn, or some other point adjacent thereto, for the term of ten years, from the first day of February, 1858, to the highest bidder therefor;

And whereas, at said sale of said ferry franchise so made by the Comptroller, on the 26th day of January, A. D. one thousand eight hundred and fifty-eight, the said James Wilson, the party of the second part hereto, became the purchaser thereof for said term of ten years, from the first day of February, A. D. one thousand eight hundred and fifty-eight, he being the highest bidder therefor.

Now, therefore, this indenture witnesseth, that the said parties of the first part, for and in consideration of the rents, covenants, provisions, articles, and agreements hereinafter mentioned, on the part and behalf of the said party of the second part, his executors, administrators and assigns, to be paid, performed, observed, fulfilled and kept, have granted, demised and to farm let, and by these presents do grant, demise and to farm let, unto the said party of the second part, his executors, administrators and assigns, all the certain grant of the right to establish and maintain a ferry, and all that certain ferry to be established and maintained, from the foot of Jackson street, East river, in the city of New York, to Hudson avenue, or some other point adjacent thereto, in the city of Brooklyn, county of Kings, and State of New York, and from said Hudson avenue, in the city of Brooklyn, back to the foot of Jackson street, in the city of New York aforesaid, with the privilege of running steamboats thereon, and including the right to erect slips, bridges, ferry houses, and all other appurtenances required for ferry purposes, and with all and singular the ferriage fees, perquisites, rents, issues, profits, privileges, advantages, and emoluments, which may arise or accrue from the said ferry.

To have and to hold the said ferry, with the appurtenances, unto the said party of the second part, his executors, administrators and assigns, for and during and until the full end and term of ten years, from the first day of February, in the year one thousand eight hundred and fifty-eight, and fully to be complete and ended.

Yielding and paying rent therefor, yearly and every year during the said term of ten years, the annual rent or sum of five hundred dollars, lawful money of the United States, in quarter-yearly payments, on the first days of August, November, February, and May, in each and every year during the said term.

Provided always, that if it should so happen that the said yearly rent, or any part thereof, shall be behind or unpaid for the space of ten days after any day of payment on which the same ought to be paid, as aforesaid, or if the said party of the second part, his executors, administrators or assigns, do or shall neglect or omit to pay, perform, fulfill, observe and keep, any or either of the payments, articles, covenants, clauses, agreements, provisions, matters or things, herein contained, which, on the part and behalf of the said party of the second part, his executors, administrators or assigns, are to be paid, performed, observed, fulfilled and kept, during the said term of ten years, according to the true intent and meaning of these presents; that then, and in every and all such case and cases, it shall and may be lawful for the said parties of the first part, their successors or assigns, to enter into or upon the premises hereby demised, and to have, possess and enjoy the same again, as fully as though these presents had never been made; any thing herein contained to the contrary notwithstanding.

And the said party of the second part, for himself, his heirs, executors, administrators, and assigns, doth covenant and agree to and with the said parties of the first part, their successors and assigns, by these presents, in manner following, that is to say: that the said party of the second part, his executors, administrators, and assigns, shall and will yearly, and every year, during the said term hereby demised, well and truly pay unto the said parties of the first part, their successors and assigns, the said yearly rent or sum of money hereinbefore mentioned, at the days and times above specified for the payment thereof, without fraud or delay.

And, also, that he, the said party of the second part, shall and will, at his own proper costs, charges, and expenses, furnish, provide, and navigate upon the said ferry to and from the foot of Jackson street, aforesaid, to Hudson avenue, Brooklyn aforesaid, one good and substantial steam ferry-boat, and keep the said steam ferry-boat at all reasonable times continually employed on the said ferry during the term hereby granted; and, also, shall and will, whenever thereunto required by the said parties of the first part, at the proper costs, charges, and expenses of the party of the second part, provide and navigate upon the said ferry one other good and substantial steam ferry-boat, which said steam ferry-boat shall be approved by the Common Council of the Corporation of the city of New York, and shall be used to carry, transport, and convey carriages, horses, passengers, and effects upon the said ferry, and that the said steamboats shall always, during the said term, be kept in good repair, and furnished with all necessary and proper implements and machinery, adapted to their respective kind, and to be manned with a sufficient number of able-bodied men, skilled in water service, to manage the same, and that the said men, so to be employed in all and each of the said boats, shall and will at all times be ready and willing to give their constant attendance at the said ferry, for the prompt and convenient transportation of passengers and effects, horses and carriages, across the said ferry; and, also, that he, the said party of the second part, his executors, administrators, and assigns, shall conduct and manage the said ferry agreeably to such rules, regulations, and restrictions as from time to time and during the said term shall, by any by-law, ordinance, order, or resolution of the said parties of the first part, or their successors, in Common Council convened, be made or passed in relation to the said ferry.

And, also, that he, the said party of the second part, his executors, administrators, or assigns, shall and will, at their own proper costs, charges, and expenses, build, erect, make and finish, and at all times, during the said term hereby demised, well and sufficiently repair, uphold, sustain, amend, maintain, and keep all and singular the floats, racks, fenders, bridges, and other ferry fixtures at each landing place of the said ferry, and shall and will also keep in repair the piers adjoining both slips used for the said ferry, both at Brooklyn and New York, or such parts and proportions of said premises as may belong to the said parties of the first part.

And, also, that the said party of the second part, his executors, administrators, or assigns, shall and will, at the expiration of the said term hereby demised, peaceably and quietly leave, surrender, and yield up the said ferry and other hereby demised premises, and the said piers, in good order and condition, into the hands and possession of the said parties of the first part, their successors or assigns.

And, also, that the said party of the second part, his executors, administrators, and assigns, shall not nor will, during the said term, transfer, assign, or set over, let or underlet, or in any other manner convey this present lease, or any part thereof, or their estate or interest therein, or in or to the above demised premises, or any part of the same, without the leave and consent of the said parties of the first part, their successors or assigns, in writing, under their common seal, had and obtained.

And it is hereby mutually agreed, by and between the respective parties to these presents, that the said parties of the first part, or their successors, shall and may, at any time and from time to time, extend the piers at the foot of Jackson street aforesaid, or any or either of them, to such distance into the East river as said parties of the first part shall deem expedient, by resolution duly passed in their legislative capacity, without making to the said party of the second part, his executors, administrators, or assigns, any compensation for the supposed damage they may thereby sustain, and without being liable to any action, suit, or proceeding, by reason of such extension, by or on behalf of the said parties of the second part, their executors, administrators, or assigns, and without any alteration of the rent hereby demised.

And it is further mutually covenanted and agreed, by and between the parties to these presents, and these presents are upon the express understanding, that nothing herein contained shall be taken or construed to operate as a covenant, by the said parties of the first part, or their successors, for possession or quiet enjoyment by the said party of the second part, or his executors, administrators, or assigns, of the said ferry or right of ferriage; nor shall the same be taken or construed to interfere, in any manner, with any previous grant or right made by the said parties of the first part, nor with the right to grant any future ferries to and from Brooklyn, or to and from elsewhere wheresoever; nor to operate further than to grant the possession of the estate, right, title, or interest which the said parties of the first part may have or lawfully claim in the said ferry and right of ferriage hereby demised, by virtue of their several charters and the various acts of the Legislature of the people of the State of New York.

In witness whereof, to one part of these presents, remaining with the said parties of the first part, the said party of the second part has set his hand and seal; and to the other part thereof, remaining with the said party of the second part, the said parties of the first part have caused the common seal of the city of New York to be affixed, the day and year first above written.

JAMES WILSON. [L. S.]

Attest, A. S. CADY.
City and County of New York, ss. :

On the 17th day of May, 1858, before me personally

came James Wilson, to me known to be the person described in, and who executed the foregoing lease, and acknowledged that he executed the same for the purposes therein named.

A. S. CADY,
Commissioner of Deeds.

This lease was confirmed by the Common Council, June 22d, 1858.

Know all men by these presents, That we   of the city of New York, and   of said city, are held and firmly bound unto the Mayor, Aldermen, and Commonalty of the city of New York, in the sum of $1,000 lawful money, to be paid to the said Mayor, Aldermen, and Commonalty of the city of New York, for which payment, well and truly to be made, we bind ourselves, our heirs, executors, administrators, firmly by these presents.

Sealed with our seals, dated the   1858.

Whereas   of the city of New York, has purchased from the Mayor, Aldermen, and Commonalty of the city of New York, the lease of the ferry from the foot of Jackson street, East river, to Hudson avenue, Brooklyn, for the term of ten years, from the 1st day of February, in the year 1858, at the yearly rent or sum of $500;

Now, the condition of the above obligation is such that, if the above bounden   shall well and truly pay, or cause to be paid, unto the said the Mayor, Aldermen, and Commonalty of the city of New York, quarterly, on the first days of May, August, November, and February, in each and every year, for the full end and term of ten years, from the first day of February, in the year 1858, the yearly rent or sum of $500, then this obligation to be void, otherwise to remain in full force and virtue.

J. L. BROWN, [L. S.]
HENRY MATTHEWS. [L. S.]

Sealed and delivered in the presence of
A. S. CADY.

FERRY FROM

GRAND STREET TO WILLIAMSBURGH.

THIS INDENTURE, made the 20th day of April, 1859, between the Mayor, Aldermen, and Commonalty of the city of New York, of the first part, and Jeremiah V. Meserole, Fleming Duncan, Gerrit Smith, William R. Painter, John O'Donohue, Francis Dubois, and Loftus Wood, of the counties of "New York" and "Kings," in the State of New York, parties of the second part—

Witnesseth, that the said parties of the first part, for and in consideration of the rents, covenants, and agreements hereinafter mentioned and contained, on the part of the said parties of the second part, their executors, administrators, and assigns, well and truly to be paid, observed and performed, fulfilled and kept, according to the true intent and meaning of these presents, have granted, demised, and to farm let, and by these presents do grant, demise, and to farm let, unto the said parties of the second part, and their executors, administrators, and assigns, all that ferry established from the foot of Grand street in the city of New York, over and across the East River to the foot of Grand street, in the city of Brooklyn (E. D) late town of Williamsburgh, with all and singular the rights, privileges, and advantages thereof, belonging to the said parties of the first part.

To have and to hold the same unto the said parties of the second part, their executors, administrators, and assigns, for and during, and until the full end and term of ten years, from and after the first day of May, in the year of our Lord one thousand eight hundred and fifty-nine, yielding and paying therefor, yearly and every year during the said term, the yearly rent of $15,000, in quarter-yearly payments, on the usual days of payment, to wit: on the first day of August, November, February, and May, in each and every year during the term hereby demised.

And the said parties of the second part, for themselves, their executors, administrators and assigns, do covenant and agree to and with the said parties of the first part, their successors and assigns, that they, the said parties of the second part, their executors, administrators and assigns, shall and will well and truly pay or cause to be paid unto the said parties of the first part, their successors and assigns, the said yearly rent above reserved, at the several times above limited and appointed for the payment thereof; and also, that they, the said parties of the second part, their executors, administrators or assigns, shall and will, from the first day of May next, at their own proper costs and expenses, furnish, provide and navigate on said ferry, from the foot of Grand street, in the city of New York, to the foot of Grand street, in the city of Brooklyn (E. D.), two swift, good and substantial single-keeled steamboats; that the said steam ferry-boats shall not be less than 100 feet in length, and of corresponding dimensions; that all of said boats shall be finished and furnished in a style equal to that of the boats now running on said ferry from the foot of Grand street aforesaid; and each of said boats shall have attached to its engine a fire apparatus or force-pump, with not less than 400 feet of hose of the same quality and dimensions as that used by the Fire Department of the city of New York, which fire apparatus or force-pump shall be used for the extinguishment of fires, whenever required, by the Chief Engineer of the Fire Department of the city of New York, or his assistants; for which service the parties of the second part shall be entitled to, and shall receive from the parties of the first part, the sum of $20 per hour for each hour engaged; but no time shall be counted less than one hour.

And said ferry-boats shall, in all respects, be such as shall be approved by the Comptroller of the said parties of the first part.

And the said parties of the second part shall and will further, from the first day of May next, at their own proper costs and expenses, furnish and provide an additional steam ferry-boat of the same character and description of those hereinbefore described, to be in like manner approved by the said Comptroller of the said parties of the first part; which said boat shall be in readiness to be used, and shall be used, on the said ferries, to supply the place of either of the regular boats, which, from any cause, may be prevented from making its regular trips.

The said parties of the second part shall and will further

keep the said steam ferry-boats employed on said ferry in such manner and at such times as the public accommodation shall require, and as shall be directed by the said Comptroller of the said parties of the first part; and shall and will, at all times, cause one or other of said boats to leave each of the said landings as often as is hereinafter specified, viz., once in every five minutes, beginning one hour before sunrise, and continuing until one hour after sunset; and once in every quarter hour from one hour after sunset until one hour before sunrise, or as fast as the passengers and freight can be discharged from the said steam ferry-boats.

And the said steamboats shall always, during the said term, be furnished and manned with a sufficient number of able-bodied men, skilled in water service, to sail and manage the same, and that the men so to be employed in all and every of said boats shall, at all reasonable times, be ready and willing to give their ready and constant attendance at the said ferries, for the prompt and convenient transportation of horses, carriages, passengers, and effects across the said river, and that the said parties of the second part, their executors, administrators, and assigns, shall not ask, demand, or receive any higher or greater commutation for passengers, carriages, horses, or effects, than such as is specified in the schedule of rates of ferriage which is hereunto annexed.

And the said parties of the second part, their executors, administrators, or assigns, shall and will, at their own proper costs and charges, keep good and sufficient bridges, floats, ferry accommodations and fixtures at each landing-place of the said ferry, to the extent the same may be required or necessary, and that the said parties of the second part, their executors, administrators, or assigns, shall and will, at their own proper costs and charges, at all times during the term hereby demised, well and sufficiently uphold, maintain and keep in good and substantial repair, all such necessary bridges, floats, ferry accommodations and fixtures as aforesaid.

It is understood that all the bulkheads, docks, floats, bridges, ferry-houses, and fixtures, at the foot of Grand street, New York, and at the foot of Grand street, Brooklyn (E. D.), belonging to the Corporation of the city of New York, and leased by these presents, the parties of the second part hereby agree to keep in good order and repair, at their own proper costs and expenses, and to make and keep in repair such further fixtures as may be required for properly conducting the said ferry, and that in the event of any damage to the adjoining bulkheads or piers from collision by the ferry-boats or otherwise, or from any action or operation of the said parties of the second part, that the said parties of the second part shall and will repair and restore the said bulkheads or piers to their former good condition, at their own proper costs and expenses.

And also that the said parties of the second part, their executors, administrators, and assigns, shall not, nor will, during the said term, assign, transfer, set over, mortgage, encumber, underlet, or in any other manner convey this present lease, or any part of the same, without the leave or consent of the said parties of the first part, their successors or assigns, in writing, first had and obtained.

And also that the said parties of the second part, their

executors, administrators, and assigns, shall at all times during the said term conduct and manage the said ferry agreeably to such rules, regulations, rates of ferriage, times of running and restrictions as now are or may from time to time hereafter, during the said term, by any bylaw, ordinance, or resolution of the said parties of the first part, or their successors, be made or passed in relation thereto.

Provided always, nevertheless, and these presents are upon this express condition, that if the said yearly rent or any part thereof shall be behind and unpaid for the space of ten days after any day of payment on which the same ought to be paid as aforesaid, or if the said parties of the second part, their executors, administrators, or assigns, shall neglect to perform, fulfill, and keep any or either of the articles, clauses, or agreements herein contained, which are on their part to be performed, fulfilled, and kept, according to the true intent and meaning of these presents, then and in such case it shall be lawful for the said parties of the first part, their successors or assigns, to declare in writing to the said parties of the second part, their executors, administrators, and assigns, that these presents and the estate hereby created shall be null and void, in which case every clause, article, or thing herein contained, shall be thenceforth null and void.

In witness whereof, to one part of these presents, remaining with the said parties of the first part, the said parties of the second part have set their several hands and seals, and to the other part of these presents, remaining with the said parties of the second part, the said parties of the first part have caused their common seal to be affixed, the day and year first above written.

J. V. MESEROLE. [L. S.]
F. DUNCAN [L. S.]
GERRIT SMITH. [L. S.]
W. R. PAINTER. [L. S.]
J. O'DONOHUE. [L. S.]
FRANCIS DUBOIS.[L. S.]
LOFTUS WOOD. [L. S.]

Sealed and delivered in presence of
  JAMES SANDFORD.

City and County of New York, ss.:

On the 20th day of April, A. D. 1859, before me personally came J. V. Meserole, F. Duncan, W. R. Painter, J. O'Donohue, and F. Dubois, and on the 21st day of April, A. D. 1859, before me personally came Gerrit Smith and Loftus Wood, all of whom were known to me to be the individuals described in, and who executed the foregoing lease, and severally acknowledged to me that they executed the same.

JAMES SANDFORD,
Com. of Deeds.

ABRAHAM MESEROLE. } *Securities.* ($30,000.)
JOHN O'DONOHUE.

SCHEDULE *of the rates of ferriage referred to in the foregoing lease:*

For every foot passenger	03
Commutation for foot passenger per year	$10 00
For man and horse	12
One-horse pleasure carriage, two persons	25
Gig or sulky	25
Two-horse pleasure carriage, four persons & driver	37
One-horse wagon, loaded	25
One-horse wagon, light	18
Two-horse wagon, loaded	37
Two-horse wagon, light	25
Two-horse wagon, hay or straw	50
Every steer, ox, or cow	12
Every score of sheep, or hogs	75
Every calf	03
Every dead hog, weighing 100 lbs. or under	06
Every dead hog, weighing over 100 lbs	08
Every 100 lbs. iron, butter, cheese, &c	04
Every bbl. cider, liquor, or pork	06
Every milk wagon, one-horse, commutation per month	4 00
Every bbl. flour	04

All other articles, not enumerated, in proportion, at the above rates.

NEW YORK, April 20, 1859.

NOTE.—Vide preamble and resolution following lease of Peck slip Ferry, on page 42.

FERRY FROM
NORTH OF GRAND STREET TO SOUTH SEVENTH STREET, WILLIAMSBURGH.

The following resolution passed the Common Council in relation to this Ferry:

Resolved, That the Comptroller is hereby authorized and directed to advertise and sell at public auction a lease of a ferry from the present ferry slip, north of and immediately adjoining the present ferry slip at the foot of Grand street, New York, to the foot of South Seventh street, in the city of Brooklyn, E. D., for the period of ten years, from the first day of May next; and the parties purchasing such ferry lease at such sale shall procure at their own risk and expense the slips above designated; and that until such ferry is put in operation, under and in pursuance of such sale, the Brooklyn Ferry Company is authorized to run ferry-boats for the accommodation of the public, and to charge rates of ferriage not exceeding those which have heretofore been charged on said ferry by the Williamsburgh Ferry Company.

Passed by the Board of Councilmen, over the Mayor's veto, August 8th, 1859.

Passed by the Board of Aldermen, over the Mayor's veto, September 5th, 1859.

The Comptroller, however, made no sale under the above resolution, and a ferry has been running between the two points without authority, against the parties engaged in which, the Comproller has commenced proceedings at law; and at the date of putting this work finally in press, the compiler is informed at the Comptroller's office that the matter is still in litigation. There is, therefore, no rent being paid for this ferry.

FERRY FROM

HOUSTON STREET TO WILLIAMSBURGH.

THIS INDENTURE, made the twelfth day of January, in the year of our Lord one thousand eight hundred and fifty-two, between The Mayor, Aldermen, and Commonalty of the City of New York, of the first part, and Gerard Stuyvesant, Reuben Withers, James M. Waterbury, and William W. Winans, John C. Winans, Susan Stevens, Catherine Winans, and Margaret Green, wife of David Green, heirs at law and legal representatives of Anthony V. Winans, late of the City of New York, deceased, parties of the second part:

Witnesseth, that the said parties of the first part, for and in consideration of the rents, covenants, payments, agreements, and articles hereinafter mentioned and contained, on the part and behalf of the said parties of the second part, their several respective executors, administrators and assigns, to be paid, done, performed and kept have demised, granted, and to farm letten, and by these presents do demise, grant, and to farm let, unto the said parties of the second part, their executors, administrators and assigns, all that ferry established from the foot of Houston street, in the City of New York, over and across the East river, to a point immediately adjoining the ferry now established at the foot of Grand street, in the Village of Williamsburgh, in the County of Kings, and from thence to the foot of Houston street, as aforesaid, together with all and singular the ferriage fees, perquisites, issues, profits, benefits and emoluments thereof.

To have and to hold, the said ferry, and the premises now used and occupied by the said ferry, with the appurtenances, unto the said parties of the second part, their executors, administrators, and assigns, for and during the full end and term of ten years, from the first day of May, in the year one thousand eight hundred and fifty-three: Yielding and paying therefor, unto the said parties of the first part, their successors and assigns, yearly and every year during the said term, the sum of six thousand five hundred dollars. And the said parties of the first part shall build and complete piers at the foot of Houston street, in said city; that from the completion thereof, the said rent shall be seven thousand five hundred dollars per annum, to be paid in quarter-yearly payments, to wit, on the first days of August, November, February, and May, in each and every year, during the said term hereby demised.

Provided always, and these presents and the premises hereby demised are upon this express condition, that if the said yearly rent, or any part thereof, should be behind or unpaid, for the space of ten days after any day of payment on which the same or any part thereof ought to be paid as aforesaid, or if the said parties of the second part, their executors, administrators, or assigns, shall neglect to pay, perform, fulfill, and keep any or either of the payments, articles, covenants, clauses, agreements, matters and things herein contained, which on their part are to be paid, performed, fulfilled and kept, during the term aforesaid, according to the true intent and meaning of these presents, that then, and in every such case, it shall and may be lawful for the said parties of the first part, their successors and assigns, to enter into and upon the premises hereby demised, and to have, possess, and enjoy the same, as fully as though these presents had not been made, anything herein contained to the contrary notwithstanding.

And the said parties of the second part, for themselves, their executors, administrators, and assigns, do covenant and agree, to and with the said parties of the first part, their successors and assigns, by these presents, that they, the said parties of the second part, their executors, administrators, and assigns, shall and will, yearly and every year during the said term, well and truly pay unto the said parties of the first part, their successors or assigns, the said yearly rent or sums of money hereinbefore mentioned, at the days and times above specified for the payment thereof, without fraud or delay.

And also, that they, the said parties of the second part, their executors, administrators, and assigns, shall and will, on or before the first day of May, in the year of our Lord one thousand eight hundred and fifty-three, and thenceforth during the continuance of the said term hereby demised, at their own proper cost and expense, furnish, provide, and navigate, upon the said ferry, one good and substantial steam ferry-boat, to be approved of by the ferry committee for the time being of the said parties of the first part, or their successors, to carry, transport, and convey passengers, horses, cattle, carts, carriages and wagons, goods, merchandise, and other things whatsoever, on the said ferry, between Houston street and Williamsburgh, as aforesaid, with safety, convenience, and expedition, in such manner as that the said steam ferry-boat shall leave the landing place of said ferry at the foot of Houston street at least once in every half hour, unless prevented by the elements, from sunrise to eight o'clock in the evening of each day; and also, that they shall and will, whenever required by any resolution of the said parties of the first part, or their successors, passed in Common Council, at any time during the said term hereby demised, place and navigate one or more additional steam ferry-boats, to be approved of as aforesaid, upon the said ferry; and that the said boat or boats shall at all times during the said term be kept in good repair, and properly furnished and provided with the necessary implements and tackle, and with a sufficient number of sober, skillful, and able-bodied men, who shall be competent to manage the same, and shall, at all reasonable times, give their constant and ready attendance at the said ferry, for the prompt and expeditious transportation of passengers, horses, cattle, carts, carriages, wagons, goods, merchandise, and other things, whatsoever, across the said river.

And also, that they shall conduct and manage the said ferry agreeably to such rules, regulations, rates of ferriage, times of running, and restrictions, as now are, or may from time to time hereafter, during the said term, by any by-law, ordinance, or resolution of the said parties of the first part, or their successors, or by any statute of this State, be made or passed in relation to the same. *Also,* that they, the said parties of the second part, their executors, administrators, and assigns, shall and will, at their own proper costs, charges, and expenses, build, erect, make, and furnish, and at all times during the term hereby demised, will well and sufficiently uphold, maintain, and keep in good and substantial repair, the necessary bridges and floats, and other fixtures at each landing place of the said ferry, and the necessary docks and piers on the Long Island shore; and that they will likewise keep in like good repair, during the term hereby demised, the bulkhead, docks and piers, made and erected, and to be made and erected by the said parties of the first part, or their successors, for the accommodation of said ferry, at the foot of Houston street, as aforesaid; and also all the bulkhead, piers, ferry houses, and fixtures belonging to the said parties of the first part, at Williamsburgh aforesaid, and now used for the purposes of said ferry. *And* will likewise keep in like good repair, during the said term, the street in front of the bulkhead at the foot of Houston street, to the extent of twenty-five feet back from the said bulkhead, and to the full width thereof.

And the said parties of the second part further covenant and agree, that whenever Tompkins street, at Houston street, in said city, shall be extended to the present exterior line of said city, they will remove, at their own proper cost and expense, the ferry houses, fifty feet from the easterly line of said street.

And that, at the expiration, or other sooner determination of the said term hereby demised, they, the said parties of the second part, their executors, administrators or assigns, shall and will peaceably and quietly leave, surrender, and yield up the said ferry, and every thing hereby demised, together with the bulkheads, piers, docks, floats, bridges and other fixtures and improvements which may have been erected or made by either of the parties, for the use of the said ferry, at the foot of Houston street, or at the termination of said ferry in Williamsburgh, in good order and condition, into the possession of the said parties of the first part, their successors or assigns, without fraud or delay.

And, also, that the said parties of the second part, their executors, administrators and assigns, shall not, nor will, during the said term, assign, transfer, set over, mortgage, encumber, underlet, or in any other manner convey this present lease, or any part thereof, or the above demised premises, or any part of the same, without the leave and consent of the said parties of the first part, their successors or assigns, in writing first had and obtained.

And it is hereby expressly understood and agreed, that nothing contained in these presents shall prevent the establishment of any other ferry or ferries across the said East river, at any place, or at any time previous to the expiration of the said term hereby granted by the said parties of the first part.

And the said parties of the first part, for themselves and their successors, do covenant and agree to and with the said parties of the second part, their executors, administrators and assigns, in manner and form following, that is to say: that if, at any time during the said term, the said parties of the first part, or their successors, shall require any part of the said premises, for the purpose of docking out and building Tompkins street, that in such case the said parties of the first part, or their successors, shall be, and are hereby, authorized to make such improvements, without any manner of claim for damage, or any abatement of rent or otherwise, on the part of the parties of the second part, their executors, administrators or assigns, by reason thereof. *But,* if made, the new slip to be left in such suitable condition, for ferry use, as the same shall be in at the commencement of this term, and a slip for a temporary landing place to be provided during said interruption, by the said parties of the first part. All fixtures to be at the expense of the said parties of the second part.

And it is hereby expressly understood and agreed, by

and between the parties aforesaid, that nothing in this lease contained shall, in any respect, vary or affect any clause, covenant, article, or agreement, in the lease heretofore executed between the said parties of the first part and Williamsburgh Ferry Company, dated on the eighth day of October, one thousand eight hundred and twenty-seven.

In witness whereof, to one part of these presents, remaining with the said parties of the second part, the said parties of the first part have caused the common seal of the said city of New York to be affixed; and to the other part thereof, remaining with the said parties of the first part, the said parties of the second part have affixed their hands and seals, the day and year first above written.

Sealed and delivered in the presence of

GEO. L. TAYLOR, as to MRS. GREEN.
CHAS. W. LAWRENCE, as to others.

GERARD STUYVESANT. [L. S.]
R. WITHERS. [L. S.]
JAS. M. WATERBURY. [L. S.]
WILLIAM W. WINANS. [L. S.]
JOHN C. WINANS, [L. S.]
Per Att'y, WILLIAM W. WINANS.
SUSAN STEVENS, [L. S.]
Per Att'y, A. W. WINANS.
CATHARINE WINANS, [L. S.]
Per Att'y, A. W. WINANS.
MARGARET GREEN. [L. S.]

City and County of New York, ss.:

On this 18th day of February, 1852, before me came Charles W. Lawrence, subscribing witness to the above conveyance, to me personally known, who, being by me duly sworn, did depose and say, that he resides in the city of New York, that he is acquainted with Gerard Stuyvesant, R. Withers, Jas. M. Waterbury, William W. Winans, John C. Winans, Susan Stevens and Catharine Winans, (the three last of whom executed the same through William W. Winans and A. W. Winans, as attorneys,) that he knows said persons to be the same individuals described in and who executed the within conveyance, and that they acknowledged, in his presence, that they executed the same, and that he subscribed his name as a witness thereto; and, on the same day, before me came Margaret Green, wife of David Green, to me known to be the same person described in, and who executed the above conveyance, and acknowledged that she executed the same; and on a private examination by me, apart from her said husband, acknowledged that she executed the same freely, and of her own consent, and without any fear or compulsion of her said husband.

GEO. L. TAYLOR,
Com'r of Deeds.

Resolved, That the Houston street Ferry Company be, and they hereby are, directed to have a suitable lamp placed at the entrance of the ferry house, foot of Houston street.

Adopted by the Board of Councilmen, June 4, 1855.

Adopted by the Board of Aldermen, June 5, 1855.

Approved by the Mayor, June 7th, 1855.

FERRY FROM

TENTH STREET, EAST RIVER, TO GREENPOINT, L. I.

This ferry is and has been running in connection with the Twenty-third street Ferry, by the same Company, and without any apparent authority. There is no lease, and consequently, no rent is paid for it.

FERRY FROM

FOURTEENTH STREET TO GREENPOINT, L. I.

THIS INDENTURE, made the twenty-sixth day of September, in the year of our Lord one thousand eight hundred and fifty-one, between the Mayor, Aldermen, and Commonalty of the city of New York, parties of the first part, and Alexander H. Schultz, of the City of New York, party of the second part:

Whereas, on the first day of December, A. D. eighteen hundred and forty-nine, a certain resolution, passed by the Common Council of the city of New York, was approved of by the Mayor of said city, which said resolution was in the words and figures following, to wit:

Resolved, That a ferry lease be granted to Nezeiah Bliss and Hezekiah Bradford, from the foot of Sixteenth street, East River, to the foot of J, K, or L street, Green Point, Long Island, for the term of ten years, from the first day of May, one thousand eight hundred and fifty, at an annual rent of two hundred and fifty dollars, payable quarterly; the said Nezeiah Bliss and Hezekiah Bradford to make such improvements as may be necessary for the accommodation of such ferry, at their own cost and expense; and to place on such ferry good and substantial steam ferry-boats, and run the same under such regulations as may be approved of by the Comptroller and the Counsel of the Corporation; and that the Counsel of the Corporation be, and he is hereby, instructed to prepare a lease for said ferry on the above terms, to be approved of by the Comptroller.

And whereas, a lease was made and executed to the said Bliss and Bradford, pursuant to the terms of said resolution; and which said lease has been assigned to, and is now held by and owned by the said party hereto of the second part:

And whereas, on the twenty-sixth day of September, eighteen hundred and fifty-one, a certain resolution, passed by the Common Council of the city of New York, was approved of by the Mayor of said city, which said last mentioned resolution was in the words and figures followlowing, to wit:

Resolved, That a lease be granted to Alexander H. Schultz, for permission to run a ferry from the foot of Fourteenth street, East River, to Green Point, Long Island, for a term equal to the unexpired term of the lease of the ferry to Green Point, authorized by a resolution of the Common Council, approved by the Mayor, December the 1st, eighteen hundred and forty-nine, with an addition of five years thereto, at an annual rent of two hundred and fifty dollars for the unexpired term of the present lease; and seven hundred and fifty dollars per annum, for the additional five years hereby granted, and upon the same terms and conditions contained in the lease heretofore granted for said ferry. The ferry thus authorized, to be put in complete order, with boats running on the same within one year from the approval of this resolution by his Honor, the Mayor.

Now, this Indenture witnesseth, that the said parties of the first part, for and in consideration of the rents, covenants, provisions, articles, and agreements hereinafter mentioned, on the part and behalf of the said party of the second part, his executors, administrators and assigns, to be had, performed, observed, fulfilled and kept, have granted, demised, and to farm letten, and by these presents, do grant, demise, and to farm let, unto the said party of the second part, his executors, administrators and assigns, all that certain ferry established and located at and from the foot of Fourteenth street East River, in the city of New York, over and across the East River, to Green Point, Long Island, and from Green Point aforesaid, back to the foot of Fourteenth street aforesaid, with the privilege of running steamboats thereon, and with all and singular the ferriage fees, perquisites, rents, issues, profits, benefits and advantages whatsoever, which may arise or accrue from the said ferry; to have and to hold the said ferry, with the appurtenances, unto the said party of the second part, his executors, administrators and assigns, from the first day of May, eighteen hundred and fifty-one, for and during, and until the full end and term of fourteen years, from thence next ensuing, and fully to be complete and ended, yielding and paying therefor, yearly, and every year during the first nine years of the term of lease to Bliss and Bradford, unto the said parties of the first part, their successors and assigns, the yearly rent or sum of two hundred and fifty dollars; and seven hundred and fifty dollars per annum, for the remainder of said term of five years, lawful money of the United States of America, in quarter-yearly payments, on the usual quarter days for the payment of rent in the said city of New York; that is to say: one fourth part thereof on the first days of August, November, February and May, in each and every year during the said term; the first payment to be made on the first day of November next: provided always, that if it should so happen that the said yearly rent, or any part thereof, should be behind or unpaid, for the space of ten days after any day of payment, on which the same ought to be paid as aforesaid; or if the said party of the second part, his executors, administrators or assigns, shall neglect or omit to pay, perform, fulfill, observe and keep, any or either of the payments, articles, covenants, clauses, agreements, provisions, matters or things herein contained, which, on the part and behalf of the said party of the second part, his executors, administrators or assigns, are to be paid, performed, fulfilled, and kept, during the said term of fourteen years, according to the true intent and meaning of these presents, that then, and in every and all such case and cases, it shall and may be lawful for the said parties of the first part, their successors or assigns, to enter into and upon the premises hereby demised; and to have, possess and enjoy the same again, as fully as though these presents had never been made, anything herein contained to the contrary notwithstanding.

And the said party of the second part, for himself, his heirs, executors, administrators and assigns, doth covenant and agree, to and with the said parties of the first part, their successors and assigns, by these presents, in manner following; that is to say, That the said party of the second part, his executors. administrators and assigns. shall and will yearly, and every year during the said term hereby demised, well and truly pay unto the said parties of the first part, their successors or assigns, the said yearly rent or sum of money hereinbefore mentioned, at the days and times above specified for the payment thereof, without fraud or delay. And also, that he, the said party of the second part, shall and will, at his own proper costs, charges, and expenses, furnish, provide, and navigate upon the said ferry, to and from the foot of Fourteenth street, to Green Point aforesaid, one good and substantial steam ferry-boat, and keep the said steam ferry-boat at all reasonable times continually employed on the said ferry, during the term hereby granted; and also shall and will, whenever there nto required by the said parties of the first part, at their own proper costs, charges, and expenses, provide and navigate, upon the said ferry, one other good and substantial steam ferry-boat; which steam ferry-boat shall be approved by the Street Commissioner of the Corporation of the said city of New York; and shall be used to carry, transport, and convey carriages, horses, passengers, and effects, upon the said ferry, and that the said steamboats shall always, during the said term, be kept in good repair, and furnished with all necessary and proper implements and machinery adapted to their respective kind, and be manned with a sufficient number of able-bodied men, skilled in water service, to manage the same; and that the said men so to be employed, in all and each of the said boats, shall and will, at all times, be ready and willing to give their constant attendance at the said ferry, for the prompt and convenient transportation of passengers and effects, horses and carriages, across the said ferry. And also that the said party of the second part, his executors, administrators and assigns, shall not ask, demand, or receive any higher or greater toll, fare, and rate of ferriage, or any greater commutation for passengers, carriages, horses or effects, than such as is specified in the schedule of rates of ferriage hereto annexed. And also, that he, the said party of the second part, his executors, administrators, and assigns, shall conduct and manage the said ferry agreeably to such rules, regulations, rates of ferriage, times of running, and restrictions, as are now, or from time to time, during said term, shall, by any by-law, ordinance, order, or resolution of the said parties of the first part, or their successors in Common Council convened, be made or passed in relation to the said ferry.

And also, that he, the said party of the second part, his executors, administrators, and assigns, shall and will, at his own proper costs, charges, and expenses, build, erect, make, and finish, and, at all times during the said term hereby demised, well and sufficiently repair, uphold, sustain, amend, maintain, and keep, all and singular, the floats, racks, fenders, bridges, and other ferry fixtures, at each landing place of the said ferry; and shall and will also keep in repair the piers hereafter to be erected adjoining both slips used for the said ferry, both at Green Point and New York, or such parts or proportions of the said piers as may belong to the said parties of the first part.

And the said party of the second part, for himself, his heirs, executors, administrators, and assigns, doth covenant and agree to, and with the said parties of the first part, their successors and assigns, that he, the said party of the second part, his executors, administrators, and assigns, will put the ferry, hereby authorized, in complete order, with the boats running on the same, as hereinbefore covenanted and agreed, within one year from the twenty-sixth day of September, eighteen hundred and fifty-one, being the date of the approval by the Mayor of the second resolution hereinbefore set forth.

And also, that the said party of the second part, his executors, administrators and assigns, shall and will, at the expiration of the said term, hereby demised, peaceably and quietly leave, surrender and yield up the said ferry and other hereby demised premises and the piers, in good order and condition, into the hands and possession of the said parties of the first part, their successors or assigns. And also, that he, the said party of the second part, his executors, administrators and assigns, shall not nor will, during the said term, transfer, assign, or set over, let or underlet, or in any other manner convey this present lease, or any part thereof, or his estate or interest therein, or in or to the above demised premises, or any part of the same, without the leave or consent of the said parties of the first part, their successors or assigns, in writing, under their common seal, first had and obtained.

And it is hereby mutually agreed, by and between the respective parties to these presents, that the said parties of the first part, or their successors, shall and may, at any time and from time to time, extend the piers at the foot of Fourteenth street aforesaid, or any or either of them, to such distance into the East river, as said parties of the first part shall deem expedient, by resolution duly passed in their legislative capacity, without making to the said party of the second part, his executors, administrators or assigns, any compensation for the supposed damage he may sustain; and without being liable to any action, suit or proceeding, by reason of such extension, by or on behalf of the said party of the second part, his executors, administrators or assigns, and without any alteration of the rent hereby reserved.

And it is hereby mutually covenanted and agreed, by and between the parties to these presents, and these presents are upon the express understanding, that nothing herein contained shall be taken or construed to operate as a covenant, by the said parties of the first part or their successors, for possession or quiet enjoyment by the said party of the second part, or his executors, administrators or assigns, of the said ferry or right of ferriage; nor shall the same be taken or construed to interfere, in any manner, with any previous grants or rights made by the said parties of the first part, nor with the right to grant any future ferries, to and from Green Point, or to and from elsewhere wheresoever; nor to operate further than to grant the possession of the estate, right, title or interest, which the said parties of the first part may have or lawfully claim, in the said ferry and right of ferriage hereby demised, by virtue of their several charters, and the various acts of the Legislature of the people of the State of New York.

SCHEDULE *of the Rates of Ferriage referred to in the foregoing lease.*

For every foot passenger,	$0 03
Commutation of foot passenger, per year,	10 00
For man and horse,	12½
One-horse pleasure carriage, two persons,	25
Gig or sulky,	25
Two-horse pleasure carriage, with four persons and driver,	37½

One-horse wagon, loaded,	25
One-horse wagon, light,	$18\frac{3}{4}$
Two-horse wagon, loaded,	$37\frac{1}{2}$
Two-horse wagon, light,	25
Two-horse wagon, hay or straw,	50
For every steer, ox, or cow,	$12\frac{1}{2}$
For every score of sheep or hogs,	75
For every calf,	03
For every dead hog, weighing 100 lbs., or under,	$06\frac{1}{4}$
For every dead hog, weighing over 100 lbs.	08
For every 100 lbs. iron, butter, cheese, &c.,	04
For every barrel cider, liquors, or pork,	$06\frac{1}{4}$
For every milk wagon, with one horse,—commutation, per month,	4 00
For every barrel of flour,	04

In witness whereof, to one part of these presents, remaining with the said parties of the first part, the said party of the second part hath set his hand and seal; and to the other part thereof, remaining with the said party of the second part, the said parties of the first part have caused the common seal of the city of New York to be affixed, the day and year first above written.

Sealed and delivered in the presence of
   Jos. C. PINCKNEY.
           ALEX'R H. SCHULTZ. [L. S.]

The Mayor, Aldermen and Commonalty of the city of New York hereby give permission for the transfer of this lease to Gideon Lee Knapp.

New York, March 18, 1852.
           JOS. R. TAYLOR,
                Comptroller.

NOTE.—"Hundred," eighth line, page "148," interlined.

FERRY FROM

SIXTEENTH STREET TO GREENPOINT. L. I.

This Indenture, made the first day of December, in the year of our Lord one thousand eight hundred and forty-nine, between The Mayor, Aldermen, and Commonalty of the City of New York, parties of the first part, and Nezeiah Bliss, of the town of Bushwick, in the County of Kings, and Hezekiah Bradford, of the city of New York, parties of the second part:

Whereas, on the first day of December, A. D. eighteen hundred and forty-nine, a certain resolution, passed by the Common Council of the city of New York, was approved of by the Mayor of said city, which said resolution was in the words and figures following, to wit:

Resolved, That a ferry lease be granted to Nezeiah Bliss and Hezekiah Bradford, from the foot of Sixteenth street, East River, to the foot of J, K, or L street, Green Point, Long Island, for the term of ten years, from the 1st day of May, one thousand eight hundred and fifty, at an annual rent of two hundred and fifty dollars, payable quarterly, the said Nezeiah Bliss and Hezekiah Bradford to make such improvements as may be necessary, for the accommodation of such ferry, at their own cost and expense; and to place on such ferry good and substantial steam ferry-boats, and run the same under such regulations as may be approved of by the Comptroller and the Counsel of the Corporation; and that the Counsel of the Corporation be, and he is hereby, instructed to prepare a lease for said ferry, on the above terms, to be approved of by the Comptroller.

Now, this Indenture witnesseth, that the said parties of

the first part, for and in consideration of the rents, covenants, provisions, articles, and agreements, hereinafter mentioned, on the part and behalf of the said parties of the second part, their executors, administrators and assigns, to be paid, performed, observed, fulfilled and kept, have granted, demised, and to farm letten, and by these presents do grant, demise, and to farm let, unto the said parties of the second part, their executors, administrators and assigns, all that certain ferry established and located at and from the foot of Sixteenth street, East River, in the city of New York, over and across the East River, to the foot of J, K, or L street, Green Point, Long Island, and from J, K, or L street, aforesaid, back to the foot of Sixteenth street, aforesaid, with the privilege of running steamboats thereon, and with all and singular the ferriage fees, perquisites, rents, issues, profits, benefits and advantages whatsoever, which may arise or accrue from the said ferry; to have and to hold the said ferry, with the appurtenances, unto the said parties of the second part, their executors, administrators and assigns, from the first day of May, eighteen hundred and fifty, for and during, and until the full end and term of ten years, from thence next ensuing, and fully to be complete and ended, yielding and paying therefor, yearly, and every year during the said term, unto the said parties of the first part, their successors or assigns, the yearly rent or sum of two hundred and fifty dollars, lawful money of the United States of America, in quarter yearly payments, on the usual quarter days for the payment of rent in the said city of New York; that is to say, one fourth part on the first days of August, November, February and May, in each and every year during the said term; the first payment to be made on the first day of August next: Provided always, that if it should so happen that the said yearly rent, or any part thereof, shall be behind or unpaid, for the space of ten days after any day of payment, on which the same ought to be paid, as aforesaid; or if the said parties of the second part, their executors, administrators, or assigns, do, or shall neglect to pay, perform, fulfill, observe and keep, any or either of the payments, articles, covenants, clauses, agreements, provisions, matters or things herein contained, which, on the part and behalf of the said parties of the second part, their executors, administrators, or assigns, are to be paid, performed, observed, fulfilled and kept, during the said term of ten years, according to the true intent and meaning of these presents, that then, and in every and all such case and cases, it shall and may be lawful for the said parties of the first part, their successors or assigns, to enter into and upon the premises hereby demised, and to have, possess and enjoy the same again, as fully as though these presents had never been made, anything herein contained to the conrary notwithstanding.

And the said parties of the second part, for themselves, their heirs, executors, administrators and assigns, do covenant and agree, to and with the said parties of the first part, their successors and assigns, by these presents, in manner following, that is to say : That the said parties of the second part, their executors, administrators and assigns, shall, and will yearly, and every year during the said term hereby demised, well and truly pay unto the said parties of the first part, their successors or assigns, the said yearly rent or sum of money hereinbefore mentioned, at the days and times above specified for the payment thereof, without fraud or delay. And also, that they, the said parties of the second part, shall and will, at their own proper costs, charges and expenses, furnish, provide and navigate upon the said ferry, to and from the foot of Sixteenth street, to Green Point aforesaid, one good and substantial steam ferry boat, and keep the said steam ferry boat at all reasonable times continually employed on the said ferry, during the term hereby granted; and also shall and will, whenever thereunto required by the said parties of the first part, at their own proper costs, charges and expenses, provide and navigate, upon the said ferry, one other good and substantial steam ferry boat, which steam ferry boat shall be approved by the Street Commissioner of the Corporation of the said city of New York, and shall be used to carry, transport, and convey carriages, horses, passengers and effects, upon the said ferry, and that the said steamboats shall always, during the said term, be kept in good repair, and furnished with all necessary and proper implements and machinery adapted to their respective kind, and be manned with a sufficient number of able-bodied men, skilled in water service, to manage the same; and that said men so to be employed, in all and each of the said boats, shall and will, at all times, be ready and willing to give their constant attendance at said ferry, for the prompt and convenient transportation of passengers and effects, horses and carriages, across the said ferry. And also that the said parties of the second part, their executors, administrators nd assigns, shall not ask, demand, or receive, any higher and greater toll, fare, and rate of ferriage, or any greater commutation for passengers, carriages, horses, or effects, than such as is specified in the schedule of rates of ferriage hereto annexed. And also, that they, the said parties of the second part, their executors, administrators and assigns, shall conduct and manage said ferry agreeably to such rules, regulations, rates of ferriage, times of running and restrictions, as now are, or, from time to time during said term, shall, by any by-law, ordinance, order, or resolution, of the said parties of the first part, or their successors in Common Council convened, be made or passed in relation to the said ferry.

And also that they, the said parties of the second part, their executors, administrators and assigns, shall and will, at their own proper costs, charges, and expenses, build, erect, make and finish, and, at all times during the said term hereby demised, well and sufficiently repair, uphold, sustain, amend, maintain and keep, all and singular the floats, racks, fenders, bridges and other ferry fixtures, at each landing place of the said ferry; and shall and will also keep in repair the piers adjoining both slips used for the said ferry, both at Green Point and New York, or such parts or proportions of said piers as may belong to the said parties of the first part.

And also, that the said parties of the second part, their executors, administrators or assigns, shall and will, at the expiration of the said term hereby demised, peaceably and quietly leave, surrender and yield up the said ferry and other hereby demised premises and the piers, in good order and condition, into the hands and possession of the said parties of the first part, their successors or assigns. And also, that the said parties of the second part, their executors, administrators and assigns, shall not nor will, during the said term, transfer, assign, or set over, let or underlet, or in any other manner convey this present lease or any part thereof, or their estate or interest therein, or in or to the above demised premises or any part of the same, without the leave or consent of the said parties of the first part, their successors or assigns, in writing, under their common seal, first had and obtained.

And it is hereby mutually agreed, by and between the respective parties to these presents, that the said parties of the first part, or their successors, shall and may, at any time, and from time to time, extend the piers at the foot of Sixteenth street aforesaid, or any or either of them, to such distance into the East river as said parties of the first part shall deem expedient, by resolution duly passed in their legislative capacity, without making to the said parties of the second part, their executors, administrators or assigns, any compensation for the supposed damage they may thereby sustain; and without being liable to any action, suit or proceeding, by reason of such extension, by or on behalf of the said parties of the second part, their executors, administrators or assigns, and without any alteration of the rent hereby reserved.

And it is hereby mutually covenanted and agreed, by and between the parties to these presents, and these presents are upon the express understanding, that nothing herein contained shall be taken or construed to operate as a covenant, by the said parties of the first part or their successors, for possession or quiet enjoyment by the said parties of the second part, or their executors, administrators and assigns, of the said ferry or right of ferriage, nor shall the same be taken or construed to interfere, in any manner, with any previous grants or rights made by the said parties of the first part, nor with the right to grant any future ferries, to and from Green Point or to and from elsewhere wheresoever; nor to operate further than to grant the possession of the estate, right, title or interest, which the said parties of the first part may have or lawfully claim, in the said ferry and right of ferriage hereby demised, by virtue of their several charters, and the various acts of the Legislature of the people of the State of New York.

Schedule *of the Rates of Ferriage, referred to in the foregoing lease.*

For every foot passenger,....three (3) cents....	$0 03
Commutation of foot passenger, per year,.......	10 00
For man and horse,............................	12½
One-horse pleasure carriage, two persons,.......	25
Gig or sulky,................................	25
Two-horse pleasure carriage, with four persons and driver,.............................	37½
One-horse wagon, loaded,......................	25
One-horse wagon, light,.......................	18¾
Two-horse wagon, loaded,......................	37½
Two-horse wagon, light,.......................	25
Two-horse wagon, hay or straw,................	50
For every steer, ox, or cow,...................	12½
For every score of sheep or hogs,..............	75
For every calf,...............................	03
For every dead hog, weighing 100 lbs. or under,.	06¼
For every dead hog, weighing over 100 lbs......	08
For every 100 lbs. iron, butter, cheese, &c.,.....	04
For every barrel cider, liquors or pork,.........	06¼
For every milk wagon, with one horse,—commutation, per month,.......................	4 00
For every barrel of flour,......................	04

In witness whereof, to one part of these presents, remaining with the said parties of the first part, the said parties of the second part have set their hands and seals; and to the other part thereof, remaining with the said parties of the second part, the said parties of the first part have caused the common seal of the city of New York to be affixed, the day and year first above written.

Sealed and delivered in the presence of
  JOS. C. PINCKNEY.

    NEZEIAH BLISS.   [L. S.]
    HEZEKIAH BRADFORD. [L. S.]

City and County of New York, ss.:

On this 29th May, 1850, before me came Nezeiah Bliss and Hezekiah Bradford, to me personally known to be the individuals described in, and who executed the foregoing instrument—and severally acknowledged to me that they executed the same for the purposes therein mentioned.

    JOS. C. PINCKNEY,
      Commissioner of Deeds.

The New York terminus of this Ferry was changed to the foot of Fourteenth street, East River, as appears by the following resolution passed by the Common Council, and approved by the Mayor on the 26th September, 1852:

Resolved, That a lease be granted to Alexander H. Schultz, for permission to run a ferry from the foot of Fourteenth street, East River, to Green Point, Long Island, for a term equal to the unexpired term of the lease of the ferry to Green Point, authorized by a resolution of the Common Council—approved by the Mayor, December the first, eighteen hundred and forty-nine—with an addition of five years thereto, at an annual rent of two hundred and fifty dollars for the unexpired term of the present lease; and seven hundred and fifty dollars per annum for the additional five years hereby granted, and upon the same terms and conditions contained in the lease heretofore granted for said ferry. The ferry thus authorized, to be put in complete order, with boats running on the same, within one year from the approval of this resolution by his Honor the Mayor.

FERRY FROM

TWENTY-THIRD STREET TO GREENPOINT, L. I.

This Indenture, made this eighth day of November, in the year of our Lord one thousand eight hundred and fifty-one, between the Mayor, Aldermen and Commonalty of the city of New York, parties of the first part; and the Trustees of St. Patrick's Cathedral, in the city of New York, parties of the second part:

Whereas, on the twenty-second day of October, A. D. eighteen hundred and fifty-one, a certain resolution, passed by the Common Council of the city of New York, was approved of by the Mayor of said city, which said resolution was in the words and figures following; to wit,

Resolved, That a lease for a right to run a ferry from the foot of *Twenty-third street* to the grounds of the *Calvary Cemetery*, the present terminus, be granted to the Trustees of St. Patrick's Cathedral and to their successors, the present lessees, for the term of ten years from the termination of the present lease, at the annual rent of one hundred dollars, payable quarterly; and that, from and after the approval of these resolutions, said lessees have the usual ferry privileges.

Resolved, That the Counsel to the Corporation be directed to prepare a lease, in conformity with the preceding report and resolution; and that said lease be prepared and executed within twenty days after the approval of these resolutions.

Now, this indenture witnesseth, that the said parties of the first part, for and in consideration of the rents, covenants, provisions, articles and agreements, hereinafter mentioned, on the part and behalf of the said parties of the second part, their successors and assigns, to be had, performed, observed, fulfilled and kept, have granted, demised and to farm letten, and by these presents do grant, demise and to farm let, unto the said parties of the second part, their successors and assigns, all the right to keep and maintain a ferry from the bulkhead at the north side of, and contiguous to the foot of Twenty-third street, in the city of New York, to and from said last mentioned point, and to and from the grounds of the Calvary Cemetery, known as the Ferry Bridge, on Long Island; and also, all the right to use so much of the bulkhead aforesaid as shall be necessary and required, in order to erect and prepare such suitable fixtures and necessary arrangements as are required in order to effect a landing for the boats used and employed on said ferry; and also to erect and place in front of said bulkhead such usual and necessary fixtures as may be required for the purpose aforesaid, such portion of said bulkhead and the position of such fixtures being particularly designated on a map annexed, and considered a part of this indenture.

Provided, however, that nothing herein contained shall authorize the said parties of the second part to use more of the water in front of said bulkhead, for the erection of any structures or fixtures, than such breadth of opening as shall or may be necessary, safely and conveniently to admit such boats, as may be employed by the said parties of the second part, for the purpose aforesaid.

To have and to hold the said demised premises unto the said parties of the second part, their successors and assigns for and during, and until the full end and term of ten years, from the twenty-seventh day of December, one thousand eight hundred and fifty-three; yielding and paying, therefor, yearly, and every year during the said term, unto the said parties of the first part, their successors and assigns, the yearly rent or sum of one hundred dollars, in quarter-yearly payments, on the usual quarter days for the payment of rent in the City of New York, that is to say, on the first days of February, May, August, and November, in each and every year during the said term.

And the said parties of the second part, for themselves, their successors and assigns, do covenant to and with the said parties of the first part, their successors and assigns, well and truly to pay the rents herein reserved, at the several times that the same are payable, as hereinbefore contained; and, also, to do and perform, and to abide by all and singular, the covenants, agreements, stipulations and conditions herein contained, on the part of the said parties of the second part, to be done, performed, fulfilled, and kept, during the said term of ten years. *And*, also, that they, the said parties of the second part, shall and will, at their own proper costs, charges and expenses, furnish, provide and navigate upon the said ferry, to and from Twenty-third street, to Long Island aforesaid, one good and substantial steam ferry-boat, and keep the said steam ferry-boat, at all reasonable times, continually employed on the said ferry during the term hereby granted; and, also, shall and will, whenever thereunto required by the said parties of the first part, at their own proper costs, charges and expenses, provide and navigate upon the said ferry, one other good and substantial steam ferry-boat, which said steam ferry-boat shall be approved by the Street Commissioner of the Corporation of the said City of New York, and shall be used to carry, transport and convey carriages, horses, passengers and effects, upon the said ferry; and, that said steam ferry-boats shall always, during the said term, be kept in good repair, and furnished with all necessary and proper implements and machinery, adapted to their respective kind, and be manned with a sufficient number of able-bodied men, skilled in water service, to manage the same, and that the said men, so to be employed in all and each of the said boats, shall and will, at all times, be ready and willing to give their constant attendance at the said ferry, for the prompt and convenient transportation of passengers and effects, horses and carriages, across the said ferry. *And*, also, that they, the said parties of the second part, their successors and assigns, shall conduct and manage the said ferry, agreeably to such rules, regulations and restrictions, as, from time to time, during the said term, shall, by any by-law, ordinance, order or resolution of the said parties of the first part, or their successors, in Common Council convened, be made or passed in relation to the said ferry.

And, also, that they, the said parties of the second

part, their successors and assigns, shall and will, at their own proper costs, charges and expenses, build, erect, make and finish, and at all times during the said term hereby demised, well and sufficiently repair, uphold, sustain, amend, maintain and keep, all and singular, the floats, racks, fenders, bridges, and other ferry fixtures, at each landing place of the said ferry; and shall and will also keep in repair the piers adjoining both slips used for the said ferry at New York, or such parts or proportions of said piers as may belong to the said parties of the first part.

And, also, that the said parties of the second part, their successors or assigns, shall and will, at the expiration of the said term hereby demised, peaceably and quietly leave, surrender and yield up the said ferry, and other hereby demised premises, and the said piers, in good order and condition, into the hands and possession of the said parties of the first part, their successors or assigns; *And*, also, that the said parties of the second part, their successors or assigns, shall not, nor will, during the said term, transfer, assign or set over, let or underlet, or in any other manner convey this present lease, or any part thereof, or their estate or interest therein, or in or to the above demised premises, or any part of the same, without the leave or consent of the said parties of the first part, their successors or assigns, in writing, first had and obtained. *And*, it is hereby further mutually covenanted and agreed, by and between the parties to these presents; and these presents are upon the express understanding, that nothing herein contained shall be taken or construed to operate as a covenant, by the said parties of the first part, or their successors, for possession or quiet enjoyment, by the said parties of the second part, or their successors or assigns, of the said ferry or right of ferriage, nor shall the same be taken or construed to interfere in any manner with any previous grants or rights, made by the said parties of the first part, nor with the right to grant any future ferries to and from Long Island, or to and from elsewhere wheresoever, nor to operate further than to grant the possession of the estate, right, title or interest, which the said parties of the first part may have, or lawfully claim, in the said ferry or right of ferriage hereby demised, by virtue of their several charters, and the various acts of the Legislature of the People of the State of New York.

In witness whereof, to one part of these presents, remaining with the said parties of the first part, the said parties of the second part have put their corporate seal, attested by the signatures of their President and Secretary; and, to the other part thereof, remaining with the said parties of the second part, the said parties of the first part have caused the common seal of the City of New York to be affixed, the day and year first above written.

Sealed and delivered in the presence of
CHAS. W. LAWRENCE.

DINES CAROLIN,
President pro tem.

Seal of
The Trustees of
St. Patrick's Cathedral,
New York.

Attest,

B. O'CONNOR,
Secretary.

May 4, 1853, Comptroller consents to assignment of this lease to Gideon Lee Knapp.

Resolved, That the lessee of the Twenty-third street ferry

NOTE.—"Demised," interlined, 23d line, 142d page.

be, and is hereby granted permission to change, at his own expense, the Long Island terminus of said ferry, from Penny Bridge on Newtown Creek to the foot of "L" street, Green Point; providing that the said lessee pay to this corporation the sum of one thousand dollars, in addition to the amount to be paid for the remainder of his lease.

Adopted by the Board of Councilmen, May 16, 1856.

Adopted by the Board of Aldermen, August 4, 1856.

Received from his honor the Mayor, September 4, 1856, without his approval or objections thereto; therefore, under the provisions of the amended charter, the same became adopted.

Resolved, That the proprietors of the Twenty-third street ferry be compelled, forthwith, to run their boats up Newtown Creek, according to their lease, until such time as they can build ferry slips on Green Point to run in, as the up town population, who have to cross to Long Island daily, are suffering a great deal of hardship and inconvenience, by having to travel down to Tenth street ferry, which is nearly a mile further, in consequence of the Twenty-third street ferry being stopped running since last fall.

Adopted by the Board of Aldermen, March 2, 1857.

Adopted by the Board of Councilmen, March 2, 1857.

Approved by the Mayor, March 5, 1857.

Whereas, The citizens having occasion to avail themselves of the ferry at the foot of Twenty-third street are greatly inconvenienced by the irregularity and incompleteness of the service of the same, being sometimes obliged to wait for the space of half or three-quarters of an hour for the running of the boat, for the running of which there appears to be no set hours; and

Whereas, one boat is not adequate for the proper service of said ferry, therefore be it

Resolved, That the lessee or lessees of the ferry from the foot of Twenty-third street to Green Point be, and are hereby directed forthwith to place two good and sufficient boats upon the said ferry, and to run the same so that a boat shall leave the pier at the foot of Twenty-third street at least every fifteen minutes, between the hours of twelve M. and eight P. M., and to continue the same throughout the year.

Adopted by the Board of Councilmen, Nov. 26, 1858.

Adopted by the Board of Aldermen, Nov. 29, 1858

Approved by the Mayor, Dec. 13, 1858.

FERRY FROM

THIRTY-FOURTH STREET, EAST RIVER, TO HUNTER'S POINT, L. I.

THIS INDENTURE, made the first day of August, in the year of our Lord 1857, between the Mayor, Aldermen, and Commonalty of the city of New York, parties of the first part, and Anthony W. Winans, of the city of New York, party of the second part:

Whereas, on the 26th day of November, in the year 1855, a certain resolution, passed by the Common Council of the city of New York, was approved by the Mayor of said city, which resolution was in the words and figures following; to wit,

Resolved, That a ferry across the East river be established from the foot of 34th street, East river, to Hunter's Point, Long Island, the terminus of the Flushing Railroad, and the Comptroller is hereby authorized and directed to carry this resolution into effect, and lease said ferry in pursuance of the 7th section of the act further to amend the charter of the city of New York, passed April 12, 1853.

Resolved, That the Comptroller be, and he is hereby directed to advertise the lease of said ferry and bulkhead for 10 years, for sale at public auction, by a notice in the Corporation papers for 30 days, and to lease the same to the highest bidder, who will give adequate security, and that the Corporation Counsel prepare a lease to said highest bidder, in pursuance of the 7th section of the act further to amend the charter of the city of New York, passed April 12, 1853; provided the lessee of said ferry shall enter into a contract, with good and sufficient security for the fulfillment of the same, to be approved by the Comptroller of the city, and that, at the commencement of the term of said lease, the land and water front at Hunter's Point, adjacent to the New York and Flushing Railroad, requisite for the purposes of this ferry, shall be conveyed to the Corporation of the city of New York, in fee simple, to be used for ferry purposes.

Now, therefore, this Indenture witnesseth, that the said parties of the first part, for and in consideration of the rents, covenants, provisions, articles, and agreements, hereinafter mentioned, on the part and behalf of the said party of the second part, to be paid, performed, observed, fulfilled, and kept, have granted, demised, and to farm let, and by these presents do grant, demise, and to farm let, unto the said party of the second part, all that certain grant of the right to establish and maintain a ferry from the foot of 34th street, East river, in the city of New York, over and across the East river to Hunter's Point, Long Island, the terminus of the Flushing Railroad, together with all the right, title, and interest which the said parties of the first part now have in and to the following described premises, viz.: All that certain lot, piece, or parcel of land situate at Long Island, Queens county, and State of New York, which on a certain map of the Hunter's farm, made by Charles Perkins, dated 1853, and filed in the Register's office, in said county of Queens, and State of New York, is bounded and described as follows: Beginning at a point 10 feet north of the north line of West First street, at the present high water mark, 45 feet westerly from the westerly line of West avenue, and running thence westerly in a straight line parallel to said street, as laid down on said map, to the exterior line of water grant, as established by the Commissioners of the Land Office; thence southerly along the exterior line of water grant, as the same runs, 100 feet; thence easterly and parallel to said north line to present high water mark; thence along said high water mark to the place of beginning; the said premises situate and being adjacent to the terminus of the Flushing Railroad, at Hunter's Point, requisite for the purpose of a ferry to 34th street, East river, New York (the said premises to be kept always open and free as a public highway), and from thence back again to the foot of 34th street, aforesaid. Together with all and singular the bulkhead at the foot of 34th street, aforesaid, as now owned by the parties of the first part, under and by virtue of a certain indenture of re-lease from the Farmers' Loan and Trust Company, bearing date the 23d day of July, 1856, together with all the usual accustomed ferriage fees, perquisites, rents, issues, profits, and advantages whatsoever, to the said ferry belonging, or therewith used, or thereout arising.

To have and to hold the said ferry with the appurtenances, and other hereby granted premises, unto the said party of the second part, his heirs, executors, administrators and assigns for and during the full end and term of ten years, from the 1st day of August, in the year of our Lord 1857, yielding and paying therefor, yearly and every year, during the said term, unto the said parties of the first part, their successors or assigns, the yearly rent or sum of $100, payable quarterly, on the usual days for the payment of rent in the city of New York, that is to say: one fourth part on the 1st day of August, November, February, and May, in each and every year during the said term.

Provided always, and these presents and the premises hereby demised are upon this express condition, that if it should so happen that the said yearly rent, or any part thereof, should be behind or unpaid for the space of ten days after any day of payment on which the same, or any part thereof, ought to be paid as aforesaid, or if the said party of the second part, his heirs, executors, administrators, or assigns, shall neglect to pay, perform, fulfill, and keep any or either of the payments, articles, covenants, clauses, provisions, or agreements herein contained, which on his or their part are to be paid, performed, fulfilled, observed, and kept during the term aforesaid, according to the true intent and meaning of these presents, that then and in every such case or cases it shall and may be lawful to and for the said parties of the first part, their successors and assigns, to enter into and upon the premises hereby demised, and to have, possess, and enjoy the same as fully as though these presents had not been made, anything herein contained to the contrary notwithstanding. And the said party of the second part, for himself, his heirs, executors, administrators, or assigns, doth covenant and agree to and with the said parties of the first part, their successors and assigns, by these presents, that he, the said party of the second part, shall and will yearly and every year, during the said term, well and truly pay unto the said parties of the first part, their successors and assigns, the said yearly rent or sum of money hereinbefore mentioned, at the days and times above specified for the payment thereof, without fraud or delay.

And, also, that he, the said party of the second part, his heirs, executors, administrators, or assigns, shall and will, on or before the first day of May in the year 1858, and during the remainder of the said term, at his or their own proper cost and expense, furnish, provide, and navigate upon the said ferry, from the foot of Thirty-fourth street, East river, in the city of New York, to Hunter's Point, Long Island, as aforesaid, one good and substantial steam ferry-boat, suitable for the said ferry, and approved by the Mayor or Comptroller of the city of New York, for the time being, until the Common Council of the city of New York shall direct another or other boats to be put on said ferry, and keep the said steam ferry-boat or boats at all reasonable times continually employed on the said ferry during the remainder of the term hereby granted, after the expiration of the said period of nine months, and will run the same as frequently on every day as the public convenience may require, and that the said steamboat or boats shall always, during the said period, be kept in good repair and furnished with all necessary and proper implements and machinery adapted to their respective kind, and be manned with a sufficient number of able-bodied men, skilled in water service, to manage the same, and that said men so to be employed in said boat or boats shall and will at all times be ready and willing to give their constant attendance at said ferry, for the prompt, safe, expeditious, and convenient transportation of passengers and effects, horses and carriages, across the said ferry.

And, also, that he, the said party of the second part, his heirs, executors, administrators, or assigns, shall and will keep the frames, ferry stairs, bridges, and fixtures, of what kind soever, connected with the said ferry, and all the appurtenances used at the said ferry, on each side of the same, in good order and repair at their own expense, during the continuance of this lease.

And it is understood that no expense whatever is to be incurred by the parties of the first part for or in connection with said premises or any part thereof.

And, also, that the said party of the second part, or his heirs, executors, administrators, or assigns, shall not, nor will, at any time during the said term, in any manner grant, assign, or transfer this present lease, or let, underlet, or set over the said ferry, or any part thereof, or their estate, or interest therein, without the leave or consent of the Comptroller of said city for the time being, in writing first had and obtained. Nor shall, nor will do, commit, or suffer any act or acts, thing or things, either by commission or otherwise, which shall create a forfeiture of these presents or the premises hereby demised, or in any way lessen, injure, or encumber the same or the rents or revenues thereof, but that he, the said party of the second part, his heirs, executors, administrators, or assigns, shall and will conduct and manage the said ferry, and run said boat or boats, and place on additional boats, agreeably to such rules, regulations, and restrictions as now are, or from time to time hereafter, during the said term, shall be by any by-law, ordinance, or resolution of the said parties of the first part or their successors, made or passed in relation thereto.

And also, that he, the said party of the second part, his heirs, executors, administrators, or assigns, shall and will, on the last day of the term hereby granted, or other sooner determination of these presents, well and truly deliver up the said hereby demised premises, with the rights, privileges, and appurtenances thereunto belonging, into the hands and possession of the said parties of the first part, their successors and assigns, without fraud or delay.

And the said party of the second part, for himself, his heirs, executors, administrators, or assigns, and the said parties of the first part, for themselves and their successors, do mutually covenant and agree, to and with each other respectively, in manner following, that is to say:

That, at the expiration or other sooner determination of the said term hereby granted, the steamboats, and all other boats and furniture of what description soever actually necessary for the purposes of said ferry, and which shall be actually used and employed upon the said ferry at that time, and also all the buildings, bridges, and other fixtures and property actually necessary for and used in connection with the said ferry, shall be valued by three indifferent persons or appraisers, one of whom shall be chosen by the parties of the first part or their successors, and one by the party of the second part, his executors, administrators, or assigns, and the third by the two thus selected, and before proceeding to make such valuation; that, in case of disagreement, the concurrence of any two of such appraisers shall be conclusive; that the said appraisers, or any two of them, after making a valuation of said steamboats and other boats and furniture, and of the said buildings, bridges, and other fixtures and property, shall certify the same under their hands and shall notify the parties to these presents thereof, and that such valuation so made shall be binding and conclusive upon the said parties; and the said parties of the first part do hereby covenant and agree that, in ten days after the making of the said valuation, every person and persons requiring and obtaining the ferry lease and franchise hereby demised, subsequent to the expiration of the term hereby granted, shall purchase such steamboats and other boats and furniture, and said buildings, bridges, and other fixtures and property, at such valuation and shall pay to the party of the second part, his heirs, executors, administrators, or assigns, the amount of such valuation. Provided, however, that thereupon the said steamboats and other boats and furniture, and the said buildings, bridges, and other fixtures and property, shall be assigned and delivered over to the person or persons so requiring and obtaining the ferry lease and franchise hereby demised, subsequent to the expiration of the term hereby granted, free and clear from any claim or demands of any person or persons whomsoever.

And it is hereby expressly understood and agreed, that the said party of the second part, his heirs, executors, administrators, or assigns, shall be bound to place, provide and navigate such additional boat or boats on the said ferry, at his or their own proper cost, charges and expenses, and at such time or times during the said term hereby granted, as may be required by the said parties of the first part, or their successors; which said additional boat or boats shall be approved by the Mayor or Comptroller of the city of New York, for the time being, and shall be used, as well as the other boat or boats upon the said ferry, to carry, transport and convey carriages, horses, passengers and effects across the said ferry.

And it is hereby further mutually covenanted and agreed by and between the parties to these presents, and these presents are upon the express condition, that nothing herein contained shall be taken or construed to interfere in any manner with any provisions, grants, or rights, made by the said parties of the first part, of other premises, nor with the right to grant any future ferries to and from the city of New York, or to and from elsewhere wheresoever. Nor, so far as regards the said ferry and demised premises, to operate further than to grant the possession of the estate, right, title, or interest, which the said parties of the first part may have or lawfully claim in the said ferry and right of ferriage and other premises hereby demised by virtue of their several charters, and the various acts of the Legislature of the people of the State of New York.

In witness whereof, to one part of these presents, remaining with the said parties of the first part, the said party of the second part hath set his hand and seal, and to the other part thereof, remaining with the said party of the second part, the said parties of the first part have caused the common seal of the city of New York to be affixed, the day and year first above written.

A. W. WINANS. [L. S.]

Attest, JAMES SANDFORD.

City and County of New York, ss.:

On this 6th day of August, A. D. 1857, before me personally came Anthony W. Winans, to me known to be the individual described in, and who executed the foregoing instrument, and acknowledged to me that he executed the same.

JAMES SANDFORD,
Commissioner of Deeds.

Know all men by these presents: That we, Anthony W. Winans, of the city of New York, and John C. Winans, of the said city, are held and firmly bound unto the Mayor, Aldermen, and Commonalty of the city of New York, in the sum of two hundred dollars, lawful money, to be paid to the said Mayor, Aldermen, and Commonalty of the city of New York, for which payment, well and truly to be made, we bind ourselves, our heirs, executors, administrators, firmly by these presents.

Sealed with our seals. Dated the 6th day of August, 1857.

Whereas, Anthony W. Winans, of the city of New York, has purchased from the Mayor, Aldermen, and Commonalty of the city of New York the lease of the ferry from the foot of Thirty-fourth street to Hunter's Point, Long Island, commonly called "Hunter's Point Ferry," for the term of ten years from the first day of August, in the year 1857, at the yearly rent or sum of one hundred dollars.

Now, the condition of the above obligation is such that if the above bounden Anthony W. Winans shall well and truly pay or cause to be paid unto the said the Mayor, Aldermen, and Commonalty of the city of New York, quarterly, on the first days of August, November, February and May, in each and every year, for the full end and term of ten years from the first day of August, in the year 1857, the yearly rent or sum of one hundred dollars, then this obligation to be void, otherwise to remain in full force and virtue.

A. W. WINANS. [L. S.]
J. C. WINANS. [L. S.]

Sealed and delivered in presence of
JAMES SANDFORD.

FERRY FROM

HORNE'S HOOK, EIGHTY-SIXTH STREET, E. R., TO ASTORIA.

This ferry was leased to one Halsey, whose lease expired in April, 1857, at the rate of $150 per annum. Shortly before the expiration of his term of office, the late Comptroller, A. C. Flagg, was directed by the Commissioners of the Sinking Fund to sell the lease at auction, which he attempted to do; but there was no bid made, upon which, he gave permission to the said Mr. Halsey to continue the running of his boats at the rent of $50 per annum.

The ferry is now running upon this permission, and paying the aforesaid rent. At some future time this privilege may be valuable, but at present it is not remunerative.

FERRY FROM

PIER NO. 2, NORTH RIVER, TO NORTH SIDE OF STATEN ISLAND.

A ferry has been running from this pier without authority; established by parties holding no lease and paying no rent therefor.

FERRY FROM

CORTLANDT STREET TO JERSEY CITY.

This Indenture, made the   day of January, in the year of our Lord eighteen hundred and fifty-seven, between the Mayor, Aldermen, and Commonalty of the city of New York, of the first part, and the New Jersey Railroad and Transportation Company, of the second part:

Whereas, The said parties of the first part, by an indenture of lease bearing date the twenty-sixth day of September, in the year of our Lord eighteen hundred and twenty-five, demised and leased, and to farm let unto Francis B. Ogden, Cadwallader D. Colden, and Samuel Swartout, all the ferry and rights of ferriage from the city of New York to so much of the Jersey shore as lies between a point immediately south of Hoboken and a point due west from the Battery castle, with the appurtenances, for the term of fifteen years and six months, next ensuing the first day of November, which was in the year last aforesaid, at and for the yearly rent of one thousand five hundred dollars ($1,500), and for, upon, and in consideration of divers covenants agreements and stipulations therein contained and set forth. And whereas, the New Jersey Railroad and Transportation Company, the parties of the second part hereto, appear to have acquired, by virtue of certain assignments and conveyances, upon the first day of January, A. D. eighteen hundred and thirty-nine, all the right, title, and interest which the said Francis B. Ogden, Cadwallader D. Colden, and Samuel Swartout, their heirs, executors, administrators, or assigns, under the lease hereinbefore recited, may have acquired, or at the time last aforesaid, had or possessed of, in or to the then unexpired term of said lease. And whereas, a resolution of the Common Council of the city of New York was duly adopted and approved, bearing date the eleventh day of May, A. D. eighteen hundred and forty-one, renewing and extending the aforesaid lease to the New Jersey Railroad and Transportation Company, the said parties of the second part hereto, for the term of seven years, during which term the said parties of the second part continued to enjoy the premises demised in said lease, making quarterly payments of the rents as stipulated in said resolution, during the said term of seven years. And whereas, a subsequent resolution of of the Common Council of the city of New York, was duly adopted and approved, bearing date the sixth day of February, eighteen hundred and forty-nine, renewing and extending the aforesaid lease to the said parties of the second part, for the term of seven years, at the annual rent of five thousand five hundred dollars ($5,500), during which time the said parties of the second part have continued to enjoy the premises demised in said lease, making quarterly payments of the rents, as stipulated in said resolution, during the said term of seven years.

And whereas, the Comptroller of the city of New York, in pursuance of the authority vested in him by the laws of the State and the ordinances of the Common Council of the city of New York, did sell, at public auction, on Wednesday the 23d day of April, A. D. 1856, at 12 o'clock M., at the City Hall, in the city of New York, a ferry lease, from the slip at the foot of Cortlandt street to Jersey city, together with the ferry slip at the foot of Cortlandt street, including one-half of the pier on the north side of said slip, now occupied by the New Jersey Railroad and Transportation Company, for the term of ten years, from the 1st day of May, A. D. 1856, to the highest bidder therefor. And whereas, at said sale of said ferry lease, so made by the Comptroller, on the 23d day of April, A. D. 1856, the said the New Jersey Railroad and Transportation Company, the parties of the second part hereto, became the purchasers thereof for said term of ten years, from the 1st day of May, A. D. 1856, they being the highest bidder therefor. Now, therefore, this indenture witnesseth, that for and in consideration of said parties of the second part covenanting and agreeing to perform, fulfill, and keep the several covenants, agreements, and stipulations hereinafter contained and set forth, and for and in consideration of the rents hereinafter agreed to be paid to the said parties of the first part, the said parties of the first part have granted, demised, and to farm let, unto the said parties of the second part, all the said premises, ferry and right of ferriage, from the city of New York, to so much of the Jersey shore as lies between a point immediately south of Hoboken and a point due west from the Battery castle, together with all and singular the rights, members, privileges, and appurtenances thereto belonging, and, also, together with the ferry slip at the foot of Cortlandt street, including half of the pier on the north side of said slip, now occupied by the New Jersey Railroad and Transportation Company. To have and to hold the said ferriage and right of ferriage unto the said parties of the second part, for and during and until the full end and term of ten years, from the first day of May, in the year 1856, upon the same covenants, agreements, and stipulations, and with the same rights and privileges, as in the said above first-mentioned indenture of lease are contained and set forth, except so far as the same may be inconsistent with the provisions herein contained. They, the said parties of the second part, paying and yielding therefor, unto the said parties of the first part, for and during each and every year of the term herein and hereby granted, the yearly sum of five thousand dollars ($5,000), payable, in equal quarterly payments, upon the first days of May, August, November, and February following in each and every year of the term aforesaid. And the said parties of the second part, for themselves, their successors, and assigns, covenant to and with the said parties of the first part, their successors and assigns, to pay unto the said parties of the first part, their successors and assigns, the said yearly sum, at the times and in the manner hereinbefore specified and prescribed, and to do and perform every covenant, agreement, and stipulation herein and in the said first above-mentioned indenture of lease contained, when the same are not wholly inconsistent with any matter or thing herein contained, and to abide by all the conditions, restrictions, and reservations in the said former lease herein mentioned contained, as fully and completely as the said grantees would have, had they held the same, and had that lease been renewed or extended to them for the further term of ten years herein contained.

And the said parties of the second part do further covenant and agree, to and with the said parties of the first part, their successors and assigns, that they will establish a ferry to Jersey city from some other point in the immediate vicinity of Canal street, in the said city of New York, whenever required to do so by the Common Council of said city of New York, said ferry, when established, to become and be in all respects subject to the provisions of this lease. And that the said parties of the second part will continue the regular fifteen-minute trips to one hour after sunset in the winter, and to two hours after sunset in the summer, and, also, to continue the half-hourly trips at night until twelve (12) o'clock, and, also, that the citizens of New York shall, from time to time, during the continuance of this lease, be entitled to all the rights, benefits, and privileges of commutation, and upon the same terms and conditions as enjoyed by the inhabitants of Jersey city aforesaid; and the said parties of the first part, for themselves, their successors and assigns, covenant to and with the said parties of the second part, that the said parties of the second part shall peaceably and quietly use, possess, and enjoy all the rights and franchises of ferry, with the privileges thereunto appertaining, under and by virtue of the first above mentioned lease, as fully in all respects as the same have been, or may be, enjoyed under and by virtue of the aforesaid lease, without the let, suit, hindrance or erection of the parties of the first part, or any other party or person or persons, or body corporate, whatever.

In witness whereof, to one part of these presents, remaining with the said parties of the first part, the said parties of the second part have caused the corporate seal of the New Jersey Railroad and Transportation Company to be attached; and to the other part of these presents, remaining with the said parties of the second part, the said parties of the first part have caused the common seal of the city of New York to be affixed, the day and year the first above written, and the same to be signed by their Treasurer.

JOHN S. DARSY,
Prest. N. J. R. R. & Transp. Co.

In presence of
A. S. CADY.

FERRY FROM
BARCLAY STREET TO HOBOKEN, N. J.

THIS INDENTURE, made the 15th day of May, in the year of our Lord 1855, between the Mayor, Aldermen, and Commonalty of the city of New York, of the first part, and John C. Stevens, Robert L. Stevens and Edwin A. Stevens, of the second part, witnesseth : That the said parties of the first part, for and in consideration of the rents, covenants, articles and agreements, hereinafter mentioned, on the part and behalf of the said parties of the second part, their executors, administrators and assigns, well and truly to be paid, done, performed and kept, according to the purport, true intent and meaning of these presents, have demised, granted and to farm letten, and by these presents do demise, grant and to farm let, unto the said parties of the second part, their executors, administrators and assigns, the privileges of conducting all that ferry established from the foot of Barclay street, in the city of New York, across the North river to Hoboken, in the State of New Jersey, and commonly called and known by the name of the Hoboken ferry, together with all and singular the rights, members, profits, advantage, and appurtenance thereof.

To have and to hold the same, unto the said parties of the second part, their executors, administrators and assigns, subject to whatever may be the right of the heirs, or legal representatives, of William Rhinelander, deceased, to the bulkhead at the foot of Barclay street, or any part thereof, or to the wharfage or profits to accrue therefrom, for and during the full end and term of ten years, from the 1st day of May, in the year of our Lord 1855, yielding and paying therefor, unto the said parties of the first part, their successors, or assigns, yearly and every year during the said term, in equal quarter-yearly payments, on the first days of August, November, February and May, the yearly rent of $100.

Provided always, nevertheless, that if it should so happen that either of the said quarterly payments, or any part thereof, shall be in arrear and unpaid, for the space of ten days after the time limited for the payment thereof, as aforesaid, or if the said parties of the second part, their executors, administrators or assigns, shall, or do neglect or omit to pay, perform, fulfill, or keep any or either of the payments, articles, covenants, clauses, agreements, matters, or things herein contained, which, on the part and behalf of the said parties of the second part, their executors, administrators, or assigns, are to be paid, performed, fulfilled, or kept during the said term of ten years, according to the true intent and meaning of these presents, then, and in every and all such case or cases, it shall be lawful for the said parties of the first part, their successors or assigns, thereupon, into the said premises wholly to re-enter, repossess, and them, the said parties of the second part, their executors, administrators, or assigns, and other occupiers thereof, to expel, remove and put out, and from thenceforward, for them, the said parties of the first part, to occupy and enjoy the said premises again, as fully as though these presents had not been made, any thing herein contained to the contrary notwithstanding.

And the said parties of the second part do, for themselves, their heirs, executors and administrators, covenant, promise and agree, to and with the said parties of the first part, their successors and assigns, in manner and form following; that is to say; That the said parties of the second part, their executors, administrators, or assigns, during the term or time for which the said premises are hereby granted, shall and will well and truly pay, or cause to be paid, unto the said parties of the first part, their successors or assigns, the aforesaid rent, on the days hereinbefore limited and appointed for the payment thereof, agreeably to the true intent and meaning thereof.

Also, that the said parties of the second part, their executors, administrators and assigns, at their own proper cost and expense, shall, during the term hereby demised and granted, provide and keep a sufficient number of good and substantial steam ferry-boats, sufficiently large, and adapted as well to carry and transport carriages and horses, as passengers and effects, across the said river, at the place appointed and now used for the said ferry, with convenience and safety, and that the said boats shall always, during the said term, be furnished and manned at the expense of the parties of the second part, with a sufficient number of sober and able-bodied men, skilled in water service, to manage the same, and that the men to be employed shall, at all reasonable times, be ready and willing to give their constant attendance at the said ferry, for the prompt and convenient transportation of passengers and effects across the said ferry ; also, that the said parties of the second part, their executors, administrators and assigns, shall and will, when required by a resolution of the said parties of the first part, or their successors, passed in Common Council, place and employ an additional boat or boats upon the said ferry. Also, that the said parties of the second part, their executors, administrators or assigns, or any other person or persons employed by them, shall not nor will, during the said term thereby demised, ask, demand, or receive, any higher or greater toll or fare for the transportation of passengers, horses, or effects, across the said river, in the boats of the said ferry, than the rates taken at the time of the execution of the former lease of the said ferry, by the said parties of the first part, to John Stevens, dated the 30th day of April, 1836, and to which the ferriage had then lately been reduced.

Also, that the said parties of the second part, their executors, administrators or assigns, shall not, during the said term, sell, transfer or grant this lease, or any part thereof, directly or indirectly, to any person or persons whomsoever, or encumber the same, without the leave of the parties of the first part, or their executors, first had and obtained, nor shall commit, or suffer to be done, anything which may create a forfeiture of the said ferry, or lessen, injure or encumber the same or the revenues thereof.

And also, that they shall and will conduct and manage the said ferry agreeably to such rules and regulations as now are, or from time to time hereafter during the said term shall, by any by-law, ordinance, or resolution of the said parties of the first part, or their successors, be reasonably made or passed in relation to the same. And it is hereby further understood and agreed, by and between the parties to these presents, that these presents and the privileges hereby granted are subject to whatever rights the heirs or representatives of William Rhinelander, deceased, may legally claim to the bulkhead at the foot of Barclay street, or to any part thereof, or to any wharfage or profits to accrue therefrom.

In witness whereof, to one part of these presents, remaining with the said parties of the first part, the said parties of the second part have set their hands and seals; and to the other part thereof, remaining with the said parties of the second part, the said parties of the first part have caused the common seal of the city of New York to be affixed, the day and year first above written.

[Not executed, but ferry in operation.]

FERRY FROM

CHAMBERS STREET TO PAVONIA, N. J.

THIS INDENTURE, made this 15th day of February, in the year of our Lord one thousand eight hundred and fifty-four, between the Mayor, Aldermen, and Commonalty of the city of New York, parties of the first part, and " The Pavonia Ferry Company," of the State of New Jersey, parties of the second part: Whereas, on the 15th day of February, in the year 1854, a certain resolution, passed by the Common Council of the city of New York, was approved by the Mayor of said city, which resolution was in the words and figures following, to wit:

" *Resolved*, That a ferry, across the North or Hudson river, be established from the foot of Chambers street to Pavonia avenue, in the State of New Jersey, or to such other street or avenue, contiguous or near the said Pavonia avenue, as the purchaser may select, under the permission of the Comptroller of the city and county of New York and the Corporation of Jersey City, and that the lease of said ferry include the pier and bulkhead at the foot of Chambers street, and be for the term of ten years, from the expiration of the lease at present existing for said pier at the foot of Chambers street, and that the Comptroller be, and he is hereby, directed to carry out this resolution and lease the said ferry in pursuance of the seventh section of the Act further to amend the Charter of the city of New York, passed April 12, 1853.

"*Resolved*, That the Comptroller be, and he is hereby, directed to advertise anew the lease of said ferry, pier, and bulkhead for ten years, for sale at public auction, by a notice in the Corporation papers for ten days, and to lease the same to the highest bidder, who will give adequate security, and that the Corporation Counsel prepare a lease to said highest bidder, in pursuance of the provisions of the seventh section of the Act further to amend the Charter of the city of New York, passed April 12, 1853."

Now, therefore, this indenture witnesseth, that the said parties of the first part, for and in consideration of the rents, covenants, premises, articles, and agreements hereinafter mentioned, on the part and behalf of the said parties of the second part, their successors and assigns, to be paid, performed, observed, fulfilled, and kept, have granted, demised, and to farm let, and by these presents do grant, demise, and to farm let unto the said parties of the second part, their successors and assigns, all that certain ferry to be established from the foot of Chambers street, in the city of New York, over and across the North or Hudson river, to the foot of Pavonia avenue, in the State of New Jersey, or to such other avenue or street, contiguous to or near the said Pavonia avenue, as may be selected by the parties to these presents of the second part, under the permission, in writing, of the Comptroller of the city of New York and the Corporation of Jersey City, and from said Pavonia ave-

nue, or such point as may be selected as aforesaid, back to
the foot of Chambers street aforesaid, with all and singular
the usual accustomed ferriage fees, perquisites, rents, issues,
benefits, profits, and advantages whatsoever to the said
ferry belonging, or therewith used, or thereout arising.
And also, the whole of that certain pier, known as Pier
No. 30, North river, at the foot of Chambers street, in the
city of New York, and one-half of the bulkhead, and one-
half of the slip between said pier and Pier No. 31. Also,
the erection on the upper side of said Pier No. 30, which
originally formed an L, the said Pier No. 30 and said half
of said bulkhead and slip being delineated upon the map
hereunto annexed, dated New York, April, 1854, made by
John J. Sewell, City Surveyor, said map being considered
a part of this indenture, and to which reference may be had
for a more particular designation of the premises hereby
granted. And also, the use of the slip on the south or
lower side of said Pier No. 30, for all the purposes of col-
lecting wharfage that would be enjoyed by the lessee of
the pier for commercial purposes, together with all the
dockage, wharfage, rights, benefits, appurtenances, and advantages to the said pier, slips and bulkhead belonging, or
in any wise appertaining. To have and to hold the said
ferry, with the appurtenances and other hereby granted
premises, unto the said parties of the second part, their
successors and assigns, for and during the full end and
term of ten years, from the first day of May, in the year of
our Lord one thousand eight hundred and fifty-four, yielding and paying therefor, yearly and every year during the
said term, unto the said parties of the first part, their successors, or assigns, the annual rent or sum of $9,050, pay-
able quarterly, on the usual days for the payment of rent
in the city of New York, that is to say, one-quarter part

on the first day of August, November, February, and May, in each and every year during the said term.

Provided always, and these presents and the premises hereby demised are upon this express condition, that, if it should so happen that the said yearly rent, or any part thereof should be behind and unpaid for the space of ten days after any day of payment on which the same or any part thereof ought to be paid as aforesaid, or if the said parties of the second part, their successors, or assigns, shall neglect to pay, perform, fulfill and keep any or either of the payments, articles, clauses, covenants, provisions, agreements, matters and things herein contained, which on their part are to be paid, performed, fulfilled, observed and kept during the term aforesaid, according to the true intent and meaning of these presents, that then and in every such case or cases it shall and may be lawful to and for the said parties of the first part, their successors and assigns, to enter into and upon the premises hereby demised, and to have, possess and enjoy the same as fully as though these presents had not been made, any thing herein contained to the contrary notwithstanding. And the said parties of the second part, for themselves, their successors and assigns, do covenant and agree to and with the said parties of the first part, their successors and assigns, by these presents, that they, the said parties of the second part, their successors and assigns, shall and will, yearly and every year during the said term, well and truly pay unto the said parties of the first part, their successors or assigns, the said yearly rent or sum of money hereinbefore mentioned, at the days and times above specified for the payment thereof, without fraud or delay. And also that they, the said parties of the second part, their successors and assigns, shall and will, within twelve months from the beginning of the said term and during the remainder of the said term, at their own proper cost and expense, furnish, provide and navigate upon the said ferry from the foot of Chambers street, in the city of New York, to the State of New Jersey, as aforesaid, two good and substantial steam ferry-boats, suitable for the said ferry and approved by the Mayor or Comptroller of said city, for the time being, and keep the said steam ferry-boats at all reasonable times continually employed on the said ferry, during the remainder of the term hereby granted after the expiration of the said period of twelve months, and will run the same as frequently on every day as the public convenience may require; and that the said steamboats shall always during the said period be kept in good repair and furnished with all necessary and proper implements and machinery adapted to their respective kind, and be manned with a sufficient number of able-bodied men, skilled in water service, to manage the same, and that said men, so to be employed on all and each of the said boats, shall and will at all times be ready and willing to give their constant attendance at said ferry, for the prompt, safe, expeditious and convenient transportation of passengers and effects, horses and carriages, across the said ferry. And, also, that the said parties of the second part, their successors or assigns, shall not during the term of this lease charge or receive, as rates of ferriage, a sum or sums exceeding those laid down in the schedule marked A, hereinafter set forth, the same being a part of these presents; and, also, that they, the said parties of the second part, their successors or assigns, shall not, nor will, at any time during the continuance of this lease, permit or cause to be erected any obstruction whatever on the lower or south side of Pier No

30, nor permit or cause to be sunk, in any of the waters covered by this lease, any block or blocks of any kind, except, and this covenant is not intended to prohibit the construction of, a pile bridge for the accommodation of the said ferry, from the L aforesaid to the bulkhead embraced in this lease. And the said parties of the second part, for themselves, their successors and assigns, do covenant and agree that all the fixtures in the water, for the use of said ferry, shall be made on the side of Pier No. 30 where the L is, and all the arrangements for the ferry-boats shall be made from the outside of said L; and, also, the fenders for the guidance of the boats shall in no case extend beyond half the width of the slip, nor further out into the river than on a line with the outer end of Pier No. 36; and, also, that they, the said parties of the second part, their successors and assigns, shall and will keep the frames, ferry-stairs, bridges, and fixtures, of what kind soever, connected with the said ferry, and all the appurtenances used at the said ferry, on each side of the same, in good order and repair, at their own expense, during the continuance of this lease, and it is understood that no expense whatever is to be incurred by the parties of the first part, for or in connection with said premises, or any part thereof; and, also, that the said parties of the second part, or their successors, shall not, nor will at any time during the said term, in any manner grant, assign, or transfer this present lease, or let, underlet, or set over the said ferry, or any part thereof, or their estate or interest therein, without the leave or consent of the Comptroller of said city, for the time being, in writing, first had and obtained, nor shall nor will do, commit, or suffer any act or acts, thing or things, either by commission or omission, which shall create a forfeiture of these presents or the premises hereby demised, or in any wise lessen, injure, or encumber the same, or the rents or revenues thereof, but that they, the said parties of the second part, their successors, or assigns, shall and will conduct and manage the said ferry, and run said boats, and place on additional boats, agreeably to such rules, regulations and restrictions, as now are or from time to time hereafter, during the said term, shall be, by any by-law, ordinance, or resolution of the said parties of the first part, or their successors, made or passed in relation thereto; and, also, that they, the said parties of the second part, their successors, or assigns, shall and will on the last day of the term hereby granted, or other sooner determination of these presents, well and truly deliver up the said hereby demised premises, with the rights, privileges, and appurtenances, thereunto belonging, into the hands and possession of the said parties of the first part, their successors, or assigns, without fraud or delay. And the said parties of the second part, for themselves, their successors and assigns, and the said parties of the first part, for themselves and their successors, do mutually covenant, grant, and agree, to and with each other respectively, in manner following, that is to say: that at the expiration or other sooner determination of the said term, hereby granted, the steamboats and all other boats and furniture, of what description soever, actually necessary for the purposes of the said ferry, and which shall be actually used or employed upon the said ferry at that time, and also all the buildings, bridges, and other fixtures and property, actually necessary for and used in connection with the said ferry, shall be valued by three indifferent persons or appraisers, one of whom shall be chosen by the parties of the first part, or their successors, and one by the parties of the second part, their successors or assigns, and the third by the two thus selected, and before proceeding to make such valuation; that, in case of disagreement, the concurrence of any two of such appraisers shall be conclusive; that the said appraisers, or any two of them, after making a valuation of the said steamboats, and other boats, and furniture, and of the said buildings, bridges, and other fixtures and property, shall certify the same under their hands, and shall notify the parties to these presents thereof; and that such valuation so made shall be binding and conclusive upon the said parties; and the said parties of the first part do hereby covenant and agree that, in ten days after the making of the said valuation, every person and persons requiring and obtaining the ferry lease and franchise hereby demised, subsequent to the expiration of the term hereby granted, shall purchase such steamboats and other boats, and furniture and said buildings, bridges and other fixtures and property, at such valuation, and shall pay to the parties of the second part, their successors or assigns, the amount of such valuation. Provided, however, that thereupon the said steamboats and other boats, and furniture, and the said buildings, bridges, and other fixtures and property, shall be assigned and delivered over to the person or persons last mentioned, free and clear from any claim or demands of any person or persons whomsoever. And it is hereby expressly understood and agreed that the said parties of the second part, their successors and assigns, shall be bound to place, provide and navigate such additional boat or boats on the said ferry, at their own proper costs, charges and expenses, and at such time or times, during the said term hereby granted, as may be required by the said parties of the first part, or their successors, which said additional boat or boats shall be approved of by the Mayor or Comptroller of the city of New York, for the time being, and shall be used, as well as all the other boats upon the said ferry, to carry, transport and convey carriages, horses, passengers and effects, across the said ferry; and it is hereby further mutually understood and agreed, that in case any of the persons to be employed upon the said ferry by the said parties of the second part, their successors, or assigns, shall conduct himself improperly while in the discharge of his duties, or shall conduct himself in such manner as to give offense to the public, for whose convenience these presents have been made and this lease granted by the said parties of the first part, that then and in such case the said parties of the second part, their successors or assigns, shall and will, upon being requested so to do by the Street Commissioner for the time being of the said parties of the first part, discharge such person from their employment at such ferry. And it is hereby further mutually covenanted and agreed, by and between the parties to these presents, and these presents are upon the express understanding, that nothing herein contained shall be taken or construed to operate as a covenant by the said parties of the first part, or their successors, for possession or quiet enjoyment by the said parties of the second part, or their successors or assigns, of the said ferry or right of ferriage, nor shall the same be taken or construed to interfere in any manner with any provisions, grants, or rights made by the said parties of the first part of other premises nor with the right to grant any future ferries to and from the State of New Jersey, or to and from elsewhere wheresoever. Nor, so far as regards the said ferry and demised premises, to operate further than to grant the possession of the estate, right, title, or interest, which the said parties of the first part may have or lawfully claim in the said ferry and right of ferriage, and other premises hereby demised, by virtue of their several charters and the various acts of the Legislature of the people of the State of New York.

In witness whereof, the parties to these presents have interchangeably set their corporate seals, the day and year first above written.

Sealed and delivered in the presence of

[This lease is not executed, nor is the ferry in operation, but the rent is paid by the Erie Railroad Company.]

Schedule A.

The following are the rates of ferriage referred to in the foregoing lease, viz.: for the ferry from the foot of Chambers street, in the city of New York, across the North or Hudson river, to, or near, the foot of Pavonia avenue, in the State of New Jersey.

For each passenger...............................	$0 03
Every four-wheeled carriage drawn by four horses.	37½
Every four-wheeled carriage drawn by two horses.	25
Every four-wheeled carriage drawn by one horse..	18¾
Every two-wheeled carriage drawn by two horses.	20
Every two-wheeled carriage drawn by one horse..	15
Every market carriage, with their drivers, going to or returning from market, with four wheels, drawn by two horses, and loaded............	25
Every market carriage, with their drivers, going to or returning from market, with four wheels, drawn by two horses, and empty............	18¾
Every market carriage, with their drivers, going to or returning from market, with four wheels, drawn by one horse, loaded or empty	12½

All passengers in carriages, except the drivers thereof, each.	03
Carriages of burden, including charcoal wagons, tin wagons, and peddlers' wagons, with their drivers, drawn by two horses, loaded, each.	25
Carriages of burden, including charcoal wagons, tin wagons, and peddlers' wagons, with their drivers, drawn by two horses, unloaded, each.	18¾
Carriages of burden, including charcoal wagons, tin wagons, and peddlers' wagons, with their drivers, drawn by one horse, empty or loaded, each.	12½
Hay, straw, hemp, flax, and other bulky articles, for two-horse load.	37½
For carriages calculated to convey hay, straw, hemp, flax, and other bulky articles, two horses, unloaded.	20
For carriages calculated to convey hay, straw, hemp, flax, and other bulky articles, one-horse load.	20
For carriages calculated to convey hay, straw, hemp, flax, and other bulky articles, unloaded	12½
For burden and other carriages, drawn by oxen or mules, to be rated the same as if drawn by horses.	
For each additional horse, ox, or mule.	06
For marketing, a barrel to be rated equal to two bushel baskets; and tubs, chests, and scow baskets, rated according to the number of bushels they contain, for each bushel.	02
All articles, having contained marketing, to return free, if empty, otherwise to pay the usual rates.	

A two-horse load, with or without the carriage, not otherwise rated	20
Barrel of salt, plaster, flour, sugar, liquor, &c	04
Hogshead of liquor, sugar, molasses, &c	15
Lime, per hogshead	10
Stoves of cast iron, of six or more plates	06
Salt, plaster, grain, clover, and other grass seeds, per bushel	02
Flour, beef, pork, iron, &c., per cwt	03
Coffee, per bag, chest, large trunk	03
Soap, candles, glass, chocolate, per box	02
Chairs, per dozen, and for bureaus, bedsteads, clock cases	06
Lumber, per 100 feet	06
Live calves and fat hogs, per head	03
For sheep and store-hogs, per head	$0 02
Fat cattle, per head	12½
A cow and calf	12½
Store-cattle, horses and mules, each	09
Saddle-horse and rider	09
Sideboard, desk, or secretary, each	10
Table, stand, feather-bed, mattress, large chest of tea, each	03
Crate or tierce of earthenware, or hamper of bottles, each	12½
Fresh shad, per 100, or herring, per 1000	20

And all animals and things not herein enumerated shall be charged proportionably to the foregoing rates.

FERRY FROM

HOBOKEN STREET TO HOBOKEN, N. J.

THIS INDENTURE made the eleventh day of May, in the year of our Lord 1850, between the Mayor, Aldermen and Commonalty of the City of New York, of the first part, and John C. Stevens, Robert L. Stevens, and Edwin A. Stevens, of the second part; witnesseth that the said parties of the first part, for and in consideration of the rents, covenants and agreements hereinafter mentioned, on the part and behalf of the said parties of the second part, their executors, administrators and assigns, well and truly to be observed, performed and kept, according to the true intent and meaning of these presents, have granted demised and to farm letten, and, by these presents, do grant, demise, and to farm let, unto the said parties of the second part, their executors, administrators and assigns, all that certain bulkhead at the foot of Hoboken street, and the ferry established from the foot of Hoboken street, in city of New York, across the North or Hudson river, to Hoboken, in New Jersey, and thence back again, together with all the profits, privileges, advantages and emoluments arising therefrom: to have and to hold the same, unto the said parties of the second part, their executors, administrators and assigns, for and during the full end and term of eight years, from the first day of May, in the year of our Lord one thousand eight hundred and fifty-two, fully to be complete and ended. Yielding and paying therefor, yearly and every year during the said term hereby granted and demised, the yearly rent or sum of six hundred dollars, in equal quarter-yearly payments, on the first days of August, November, February, and May, in each and every year during the said term. And the said parties of the second part, for themselves, their heirs, executors, administrators, and assigns, do covenant, grant, promise, and agree, to and with the said parties of the first part, their successors and assigns, that they, the said parties of the second part, their executors, administrators and assigns, shall and will well and truly pay or cause to be paid, to the said parties of the first part, their successors and assigns, the said yearly rent herein before mentioned, at the several and respective times above limited and appointed for the payment thereof as aforesaid.

And also, that they shall and will, at their own proper costs, charges, and expenses, at all times during the said term, find, furnish and provide, maintain, keep and navigate, one good and substantial steam ferry boat, of the same size, construction and efficiency, as the steam boat now on the Barclay street ferry, and such as may be approved by the Ferry Committees for the time being, of the said parties of the first part or their successors, to carry, transport and convey passengers, horses, cattle, carts, carriages and wagons, goods, merchandise, and other things whatsoever, across the said river, between the places aforesaid, with safety, convenience, and expedition.

And also, to keep the said steam ferry boat, at all times during the said term hereby granted and demised, in good repair; and to furnish the same, at all times, with a sufficient number of proper implements, tackle, and necessaries, at the proper costs and charges of the said parties of the second part, their executors, administrators and assigns.

And also, that the said parties of the second part, their executors, administrators, and assigns, shall and will, at all times during the term hereby granted, provide and maintain a sufficient number of sober, honest, skillful, and ablebodied men, who shall be competent to manage the boats used on the said ferry. And also, that the said men, so to be employed, shall at all reasonable times give their constant and ready attendance at the said ferry, on both sides, for the prompt and expeditious transportation of passengers, horses, cattle, merchandise, goods, effects, and things, as aforesaid, across the said river; and in such manner, as that the said steam boat may leave the landing place of the said ferry, at the foot of Hoboken street aforesaid, for Hoboken aforesaid, once at least in every hour, from sunrise to sunset of each day.

And also, that the said parties of the second part, their executors, administrators, and assigns, shall not, nor will, during the said term hereby demised, in any manner grant, assign, transfer, or set over, this present lease or any part thereof, without the leave or consent of the said parties of the first part, or their successors, first had and obtained. And also, that they shall and will conduct and manage the said ferry, agreeably to such rules, regulations, and restrictions, as now are, or from time to time hereafter during the said term shall, by any by-law, ordinance, or resolution, of the said parties of the first part or their successors, be reasonably made or passed in relation to the same. And also, quietly and peaceably to yield and deliver up the possession of the said premises, and every part thereof, at the expiration or other sooner determination of the said term of years, to the said parties of the first part or their successors.

And it is hereby expressly understood and agreed, that the said parties of the second part, their executors, administrators, and assigns, shall be bound to place such additional boats on the said ferry, and at such time or times during the said term hereby granted, as may be required by the said parties of the first part or their successors; also, that nothing contained in these presents shall prevent the establishment of any other ferry or ferries across the said North or Hudson River, pervious to the expiration of the said term hereby granted by the said parties of the first part or their successors.

And further, that the rates of ferriage on the said ferry shall not, during the said term, be raised to any larger amount than the rates taken at the time of the execution of the former lease of the said ferry by the said parties of the first part to John Stevens, dated the thirtieth day of April, one thousand eight hundred and thirty-six, and of which the present lease is a renewal.

Provided always, nevertheless, that if the said yearly rent so reserved, or any part thereof, shall be behind or unpaid for the period of ten days after any day of payment, on which the same ought to be paid as aforesaid; or if the said parties of the second part, their executors, administrators or assigns, do or shall neglect or omit to pay, perform, fulfill or keep, any or either of the payments, articles, covenants, clauses, arrangements, matters or things, herein contained, which, on the part and behalf of the said parties of the second part, their executors, administrators and assigns, are to be paid, performed, fulfilled and kept, during the said term hereby demised, according to the true intent and meaning of these presents; that then, and in every or all such case or cases, all the covenants, articles, stipulations and agreements, on the part and behalf of the said parties of the first part or their successors, herein mentioned and contained, to be by them done, performed or complied with, shall be utterly null and void ; and it shall be lawful, to and for the said parties of the first part and their successors, to re-enter upon the premises hereby demised, and to have, possess, and enjoy the same again, as fully and completely as though these presents had never been made, any thing herein contained to the contrary thereof in any wise notwithstanding.

In witness whereof, to one part of these presents, remaining with the said parties of the first part, the said parties of the second part have set their hands and seals ; and to the other part, remaining with the said parties of the second part, the said parties of the first part have caused the common seal of the city of New York to be affixed, the day and year first above written.

Sealed and delivered in
the presence of
  CHAS. W. LAWRENCE.

    JOHN C. STEVENS. [L. S.]
    ROB'T L. STEVENS. [L. S.]
    E. A. STEVENS. [L. S.]

City and County of New York, ss.:

On this first day of May, 1852, before me came Charles W. Lawrence, subscribing witness to the foregoing lease, to me known, who, being by me duly sworn, did depose and say, that he resides in the city of New York, that he is acquainted with John C. Stevens, Robert L. Stevens, and Edwin A. Stevens, and knows them to be the same individuals described in, and who executed the foregoing indenture of lease, that he saw them sign the same—that they acknowledged in his presence that they executed the same, and that he subscribed his name as a witness thereto.

GEORGE L. TAYLOR,
Commissioner of Deeds.

FERRY FROM

CANAL STREET TO JERSEY CITY.

Resolved, That the New Jersey Railroad and Transportation Company be, and they are hereby, directed to establish a ferry from some point in the immediate vicinity of Canal street, in conformity to the conditions of their lease, and the adoption of a resolution of the Common Council, dated the 6th day of February, 1849, transcribed in said lease, and that the Comptroller be, and is hereby, directed to have the same carried into operation.

Adopted by the Board of Aldermen, May 5, 1851.
Adopted by the Board of Assistants, May 10, 1851.
Approved by the Mayor, May 15, 1851

FERRY FROM

CHRISTOPHER STREET TO HOBOKEN, N. J.

This Indenture, made this twentieth day of March, in the year of our Lord one thousand eight hundred and fifty-one, between the Mayor, Aldermen, and Commonalty of the city of New York, of the first part, and John C.

Stevens, Robert L. Stevens, and Edwin A. Stevens, of the second part, Witnesseth, that the said parties of the first part, for and in consideration of the rents, covenants and agreements hereinafter mentioned on the part and behalf of the said parties of the second part, their executors, administrators and assigns, well and truly to be observed, performed and kept, according to the true intent and meaning of these presents, have granted, demised and to farm letten, and by these presents do grant, demise and to farm let, unto the said parties of the second part, their executors, administrators and assigns, all that certain bulkhead on West street, commencing at a point seventy-seven feet south of the pier at the foot of Christopher street, in said city, and running in a southerly direction eighty feet, and the ferry established from the foot of Christopher street, in the city of New York, across the North or Hudson river, to Hoboken, in New Jersey, and thence back again, together with all the profits, privileges, ferriages, advantages and emoluments arising therefrom.

To have and to hold the same unto the said parties of the second part, their executors, administrators and assigns, for and during the full end and term of ten years, from the first day of May, in the year of our Lord one thousand eight hundred and fifty-two, fully to be complete and ended. Yielding and paying therefor, yearly and every year, for the first five years of the term hereby granted, the sum of three hundred and fifty dollars; and during the remaining five years of the said term hereby granted and demised, the yearly rent to be fixed by appraisers, one of whom shall be chosen by each of the parties hereto, and in case of their disagreement, they to choose a third appraiser; and said rent of three hundred and fifty dollars, and said rent as fixed by said appraisers, shall be paid in equal quarter-yearly payments, on the first days of August, November, February and May, in each and every year during the said term. And the said parties of the second part, for themselves, their heirs, executors, administrators and assigns, do covenant, grant, promise and agree, to and with the said parties of the first part, their successors and assigns, that they, the said parties of the second part, their executors, administrators and assigns, shall and will well and truly pay, or cause to be paid, to the said parties of the first part, their successors and assigns, the said yearly rent hereinbefore mentioned, at the several and respective times above limited and appointed for the payment thereof as aforesaid.

And also, that they shall and will, at their own proper costs, charges and expenses, at all times during the said term, find, furnish and provide, maintain, keep and navigate, one good and substantial steam ferry-boat, of the same size, construction and efficiency as the steam boat now on the Barclay street ferry, and such as may be approved by the Ferry Committees for the time being, of the said parties of the first part, or their successors, to carry, transport and convey passengers, horses, cattle, carts, carriages and wagons, goods, merchandise, and other things whatsoever, across the said river, between the places aforesaid, with safety, convenience and expedition; and also, to keep the said steam ferry-boat, at all times during the said term hereby granted and demised, in good repair, and to furnish the same at all times with a sufficient number of proper implements, tackle and necessaries, at the proper costs and charges of the said parties of the second part, their executors, administrators and assigns.

And also, that the said parties of the second part, their executors, administrators and assigns, shall and will, at all times during the said term hereby granted, provide and maintain a sufficient number of sober, honest, skillful and able-bodied men, who shall be competent to manage the boats used on the said ferry. And also, that the said men so to be employed shall, at all reasonable times, give their constant and ready attendance at the said ferry, on both sides for the prompt and expeditious transportation of passengers, horses, cattle, merchandise, goods, effects and things, as aforesaid, across the said river, and in such manner as that the said steam boat may leave the landing place of the said ferry at the foot of Christopher street aforesaid, for Hoboken aforesaid, once at least in every hour, from sunrise to sunset of each day And also, that the said parties of the second part, their executors, administrators and assigns, shall not, nor will, during the said term hereby demised, in any manner grant, assign, transfer or set over this present lease, or any part thereof, without the leave or consent of the said parties of the first part, their successors, first had and obtained. And also, that they shall and will conduct and manage the said ferry, and run said boats at such times, and charge such rates of fare, agreeably to such rules, regulations and restrictions as now are, or from time to time hereafter, during the said term, shall, by any by-law, ordinance or resolution of the said parties of the first part, or their successors or assigns, be reasonably made or passed in relation to the same. And also, quietly and peaceably to yield and deliver up the possession of the said premises, and every part thereof, at the expiration or other sooner determination of the said term of years, to the said parties of the first part, or their successors.

And it is hereby expressly understood and agreed, that the said parties of the second part, their executors, administrators and assigns, shall be bound to place such additional boats on the said ferry, and at such time or times during the said term hereby granted, as may be required by the said parties of the first part, or their successors. Also, that nothing contained in these presents shall prevent the establishment of any other ferry or ferries across the said North or Hudson river, previous to the expiration of the said term hereby granted, by the said parties of the first part, or their successors. And further, that the rates of ferriage on the said ferry shall not, during the said term, be raised to any larger amount than the rates taken at the time of the execution of the former lease of the said ferry, by the said parties of the first part, to John Stevens, dated the thirtieth day of April, one thousand eight hundred and thirty-six.

And the said parties of the second part do hereby covenant and agree, to and with the said parties of the first part, that they, the said parties of the second part, will remove and set back their ferry houses and gates at said ferry, thirty-five feet west of West street, and extend their racks at said ferry, so as to give free ingress and egress to the adjoining piers, under such directions as shall be given for that purpose by the Street Commissioner of the said parties of the first part.

Provided always, nevertheless, that if the said yearly rent so reserved, or any part thereof, shall be behind or unpaid for the period of ten days after any day of payment on which the same ought to be paid as aforesaid, or if the said parties of the second part, their executors, administrators, and assigns, do or should neglect or omit to pay, perform, fulfill, or keep, any or either of the payments, articles, covenants, clauses, arrangements, matters, or things herein contained, which, on the part and behalf of the said parties of the second part, their executors, administrators or assigns, are to be paid, performed, fulfilled, and kept, during the said term hereby demised, according to the true intent and meaning of these presents, that then and in every or all such case or cases, all the covenants, articles, stipulations, and agreements on the part and behalf of the said parties of the first part, or their successors, herein mentioned and contained, to be by them done, performed, or complied with, shall be utterly null and void; and it shall be lawful to and for the said parties of the first part and their successors to re-enter upon the premises hereby demised, and to have, possess, and enjoy the same again, as fully and completely as though these presents had never been made, anything herein contained to the contrary thereof in anywise notwithstanding.

In witness whereof, to one part of these presents, remaining with the said parties of the second part, the said parties of the first part have caused the common seal of the city of New York to be affixed; and to the other part thereof, remaining with the said parties of the first part, the said parties of the first part have set their hands and seals, the day and year first above written.

JOHN C. STEVENS. [L. S.]
ROBT. L. STEVENS. [L. S.]
E. A. STEVENS. [L. S.]

Sealed and delivered in the presence of
    GEO. L. TAYLOR.

City and County of New York, ss.:

On this first day of May, 1852, before me came John C. Stevens, Robert L. Stevens, and Edwin A. Stevens, to me personally known to be the same individuals described in, and who executed the foregoing conveyance, and acknowledged that they executed the same, for the purposes therein mentioned.

GEO. L. TAYLOR,
Com'r of Deeds.

NOTE.—The appraisement, by which the rent of this Ferry for the last five years was to have been fixed, in accordance with the terms of the lease, never was made; and the rent has therefore been continued at the rate specified in the lease.

FERRY FROM

THIRTY-NINTH STREET TO BULL'S FERRY.

THIS INDENTURE, made the 9th day of July, in the year of our Lord 1852, between the Mayor, Aldermen, and Commonalty of the city of New York, parties of the first part, and Sophia V. D. Laing, sole executrix and trustee, under the will of Edgar H. Laing, party of the second part: Whereas, on the 20th of August, 1851, a certain resolution, passed by the Common Council of the city of New York, was approved of by the Mayor of said city, which said resolution was in the words and figures following, to wit. *Resolved*, that a lease be granted to E. H. Laing, for a ferry from the foot of 39th street, North river, to a point at or near Bull's ferry, for the term of ten years, from the 1st of August, 1852, at an annual rent of one hundred dollars ($100) for the the first five years, and two hundred dollars ($200) for the last five years of said term, payable quarterly, and the said E. H. Laing to make such improvements as may be necessary for the accommodation of such ferry, at his own cost and expense, and to place on such ferry good and substantial steam ferry-boats, and run the same under such regulations as may from time to time be prescribed by the Common Council, said lease to contain the usual covenants and restrictions contained in ferry leases, and the Comptroller be, and he is hereby, directed to carry the same into effect. Now, this indenture witnesseth, that the said parties of the first part, for and in consideration of the rents, covenants, provisions, articles, and agreements, hereinafter mentioned on the part and behalf of the said party of the second part, her executors, administrators, and assigns, to be had, performed, observed, fulfilled, and kept, have granted, demised, and to farm letten, and by these presents do grant, demise, and to farm let, unto the said party of the second part, her executors, administrators, and assigns, all that certain ferry established, or to be established, and located at and from the foot of 39th street, North river, in the city of New York, over and across the North river to a point at or near Bull's ferry, and from a point at or near Bull's ferry aforesaid back to the foot of 39th street aforesaid, with the privilege of running steamboats thereon, and with all and singular the ferriage fees, perquisites, rents, issues, profits, benefits, and advantages whatsoever, which may arise or accrue from the said ferry, to have and to hold the said ferry, with the appurtenances, unto the said party of the second part, her executors, administrators, and assigns, from the time of the establishment thereof as hereinafter covenanted and agreed, for and during and until the full end and term of ten years from thence next, ensuing, and fully to be complete and ended, yielding and paying therefor, yearly and every year during the first five years of said term, the annual rent or sum of one hundred dollars, and for the remaining five years of said term the annual rent or sum of two hundred dollars, lawful money of the United States of America, in quarter-yearly payments, on the usual quarter days for the payment of rent in the said city of New York, that is to say, one-fourth part thereof on the first days of August, November, July, and May, in each and every year during the said term, the first payment to be made on the first quarter day after the date of this lease; provided, always, that if it should so happen that the said yearly rent, or any part thereof, shall be behind and unpaid for the space of ten days after any day of payment on which the same ought to be paid as aforesaid, or if the said party of the second part, her executors, administrators, or assigns, shall neglect or omit to pay, perform, fulfill, observe, and keep any or either of the payments, articles, covenants, clauses, agreements, provisions, matters, or things herein contained, which on the part and behalf of the said party of the second part, her executors, administrators, or assigns, are to be paid, performed, observed, fulfilled, and kept during the said term of ten years, according to the true intent and meaning of these presents, that then, and in every and all such case or cases, it shall and may be lawful for the said parties of the first part, their successors, or assigns, to enter into and upon the premises hereby demised, and to have, possess, and enjoy the same again as fully as though these presents had never been made, any thing herein contained to the contrary notwithstanding.

And the said party of the second part, for herself, her heirs, executors, administrators, and assigns, doth covenant and agree, to and with the said parties of the first part, their successors and assigns, by these presents, in manner following, that is to say · that the said party of the second part, her executors, administrators, and assigns, shall and will yearly, and every year during the said term hereby demised, well and truly pay unto the said parties of the first part, their successors or assigns, the said yearly rent or sum of money hereinbefore mentioned, at the days and times above specified for the payment thereof, without fraud or delay. And also, that she, the said party of the second part, shall and will, at her own proper costs, charges, and expenses, furnish, provide, and navigate upon the said ferry, to and from the foot of 39th street to Bull's ferry aforesaid, good and substantial steam ferry-boats, and keep the said steam ferry-boats at all reasonable times continually employed on the said ferry during the term hereby granted, and also shall and will, whenever thereunto required by the said parties of the first part, at her own proper cost, charges, and expenses, provide and navigate upon the said ferry one other good and substantial steam ferry-boat, which said steam ferry-boat shall be approved by the Street Commissioner of the Corporation of the city of New York, and shall be used to carry, transport, and convey carriages, horses, passengers, and effects upon the said ferry, and that the said steamboats shall always, during the said term, be kept in good repair, and furnished with all necessary and proper implements and machinery adapted to their respective kind, and be manned with a sufficient number of able-bodied men, skilled in water service, to manage the same, and that the said men, so to be employed in all and each of the said boats, shall and will, at all times, be ready and willing to give their constant attendance at the said ferry for the prompt and convenient transportation of passengers and effects, horses and carriages, across the said ferry; and also, that the said party of the second part, her executors, administrators, administrators, and assigns, shall conduct and manage the said ferry agreeably to such rules, regulations, rates of ferriage, times of running, and restrictions, as from time to time during the said term shall, by any by-law, ordinance, order, or resolution of the said parties of the first part, or their successors, in Common Council convened, be made or passed in relation to the said ferry; and also, that the said party of the second part, her executors, administrators, or assigns, shall and will, at her or their own proper cost, charges, and expenses, build, erect, make, and furnish, or cause to be built, erected, made, and furnished, such improvements as may be necessary for the accommodation of such ferry, and at all times during the said term hereby demised well and sufficiently repair, uphold, sustain, amend, maintain, and keep all and singular the floats, racks, fenders, bridges, and other ferry fixtures at each landing-place of the said ferry, and shall and will also keep in repair the piers adjoining, or which may be made or built adjoining, both slips used for the said ferry, both at Bull's ferry and New York, or such parts or proportions of said piers as may belong to the said parties of the first part, and also that the said party of the second part, her executors, administrators, or assigns, shall and will, at the expiration of the said term hereby demised, peaceably and quietly leave, surrender, and yield up the said ferry, and other hereby demised premises and the piers, in good order and condition, into the hands and possession of the said parties of the first part, their successors or assigns; and also, that the said party of the second part, her executors, administrators, and assigns, shall not, nor will, during the said term, transfer, assign, or set over, let, or underlet, or in any other manner convey their present lease, or any part thereof, or their estate or interest therein, or in or to the above demised premises, or any part of the same, without the leave or consent of the said parties of the first part, their successors or assigns, in writing first had and obtained; and it is hereby mutually agreed, by and between the respective parties to these presents, that the said parties of the first part, or their successors, shall and may, at any time, and from time to time extend the piers at the foot of 39th street aforesaid, or any or either of them, to such distance into the North river as said parties of the first part shall deem expedient, by resolution duly passed in their legislative capacity, without making to the said party of the second part, her executors, administrators, or assigns, any compensation for the supposed damage they may sustain, and without being liable to any action, suit, or proceeding, by reason of such extension, by or on behalf of the said party of the second part, her executors, administrators, or assigns, and without any alteration of the rent hereby reserved.

And it is hereby mutually covenanted and agreed, by and between the parties to these presents, and these presents are upon the express understanding, that nothing herein contained shall be taken or construed to operate as a covenant, by the said parties of the first part, or their successors, for possession or quiet enjoyment, by the said party of the second part, her executors, administrators, or assigns, of the said ferry, of right of ferriage; nor shall the same be taken or construed to interfere in any manner with any previous grants or rights made by the said parties of the first part, nor with the right to grant any future ferries to and from Bull's ferry, or to and from elsewhere wheresoever, nor to operate further than to grant the possession of the estate, right, title, or interest, which the said parties of the first part may have, or lawfully claim, in the said ferry and right of ferriage, hereby demised by virtue of their several charters, and the various acts of the Legislature of the people of the State of New York.

In witness whereof, to one part of these presents, remaining with the said parties of the first part, the said party of the second part hath set her hand and seal; and to the other part thereof, remaining with the said party of the second part, the said parties of the first part have caused the common seal of the City of New York to be affixed, the day and year first above written.

SOPHIA V. D. LAING. [L. S.]

In the presence of
THOS. W. LAWRENCE.

Rent in this lease to commence from Aug. 1, 1852.

FERRY FROM

FORTY-SECOND ST., NORTH RIVER, TO WEHAWKEN. N. J.

THIS INDENTURE, made the 21st day of June, in the year 1858, between the Mayor, Aldermen, and Commonalty of the city of New York, parties of the first part, and Francis Price, of Weehawken, Hudson county, State of New Jersey, party of the second part—

Whereas, on the 10th day of July, 1856, a certain resolution, passed by the Common Council of the city of New York, was approved by the Mayor of said city, which said resolution was in the words and figures following, to wit:

"*Resolved*, That a ferry across the North river be established, from the foot of Forty-second street to the nearest practicable point on the opposite or New Jersey shore; and that the Comptroller be, and he hereby is, authorized and directed to carry this resolution into effect, and to give a lease for such a ferry pursuant to the Charter and the amendments thereto; such lease and privileges of a ferry to be for a term of ten years, and to be sold at public auction, after thirty days' notice, and to be given to the highest bidder, with adequate security; which lease shall be prepared by the Counsel to the Corporation, and shall contain, so far as applicable, all the covenants and conditions, for the benefit and protection of the city, which are contained in the lease of the Houston and Williamsburgh Ferry."

And whereas, the Comptroller of the city of New York, in pursuance of the authority vested in him by the foregoing resolution of the Common Council of the city of New York, and by the laws of the State of New York, did sell, at public auction, on the 19th day of August, 1856, at the City Hall, in the city of New York, a grant of the right to establish and maintain a ferry from the foot of Forty-second street, North river, in the city of New York, to a point nearly opposite thereto, in New Jersey, at the landing heretofore conveyed, by the party of the second part hereto, to the said the Mayor, Aldermen, and Commonalty of the city of New York, including the right to erect slips, bridges, ferry-houses, and all other appurtenances required for ferry purposes, with all the profits, privileges, advantages, and emoluments arising from said ferry, for the term of ten years.

And whereas, at said sale of said grant so made, by the Comptroller, on the 19th day of August, A. D. 1856, the said Francis Price, the party of the second part hereto, became the purchaser thereof, for said term of ten years, he being the highest bidder therefor.

Now, therefore, this indenture witnesseth, that the said parties of the first part, for and in consideration of the rents, covenants, payments, agreements and articles hereinafter mentioned and contained, on the part and on behalf of the said party of the second part, his executors, administrators and assigns, to be paid, done, performed and kept, have demised, granted, and to farm letten, and by these presents do demise, grant, and to farm let, unto the said party of the second part, his executors, administrators and assigns, all the certain grant of the right to establish and maintain a ferry, and all that certain ferry to be established and maintained, from the foot of Forty-second street, North river, in the city of New York, to a point nearly opposite thereto, in the State of New Jersey, at the landing heretofore conveyed, by the party of the second part hereto, to the Mayor, Aldermen, and Commonalty of the city of New York, including the right to erect slips, bridges, ferry-houses, and all other appurtenances required for ferry purposes, and with all and singular the ferriage fees, perquisites, issues, profits, benefits, and emoluments thereof.

To have and to hold the said ferry, with the appurtenances, unto the said party of the second part, his executors, administrators and assigns, for and during, and until the full end and term of ten years, from the 1st day of November, in the year 1856.

Yielding and paying rent therefor, unto the said parties of the first part, their successors and assigns, yearly and every year, during the said term, the annual rent of $50, lawful money of the United States, in quarter-yearly payments, on the 1st day of August, November, February and May, in each and every year during the said term.

Provided always, and these presents and the premises hereby demised are upon the express condition, that if the said yearly rent, or any part thereof, should be behind or unpaid for the space of ten days after any day of payment, on which the same, or any part thereof, ought to be paid, as aforesaid, or if the said party of the second part, his executors, administrators, or assigns, shall neglect to pay, perform, fulfill, and keep any, or either of the payments, articles, covenants, clauses, agreements, matters and things herein contained, which on his part or their part are to be paid, performed, fulfilled and kept, during the term aforesaid, according to the true intent and meaning of these presents, that then, and in every such case, it shall and may be lawful for the said parties of the first part, their successors or assigns, to enter into and upon the premises hereby demised, and to have, possess and enjoy the same again, as fully as though these presents had not been made, anything herein contained to the contrary notwithstanding.

And the said party of the second part, for himself, his heirs, executors, administrators and assigns, doth covenant and agree to and with the said parties of the first part, their successors and assigns, that he, the said party of the second part, his executors, administrators and assigns, shall and will yearly, and every year during the said term hereby demised, well and truly pay unto the said parties of the first part, their successors or assigns, the said yearly rent, or sum of money hereinbefore mentioned, at the days and times above specified for the payment thereof, without fraud or delay.

And also that he, the said party of the second part, shall and will, at his own proper costs, charges and expenses, furnish, provide, and navigate, upon the said ferry, at least one good and substantial steam ferry-boat, to carry, transport, and convey passengers, horses, cattle, carts, carriages, wagons, goods, merchandise, and other things whatsoever, on the said ferry with safety, convenience, and expedition. in such manner as that the said steam ferry-boat shall leave the landing-place of said ferrry, at the foot of Forty-second street, North river, at least once in every half-hour, unless prevented by the elements, from sunrise to sunset of each day, and also that he shall and will, whenever required by any resolution of the said parties of the first part, or their successors, passed in Common Council, at any time during the said term hereby demised, at the proper costs, charges and expenses of the said party of the second part, provide and navigate upon the said ferry one or more additional steam ferry-boats, which said steam ferry-boat or boats shall be approved, and that the said boat or boats shall at all times during the said term be kept in good repair, and properly furnished and provided with the necessary implements and tackle, and with a sufficient number of sober, skillful, and able-bodied men, who shall be competent to manage the same, and shall at all reasonable times give their constant and ready attendance at the said ferry, for the prompt and expeditious transportation of passengers, horses, cattle, carts, carriages, wagons, goods, merchandise, and other things whatsoever, across the said river.

And also that he, the said party of the second part, his executors, administrators and assigns, shall conduct and manage the said ferry agreeably to such rules, regulations, rates of ferriage, times of running, and restrictions, as from time to time during the said term shall, by any by-law, ordinance, or resolution of the said parties of the first part, or their successors, in Common Council convened, be made or passed in relation to the said ferry.

And also that he, the said party of the second part, his executors, administrators or assigns, shall and will, at his or their own proper costs, charges and expenses, build, erect, make and furnish, and at all times, during the term hereby demised, will well and sufficiently uphold, maintain, and keep in good and substantial repair, the necessary bridges and floats, and other fixtures, at each landing-place of the said ferry, and the necessary docks and piers on the New Jersey shore, and that he or they will likewise keep in like good repair, during the term hereby demised, the bulkheads, docks and piers made and erected, and to be made and erected, by the said parties of the first part, or their successors, for the accommodation of said ferry at the foot of Forty-second street, aforesaid, which may be made or built adjoining the slips used for the said ferry, or such parts or proportions of said piers as may belong to the said parties of the first part, and used by the parties of the second part, and will likewise keep in like good repair, during the said term, the street in front of the bulkhead at the foot of Forty-second street, aforesaid, to the extent of twenty-five feet back from the said bulkhead, and to the full width thereof.

And, also, that the said party of the second part, his executors, administrators, or assigns, shall and will, at the expiration of the said term hereby demised, peaceably and quietly leave, surrender and yield up the said ferry and everything hereby demised, together with the bulkheads, piers, docks, floats, bridges, and other fixtures and improvements which may have been directed or made by either of the parties for the use of the said ferry, at the foot of Forty-second street, or at the termination of said ferry in New Jersey, in good order and condition, into the possession of the said parties of the first part, their successors or assigns, without fraud or delay, according to the provisions of the charter of the said parties of the first part.

And it is hereby mutually agreed, by and between the respective parties to these presents, that the said parties of the first part, or their successors, shall and may, at any time and from time to time, extend the piers at the foot of Forty-second street aforesaid, or any or either of them, to such distance into the North river as said parties of the first part shall deem expedient, by resolution duly passed in their legislative capacity, without making to the said party of the second part, his executors, administrators or assigns, any compensation for the supposed damage they may sustain, and without being liable to any action, suit, or proceeding, by reason of such extension by or on behalf of the said party of the second part, his executors, administrators, or assigns, and without any alteration of the rent hereby reserved.

And it is hereby mutually covenanted and agreed, by and between the parties to these presents, and these presents are upon the express understanding, that nothing herein contained shall be taken or construed to operate as a covenant by the said parties of the first part, or their successors, for possession or quiet enjoyment of the said party of the second part, his executors, administrators or assigns, of the said ferry or right of ferriage, nor shall the same be taken or construed to interfere in any manner with any previous grants or rights made by the said parties of the first part, nor with the right to grant any future ferries to and from the State of New Jersey, or to and from elsewhere wheresoever, nor to operate further than to grant the possession of the estate, right, title, or interest, which the said parties of the first part may have or lawfully claim, in the said ferry and right of ferriage hereby demised, by virtue of their several charters and the various acts of the Legislature of the State of New York.

In witness whereof, to one part of these presents, remaining with the said parties of the first part, the said party of the second part hath set his hand and seal; and to the other part thereof, remaining with the said party of the second part, the said parties of the first part have caused the common seal of the city of New York to be affixed, the day and year first above written.

JAMES PRICE. [L. S.]

Sealed and delivered in presence of
  JAMES SANDFORD.

State of New York, City and County of New York, ss.:

On this 21st day of June, A. D. 1858, before me personally came Francis Price, to me known to be the individual described in, and who executed the foregoing lease, and acknowledged to me that he executed the same.

JAMES SANDFORD,
Commissioner of Deeds.

August 3d, 1859.

Consent this day given that this lease may be assigned to the Weehawken Ferry Company.

ROBERT T. HAWS,
Comptroller.

Securities—NATHANIEL DOLE and J. LOTHROP.
$100.

FERRY FROM

EIGHTY-SIXTH STREET TO BULL'S FERRY.

THIS INDENTURE, made the twentieth day of August, in the year of our Lord one thousand eight hundred and fifty-one, between the Mayor, Aldermen, and Commonalty of the city of New York, parties of the first part; and Henry Conklin, of said city, party of the second part:

Whereas, on the twentieth of August, one thousand eight hundred and fifty-one, a certain resolution, passed by the Common Council of the city of New York, was approved of by the Mayor of said city, which said resolution was in the words and figures following; to wit:

Resolved, That a ferry lease be granted to Henry Conklin, to establish and conduct a ferry from the foot of Eighty-sixth street, North river, to a point at or near to Bull's Ferry, for the term of ten years, at an annual rent of one hundred dollars for the first five years, and two hundred dollars for the last five years, to be paid quarterly; said ferry to be established within one year after Eighty-sixth street is regulated to the North river; the said Henry Conklin to make such improvements as may be necessary for the accommodation of such ferry, at his own cost and expense ; and to place on such ferry good and substantial steam ferry-boats, and run the same under such regulations as may, from time to time, be prescribed by the Common Council—said lease to contain the usual covenants and restrictions contained in ferry leases ; and the Comptroller be and he is hereby directed to carry the same into effect.

Now, this indenture witnesseth, that the said parties of the first part, for and in consideration of the rents, covenants, provisions, articles, and agreements hereinafter mentioned, on the part and behalf of the said party of the second part, his executors, administrators and assigns, to be had, performed, observed, fulfilled, and kept, have granted, demised, and to farm letten, and by these presents, do grant, demise and to farm let, unto the said party of the second part, his executors, administrators, and assigns, all that certain ferry established or to be established and located at and from the foot of Eighty-sixth street, North river, in the city of New York, over and across the North river, to a point at or near to Bull's Ferry, and from a point at or near Bull's Ferry aforesaid, back to the foot of Eighty-sixth street aforesaid, with the privilege of running steam boats thereon ; and with all and singular, the ferriage fees, perquisites, rents, issues, profits, benefits, and advantages whatsoever, which may arise or accrue from the said ferry.

To have and to hold, the said ferry, with the appurtenances, unto the said party of the second part, his executors, administrators and assigns, from the time of the establishment thereof, as hereinafter covenanted and agreed, for and during and until the full end and term of ten years from thence next ensuing, and fully to be complete and ended ; yielding and paying therefor, yearly, and every year during the first five years of said term, the annual rent or sum of one hundred dollars, and for the remaining five years of said term, the annual rent or sum of two hundred dollars, lawful money of the United States of America, in quarter-yearly payments, on the usual quarter days for the payment of rent in the said city of New York ; that is to say, one fourth part thereof on the first days of August, November, February, and May, in each and every year during the said term, the first payment to be made on the first quarter day after the establishment of said ferry

Provided always, that if it should so happen, that the said yearly rent, or any part thereof, shall be behind and unpaid, for the space of ten days after any day of payment on which the same ought to be paid as aforesaid, or if the said party of the second part, his executors, administrators, or assigns, shall neglect or omit to pay, perform, fulfill, observe and keep any or either of the payments, articles, covenants, clauses, agreements, provisions, matters or things herein contained, which on the part and behalf of the said party of the second part, his executors, administrators, or assigns, are to be paid, performed, observed, fulfilled, and kept, during the said term of ten years, according to the true intent and meaning of these presents, that then and in every and all such case or cases, it shall and may be lawful for the said parties of the first part, their successors, or assigns, to enter into and upon the premises hereby demised, and to have, possess and enjoy the same again, as fully as though these presents had never been made, anything herein contained to the contrary notwithstanding.

And the said party of the second part, for himself, his heirs, executors, administrators and assigns, doth covenant and agree, to and with the said parties of the first part, their successors and assigns, by these presents, in manner following; that is to say, That the said party of the second part, his executors, administrators and assigns, shall and will, yearly and every year during the said term hereby demised, well and truly pay unto the said parties of the first part, their successors or assigns, the said yearly rent or sum of money herein before mentioned, at the days and times above specified for the payment thereof, without fraud or delay. And also, that he, the said party of the second part, shall and will, at his own proper costs, charges and expenses, furnish, provide and navigate, upon the said ferry to and from the foot of Eighty-sixth street to Bull's Ferry aforesaid, good and substantial steam ferry-boats, and keep the said steam ferry-boats at all reasonable times continually employed on the said ferry during the term hereby granted: and also shall and will, whenever thereunto required by the said parties of the first part, at their own proper costs, charges and expenses, provide and navigate upon the said ferry one other good and substantial steam ferry-boat; which said steam ferry-boat shall be approved by the Street Commissioner of the Corporation of the City of New York, and shall be used to carry, transport and convey carriages, horses, passengers and effects, upon the said ferry; and that the said steamboats shall always, during the said term, be kept in good repair, and furnished with all necessary and proper implements and machinery adapted to their respective kind; and manned with a sufficient number of able-bodied men, skilled in water service, to manage the same; and that the said men, so to be employed in all and each of the said boats, shall and will, at all times, be ready and willing to give their constant attendance at the said ferry, for the prompt and convenient transportation of passengers and effects, horses and carriages, across the said ferry. And also, that he, the said party of the second part, his executors, administrators and assigns, shall conduct and manage the said ferry agreeably to such rules, regulations, rates of ferriage, times of running, and restrictions, as, from time to time during the said term, shall, by any by-law, ordinance, order or resolution, of the said parties of the first part, or their successors, in Common Council convened, be made or passed in relation to the said ferry. And also, that he, the said party of the second part, his executors, administrators or assigns, shall and will, at his own proper costs, charges and expenses, build, erect, make and finish, such improvements as may be necessary for the accommodation of such ferry, and at all times during the said term hereby demised, well and sufficiently repair, uphold, sustain, amend, maintain and keep, all and singular the floats, racks, fenders, bridges, and other ferry fixtures, at each landing place of the said ferry; and shall and will also keep in repair the piers adjoining, or which may be made or built adjoining both slips used for the said ferry, both at Bull's Ferry and New York, or such parts or proportions of said piers as may belong to the said parties of the first part.

And also, that the said party of the second part, his executors, administrators or assigns, shall and will, at the expiration of the said term hereby demised, peaceably and quietly leave, surrender and yield up the said ferry and other hereby demised premises and the piers, in good order and condition, into the hands and possession of the said parties of the first part, their successors or assigns.

And also, that the said party of the second part, his executors, administrators and assigns, shall not nor will during the said term transfer, assign or set over, let or underlet, or in any other manner convey, this present lease or any part thereof, or their estate or interest therein, or in or to the above demised premises, or any part of the same, without the leave or consent of the said parties of the first part, their successors or assigns, in writing first had and obtained.

And it is hereby mutually agreed, by and between the respective parties to these presents, that the said parties of the first part, or their successors, shall and may, at any time and from time to time, extend the piers at the foot of Eighty-sixth street aforesaid, or any or either of them, to such distance into the North river, as said parties of the first part shall deem expedient, by resolution duly passed in their legislative capacity, without making to the said party of the second part, his executors, administrators or assigns, any compensation for the supposed damage they may sustain, and without being liable to any action, suit, or proceeding by reason of such extension, by or on behalf of the said party of the second part, his executors, administrators or assigns, and without any alteration of the rent hereby reserved.

And it is hereby mutually covenanted and agreed, by and between the parties to these presents, and these presents are upon the express understanding, that nothing herein contained shall be taken or construed to operate as a covenant by the said parties of the first part, or their successors, for possession or quiet enjoyment by the said party of the second part, his executors, administrators or assigns, of the said ferry or right of ferriage; nor shall the same be taken or construed to interfere, in any manner, with any previous grants or rights made by the said parties of the first part, nor with the right to grant any future ferries to and from Bull's Ferry, or to and from elsewhere wheresoever, nor to operate further, than to grant the possession of the estate, right, title, or interest which the said parties of the first part may have or lawfully claim, in the said ferry and right of ferriage hereby demised, by virtue of their several charters and the various acts of the Legislature of the people of the State of New York.

In witness whereof, to one part of these presents, remaining with the said parties of the first part, the said party of the second part hath set his hand and seal; and to the other part thereof, remaining with the said party of the second part, the said parties of the first part have caused the common seal of the City of New York to be affixed, the day and year first above written.

Sealed and delivered, in the presence of
 ·CHARLES W. LAWRENCE,
      HENRY CONKLIN. [L. S.]

I hereby consent that the within lease be assigned to Horace P. Russ, Geo. W. Reid, and Edmund Griffin, in such proportions as they may agree upon. Dec. 21, 1853.

      A. C. FLAGG,
        Comptroller.

NOTE.—"Five," 18th line, page 153, interlined: and "to," 5th line from bottom, page 156, written on an erasure.

RAILROADS

AND

RAILROAD GRANTS

IN THE

CITY OF NEW YORK.

SECOND AVENUE RAILROAD.

This Agreement, made this fifteenth day of December, in the year one thousand eight hundred and fifty-two, between the Mayor, Aldermen and Commonalty of the city of New York, parties of the first part, and Denton Pearsall, Joseph C. Skaden, Abraham B. Rapelyea, William L. Hall, Richard T. Mulligan, Charles Miller, Daniel J. Sherwood, Abraham Allen and Henry Goff, parties of the second part, being the persons named in the resolutions hereinafter set forth, to whom permission is given to lay or build a railroad track, in accordance with said resolutions.

Whereas, The said parties of the first part, in Common Council convened, did, on the eleventh day of December, one thousand eight hundred and fifty-two, duly pass and adopt the following resolutions, which that day became operative and binding, in the words and figures following:

Resolved, That permission is hereby given to Denton Pearsall, Joseph C. Skaden, Abraham B. Rapelyea, Wm. L. Hall, R. T. Mulligan, Charles Miller, Daniel J. Sherwood, Abraham Allen and Henry Goff, to lay a grooved railroad track in the following streets and avenues of the city of New York, viz.: Commencing at a point in the 2d avenue, at or near to 42d street, thence running down the 2d avenue to 23d street, with a double track, through 23d street, with a single track, to the 1st avenue; down 1st avenue to Allen street, through Allen street to Grand street, through Grand street to the Bowery, down the Bowery to Chatham street, across Chatham street to Oliver street, through Oliver street to South street, through South street to Roosevelt street, across Roosevelt street to Front street, through Front street to Peck slip, the terminus. Returning, with a single track, as follows: Through Peck slip to Pearl street, through Pearl street to Chatham street, through Chatham street to the Bowery, through the Bowery to Grand street, through Grand street to Chrystie street, through Chrystie street to the 2d avenue, to 23d street, where it intersects the double track, and so on to its termination, opposite the Harlem river, with a double track.

Provided, however, That all the said rails shall be laid down in such manner, and in such parts of the said streets and avenues, as shall be approved by the Street Commissioner, so as to cause no impediment to the common and ordinary use of the streets and avenues for all other purposes; and that the water courses of the streets shall be left free and unobstructed, and that the said company shall pave the streets in and about the rails in a permanent manner, and keep the same in repair to the entire satisfaction of said Street Commissioner;

And Provided, further, That no motive power, except horses, be used below 42d street; and further, that they run a car on said road for the convenience of public travel, each and every day, both ways, as often as every 15 minutes, from 5 to 6 o'clock, A. M., every 4 minutes, from 6 A. M. to 8 P. M., every 15 minutes, from 8 P. M. to 12 o'clock, P. M., and every 30 minutes, from 12 o'clock P. M. to 5 o'clock, A. M., and as much oftener as public convenience may require, under such directions as the Common Council may from time to time prescribe.

Also, that the rate of passage on said railroad shall not

exceed a greater sum than 5 cents to 42d street, and also that the Common Council shall have power to regulate the fare for the entire length of said road, when it shall be completed to Harlem river.

Also, that said road shall be commenced within six months, and completed to 42d street within one year, and from 42d street to Harlem river within three years from the passage of this resolution.

Resolved, That the said parties shall, in all respects, comply with the direction of the Street Commissioner and of the Common Council, in the building of said railroad, and in the running of the cars thereon, and in any other matters connected with the regulation of said railroad.

Resolved, That the said parties shall, before this permission takes effect, enter into a good and sufficient agreement with the Mayor, Aldermen, and Commonalty of the City of New York, to be drawn and approved by the Counsel to the Corporation, binding themselves to abide by and perform the stipulations and provisions herein contained; and also all such other regulations or ordinances as may be passed by the Common Council, relating to the said road.*

Now, therefore, this indenture witnesseth, that the said parties of the first part do make and declare this grant, and all licenses, rights and privileges and powers conferred or provided for, or intended to be conferred or provided for, in said resolutions, conditioned and dependent upon

---

* Adopted by the Board of Assistants, Nov. 9, 1852.
Adopted by the Board of Aldermen, Nov. 15, 1852.
Received from His Honor the Mayor, Dec. 11, 1852, without his approval or objection thereto; therefore, under the provisions of the amended charter, the same became adopted.

the strict observance, performance and fulfilment by the said parties of the second part, or such of them as may act, of the said resolutions and the stipulations, restrictions, regulations and provisions therein contained, and the due and faithful performance by the said parties of the following covenants and agreements: That the said parties of the second part, for themselves and their successors, do hereby covenant and agree with the said parties of the first part, and with each other, that they will well and truly observe, perform, fulfill and keep the said resolutions hereinbefore particularly set forth, and all and every the provisions, stipulations, restrictions and conditions therein contained and thereby imposed, according to the true intent and meaning thereof.

In witness whereof, to one of these presents, remaining with the said parties of the first part, the said parties of the second part have set their hands and seals; and to the other part thereof, remaining with the said parties of the second part, the said parties of the first part have caused the common seal of the city of New York to be affixed, the day and year first above written.

DENTON PEARSALL,	[L. S.]
ABRA'M ALLEN,	[L. S.]
RICHARD T. MULLIGAN,	[L. S.]
ABRA'M B. RAPELYEA,	[L. S.]
WM. L. HALL,	[L. S.]
CHAS. MILLER,	[L. S.]
DANIEL J. SHERWOOD,	[L. S.]
HENRY GOFF,	[L. S.]
JOSEPH C. SKADEN,	[L. S.]

Sealed and delivered in presence of

CHAS. H. HAWKINS.

CITY AND COUNTY OF NEW YORK, ss.:—On this 17th day of December, A. D. 1852, before me came Charles H Hawkins, subscribing witness to the within grant, to me personally known, who, being by me duly sworn, did depose and say that he is a resident of the city of New York, that he is acquainted with Denton Pearsall, Joseph C. Skaden, Abraham B. Rapelyea, William L. Hall, Richard T. Mulligan, Charles Miller, Daniel J. Sherwood, Abraham Allen and Henry Goff, and knows them to be the same individuals described in and who executed the within grant; that he saw them sign the same; that they severally acknowledged in his presence that they executed the same, and that he subscribed his name as a witness thereto.   GEORGE L. TAYLOR,

Commissioner of Deeds.

Resolved, That the route of the 2d Avenue Railroad be, and the same is hereby, changed from Front street, between Roosevelt street and Peck Slip, to South street, between the same points.

Adopted by the Board of Assistants, July 12, 1853.

Adopted by the Board of Aldermen, July 18, 1853.

Approved by the Mayor, July 20, 1853.

Resolved, That the 2d Avenue Railroad Company be, and are hereby directed to cause Grand street, from the Bowery to Allen street, to be repaired according to the terms of their grant, within 10 days from the adoption of this resolution.

Adopted by the Board of Councilmen, Feb. 13, 1854.

Adopted by the Board of Aldermen, April 3, 1854.

Approved by the Mayor, April 6, 1854.

Resolved, That the 2d Avenue Railroad Company be, and are hereby directed to pay to the City, for all pavement now laid and about to be laid in Grand street, in and about their tracks, as called for in their grant, and also Allen, between Grand and Broome streets.

Adopted by the Board of Aldermen, July 13, 1854.

Adopted by the Board of Councilmen, Oct. 6, 1854.

Approved by the Mayor, Oct. 11, 1854.

Resolved, That the 2d Avenue Railroad Company forthwith remove that portion of their track which extends from the southerly side of 49th street to the northerly side of 53d street, or so much thereof as shall, from time to time, be directed by the Street Commissioner, and that, if the said Railroad Company shall neglect or refuse so to remove the same within two days after being required so to do by the Street Commissioner, that said Street Commissioner be authorized and directed to remove the same.

Adopted by the Board of Councilmen, July 10, 1856.

Adopted by the Board of Aldermen, Aug. 4, 1856.

Approved by the Mayor, Aug. 6, 1856.

Whereas, An act passed the recent Legislature, authorizing the 2d Avenue Railroad Company to lay rails in certain streets of the city, other than those contained in their grant or permission from the Common Council, therefore, be it

Resolved, That should the said 2d avenue Railroad Company undertake to lay rails in any of the streets of the city, by the authority thus conferred upon said Company by the said Legislature, the Counsel to the Corporation is hereby authorized and directed to restrain said Company by injunction, and further, if necessary, to test the validity of said act.

By the Board of Aldermen, April 28, 1857.

By the Board of Councilmen, May 25, 1857.

Approved by the Mayor, May 27, 1857.

The President of the Croton Aqueduct Board directed to notify the 2d Avenue Railroad Company to put in good repair forthwith all the pavements in and about their rails, and, in case of neglect or refusal, to have the same done at the expense of the 2d Avenue Railroad Company.

Adopted by the Board of Aldermen, September 10, 1857.

Adopted by the Board of Councilmen, September 14, 1857.

Approved by the Mayor, September 16, 1857.

Resolved, That the Second Avenue Railroad Company be, and they are hereby, directed to have the rails between Forty-ninth and Sixty-first streets, in Second avenue, from the curb to the centre of the avenue, forthwith.*

Adopted by the Board of Aldermen, Oct. 20, 1859.

Adopted by the Board of Councilmen, Oct. 24, 1859.

---

* So printed in the proceedings of the two Boards. The resolution directed, or intended to direct, that the rails should be *removed* from the curb to the centre of the avenue.

Approved by the Mayor, Oct. 25, 1859.

Resolved, That the Second avenue, between Forty-eighth and Sixty-first streets, be paved with Belgian pavement, one-third the expense thereof to be paid by the owners of property, one-third by the Second Avenue Railroad Company, and one-third by the city, under the direction of the Croton Aqueduct Department, and that the accompanying ordinance therefor be adopted.

Adopted by Board of Councilmen, Dec. 15, 1859.

Adopted by Board of Aldermen, Dec. 30, 1859.

Approved by the Mayor, Dec. 31, 1859.

THIRD AVENUE RAILROAD.

AGREEMENT, made the first day of January, in the year one thousand eight hundred and fifty-three, between the Mayor, Aldermen and Commonalty of the city of New York, parties of the first part, and the persons named in the resolutions hereinafter set forth, who shall duly sign and execute this agreement, their successors, associates and assigns, duly becoming parties thereto, as hereinafter provided, of the second part.

Whereas, The said parties of the first part, in Common Council convened, did, on the eighteenth day of December, one thousand eight hundred and fifty-two, duly pass and adopt the following resolutions, which were afterward, and on the thirty-first day of December, in the said year, returned by the Mayor without his approval or objections, and became operative and binding, in the words and figures following :

Resolved, That Myndert Van Schaick, Horace M. Dewey, John B. Dingledein, John Murphy, James W. Flynn, James McElvaney, Patrick McElroy, Thomas Murphy, Philip Reynolds, Elijah F. Purdy, Bryant McCahill, George Caplin, Oscar F. Benjamin, and those who may hereafter become associated with them, have the authority and consent of the Common Council, and permission is hereby granted to them to lay a double track for a railroad in the following streets.

From a point at the intersection of Park row and Broadway, near the southwesterly corner of the Park, thence along Park row to Chatham street, thence along Chatham street to the Bowery, thence along the Bowery to the 3d avenue, and thence along the 3d avenue to the Harlem River, upon the following conditions, viz. :

Such track or tracks to be laid under the direction of the Street Commissioner, and on such grades as are now established, or may hereafter be established, by the Common Council, the said parties to become bound in a sufficient penalty to keep in good repair the space inside the tracks, and a space 2 feet each side of the same of each street in which the rails are laid ; and also that no steam power be used on any part of the road for propelling cars, and upon the further condition that said parties shall place new cars on said railroad, with all the modern improvements, for the convenience and comfort of passengers, and that they run cars thereon, each and every day, both ways and as often as the public convenience may require, under such prudential directions as the Common Council and the Street Commissioner may, from time to time, prescribe ; and

Provided, also, That the said parties shall in all respects comply with the directions of the Common Council in the building of the said railroad and in any other matter connected with the regulation of said railroad.

Provided, also, That the said parties shall, before this permission takes effect, enter into a good and sufficient agreement with the Mayor, Aldermen and Commonalty of the city of New York, to be drawn and approved of by the Counsel to the Corporation, binding themselves to abide by and perform the stipulations and provisions herein contained, and also all such other resolutions or ordinances as may be passed by the Common Council relating to the running of said cars over the said road.

And further, That they run a car thereon, each and every day, both ways, as often as every fifteen minutes from 5 to 6 A. M., every four minutes from 6 A. M. to 8 P. M., every fifteen minutes from 8 P. M. to 12 M., and as much oftener as public convenience may require, under such directions as the Common Council may, from time to time, prescribe.

Also, That the said passage on said railroad shall not exceed a greater sum than five cents for any distance, between the southern point of said railroad and Sixty-first street, and six cents for the entire length of said railroad.

And also, that said track or tracks shall be laid upon a good foundation, with a grooved rail, or such other rail as may be approved of by the Common Council and the Street Commissioner, even with the surface of the streets through which they may pass, and shall be commenced within six months, and completed to Forty-second street within one year from the passage of this resolution; and from Forty-second street, toward and to the Harlem River, as fast as the Third avenue shall be graded and in a proper condition to lay rails thereon.

2. *Resolved*, That said parties have the consent of the Common Council, and permission is hereby given to them, to connect their said railroad, at the junction of the Bowery and Grand street, with the Second Avenue Railroad, if constructed; and said parties, and those to whom permission may be given by the Common Council to lay a railroad through the Second avenue, shall have the free use in common of the double track from said junction through the Bowery to Chatham street, and of one of the tracks to be laid from the southerly termination of the Bowery through Chatham street to Pearl street; each of said parties to pay half the expense of constructing and keeping in repair the double and single track so to be used by them in common. Either of said parties to have the right to construct said double and single track so to be used in common, and, if constructed by either, the other of said parties shall pay half the actual cost thereof; or said parties may, by mutual agreement, construct the same jointly.

3. *Resolved*, That in consideration of the good and faithful performance of the conditions, stipulations, and agreement above prescribed, and of such other necessary re-

quirements as may hereafter be made by the Common Council, for the regulations of the said railroad, the said parties shall pay, from the date of opening the said railroad, the annual license fee for each car now allowed by law, and shall have licenses accordingly.

4. *Resolved*, That within a reasonable time after the passage of these resolutions, the said parties, or a majority in interest thereof, may form themselves into an association which shall be vested with all the rights and privileges hereby granted; and shall have power, by the votes of at least a majority in interest of the associates, to frame and establish articles of association providing for the construction, operation, and management of said railroad, and to make contracts for the purchase of property for the use or benefit of said railroad.

5. *Resolved*, That the association shall not be deemed dissolved by the death or act of any associate, but his successor in interest shall stand in his place, and the rights of each associate shall depend on his own fulfilment of the conditions imposed on him by these restrictions or the articles of association and by-laws of the association; and in case of his failure to fulfill the same his rights shall be forfeited to and devolve upon the remaining associates after twenty days' notice of such failure, from the secretary of the association, specifying the particulars of his delinquency; and the said parties or associates may, at any time, incorporate themselves under the general railroad act whenever two-thirds in interest of the associates shall require it.

And whereas, It is deemed necessary by the said parties of the first part, in order to preserve and duly effectuate the grants, objects, stipulations, and intentions of the said resolutions, and for the purpose of more specifically determining the interest of the said parties in the rights and privileges granted by said resolutions, that provision should be made for an organization or association between the said parties of the second part, their successors, associates and assigns, duly admitted, according to this agreement, defining the mode in which the necessary capital for building the said railroad shall be contributed, and the manner in which the construction and management of the said railroad shall be conducted and controlled.

Now, it is hereby mutually declared, That the separate and individual interests of any or either of the said parties of the second part, their successors, associates, and assigns, in the said grant, and all licenses, rights and privileges, and powers conferred or provided for in said resolutions shall be conditioned and dependent upon the strict observance, performance and fulfilment by such persons of the terms of said resolutions and of this agreement; and that, in case of failure to perform the same, and every part thereof, said grant shall be inoperative as to such person so failing, and his interest therein shall cease and determine; said grant remaining operative in every respect as to all others of said parties, their successors, associates and assigns, and it is hereby covenanted, agreed and declared, by and between the parties aforesaid, viz. :

First. The said parties of the second part, for themselves and their successors, associates and assigns, do hereby covenant and agree with the said parties of the first part, and with each other, that they will well and truly observe, perform, fulfill and keep the said resolutions hereinbefore particularly set forth, and all and every the provisions, stipulations, restrictions and conditions therein contained, and thereby imposed, according to the true intent and meaning thereof; it being understood that the rate of passage on said road shall not exceed five cents for any distance between the southerly point of said railroad and Sixty-first street, and six cents for the entire length of said railroad; and also that the said road shall be completed at the times and in the manner stated in said resolutions.

SECOND. The said parties of the second part, to the end that the provisions and intentions of the said resolutions may be carried into effect, the interests of the respective parties definitely ascertained, and the manner in which the construction and management of said road shall be conducted and controlled, effectually defined, do further covenant and agree with the said parties of the first part, and with each other, to associate and organize themselves together in the manner and upon the terms and conditions following, viz.:

Within ten days after this agreement is duly executed, the said parties of the second part, unless they, or a majority of them shall have previously organized themselves to the same effect as herein provided, shall and will organize themselves into an association or company, to be called the Third Avenue Railroad Company, for the purpose of constructing, operating and managing said railroad. The first meeting of the said parties to be called by the clerk of the Common Council, who shall, within three days after the due execution of this agreement, give, or cause to be given, a notice in writing, delivered to the persons composing the said parties of the second part, personally, or left at their residences or places of business, specifying the time and place when and where such meeting shall be held.

The said parties of the second part, or as many of them as shall meet, in pursuance of said order, shall thereupon proceed, as before provided, to organize themselves into the said Company, and shall have power and authority, by the votes of the majority of the parties so assembled,

1. To estimate and declare the amount of capital requisite to construct the said railroad, provide cars, motive power, stations, buildings, fixtures, and for all other expenses requisite to put the said railroad into thorough practical operation.

2. To prescribe the mode in which the said capital and all other sums that may thereafter be required for the business of said Company shall be subscribed for, and the time or times when the same shall be paid in, and the manner in which the shares or interests of the parties refusing or neglecting to subscribe or to pay may be forfeited.

3. To adopt suitable resolutions, by-laws, rules and regulations for the organization of said Company, the subscription and payment of its capital, and all other sums that may thereafter be required for its construction, operation and future business, the execution of contracts, the liability of members, the terms, compensation, accountability, election, removal and duties of its officers, the disbursement of moneys, the transfer or assignment of shares of its members and the entire management, direction and

control of its affairs, business, property and offices; such by-laws may be altered, from time to time, in the manner prescribed therein.

4. The said parties of the second part shall be entitled to subscribe equally for the amount proposed as the original capital stock of said Company, and if any of them neglect to subscribe, or shall subscribe less than his proportion, the others may subscribe equally for the remainder, so as to make up a subscription for the whole amount. If for any reasons it shall be requisite to make other subscriptions, the persons who shall then be members of said Company shall be entitled to subscribe for the amount so required in proportion to the amounts of capital stock held by them, and if any shall neglect to subscribe, or shall subscribe for less than his proportion, the others may subscribe equally for the remainder.

5. Every person refusing or neglecting to subscribe to the capital stock of said Company, as originally declared, or to any subsequent increase thereof, or to pay his subscription, or any instalment thereof, at the times prescribed at the first meeting of said Company as aforesaid, or by the resolutions or by-laws of the said Company, all his rights, powers and privileges under said grant of the parties of the first part, and all his interests therein, shall be deemed to be freely and voluntarily waived and abandoned for the benefit of said Company and its remaining members, and shall cease, determine and be utterly null and void, and he shall be no longer a member of said Company, nor have any voice in the management of its affairs, nor any title and interest in its property; but such waiver and abandonment shall not be deemed to have taken

place until twenty days shall have elapsed after such person shall have had written notice of the required subscription or payment. But such person may, by a resolution, duly adopted by said Company, be reinstated in any or all of the rights, privileges and advantages so as aforesaid waived and lost, but upon such terms and conditions as may be hereby provided.

6. Every person who shall become a member of said Company shall thereby become a party to this agreement and all its conditions and stipulations, and the Company may direct the mode by which future members shall become so obligated, and no person shall become a member except on condition of becoming so obligated by agreement in writing duly executed.

7. The said railroad grant, property, rights and appurtenances, shall belong to, and be the property of, the persons who, for the time being, shall compose the said Third Avenue Railroad Company, in proportions equivalent to their shares of said capital stock, subject, however, to the management of the same in the manner herein provided.

8. Any shareholder may transfer his share or interest after he shall have paid one-third of his original subscription, on procuring the consent of a majority in interest of the shareholders, expressed by a resolution duly adopted, subject, however, to the provisions of this agreement, and on such terms and conditions as the by-laws may prescribe.

9. This Company shall not be dissolved by the death or insolvency of any of its members, nor by act or operation

of law, but in such and the like cases shall continue, and the persons becoming lawfully entitled to the shares shall become members of the said Company, and said Company shall have authority to incorporate themselves under the general railroad act, whenever two-thirds in interest of the shareholders shall require the same.

In witness whereof, to one of these presents, remaining with the said parties of the first part, the said parties of the second part have affixed their hands and seals ; and to the other part thereof, remaining with the said parties of the second part, the said parties of the first part have caused the common seal of the city of New York to be affixed, the day and year first above written.

M. VAN SCHAICK, [L. S.]
H. M. DEWEY, [L. S.]
JOHN B. DINGELDEIN, [L. S.]
JOHN MURPHY, [L. S.]
JAMES W. FLYNN, [L. S.]
JAMES McELVANEY, [L. S.]
PATRICK McELROY, [L. S.]
THOMAS MURPHY, [L. S.]
P. REYNOLDS, [L. S.]
ELIJAH F. PURDY, [L. S.]
BRYAN McCAHILL, [L. S.]
GEORGE CALPIN, [L. S.]
OSCAR F. BENJAMIN. [L. S.]

Sealed and delivered in }
  presence of   }

    HENRY E. DAVIES.

State of New York, City and County of New York, ss.:

On this first day of January, eighteen hundred and fifty-three, before me personally appeared Henry E. Davies, the subscribing witness to the above instrument, to me known, who, being by me duly sworn, did depose and say that he resides in the city and county of New York—that he knows Myndert Van Schaick, Horace M. Dewey, John B. Dingeldein, John Murphy, James W. Flynn, James McElvancy, Patrick McElroy, Thomas Murphy, Philip Reynolds, Elijah F. Purdy, Bryan McCahill, George Calpin, and Oscar F. Benjamin, the persons described in, and who executed the within instrument—that he was present, and saw them severally sign, seal and deliver the within instrument, for and as their act and deed; and that they each severally acknowledged that they executed the same, and that thereupon he subscribed his name as a witness thereto.

J. MANSFIELD DAVIES,
Commissioner of Deeds.

Resolved, That the time within which, by the provisions of the grant dated January 1, 1853, authorizing the construction of the Third Avenue Railroad, the grantees in said grant named, and their assigns, were permitted to lay down a double track in the Bowery, south of Fifth street and along Park Row, be, and the same is hereby, extended until the expiration of three months after such time as the Third Avenue Railroad Company shall be deprived by the New York and Harlem Railroad Company of the privilege now enjoyed by the Third Avenue Railroad Company, of running their cars over the tracks of the New York and Harlem Railroad Company.

Adopted by the Board of Assistants, December 3, 1853.

Adopted by the Board of Aldermen, December 7, 1853.

Approved by the Mayor, December 9, 1853.

Resolved, That the Third Avenue Railroad Company be, and they are hereby, directed to cause Chatham street, from Pearl to Chambers street, to be repaired, according to the terms of their grant, within ten days from the adoption of this resolution.

Adopted by the Board of Councilmen, February 6, 1854.

Adopted by the Board of Aldermen, February 9, 1854.

Approved by the Mayor, February 14, 1854.

Petition of the Third Avenue Railroad Co. for privilege to build a portico and balcony in front of their new depot. Prayer of the petitioner granted.

By the Board of Aldermen, June 8, 1857.

By the Board of Councilmen, June 11, 1857.

Approved by the Mayor, June 12, 1857.

The President of the Croton Aqueduct Board directed to notify the Third Avenue Railroad Co. to put in good repair, forthwith, all the pavements on and about their rails, and, in case of neglect or refusal, to have the same done at the expense of the Third Avenue Railroad Co.

Adopted by the Board of Aldermen, Sept. 10, 1857.

Adopted by the Board of Councilmen, Sept. 14, 1857.

Approved by the Mayor, Sept. 16, 1857.

Resolved, That the Third Avenue Railroad Co. be, and they are hereby permitted to substitute the iron instead of the Belgian pavement, on the up grades of Chatham street, at their own expense, under the supervision of the Croton Aqueduct Department.

Adopted by the Board of Aldermen, April 8, 1858.

Adopted by the Board of Councilmen, May 31, 1858.

Approved by the Mayor, June 9, 1858.

Resolved, That the Third avenue, from Fifty-sixth to Eighty-sixth street, be paved with the Belgian or trap-block pavement, the Third Avenue Railroad Company to pave or cause to be paved, at their own expense, all that portion of said avenue between and outside of their rails, which, by the terms of their grant from the city, they are required to keep in repair—the city at large, and the property owners on the line of said avenue, to pay an equal portion each of the expense of paving the remaining portion of the said Third avenue, between Fifty-sixth and Eighty-sixth streets, and that the accompanying ordinance be adopted.

Adopted by the Board of Aldermen, Oct. 10, 1859.

Adopted by the Board of Councilmen, Dec. 15, 1859.

Approved by the Mayor, Dec. 20, 1859.

NEW YORK AND HARLEM RAILROAD.

ARTICLES OF AGREEMENT made this ninth day of January, one thousand eight hundred and thirty-two, between the New York and Harlem Railroad Company, parties of the first part, and the Mayor, Aldermen and Commonalty of the city of New York, parties of the second part:

Whereas, an ordinance of the Common Council of the city of New York was passed by the Board of Aldermen on the sixteenth day of December last, and by the Board of Assistants on the nineteenth day of December last, and approved by the Mayor of the said city on the twenty-second day of December last, which ordinance is in the words and figures following, to wit:

A LAW *to authorize the New York and Harlem Railroad Co. to construct their Railway.*

SECTION 1. Be it ordained, &c., that the New York and Harlem Railroad Co. be, and they are hereby, permitted to construct and lay down, in pursuance of their act of incorporation, a double or single track, or railroad, or railway, along the Fourth avenue, from 23d street to the Harlem river, in conformity with a map now on file in the Register's office, and a branch thereof along 125th street, from the Fourth avenue to the Hudson river, provided that the width of such double railroad or way shall not exceed 24 feet.

§ 2. And be it further ordained, that if, at any time after the construction of the aforesaid railways by the said New York and Harlem Railroad Co., it shall appear to the Mayor,

Aldermen, and Commonalty of the city of New York, that the said railways, or any part thereof, shall constitute an obstruction or impediment to the future regulation of the city, or the ordinary use of any street or avenue (of which the said Mayor, Aldermen, and Commonalty shall be the sole judges), the said Railroad Company, or the directors thereof, shall, on the requisition of the said Mayor, Aldermen, and Commonalty, forthwith provide a remedy for the same, satisfactory to the said Mayor, Aldermen, and Commonalty; or, if they fail to find such remedy, they shall, within one month after such requisition, proceed to remove such railway, or obstruction or impediment, and to replace the street or avenue in as good condition as it was before the said railway was laid down; and, should the said Directors decline or neglect to obey such requisition, the said Mayor, Aldermen, and Commonalty may, upon the expiration of the time limited in such notice, cause the obstruction or impediment to be removed, and the avenues or streets restored as aforesaid, at the expense of the said Railroad Company.

§ 3. That the right of regulating the description of power to be used in propelling carriages on and along said railways, and the speed of the same, as well as all other power reserved to the said Mayor, Aldermen, and Commonalty, by the act of incorporation of the said Company, or any part thereof, be, and the same is hereby, expressly retained and reserved.

§ 4. That it shall expressly be incumbent on the said New York and Harlem Railroad Co., at their own cost, to construct stone arches and bridges for all the cross streets now or hereafter to be made (which will be intersected by the embankments or excavations of the said railroad), and which, in the opinion of the Common Council, the public convenience requires to be arched or bridged, and also to make such embankments or excavations as (in the opinion of the Common Council) may be required to make the passage over the railroad and embankments, at the intersected cross streets, easy and convenient for all the purposes for which streets and roads are usually put to; and also that the said Company shall make, at their own like cost and charges, all such drains and sewers as their embankments and excavations may (in the opinion of the Common Council) make necessary; all which work to be done under the like requisition, and under like disabilities, as in the 2d section of this ordinance mentioned. And further, that the said Company shall make their railroad path, from time to time, conform to what may hereafter be the regulation of the avenue and road through which said railroad passes.

§ 5. That it shall be incumbent on the said New York and Harlem Railroad Company to commence and complete their said railroad in the respective times allowed for that purpose in their act of incorporation; and, unless they commence and complete the same in the periods of time for the said commencement and completion in said incorporation specified, that then the consent of the Common Council, and all the powers and privileges given in this ordinance, shall cease and be null and void.

§ 6. That in case the said railroad should not be completed within the times for that purpose in their charter mentioned, or if, any time after the construction of the said railroad, the same should be discontinued, or not kept up and in repair as a good and sufficient railroad, that then the strip of land, to be taken for the said railroad, should be thrown open and become a part of the street or public avenue, without any assessment on the owners of the adjoining land or the public therefor.

§ 7. That no building shall be erected on the said strip of land to be taken for said railroad, and that a railing or other erections shall be made on the outer edges of the embankments or railroad path, and also such railing or fences on the edges of the excavations, as the Common Council shall, from time to time, deem necessary, to prevent accidents and loss of lives to our fellow-citizens.

§ 8. That this ordinance shall not be considered as binding on the Common Council, nor shall the said ordinance go into effect, until the said Harlem Railroad Company shall first duly execute (under their corporate seal) such an instrument in writing (promising, covenanting, and engaging, on their part and behalf, to stand to, abide by and perform all the conditions and requirements in this ordinance contained) as the Mayor and the Counsel of the Board shall, by their certificate, approve, and not until such instrument shall be filed, so certified, in the Comptroller's office of this city.

Passed by the Board of Aldermen, December 16, 1831.

Passed by the Board of Assistants, December 19, 1831.

Approved by the Mayor, December 22, 1831.

Now, this agreement witnesseth, that for and in consideration of the premises, and in pursuance of the requirements of the eighth section of said ordinance, the said parties of the first part do hereby for themselves, and their successors, promise, covenant and engage to and with the said parties of the second part and their successors and assigns, to stand, abide by and perform all the conditions and requirements in the said ordinance contained.

In witness whereof, the said parties of the first part have hereunto affixed their corporate seal, and caused the same to be signed by their Vice President (in the absence of their President), and attested by their Secretary, the day and year aforesaid.

JOHN MASON, [L. S.]
Vice President.

Witness,
    Isaac Adriance,
        Secretary pro tem.

Resolved, If the Board of Aldermen concur herein, that the maps presented by the New York and Harlem Railroad Company, so far as the same locate the route of the said railroad, from the north side of 23d street through the centre of the 4th avenue to Harlem River, and the branch of the same through the centre of 125th street, from the 4th avenue to the Hudson River, be approved, upon condition that neither this approval, nor anything herein contained, shall be construed into a consent to the said Company to construct the said railroad, but that the said Company shall first obtain the consent of the Mayor, Aldermen, and Commonalty of the City of New York before they commence the construction of said road.

Adopted by the Board of Assistant Aldermen, October 5, 1831.

Concurred in by the Board of Aldermen, October 10, 1831.

Approved by the Mayor, October 11, 1831.

Resolved, That the New York and Harlem Railroad Company be, and are hereby, authorized to take possession of the ground owned by the Common Council, over which the line of said railroad is ordered to be constructed, and that they be permitted to use the same during the continuance of the present charter for the purpose of a railroad and that only, and, when they cease so to use it, it shall revert to the Corporation; provided always, that said land shall be so used as not to interfere with the use of the cross streets, and on condition, however, that if the said Corporation shall not commence the said railroad, and complete the same, within the time limited by their charter, then the privilege hereby granted shall cease and be void.

Adopted by both Boards, January 30, 1832.

Approved by the Mayor, February 1, 1832.

ARTICLES OF AGREEMENT, made this eighteenth·day of May, one thousand eight hundred and thirty-two, between the New York and Harlem Railroad Company, parties of the first part, and the Mayor, Aldermen and Commonalty of the city of New York, parties of the second part.

Whereas, certain resolutions of the Common Council of the city of New York were passed by the Board of Aldermen on the second day of May, instant, by the Board of

Assistants on the seventh day of May, instant, and approved by the Mayor of the said city on the tenth day of May, instant, which resolutions are in the words and figures following, to wit:

Resolved, That the New York and Harlem Railroad Company be permitted, and the Common Council hereby consent, so far as their rights extend, that the said company may extend their rails southerly from the north line of 23d street to Prince street, subject, however, to the same conditions and restrictions which the Common Council heretofore imposed upon said Company in respect to that part of the road above 23d street. That the said Company may forthwith proceed to lay down a single track through the 4th avenue, south of 23d street, Union place, Bloomingdale Road, and Broadway, and another single track through the Bowery, both as far south as Prince street, and after two months' use of a single track upon the whole distance south of 23d street, on both Broadway and the Bowery, with convenient turnings at the several terminations above mentioned, they may, unless otherwise directed by the Common Council, lay down a second track on each of the above-mentioned routes, the same to be maintained by the said Company, subject at all times to the regulations of the Common Council, and also subject to the obligation of removing the whole or any part of the railways hereby permitted to be laid down, in case the Common Council shall hereafter see fit to require the same.

Provided, however, that all the said rails shall be laid down in such manner and in such parts of the said streets as shall be approved by the Street Commissioner, so as to cause no impediment to the common and ordinary use of the streets for all other purposes; and that the water courses of the streets shall be left free and unobstructed, and that the said Company shall pave the streets in and about the rails in a satisfactory and permanent manner, and keep the width of twenty feet of said paving, including the rails, in good repair at all times during the continuance of their use thereof.

And provided further, that if, at any time after the said rails shall have been laid down, the Common Council shall deem it necessary and shall order the said rails to be taken up, the said Railroad Company shall cause the pavement of the streets to be placed in good and sufficient repair.

And provided further, that the said Company have their single rail tracks above mentioned completed on or before the 1st day of May, 1834, and that they are to charge and receive such tolls, rates, or fare for the carrying of passengers or effects upon the said rail tracks, south of Twenty-third street, as the said Common Council may prescribe.

Resolved, That the above resolution shall not be considered as binding on the Common Council, nor shall the same go into effect until the said Harlem Railroad Company shall first duly execute, under their corporate seal, such an instrument in writing, promising, covenanting and agreeing, on their part and behalf, to stand to, abide by and perform all the conditions and provisions in the said resolution contained, as the Mayor and the Counsel of the Board shall approve of, by a certificate under their hands, nor until such instrument shall be filed, so certified, in the Comptroller's office of this city.

Now this agreement witnesseth, that for and in consideration of the premises, and in pursuance of the requirements of the said resolutions, the said parties of the first part do hereby, for themselves and their successors, promise, covenant and agree to and with the said parties of the second part, and their successors and assigns, to stand to, abide by, and perform all the conditions and requirements in the said resolutions contained.

In witness whereof, the said parties of the first part have hereunto affixed their corporate seal, and caused the same to be signed by their Vice President (in the abscence of their President), and attested by their Secretary, the day and year aforesaid.

JOHN MASON, [L. S.]

Vice President.

Attested,

A. C. RAINETAUX,

Secretary.

We hereby certify that we approve of the within, as being such an instrument in writing as the New York and Harlem Railroad Company are required to execute and file in the Comptroller's office, according to the second resolution above recited.

WALTER BOWNE, *Mayor.*

R. EMMET, *Counsel.*

NEW YORK, June 14, 1832.

Resolved, That the New York and Harlem Railroad Company be permitted, and the Common Council hereby consent, so far as their rights extend, that the New York and Harlem Railroad Company may continue their rails by single or double track southerly, from the north line of Prince street to the north line of Walker street, subject to the same conditions and restrictions which the Common Council heretofore imposed upon the said Company, in respect to that part of the said road between Prince street and Twenty-third street, as provided by the ordinances of the Common Council, May 20, 1832.

Adopted by the Board of Aldermen, April 24, 1837.
Adopted by the Board of Assistants, May 1, 1837.
Approved by the Mayor, May 4, 1837.

Resolved, That the New York and Harlem Railroad Company be permitted, and the Common Council hereby consent, that the said Company may continue their rails, similar to those laid down between Thirteenth and Fourteenth streets, by a double track from the Bowery through Broome street to Centre street, and from Broome street through Centre street to Chatham street, subject to the same conditions and restrictions which the Common Council heretofore imposed upon the said Company.

Resolved, That when such rails shall be laid through Centre and Broome streets, the said Company shall cause so much of the rails as are laid in the Bowery, south of Broome street, to be removed, and the street repaired, under the direction of the Street Commissioner.

Adopted by the Board of Aldermen, April 20, 1838.

Adopted by the Board of Assistants, May 2, 1838.

Approved by the Mayor, May 4, 1838.

Resolved, That the curb-stone on the easterly side of Centre street, in front of the market, be set six feet into the walk from its present line; that the same be done at the expense of the Harlem Railroad Company, and provided that the said Railroad Company pave the space between the rails and the said curb-stone with blocks of wood, the balance of the stone pavement to be allowed to their credit in the assessment for paving the street, or so much of the said pavement as does not legitimately belong to them to make.

Adopted by the Board of Aldermen, April 29, 1839.

Adopted by the Board of Assistants, April 29, 1839.

Approved by the Mayor, May 2, 1839.

Whereas, At the time the Common Council granted permission to the Harlem Railroad Co. to lay their rails in Centre street, it was understood that the said Company should pay for paving twenty feet in width through the centre of the said street; and the said Company were assessed, and paid accordingly, for that part of Centre street between Grand and Walker streets.

And whereas, at the time the assessment was made for paving that portion of Centre street, between Walker and Chatham streets, it was believed that the said Company did not intend to avail themselves of the said privilege, and was not, therefore, assessed for the paving; and whereas, the said Railroad Company have since recently laid their rails in the said street:

Therefore, Resolved, That the Street Commissioner request the Harlem Railroad Company to pay him the cost of paving twenty feet in width through the middle of Centre street, between Walker street and Chatham street, which has been assessed to the owners of property, and that he refund to the said owners their respective proportions of the same, when collected.

Adopted by the Board of Aldermen, July 5, 1839.

Adopted by the Board of Assistants, April 27, 1840.

Approved by the Mayor, April 30, 1840.

Resolved, That the tax of $836 25, of the New York and Harlem Railroad Company, in the Sixth Ward, for the year 1840, be remitted, and that the same be charged to errors and delinquencies of said Ward.

Adopted by the Board of Aldermen, March 15, 1841.

Adopted by the Board of Assistants, March 29, 1841.

Approved by the Mayor, April 1, 1841.

Resolved, That the Comptroller be authorized and directed to lease to the New York and Harlem Railroad Company the lot on Centre street, which they at present occupy, for one year from the expiration of their present lease, at a rent of $500, payable quarterly.

Adopted by the Board of Aldermen, January 16, 1843.

Adopted by the Board of Assistants, February 1, 1843.

Approved by the Mayor, February 8, 1843.

Resolved, That the Harlem Railroad Company are hereby required, on or before the first day of August next, to discontinue the use of steam power on the Fourth avenue south of the north line of Thirty-second street.

Adopted by the Board of Aldermen, Dec. 2, 1844.

Adopted by the Board of Assistants, Dec. 11, 1844.

Approved by the Mayor, Dec. 14, 1844.

Petition of the New York and Harlem Railroad Company, that they may be allowed three months to complete the necessary buildings at Thirty-second street, prior to the removal of their depot from Twenty-seventh street, was granted; the said three months to commence from the date of the approval of the said petition by his Honor the Mayor.

By the Board of Aldermen, March 23, 1846.

By the Board of Assistants, March 23, 1846.

Approved by the Mayor, March 30, 1846.

Resolved, That the Corporation Attorney take legal measures to prevent the steam power of the Harlem Railroad Company from plying below Thirty-second street, on the Fourth avenue, as directed by the Mayor and Common Council in December, 1844.

Adopted by the Board of Aldermen, March 16, 1846.

Adopted by the Board of Assistants, March 16, 1846.

Received from his Honor the Mayor, March 30, 1846, without his approval or objections thereto; therefore, under the provisions of the amended charter, the same became adopted.

Resolved, That the Harlem Railroad Company be required to construct a bridge of sufficient strength, and proper dimensions, for the transit of vehicles across the deep cut on the Fourth avenue, at each of the intersections of Thirty-fourth and Thirty-eighth streets, and that the same be erected without delay, and that the Clerk of the Common Council notify said Company thereof, on the adoption of this resolution.

Adopted by the Board of Assistants, November 2, 1846.

Adopted by the Board of Aldermen, November 9, 1846.

Approved by the Mayor, November 14, 1846

Resolved, That the New York and Harlem Railroad Company be, and they are hereby, directed, within thirty days from the passage of these resolutions, to restore the bridge crossing their track, at the intersection of Fiftieth street and Fourth avenue, in a firm and substantial manner.

Resolved, That said Company be, and they are hereby, directed to construct two bridges, one at the intersection of Seventy-ninth street and Fourth avenue, and one at the intersection of Eighty-fifth street and Fourth avenue; said bridges to be built in a firm and substantial manner, and the same width as the bridge at Eighty-seventh street. Also, to inclose their track on Fourth avenue, with a fence or protection wall, along the edges, between Eighty-fourth street and the tunnel at or near Ninety-second street; and also, that they inclose the sides of the bridge at the intersection of Eighty-seventh street and Fourth avenue.

Adopted by the Board of Assistants, January 24, 1848.

Adopted by the Board of Aldermen, February 1, 1848.

Approved by the Mayor, February 5, 1848.

Resolved, That the Harlem Railroad Company be requested to grade and regulate the 4th avenue from 28th to 32d street, the same now being in such an uneven condition as to render it impracticable to drive across the street, in consequence of raising the rails above the level of the street.

Adopted by the Board of Aldermen, April 26, 1848.

Adopted by the Board of Assistants, April 28, 1848.

Approved by the Mayor, May 1, 1848.

Resolved, That the New York and Harlem Railroad Company be authorized to lay down rails in Canal street, from their road in Centre street, to a point 75 feet east of Broadway, to enable them to afford increased accommodation for the public, which may be required by the extension of their own road, and by their connection with the New York and New Haven Railroad, and for the purpose of establishing a depot for passengers to and from New York and New Haven Railroad, with permission to cross the side-walk from the rail tracks into any premises which either of said Companies may become the lessees or owners of, all of which to be under the direction of the Street Commissioner, the privileges hereby granted to be enjoyed by said Company during the pleasure of the Common Council.

Adopted by the Board of Aldermen, Nov. 13, 1848.

Adopted by the Board of Assistants, Nov. 13, 1848.

Approved by the Mayor, Nov. 15, 1848.

Whereas, Resolutions having passed the Common Council on the 5th day of February, 1848, directing the Harlem Railroad Company to construct a bridge at the intersection of Fourth avenue and Eighty-fifth street, and to enclose their track with sufficient protection walls on said avenue, between Eighty-fourth and Ninety-second streets; and

Whereas, Said Company have neglected to comply with the aforesaid directions, thereby endangering the lives of the inhabitants, (several having been killed) by falling in said road, caused by the said Company not complying with said resolutions; therefore be it

Resolved, That the Counsel for the Corporation be, and is hereby authorized and directed to commence a suit against the Harlem Railroad Company, for the purpose of compelling said Company to erect a suitable bridge at the intersection of Fourth avenue and Eighty-fifth street, and also to enclose said road with a good and sufficient protection wall, from Eighty-fourth to Ninety-second street.

Adopted by the Board of Assistants, Feb. 18, 1850.

Adopted by the Board of Aldermen, March 11, 1850.

Approved by the Mayor, March 19, 1850.

Resolved, That the New York and Harlem Railroad Company be, and they are hereby, allowed to lay down (under the supervision of the Street Commissioner) a single track from their road in the Bowery, through 6th street to the rear of Tompkins market, between 6th and 7th streets, for the conveyance of country produce, &c., in order to improve the business of said market, and to accommodate that portion of our city, subject to all the restrictions contained in privileges to lay rails in Centre and other streets.

Adopted by the Board of Assistants, June 10, 1850.

Adopted by the Board of Aldermen, July 9, 1850.

Approved by the Acting Mayor, July 12, 1850.

Petition of residents of Harlem that permission may be granted to the New York and Harlem Railroad Company to lay a side track, or turnout, on the Fourth avenue, between 125th and 127th streets, was referred to the Street Commissioner, with power.

By the Board of Aldermen, July 9, 1850.

By the Board of Assistants, July 12, 1850.

Approved by the Acting Mayor, July 13, 1850.

Resolved, That the accompanying plan of curves, on the line of the New York and Harlem Railroad, at the intersection of Centre and Canal streets, Centre and Broome streets, and the Bowery, be referred to the Street Commissioner for his approval, with power to grant leave to the said Company to make said curves, if, in his opinion, the public interests would not be injured.

Adopted by the Board of Aldermen, July 11, 1850.

Adopted by the Board of Assistants, July 15, 1850.

Approved by the Mayor, July 18, 1850.

Resolved, That the New York and Harlem Railroad Company be, and they are hereby, directed to make, at their own cost, sustaining and parapet walls on the 4th avenue, on each side of their railroad track, from the northerly line of 32d street to the southerly line of 34th street, and also from the northerly line of 39th street to the southerly line of 42d street; also to make, at their own cost, proper sustaining walls along each side of their railroad track from the southerly line of 34th street to the northerly line of 39th street, and also, at their own cost, to build an arch over the said railroad track, between the said southerly line of 34th street and the northerly line of 39th street, and to build parapet walls across the 4th avenue, at the ends of the said arch, on the lines of 34th and 39th street; the parapet walls to be 3 feet high, 2 feet thick at the base, and 1 foot 6 inches in thickness at the top, to be coped with cut granite, and surmounted with a neat iron railing, 2 feet in height, the sustaining walls to be of ordinary rubble masonry, 6 feet in thickness at the base, and 5 feet in thickness at the springing of the arch; the arch to be of brick, 20 inches thick, with a radius and span of 24 feet, and to be of 15 in height, from the exterior rails of their rail track to the intrados of the arch, in conformity to a plan drawn by Edwin Smith, City Surveyor, dated May 15, 1850; also that the said New York and Harlem Railroad Company be directed, upon the completion of the said arch and walls, as above, to fill in and regulate that portion of the 4th avenue, between 34th and 39th streets, in conformity to the established grade line, and that the said work be commenced by the said Company on or before the 1st day of Oct., 1850, and that the same shall be completed by the said Company on or before the 1st day of May, 1851, under such directions as may be given by the Street Commissioner.

Adopted by the Board of Aldermen, July 12, 1850.

Adopted by the Board of Assistants, Aug. 6, 1850.

Approved by the Mayor, Aug. 8, 1850.

Resolved, That the New York and Harlem Railroad Company be, and they are hereby, authorized to take up their double track from the corner of Grand and Centre streets to the Bowery, and lay down a single track in the centre of the street, from the corner of Grand street, through Centre and Broome streets, to the Bowery, down the Bowery to Grand street, and through Grand street to Centre street, under the direction of the Street Commissioner.

Adopted by the Board of Aldermen, Sept. 11, 1850.

Adopted by the Board of Assistants, Sept. 12, 1850.

Approved by the Mayor, Sept. 13, 1850.

Petition of George Baker, Vice President of the Harlem Railroad Company, for permission to construct a sewer, or drain, from the corner of Tryon row to Chatham street, to connect with sewer in William street, at their own expense, under the direction of the Croton Aqueduct Department, was granted.

By the Board of Aldermen, October 7, 1850.

By the Board of Assistants, October 8, 1850.

Approved by the Mayor, October 11, 1850.

Resolved, That the New York and Harlem Railroad Company be, and they are hereby, authorized to lay grooved rails in a permanent manner, for a single track, on the westerly side of Chatham street, from the present terminus at Centre street, to the southerly end of the Park, with a turn-out, as shown on a profile on the petitions hereunto attached, for the exclusive use and purpose of running their City line of small passenger cars upon, to that point, subject to the pleasure and order of the Common Council; that when the Common Council may, or shall hereafter, order the said track to be taken up, the Company shall comply therewith at once, and that said Company shall, before said track is laid, execute to the City an agreement to comply therewith at once, when ordered, and that they will not run any but small passenger cars thereon, and that the Comptroller be charged with the preparation and execution of said agreement, said track to be laid under the direction of the Street Commissioner; provided that the said Company shall grade the street through which the said rails shall be laid, at their own expense, and keep the same in repair; that all ordinances heretofore passed, relative to the said Company, shall not be deemed to be in any way repealed by such permission hereby granted, except so far as the same conflicts therewith; and that said rails shall not be laid within a distance of 20 feet of the cross-walk at the corner of Broadway and the southern end of the Park.

Adopted by the Board of Assistants, Jan. 31, 1851.

Adopted by the Board of Aldermen, Feb. 4, 1851.

Approved by the Mayor, Feb. 6, 1851.

THIS AGREEMENT, made this sixth day of February, in the year one thousand eight hundred and fifty-one, between the Mayor, Aldermen and Commonalty of the city of New York, of the first part, and the New York & Harlem Railroad Company, of the second part, *Witnesseth*, that the said parties of the first part, in consideration of the sum of one dollar, to them paid by the said parties of the second part, and of the premises and covenants herein contained, to be performed and kept by the said parties of the second part, do hereby give, grant and convey, to the said parties of the second part, the right and privilege of laying grooved rails in a permanent manner for a single track, on the westerly side of Chatham street, from the present terminus at Centre street to the southerly end of the Park, with a turnout as shown on the profile hereto annexed, the privilege hereby granted being for the exclusive use and purpose of the said parties of the second part, for running their city line of small passenger cars upon; the said track to be laid under the direction of the Street Commissioner of the city of New York

It is further understood, by and between the parties to these presents, that the said rails shall not be laid within a distance of twenty feet of the crosswalk at the corner of Broadway and the southern end of the Park

And the said parties of the second part, for and in consideration of the premises, do hereby covenant and agree, to and with the said parties of the first part and their successors, in manner following, namely: that the privilege and consent hereby granted to the said parties of the second part are subject to the pleasure and order of the Common Council of the said parties of the first part; and that when the said Common Council shall hereafter order or direct the said track, so permitted by these presents to be laid, to be taken up and removed, that the said parties of the second part and their successors, will comply with such order or direction forthwith, and remove said track and rails, and replace and restore that part of said street upon which the same were laid, in the same plight and condition as the same was in before the laying of said track or rails, at the expense of the said parties of the second part and their successors.

And the said parties of the second part do further covenant and agree that they will grade all that portion of the said street occupied by said track and four feet on each side thereof, and keep the same in good repair, at their own expense, so long as the same shall be occupied and used by the said parties of the second part, or their successors, for the purposes aforesaid.

And the said parties of the second part do further covenant and agree to fulfill and comply with all the stipulations and agreements herein contained, on their part to be performed and fulfilled.

And it is further mutually understood and agreed, by and between the parties to these presents, that, in case of the non-compliance by the said parties of the second part, or their successors, of any of the stipulations, covenants or agreements herein contained, on their part to be performed, fulfilled and kept, that then and from thenceforth the privilege herein granted to the said **parties** of the second part shall cease and determine.

In witness whereof, to one part of these presents, remaining with the said parties of the second part, the said parties of the first part have caused the common seal of the city of New York to be affixed; and to the other part thereof, remaining with the said parties of the first part, the said parties of the second part have caused their common seal to be affixed, the day and year first above written.

The New York and Harlem Railroad Company, by

ROBERT SCHUYLER, [L. S.]

President.

CITY AND COUNTY OF NEW YORK, ss.

On this 27th day of February, 1851, before me personally appeared Robert Schuyler, who is personally known to me, who, being by me duly sworn, did depose and say that he is the President of the New York and Harlem Railroad Company; that the seal annexed to the foregoing instrument is the seal of the said company, and was affixed thereto by authority of said company; and that he, the deponent, resides in the Fifth Ward of the city of New York.

CHARLES W. SANDFORD,

Commissioner of Deeds, New York.

Resolved, That the New York and Harlem Railroad Company be permitted to construct a branch or side track from the tracks in the 4th avenue, to a point in front of their depot on 26th street, distant 300 feet westerly from the northwesterly corner of 26th street and 4th avenue, with a single line of rails, and that such permission be granted for a period of six months from the 1st day of January, 1851, and that the rails be taken up at the expiration of the period asked for by the Company, under the direction of the Street Commissioner.

Adopted by the Board of Aldermen, Feb. 5, 1851.

Adopted by the Board of Assistants, June 3, 1851.

Approved by the Mayor, June 4, 1851.

Resolved, That the New York and Harlem Railroad Company be, and they are hereby, directed to erect, without delay, bridges across their road at 83d, 84th, and 88th streets, the same as that erected across said road at 85th street.

Adopted by the Board of Assistants, May 30, 1851.

Adopted by the Board of Aldermen, June 4, 1851.

Approved by the Mayor, June 13, 1851.

Resolved, That the Street Commissioner be, and he is hereby, directed to have the railroad track, extending from the Harlem Railroad, in Centre street, up Chambers street toward Broadway, taken up within ten days from the passage of this resolution.

Adopted by the Board of Assistants, May 6, 1851.

Adopted by the Board of Aldermen, June 4, 1851.

Approved by the Mayor, June 13, 1851.

Resolved, That a space forty feet in width, and extending through the middle of the Fourth avenue, from Thirty-fourth to Thirty-eighth street, be, and the same is hereby, appropriated for the purpose of a public park or pleasure-ground; and that the same be laid out, under the direction of the Street Commissioner, in accordance with the general plan herewith accompanied. And that the same be carried into effect, as soon as the Harlem Railroad Company shall have completed the arching of the Fourth avenue, and that the acompanying ordinance be adopted therefrom.

Adopted by the Board of Aldermen, August 19th, 1851.

Adopted by the Board of Assistants, September 9th, 1851.

Approved by the Mayor, October 7th, 1851.

Resolved, That the New York and Harlem Railroad Company be permitted to reduce the grade of the Fourth avenue, on the east side of the road, between Thirty-second and Thirty-fourth streets, to a level with their track, with a turn-out on the east side thereof, entering the block at a point north of the north side of Thirty-third street, in accordance with the accompanying diagram, on condition that they, at their own expense, widen said avenue twenty-five feet, on the west side, between Thirty-second and Thirty-fourth streets, and cause the land for this additional width to be ceded to the Corporation of the city of New York, as part of the said Fourth avenue.

Adopted by the Board of Assistants, December 10, 1851.

Adopted by the Board of Aldermen, December 26, 1851.

Approved by the Mayor, December 29, 1851.

Resolved, That the New York and Harlem Railroad Company be directed to have the iron railing, on the bridge at the crossing of Thirty-fourth street and Fourth avenue, secured in a proper manner immediately.

Adopted by the Board of Aldermen, December 16, 1851.

Adopted by the Board of Assistants, December 29, 1851.

Approved by the Mayor, December 30, 1851.

Resolved, That the New York and Harlem Railroad Company be, and they are hereby, directed to construct a new and substantial bridge for their road at 104th street immediately, under the direction of the Street Commissioner; and further, if said Company fail to comply herewith, then the Street Commissioner is hereby directed to erect the same at the expense of said New York and Harlem Railroad Company, without delay.

Adopted by the Board of Assistants, September 18, 1852.

Adopted by the Board of Aldermen, September 20, 1852.

Approved by the Mayor, September 21, 1852.

Resolved, That the New York and Harlem Railroad Company be, and they are hereby, directed to take up the rails of their track in Canal street, and relay the same with the *grooved* rail, in the same manner as that laid along the east side of the Park; said track in Canal street not to extend west of the depot near Broadway, and that the same be completed within sixty days from the passage of this resolution.

Adopted by the Board of Aldermen, October 11, 1852.

Adopted by the Board of Assistants, November 9, 1852.

Approved by the Mayor, November 10, 1852.

Resolved, That the Harlem and New Haven Railroad Company shall station a man on the northwest corner of Grand street and the Bowery, to warn persons coming down the Bowery, on foot or in vehicles, of the near approach of the cars toward the corner of Grand street and the Bowery.

Adopted by the Board of Assistants, January 14, 1853.

Adopted by the Board of Aldermen, February 9, 1853.

Approved by the Mayor, February 15, 1853.

Resolved, That the Harlem Railroad Company be, and is hereby, authorized to lay a track in connection with their railroad at Hamilton square for the accommodation of the New York State Agricultural Society, during the period of their approaching fair, the same to be removed immediately after the fair is closed.

Adopted by the Board of Councilmen, September 4, 1854.

Adopted by the Board of Aldermen, September 18, 1854.

Approved by the Mayor, September 19, 1854.

Resolved, That the New York and Harlem Railroad

Company be, and are hereby, directed to build a good substantial wooden bridge, the full width of the street, similar to the one at 86th street, across the cut at 90th street, and the same to be done under the direction of the Street Commissioner.

Adopted by the Board of Aldermen, July 6, 1854.

Adopted by the Board of Councilmen, December 19, 1854.

Approved by the Mayor, December 20, 1854.

Resolved, That no locomotive or steam engine be allowed to run on the tracks of the Harlem or New Haven Railroad Company, on 4th avenue, south of 42d street, 18 months after the passage of this ordinance.

Adopted by the Board of Aldermen, December 7, 1854.

Adopted by the Board of Councilmen, December 22, 1854.

Approved by the Mayor, December 27, 1854.

Resolved, That the Harlem Railroad Company be directed to station a flagman at the corner of the Bowery and Broome street, for the purpose of warning pedestrians and those persons driving vehicles of the nigh approach of the rail cars as they turn the corner of the said Bowery and Broome street.

Adopted by the Board of Aldermen, January 22, 1857.

Adopted by the Board of Councilmen, February 2, 1857.

Approved by the Mayor, February 3, 1857.

Resolved, That the Harlem Railroad Company be directed to place a flagman at the corner of Pearl and Centre streets, for the protection of persons crossing said streets.

Adopted by the Board of Councilmen, February 6, 1857.

Adopted by the Board of Aldermen, February 9, 1857.

Approved by the Mayor, February 10, 1857.

Resolved, That the Street Commissioner be, and he is hereby, instructed to cause the Harlem Railroad Company to put their track in thorough condition forthwith, and if the said Harlem Railroad Company fail to comply within one week after the passage of this resolution, that then the 3d Avenue Railroad Company have permission, and the permission is hereby granted to them, to lay a new track on the line of the Bowery, under the direction of the Street Commissioner, from 5th street to Grand street, instead of the old T rail; and the said 3d Avenue Railroad Company shall enjoy all the privileges now held by the Harlem Railroad Company below 5th street, on the line of the Bowery; and all permissions and privileges heretofore granted to the Harlem Railroad Company, conflicting with the above, be, and the same are hereby, annulled and repealed.

Adopted by the Board of Aldermen, Feb. 16, 1857.

Adopted by the Board of Councilmen, Feb. 18, 1857.

Approved by the Mayor, Feb. 21, 1857.

The President of the Croton Aqueduct Board directed to notify the Harlem Railroad Company to put in good repair, forthwith, all the pavements in and about their rails, and, in case of neglect or refusal, to have the same done at the expense of the Railroad Company.

Adopted by the Board of Aldermen, Sept. 10, 1857.

Adopted by the Board of Councilmen, Sept. 14, 1857.

Approved by the Mayor, Sept. 16, 1857.

Whereas, The Harlem Railroad Company having failed to coerce the Common Council in repealing the existing ordinances of the Corporation, requiring them to discontinue the use of steam below 42d street; and

Whereas, In consequence of the said failure, the said Company having determined to defy the acts of the Common Council, and positively refuse to obey the ordinances of this body, and are now, through their paid agents, endeavoring to secure the passage of an act from the Legislature of the State (a bill having been introduced for this purpose), to continue their present nuisance, in violation of the existing ordinances, and their agreement, made with the Corporation; be it therefore

Resolved, That the Counsel to the Corporation be, and he is hereby, instructed to prepare a remonstrance (in behalf of the Common Council), against the passage of any bill giving to the Harlem Railroad Company the privilege to continue the running of locomotives and the use of steam below 42d street, in violation of the ordinances of the Mayor and Commonalty of this city.

Adopted by the Board of Aldermen, Feb. 18, 1858

Adopted by the Board of Councilmen, Feb. 23, 1858.

Approved by the Mayor, Feb. 24, 1858.

Resolved, That the New York and Harlem Railroad Company be, and they are hereby, directed to take up the pavement and rail tracks in Broome street, from a point 100 feet west of Mulberry street to the easterly side of Elizabeth street, and relay the same in accordance with the original grade of that part of said street, within 10 days from the date of the passage of this resolution, and that, in case of refusal or neglect, on the part of said Company, to comply with this resolution, that the Croton Aqueduct Board be, and they are hereby, directed to remove said tracks from said part of Broome street, and to restore the carriage way thereof to the aforesaid grade without delay.

Adopted by the Board of Aldermen, March 31, 1858.

Adopted by the Board of Councilmen, April 5, 1858.

Approved by the Mayor, April 13, 1858.

Resolved, That the Harlem Railroad Company be, and they are hereby, directed to cause their small cars to be run on their track to 42d street as often and as regularly as they are now run between 27th street and Park row, the said Company to commence running said cars, as aforesaid, within four months after the approval of this resolution by his Honor the Mayor.

Adopted by the Board of Councilmen, May 10, 1858.

Adopted by the Board of Aldermen, June 21, 1858

Approved by the Mayor, July 12, 1858.

AN ORDINANCE

In relation to the New York and Harlem Railroad Company.

Be it ordained by the Mayor, Aldermen, and Commonalty of the city of New York, in Common Council convened:

SECTION. 1. The New York and Harlem Railroad Company is hereby authorized, empowered and permitted to use steam in the drawing of their passenger and freight cars upon their railroad on the Fourth avenue, to and from the northern extremity of Manhattan, or New York Island, to the south side of 42d street, and to permit the use thereof by the New York and New Haven Railroad Company to the same point, with turn-outs to the engine-houses respectively, for a period of thirty years, from the passage of this ordinance.

§ 2. Until the completion of their new machine shops at or above 42d street, the New York and Harlem Railroad Company shall be permitted to run their engines with steam, for repairs only, but without any car, truck or other vehicle attached, to and from their present machine shop at 32d street; but such permission shall not extend, in any event, beyond a period of eighteen months from the date of this ordinance

§ 3. The New York and Harlem Railroad Company are hereby authorized to lay down a double track or railway from their track in the Fourth avenue, at 42d street, up said street to Madison avenue, and up Madison avenue to

79th street, or as far as it may, from time to time, be opened, for the use of their small cars only.

§ 4. The said Company is hereby authorized to lay down in the Fourth avenue, between 42d and 50th streets, two additional tracks, for the use of themselves and the New York and New Haven Railroad Company, to enable them to land and receive their passengers, and may cover that portion thereof which extends from 42d to 44th street by a neat ornamental roof or shed, to be first approved by the Mayor of the city of New York, and that the sidewalks opposite to said building be reduced to sixteen feet on each side of said avenue, in front of the premises of said Railroad Company.

§ 5. The New York and Harlem Railroad Company shall forthwith complete the title of the Corporation of the city of New York to the strip of ground, 20 feet wide, between 33d and 34th streets, on the west side of the Fourth avenue, and also to the strip of ground, 20 feet wide, between 32d and 33d streets, agreed by them to be conveyed to the city, and shall, within six months from this date, remove their engine-house at 32d street from said last-mentioned strip of land.

§ 6. In the case the New York and Harlem Railroad Company shall fail to carry out in good faith the provisions of the second and fifth sections of this ordinance, within the times in said sections respectively limited, the privileges hereby granted shall cease and determine, and the ordinance shall be null and void.

Adopted by the Board of Aldermen, Dec. 21, 1858.

Adopted by the Board of Councilmen, Dec. 22, 1858.

Approved by the Mayor, Dec. 31, 1858.

Resolved, That Fourth avenue, from Thirty-fourth to Thirty-eighth street, be paved with trap-block or Belgian pavement, at the expense of the owners of property benefited thereby, and that the Harlem Railroad Company be compelled to reduce the grade of the Fourth avenue, at its intersection with Thirty-fourth street, in accordance with the annexed ordinance, and that the accompanying ordinance therefor be adopted.

Adopted by the Board of Councilmen, Sept. 29, 1859.

Adopted by the Board of Aldermen, Oct. 3, 1859.

Approved by the Mayor, Oct. 4, 1859.

Resolved, That the New York and Harlem Railroad Company be, and they are hereby, directed to construct a substantial bridge over their road at Seventieth street, immediately, under the direction of the Street Commissioner; the said bridge to be similar to the bridge now at Eighty-seventh street; and further, if said company fail to comply with the conditions of this resolution, then the said Street Commissioner is hereby authorized and directed to erect, or cause to be erected, the said bridge over Seventieth street, at Fourth avenue, at the expense of the said New York and Harlem Railroad Company, without delay.

Adopted by the Board of Aldermen, Oct. 24, 1859.

Adopted by the Board of Councilmen, Oct. 27, 1859.

Approved by the Mayor, Oct. 29, 1859.

NEW YORK AND NEW HAVEN RAILROAD.

Resolved, That the block of ground bounded by Centre, Franklin, Elm and White streets, be leased to the New York and New Haven Railroad Company, for the term of twenty-one years (the Arsenal buildings, on Elm and Franklin streets, to remain for the use of the military until May 1st, 1851), at an annual rent of six thousand dollars, payable quarterly, together with the taxes and assessments on the same, with covenants for renewal at the expiration of twenty-one years, at a rent to be fixed by appraisement. The said company to improve the said premises within one year from the date of their lease. Said premises to continue during said lease for a railroad depot, and the Comptroller is hereby directed to have a lease executed in accordance with this resolution, provided that nothing therein contained shall be construed or taken as a consent or assent, on the part of the Corporation of the city of New York, to the use by the said railroad company of any of the streets and avenues of said city, for the purpose of running cars thereon, by virtue of an agreement with the Harlem Railroad Company, or as a waiver of the right and power of the Common Council of said city to regulate and control the said New York and New Haven Railroad Company, to the same extent it can now control the New York and Harlem Railroad Company.

Adopted by the Board of Aldermen, September 3, 1850.

Adopted by the Board of Assistants, September 4, 1850.

Approved by the Mayor, September 5, 1850.

THIS INDENTURE, made the fifth day of September, in

the year of our Lord one thousand eight hundred and fifty, between the Mayor, Aldermen, and Commonalty of the city of New York, of the one part, and the New York and New Haven Railroad Company, of the other part—

Witnesseth, that the said Mayor, Aldermen, and Commonalty of the city of New York, for and in consideration of the rents, covenants, payments, articles and agreements, hereinafter mentioned and contained on the part of the said the New York and New Haven Railroad Company, their successors and assigns, to be paid, done, performed, fulfilled and kept, have demised and to farm letten, and by these presents do demise and to farm let, unto the said the New York and New Haven Railroad Company, ALL the certain block of ground situate, lying and being in the Sixth Ward of the city of New York, and bounded, described and containing as follows : that is to say—northerly by White street ; easterly by Centre street ; southerly by Franklin street ; and westerly by Elm street, as laid down on a map hereto annexed, drawn by John J. Sewell, City Surveyor, dated New York, September 13, 1850, said map being considered a part of this Indenture, and reference thereto had.

TO HAVE AND TO HOLD the said above-described premises unto the said the New York and New Haven Railroad Company, their successors and assigns, from the first day of September, Anno Domini one thousand eight hundred and fifty, for and during the full end and term of twenty-one years from thence next ensuing, and fully to be complete and ended, yielding and paying therefor, yearly, and every year during the said term, unto the said Mayor, Aldermen and Commonalty of the city of New York, their successors and assigns, the yearly rent of six thousand dollars, lawful money of the United States of America, which said yearly rent shall be paid on the usual quarterly days of payment; that is to say, one thousand five hundred dollars on the 1st day of August, and the like sum on the first days of November, February and May in each and every year during the said term, the first payment to be made on the first day of August next.

Provided always, That if it should so happen that the said yearly rent of 6,000 dollars, or any part thereof, shall be behind or unpaid, by the space of 10 days after any day of payment, on which the same ought to be paid as aforesaid, or if the said party of the second part, their successors or assigns, shall neglect or omit to pay, do, perform, fulfill or keep any or either of the payments, covenants, articles, clauses, agreements, matters or things herein contained, which on the part or behalf of the said party of the second part, their successors or assigns, are to be paid, done, performed, fulfilled or kept during the term aforesaid, according to the true intent and meaning of these presents, that then (and in every such case or cases), and at all times thereafter, it shall and may be lawful to and for the said Mayor, Aldermen and Commonalty of the city of New York, their successors and assigns, into all the said demised premises, and every part thereof, wholly to reenter, re-possess, and to have and to enjoy the same again as in their former estate; and the said The New York and New Haven Railroad Company, their successors or assigns thereout, and from thence to expel and remove, anything herein contained to the contrary notwithstanding. And the said The New York and New Haven Railroad Company, for themselves, their successors and assigns, doth covenant and grant to and with the said Mayor, Aldermen and Commonalty of the city of New York, their successors and assigns, by these presents, that they, the said The New York and New Haven Railroad Company, their successors and assigns, shall and will yearly, and every year during the term hereby demised, well and truly pay unto the said Mayor, Aldermen and Commonalty of the city of New York, their successors and assigns, the yearly rent of six thousand dollars, on the days and times hereinbefore limited for the payment thereof, without fraud or delay, and that they, the said The New York and New Haven Railroad Company, their successors and assigns, shall and will, at their own proper costs and charges, bear, pay and discharge all such duties, taxes, assessments, impositions and payments, extraordinary as well as ordinary, as shall, during the term hereby demised be issued or grow due and payable out of, and for the said demised premises, or which shall during the said term be laid, assessed or imposed upon the said premises, or upon the owners or occupants thereof, for and in respect to the same, by virtue of any existing or future law of the United States of America, or of any existing or future law of the Legislature of the State of New York, or of any existing or future law or ordinance of the Mayor, Aldermen and Commonalty of the City of New York: to the end that the said yearly rent hereby reserved shall, during the term demised, be received by the said Mayor, Aldermen and Commonalty, and their successors and assigns, free and clear from any deduction; and that they shall be at no expense, cost or charge whatsoever, for or in respect to the said demised premises, during the said term.

AND the said the Mayor, Aldermen and Commonalty of the City of New York, for themselves, their successors and assigns, do covenant and agree to and with the said The New York and New Haven Railroad Company, their successors and assigns, that at the expiration of the term hereby demised, they, the said the Mayor, Aldermen and Commonalty of the City of New York, will execute to the said The New York and New Haven Railroad Company a renewal of this lease for a term of twenty-one years, from the expiration of this term, with like covenants as are contained in this lease except the covenant for renewal; the rent to be paid under such lease to be ascertained and determined by two sworn appraisers, to be chosen one by the said Mayor, Aldermen and Commonalty, and one by the said Railroad Company, or by a sworn umpire to be chosen by the said appraisers in case they cannot agree upon the said rent to be paid.

AND the said The New York and New Haven Railroad Company do hereby covenant and agree to and with the said the Mayor, Aldermen and Commonalty of the city of New York, that they will, within one year from the first day of May, 1851, improve the said premises hereby demised for a railroad depot, and that they will use the said premises hereby demised for and as a railroad depot during the term of this lease.

AND it is mutually understood and agreed, by and between the parties to this lease, and it is upon the express condition that nothing herein contained shall be construed or taken as a consent, or assent, on the part of the said the Mayor, Aldermen and Commonalty of the city of New York, to the use by the said The New York and New Haven

Railroad Company, of any of the streets, avenues of the said city, for the purposes of running cars thereon by virtue of any agreement with the Harlem Railroad Company, or as a waiver of the right and power of the Common Council of said city to regulate and control The New York and New Haven Railroad Company to the same extent as it can now control **The New York and Harlem Railroad Company.**

AND it is further agreed, that the Arsenal Buildings, on Elm and Franklin streets, shall remain for the use of the military until May 1st, A. D. 1851, and the said parties of the second part agree to permit the same to be used for that purpose for the time aforesaid.

And the said The New York and New Haven Railroad Company, for themselves, their successors and assigns, do further covenant and grant, to and with the Mayor, Aldermen and Commonalty of the city of New York, their successors and assigns, that the said The New York and New Haven Railroad Company, their successors and assigns, shall and will, well and truly, on the last day of the said term, hereby demised, or other sooner determination thereof, deliver up the said hereby demised premises, into the hands and possession of the said Mayor, Aldermen, and Commonalty of the city of New York, their successors or assigns, without fraud or delay, unless the said lease shall be renewed in the manner hereinbefore mentioned: And, lastly, That if the said The New York and New Haven Railroad Company, their successors or assigns, shall and do assign, or make over, all or any part of the premises hereby demised, to any person or persons whatsoever, without the leave and approbation of the said Mayor, Aldermen and Commonalty of the city of New York first had and obtained, then and in that case this Indenture, and everything herein contained, shall cease, determine and be utterly null and void, anything herein contained to the contrary thereof notwithstanding.

IN WITNESS WHEREOF, to one part of these presents, remaining with the Mayor, Aldermen and Commonalty of the city of New York, the said The New York and New Haven Railroad Company have put their corporate seal, attested by the signatures of their President and Secretary; and to the other part thereof, remaining with the said The New York and New Haven Railroad Company, the said Mayor, Aldermen and Commonalty of the city of New York have caused the seal of the city of New York to be affixed, the day and year first above written.

The New York and New Haven
  Railroad Company, by   [L. S.]

        ROBERT SCHUYLER,

                President, &c., &c.

WILLIAM P. BURRALL,

Secretary New York and New Haven Railroad Company.

CITY AND COUNTY OF NEW YORK, ss.: On the twenty-seventh day of November, one thousand eight hundred and fifty, before me came Robert Schuyler, who is personally known to me to be the President of The New York and New Haven Railroad Company, the Corporation named in the foregoing instrument, and the said Robert Schuyler, being by me duly sworn, did depose and say that he resides in the city of New York, that the seal affixed to the said instrument is the corporate seal of the said Company, and was affixed thereto by their authority.

JOSEPH STRONG,
Commissioner of Deeds.

BROADWAY RAILROAD.

Resolved, That Jacob Sharp, Freeman Campbell, Wm. B. Reynolds, James Gaunt, J. Newton Squire, Wm. A. Mead, David Woods, John L. O'Sullivan, Wm. M. Pullis, Jonathan Roe, John W. Hawkes, James W. Faulkner, Henry Du Bois, John J. Hollister, Preston Sheldon, John Anderson, John R. Flanagan, Sargent V. Bagley, Peter B. Sweeny, Charles B. White, James W. Foshay, Robert E. Ring, Thomas Ladd, Conklin Sharp, Samuel L. Titus, Alfred Martin, D. R. Martin, William Menzies, Charles H. Glover, Gershon Cohen, and those who may, for the time being, be associated with them, all of whom are herein designated as associates of the Broadway Railway, have the authority and consent of the Common Council to lay a double track for a railway in Broadway and Whitehall, or State street, from the South Ferry to 59th street, and also, hereafter, to continue the same, from time to time, along the Bloomingdale road, to Manhattanville, which continuation they shall be required, from time to time, to make, whenever directed by the Common Council, the said grant of permission and authority being upon and with the following conditions and stipulations, to wit :

First. Such tracks shall be laid under the direction of the Street Commissioner, in, or near the middle of the street, the outer rails not exceeding 12 feet 6 inches apart, and the rails being laid flush and even with the pavement, the inner portion of the rail being of equal height with the outer, with grooves not exceeding 1 inch in width, or such other rails as shall be approved by the Street Commissioner, or the Common Council, on such grades as are now established, or may hereafter be established by the Common Council; and the said associates shall keep in good repair the space between the said rails, and one foot on each side, and no motive power, excepting horses, shall be used below 59th street.

Second. The said associates shall place new cars on said railroad, with all the modern improvements for the convenience and comfort of passengers; and they shall run cars thereon every day, both ways, as often as the public convenience may require, under such direction as the Common Counsel may, from time to time, prescribe; said cars, with the horses attached, not to exceed 45 feet in length.

Third. The said associates shall, in all respects, comply with the directions of the Common Council, in the building of such railway, and in the running of the cars thereon.

Fourth. At the Bowling Green, the said associates may divide the two tracks aforesaid, running one of them down Whitehall street, and the other down State street, should they deem such division necessary; and also whenever, in the course of their route, the said road shall pass a public square, it may be carried, with a single track, round both sides of said square instead of only one, for the better accommodation of the public on both sides thereof.

Fifth. The said associates shall be required to procure a depot at some place near or at the lower part of said route, for the purpose of keeping withdrawn from Broadway such proportion of the cars coming down in the morning as shall not be required for the accommodation of the return travel, until the afternoon; and also, they shall be required to stop a portion of the cars at the Park, and to send down, below that point, no greater proportion of the whole number employed than shall be found, by experience, to be requisite for the accommodation of the travel below that point, subject to regulation by the Common Council.

Sixth. The cars shall be so constructed as not to make provision intended for standing passengers to crowd upon the seated passengers, and also, when all the seats are full, the cars shall not be stopped to take in more passengers to be crowded into the said seats, a flag being displayed in front of the car to give notice that all the seats are full.

Seventh. The said cars shall not be allowed to stop, so as to obstruct a crossing, nor to stop more frequently in a block (unless the same be of extraordinary length), than just beyond its first crossing, except in rainy weather.

EIGHTH. The said associates shall keep an attendant, distinguishable by some conspicuous mark or badge, at every such appointed stopping place, in all the parts of the street usually much crowded with vehicles, whose duty it shall be, with attention and respect, to help in and out of the cars all passengers who may desire such assistance, and in general to watch over the safety of passengers from all dangers of passing vehicles.

NINTH. The said associates shall be required to keep, or cause to be kept in readiness, a number of sleighs adequate to the public accommodation, when the travel of the cars may be obstructed by snow.

TENTH. The said associates shall cause the said street to be well swept and cleaned every morning, and sweepings carried away, before 8 o'clock in summer and 9 o'clock in winter, except Sundays, this provision applying to the whole of the street south of Fourteenth street, above which point the same shall be done as often as twice a week, when the weather will permit.

ELEVENTH. No higher rate of fare shall be charged, for the conveyance of passengers from any one point to any other point along said route, and such combined systems of routes as may hereafter be adopted by means of cars and transient omnibuses, than five cents for each passenger.

TWELFTH. In consideration of the good and faithful performance of all these conditions, stipulations, and requirements, and of such other requirements as may hereafter be made by the Common Council, for the regulation of the said railway, as aforesaid, the said associates shall pay, for 10 years from the date of opening the said railway, the annual license fee, for each car, now allowed by law, and shall have a license accordingly; and, after that period, shall pay such amount of license fee, for further licenses as the Corporation, with permission of the Legislature, shall then prescribe; or, in default of consenting thereto, shall surrender the road, with all the equipments and appurtenances thereto belonging, to the said Corporation, at a fair and just valuation of the same.

Thirteenth. Within a reasonable time after the passing of this resolution, the said associates, or a majority in interest thereof, shall form themselves into a joint-stock association, which association shall be vested with all the rights and privileges hereby granted, and shall have power, by the votes of at least a majority in interest of the associates, to frame and establish articles of association and by-laws providing for the construction, operation, and management of the said railway, the mode of admitting new associates, and of transferring the shares or interests of any of the associates to new associates or assigns, the number, duties, mode of appointment, tenure, and compensation of officers, the manner of making contracts, amending the by-laws, and calling in assessments from the associates, and generally the means and mode of establishing the railway and carrying it on, and of controlling and managing the property and affairs of the said association.

Fourteenth. The association shall not be deemed dissolved by the death or act of any associate, but his successor in interest shall stand in his place, and the rights of each associate shall depend on his own fulfillment of the conditions imposed on him by these restrictions, or the articles of association and by-laws of the association; and, in case of his failure to fulfill the same, after 20 days' notice in writing to him so to do, his rights shall be forfeited to and devolve upon the remaining associates; and said associates may at any time incorporate themselves under the General Railroad Act, whenever two-thirds in interest of the associates shall require it.

FIFTEENTH. The associates, whose names are set forth in this resolution, shall, by writing, filed with the clerk of the Common Council, signify their acceptance thereof, and agree to conform thereto; and all new associates or assigns duly admitted, according to the provisions of the articles of association and by-laws, shall be deemed parties to such agreement.

Adopted by the Board of Aldermen, Nov. 19, 1852.

Adopted by the Board of Assistants, Dec. 6, 1852.

Board of Aldermen, Dec. 18, 1852, received from his Honor the Mayor, with his objections thereto.

Board of Aldermen, Dec. 29, 1852, taken up, reconsidered and adopted, notwithstanding the objections of his Honor the Mayor thereto, a majority of all the members elected voting therefor.

Board of Assistants, Dec. 30, 1852, taken up, reconsidered, and adopted, notwithstanding the objections of the Mayor thereto, a majority of all the members elected voting therefor; therefore, under the provisions of the amended charter, the same became adopted.

SIXTH AVENUE RAILROAD.

AGREEMENT MADE, this sixth day of September, in the year one thousand eight hundred and fifty-one, between the Mayor, Aldermen and Commonalty of the city of New York, parties of the first part, and the persons named in the resolutions hereinafter set forth, who shall duly sign and execute this agreement, and their successors, associates and assigns, duly becoming parties thereto, as hereinafter provided, of the second part.

Whereas, The said parties of the first part, in Common Council convened, did, on the fourth day of June, one thousand eight hundred and fifty-one, duly pass and adopt the following resolutions, which were afterwards, and on the thirtieth day of July, in said year, duly signed by the Mayor of said city, and became operative and binding, in the words and figures following :

Resolved, That the persons to whom permission is granted by the following resolutions, and those who may hereafter become associated with them, have the authority and consent of the Common Council to lay a double track for a railroad in the following streets, viz.: from a point at the intersection of Chambers street and West Broadway, thence along West Broadway to Canal street, thence along and down Canal street to Hudson street, along Hudson street and 8th avenue to a point at or near 51st street; and that said railroad be continued through the 8th avenue to Harlem river, whenever required by the Common Council, and as soon and as fast as said avenue is graded, upon the following stipulations and conditions, viz.: Such track or tracks to be laid under the direction of the Street Commissioner, and on such grades as are now established, or may hereafter be established, by the Common Council, the said parties to become bound, in a sufficient penalty, to keep in good repair the space between the track and the space outside the same, on either side, of at least eight feet in width, of each street in which the rails are laid, and also that no motive power, excepting horses, be used below 51st street, and upon the further condition that said parties shall place new cars on said railroad, with all the modern improvements, for the convenience and comfort of passengers, and that they run cars thereon, each and every day, both ways, as often as the public convenience may require, under such directions as the Street Commissioner and Common Council may from time to time prescribe.

And provided, also, that the said parties shall, in all respects, comply with the direction of the Street Commissioner and of the Common Council in the building of said railroad, and in the running of the cars thereon, and in any other matter connected with the regulation of said railroad.

And provided, also, that the said parties shall, before this permission takes effect, enter into a good and sufficient agreement with the Mayor, Aldermen, and Commonalty of the city of New York, to be drawn and approved of by the Counsel to the Corporation, themselves to abide by and perform the stipulations and provisions herein contained, and also all such other resolutions, or ordinances, as may be passed by the Common Council, relating to the said road.

And further, that they run a car thereon each and every day, both ways, as often as every 15 minutes, from 5 to

6 o'clock, A. M., every 4 minutes, from 6 A. M. to 8 P. M., every 15 minutes, from 8 P. M. to 12 P. M., and every 30 minutes, from 12 P. M. to 5 o'clock A. M., and as much oftener as public convenience may require, under such directions as the Common Council may from time to time prescribe.

Also, that the rate of passage on said railroad shall not exceed a greater sum than 5 cents for the entire length of said road; and also that the Common Council shall have the power to cause the same, or any part thereof, to be taken up at any time they may see fit; and also, that the said parties, or either of them, shall not assign their interest in the said road without first obtaining the consent of the Common Council thereto: also, that such track or tracks shall be laid upon a foundation of concrete, with a grooved rail, or such other rail as may be approved of by the Street Commissioner, even with the surface of the streets through which they may pass, and shall be commenced within three months, and completed to Fifty-first street within one year, and from Fifty-first street to the Harlem River within three years, from the passage of this resolution; also, that the foundation on each side of the rails shall be paved with square grooved blocks of stone, similar to the Russ pavement, as far up as Fifty-first street; that the said parties are to keep an account of the receipts of each road monthly, and report the same to the Comptroller, monthly, under oath; that the said parties shall connect their road with such other roads as the Common Council may order to be connected therewith; that they shall file with the Comptroller a statement, under oath, of the cost of each mile of road completed, and agree to surrender, convey, and transfer the said road to the Corporation of the city of New York, whenever required so to do, on payment, by the Corporation, of the cost of said road, as appears by said statement, with ten per cent. advance thereon.

That said parties, on being required at any time by the Corporation, and to such extent as the Common Council shall determine, shall take up, at their own expense, said rails, or such part thereof as they shall be required, and on failure so to do, in ten days after such requirement, the same may be done, at their expense, by the Street Commissioner.

Resolved, That the persons, to whom permission is grant- by the following resolutions, have the authority and consent of the Common Council to lay a single track in the following streets: Commencing at the corner of Chambers street and West Broadway, through Chambers street to Church street, through Church street to Canal street, through Canal street to Wooster street, through Wooster to Fourth street, to Thompson street, with a single track; thence, with a double track, through Fourth street and Sixth avenue, to Harlem; also to lay a single track in Thompson street, from Fourth to Canal street, to connect with the Eighth Avenue Railroad, and extend the same up the Sixth avenue to Harlem River, whenever required by the Common Council, and as soon and as fast as said avenue is graded sufficiently to permit such track to be laid, upon the same terms, stipulations, and conditions, as are provided in the annexed resolutions in relation to the railroad on the Eighth avenue, except that no motive power except horses shall be used below

Forty-second street; that said railroad upon the Sixth avenue shall be commenced within three months, and completed to Forty-second street within one year, and from Forty-second street to the Harlem River within three years, from the passage of this resolution; also, that the foundation on each side of the rails shall be paved with square grooved blocks of stone, similar to the Russ pavement, as far up as Thirty-second street, and that such parts of the Eighth Avenue road as may be used by the Sixth Avenue road, from the connection in Canal street and West Broadway to Chambers street, shall be built at the joint expense of said Sixth and Eighth Avenue Railroads.

Resolved, That each of said passenger-cars, to be used on said roads, shall be annually licensed by the Mayor; and there shall be paid annually for such license such sum as the Common Council may hereafter determine.

Resolved, That the permission granted to lay or build a railroad in the following streets, viz.: commencing at a point at the intersection of West Broadway and Chambers street, thence through Chambers street to Church street, through Church street to Canal street, and through Canal street to Wooster street, through Wooster street to Fourth street, with a single track; thence through Fourth street to Sixth avenue, and through Sixth avenue to Harlem, with a double track, also, to lay a single track in Thompson street, from Fourth street to Canal street, to connect with the Eighth Avenue Railroad, be given to James S. Libby, George R. Howell, William Flagg, William H. Adams, John Post, jun., Edmund Morris, Matthew D. Greene, John Ridley, William Ebbitt, Ward, Bolster & Jacacks and Finch, Sanderson and Beers.

And whereas, said parties of the first part, on the said fourth day of June, one thousand eight hundred and fifty-one, in Common Council convened, did duly pass and adopt certain other resolutions, which were likewise duly signed and approved by the said Mayor on the said thirtieth day July, one thousand eight hundred and fifty-one, and became operative and binding, providing for the laying or building of another railroad, designated as the Eighth Avenue Railroad, provided for in said resolutions hereinbefore set forth; and further providing and directing that such parts of the Eighth Avenue Railroad as may be used by the Sixth avenue road, from the connection in Canal street and West Broadway to Chambers street, should be built at the joint expense of the Sixth and Eighth avenue roads.

And whereas, it is deemed necessary by the said parties of the first part, in order to preserve and duly effectuate the grants, objects, stipulations and intentions of the said resolutions, and for the purpose of more specifically determining the interest of said parties in the rights and privileges granted by said resolutions, that provision should be made for an organization or association between said parties of the second part, their successors, associates and assigns, duly admitted according to this agreement, defining the mode in which the necessary capital for building the said railroad shall be contributed, and the manner in which the construction and management of the said railroad shall be conducted and controlled.

Now, it is hereby mutually declared that the separate and individual interest of any or either of the said parties of the second part, their successors, associates and assigns, in the said grant, and all licenses, rights, privileges and powers conferred or provided for in the said resolutions, shall be conditioned and dependent upon the strict observance, performance, and fulfilment, by such person, of the terms of said resolutions, and of this agreement; and that, in case of failure to perform the same and every part thereof, said grant shall be inoperative as to such person so failing, and his interest therein shall cease and determine—said grant remaining operative, in every respect, as to all other of said parties, their successors, associates and assigns. And it is hereby covenanted, agreed and declared, by and between the parties aforesaid, as follows, viz.:

FIRST. The said parties of the second part, for themselves and their successors, associates and assigns, do hereby covenant and agree with the said parties of the first part, and with each other, that they will well and truly observe, perform, fulfill and keep the said resolutions hereinbefore particularly set forth, and all and every the provisions, stipulations, restrictions and conditions therein contained and thereby imposed, according to the true intent and meaning thereof, it being understood that the rate of passage on said road shall not exceed five cents for any distance, and also that the road shall be completed at the times and in the manner stated in said resolutions.

SECOND. The said parties of the second part, to the end that the provisions and intentions of the said resolutions may be fully carried into effect, the interests of the respective parties definitely ascertained, and the manner in which the construction and management of said road shall be conducted and controlled effectually defined, do further covenant and agree with the said parties of the first part, and with each other, to associate and organize themselves together, in the manner and upon the terms and conditions following, viz. :

Within ten days after this agreement is duly executed, the said parties of the second part, unless they, or a majority of them, shall have previously organized themselves to the same effect as herein provided, shall and will organize themselves into an association or company, to be called The Sixth Avenue Railroad Company, for the purpose of constructing, operating and managing said railroad; the first meeting of the said parties to be called by the clerk of the Common Council, who shall, within three days after the due execution of this agreement, give, or cause to be given, a notice in writing, delivered to the persons composing the said parties of the second part personally, or left at their residences or places of business, specifying the time and place when and where such meeting shall be held. The said parties of the second part, or as many of them as shall meet in pursuance of said notice, shall thereupon proceed, as before provided, to organize themselves into the said company, and shall have power and authority, by the votes of a majority of the parties so assembled,

1. To estimate and declare the amount of capital requisite to construct the said railroad, provide cars, motive power, stations, buildings, fixtures, and for all other expenses requisite to put the said railroad into thorough practical operation.

2. To prescribe the mode in which said capital, and all other sums that may thereafter be required for the business of said company, shall be subscribed for, and the time or times when the same shall be paid, and the manner in which shares and interests of the parties refusing or neglecting to subscribe or to pay may be forfeited.

3. To adopt suitable resolutions, by-laws, rules and regulations for the organization of said company, the subscription and payment of its capital and all other sums that may thereafter be required for its construction, operation and future business, the execution of contracts, the liability of members, the term, compensation, accountability, election, removal and duties of its officers, the disbursement of moneys, the transfer or assignment of the shares of its members, and the entire management, direction and control of its affairs, business, property and officers. Such by-laws may be altered from time to time, in the manner prescribed therein.

THIRD. The said parties of the second part shall be entitled to subscribe equally for the amount proposed as the original capital stock of said company, and if any of them neglect to subscribe, or shall subscribe less than his proportion, the others may subscribe equally for the remainder, so as to make up a subscription for the whole amount. If, for any reason, it shall be requisite to make other subscriptions, the persons who shall then be members of said company shall be entitled to subscribe for the amount so required, in proportion to the amounts of capital stock then held by them, and if any shall neglect to subscribe, or shall subscribe less than his proportion, the others may subscribe equally for the remainder.

FOURTH. Every person refusing or neglecting to subscribe to the capital stock of said company as originally declared, or to any subsequent increase thereof, or to pay his subscription or any instalment thereof, at the times prescribed at the first meeting of said company as aforesaid, or by the resolutions or by-laws of the said company, all his rights, powers and privileges under said grant of the parties of the first part, and all his interest therein, shall be deemed to be freely and voluntarily waived and abandoned for the benefit of said company and its remaining members, and shall cease, determine and be utterly null and void, and he shall no longer be a member of said company, nor have any voice in the management of its affairs, nor have any title or interest in its property. But such waiver or abandonment shall not be deemed to have taken place until twenty days shall have elapsed after such person shall have had written notice of the required subscription or payment. But such person may, by a resolution duly adopted by the said company, be reinstated in any or all of the rights, privileges and advantages so as aforesaid waived and lost, but upon such terms and conditions as may be thereby provided.

FIFTH. Every person who shall become a member of said company shall thereby become a party to this agreement and all its conditions and stipulations, and the company may direct the mode by which future members shall become so obligated, and no person shall become a member except on condition of becoming so obligated by agreement in writing duly executed.

SIXTH. The said railroad grant, property, rights and appurtenances shall belong to and be the property of the persons who, for the time being, shall compose the said Sixth Avenue Railroad Company, in proportions equivalent to their shares of said capital stock; subject, however, to the management of the same in the manner herein provided.

SEVENTH. Any shareholder may transfer his shares or interest, after he shall have paid one-third of his original subscription, on procuring the consent of a majority in interest of the shareholders, expressed by resolution duly adopted; subject, however, to the provisions of this agreement, and on such terms and conditions as the by-laws may prescribe.

EIGHTH. This Company shall not be dissolved by the death or insolvency of any of its members, nor by act or operation of law, but in such and the like cases shall continue, and the persons becoming lawfully entitled to the shares shall become members of the said Company, and said Company shall have authority to incorporate themselves under the general railroad act, whenever two-thirds in interest of the shareholders shall require the same.

In witness whereof, to one part of these presents, remaining with the said parties of the first part, the said parties of the second part have affixed their hands and seals; and to the other part thereof, remaining with the said parties of the second part, the said parties of the first part have caused the common seal of the city of New York to be affixed, the day and year first above written.

JAMES S. LIBBY,	[L. S.]
GEORGE R. HOWELL,	[L. S.]
WILLIAM FLAGG,	[L. S.]
WM. H. ADAMS,	[L. S.]
JOHN POST, Jr.,	[L. S.]
EDMUND MORRIS,	[L. S.]
MATTHEW DAVIS GREENE,	[L. S.]
JOHN RIDLEY, ·	[L. S.]
WILLIAM EBBETT,	[L. S.]

Sealed and delivered in presence of
H. H. ANDERSON,
as to Libby, Howell, Flagg, Greene, Ebbett, Adams, and Morris;
In presence of CARLTON EDWARDS, as to John Post, Jr. ; and
BERNARD J. MALONE, as to J. Ridley.

CITY AND COUNTY OF NEW YORK, ss. :—On the ninth day of September, one thousand eight hundred and fifty-one, before me personally came James S. Libby, George R. Howell, William Flagg, William H. Adams, Matthew D. Greene, and William Ebbett ; and on the fifteenth day of September, in the same year, before me personally came Edmund Morris, all of whom were known to me to be persons described in and who executed the foregoing instrument, and severally acknowledged that they executed the same ; and on the nineteenth day of September, one thousand eight hundred and fifty-one, before me personally came Carlton Edwards, a subscribing witness to said instrument, to me known, who, being by me duly sworn, did depose and say that he resides in the city of New York, that he knew John Post, jr., and knew him to be one of the persons described in and who executed the foregoing instrument; that he saw him sign the same, and that he acknowledged in his presence that he executed the same, and subscribed his name as a witness thereto. And on the same day before me personally came Bernard J. Malone, one of the subscribing witnesses to said instrument, to me known, who, being by me duly sworn, did depose and say that he resides in the city of New York, that he knew John Ridley, and knew him to be one of the persons described in and who executed the foregoing instrument, that he saw him sign the same, that he acknowledged in his presence that he executed the same, and that he subscribed his name as a witness thereto.

HENRY H. ANDERSON,
Commissioner of Deeds.

Resolved, That the route of the Sixth Avenue Railroad be, and the same is hereby, changed from the present location so as to run as follows, viz.: Commencing at the intersection of Chambers street and West Broadway, running thence, with a double track, through West Broadway to Canal street, through Canal street to Varick, through Varick to Carmine street, through Carmine street and the Sixth avenue, to intersect with the original grant of the Sixth Avenue Railroad Company.

Resolved, That the portion of said railroad track to be laid down in West Broadway, from Chambers street to Canal street, shall be built jointly by the Sixth and Eighth Avenue Railroad Companies, and in the event of either party refusing or neglecting to unite in the construction of such portion of the road, or pay for their proportionate share of the expense thereof, then it shall be competent for either of said parties to proceed with the work at their own expense and for their exclusive benefit, until the other party shall actually pay their proportion of such expense; further, should any difficulty arise between said Sixth and Eighth Avenue Railroad Companies as to the cost and value of building said road and rights to run over the same, each party shall have the privilege to select a referee, not interested in any wise in either of said roads, to adjust all difficulties, but should said referees not be able to make a proper and amicable settlement of any dispute arising between the parties hereinbefore mentioned, then it shall be competent for the Common Council to select a third person as referee, who shall investigate the subject-matter in dispute, and a decision from a majority of said referees shall be final and conclusive; nothing, however, contained in this resolution shall be construed to interfere with the power and authority of the Common Council to prescribe rules and regulations, from time to time, for the control and management of said railroad.

Adopted by the Board of Assistants, June 9, 1852.

Adopted by the Board of Aldermen, June 17, 1852.

Approved by the Mayor, June 23, 1852.

Petition of James S. Libby, President of the Sixth

Avenue Railroad Company, to grant the Manhattan Gas-Light Company permission to lay their mains in the Sixth avenue to Forty-fourth street, so that the depot may be lighted with gas, was granted

By the Board of Assistants, Nov. 9, 1852.

By the Board of Aldermen, Nov. 17, 1852.

Approved by the Mayor, Nov. 19, 1852.

Resolved, That the Eighth Avenue Railroad Company have authority, and the privilege is hereby granted to them, to extend their rail (which is to be constructed in like manner as their present) through Canal street to Broadway, and also from its present termination at Chambers street, through College place to Barclay street, and through Barclay and Church streets, or across Barclay street and through the buildings which they have rented or procured, or may rent or procure, for the purpose, to and into Vesey street; through Vesey street to Broadway, and through Church street, from Vesey street to Chambers street, and through Chambers street to its present termination aforesaid, and to run their cars over the same; and when they shall have made such extension, then and thereafter they shall be at liberty to charge every passenger, who may come to and ride any distance upon any part of their road below Fifty-first street, five cents for riding on that part of their road. Anything in the resolutions or agreement, under which the said company are now acting, inconsistent with any of the privileges granted by this resolution, is hereby modified so as to conform thereto.

And also, *Resolved*, That the Sixth Avenue Railroad Company, upon paying to the said Eighth Avenue Railroad Company the half part of the cost of that portion of their road lying between Varick street and West Broadway, and of keeping it in repair from time to time hereafter, and also the half of the costs and of the repairs, from time to time, of the extensions above authorized, shall be at liberty to use and own half of the same, and run their cars thereon, and to charge every passenger, who may come to ride any distance upon any part of their road below Forty-third street, the like sum of five cents for riding on that part of their road; and anything in the resolutions or agreement, under which they are now acting, inconsistent with the said privileges, is hereby modified so as to conform to this resolution.

Adopted by the Board of Assistants, Nov. 11, 1852.

Adopted by the Board of Aldermen, Nov. 22, 1852.

Received from his Honor the Mayor, Dec. 13, 1852, without his approval or objections thereto; therefore, under the provisions of the amended charter, the same became adopted.

Whereas, A resolution has passed the Common Council, and which resolution was permitted to become a law by the non-action of the Mayor, authorizing the Sixth and Eighth Avenue Railroad Companies to extend their road through College place to and across Barclay street, or through Barclay or Vesey street to Broadway, and to return through Chambers street to its present termination; and

Whereas, It was the understanding, although not specified in the resolution, that said extension should and was to be only with a single track, yet the said Eighth Avenue Railroad Company is now engaged in constructing said road with a double track, which will have the effect to shut from said street all other travel, and be a serious detriment to the interests of the citizens generally, and to the owners of property on the line especially; and, as there seems to be a very serious misunderstanding as to whether there should be constructed a single or a double track, therefore, be it

Resolved, That the Street Commissioner be, and he is hereby, directed to cause all further proceedings of said Companies, in the construction of said roads through the streets mentioned in the preamble, to be stayed and suspended until the further action of the Common Council, except they build a single track only through said streets, and if that course be not adopted by said Companies, that then the said Street Commissioner be, and he is hereby, directed to have said streets restored to their former condition without delay.

Adopted by the Board of Aldermen, Dec. 18, 1852.

Adopted by the Board of Assistants, Dec. 20, 1852.

Approved by the Mayor, Dec. 21, 1852.

Resolved, That the Commissioner of Streets be, and he is hereby, directed to notify the Sixth Avenue Railroad Company to have the railroad alley, between Vesey and Barclay streets, closed up with suitable gates forthwith.

Adopted by the Board of Councilmen, April 24, 1854.

Adopted by the Board of Aldermen, May 19, 1854.

Approved by the Mayor, May 26, 1854.

Resolved, That the Sixth Avenue Railroad Company be, and they are hereby, directed to complete their track to Fifty-fourth street without delay, in accordance with the ordinance heretofore adopted by the Common Council, on or before the 1st of June, 1857, otherwise the Counsel to the Corporation is authorized and directed to commence proceedings against them, to compel them to complete said track.

Adopted by the Board of Aldermen, March 9, 1857.

Adopted by the Board of Councilmen, April 17, 1857.

Approved by the Mayor, April 20, 1857.

The President of the Croton Aqueduct Board directed to notify the Sixth Avenue Railroad Company to put in good repair, forthwith, all the pavements in and about their rails, and, in case of neglect or refusal, to have the same done at the expense of the Sixth Avenue Railroad Company.

Adopted by the Board of Aldermen, Sept. 10, 1857.

Adopted by the Board of Councilmen, Sept. 14, 1857.

Approved by the Mayor, Sept. 16, 1857.

Resolved, That the Sixth Avenue Railroad Company be, and they are hereby, directed to repair their track and keep the same in good order on the established grades of the streets and avenues in which their said track is laid, in accordance with the provisions of the charter granted them by the Common Council, and that the same be done within fifteen days after the approval of this resolution by his Honor the Mayor, and in case said Sixth Avenue Railroad Co. fail to comply with the provisions of this resolution, then, that the Croton Aqueduct Board be, and they are hereby, authorized and directed to cause the track of the said Sixth Avenue Railroad Co. to be repaired and put in good order, and charge the expense thereof to the Sixth Avenue Railroad Company.

Adopted by the Board of Aldermen, May 11, 1859.

Adopted by the Board of Councilmen, June 27, 1859.

Approved by the Mayor, July 28, 1859.

Resolved, That the contractor for paving Sixth avenue, between Carmine and Forty-second streets, with square-block pavement, be, and he is hereby, directed not to pave that portion of the avenue between the outside rails of the Sixth Avenue Railroad, but to continue only the paving of the avenue between the outside rails and the curbs on either side of said Sixth avenue in accordance with the contract.

Resolved, That the Sixth Avenue Railroad Company be, and they are hereby, authorized and permitted, at their own expense, to pave the space between and within the outside rails of their said road with small cobble-stones, and are hereby directed to keep the same in good order and condition, all of which to be done under the direction of the Croton Aqueduct Department.

Resolved, That the Croton Aqueduct Department be, and are hereby, requested and directed to cause the aforesaid resolutions to be carried into effect.

Adopted by the Board of Councilmen, Oct, 20, 1859.

Adopted by the Board of Aldermen, Oct. 20, 1859.

Approved by the Mayor, Oct. 27, 1859.

SEVENTH AVENUE RAILROAD.

Whereas, A bill has been introduced in the Assembly of this State, to authorize John A. Kennedy and others to construct a railroad, with a double track, upon and along the Seventh avenue at Fifty-ninth street; thence along Seventh avenue to Broadway; thence along Broadway and Union place to University place; along University place to Sixth street; thence along Sixth street to Greene street; thence along Greene street to Canal street; thence along Canal street to West Broadway; thence along West Broadway and College place to Park place; thence along Park place to Church street; thence along Church street to Fulton street; thence along Fulton street to Broadway; also along Park place to Broadway, and thence back through Park place to Church street, and thence through Church street to Canal street; thence along Canal street to Mercer street; thence along Mercer street to Waverley place (or Sixth street), to connect with the track in University place; and

Whereas, It is believed that no public emergency requires any such railroad, but, on the contrary, the citizens of New York, and particularly those living on the route aforesaid, are wholly opposed to the measure; therefore be it

Resolved, That this Common Council do most earnestly remonstrate against the said project, and is opposed to the passage of any law which tends to obstruct the streets, avenues or highways of the city by laying rail-tracks therein.

Adopted by the Board of Councilmen, April 9, 1857.

Adopted by the Board of Aldermen, April 10, 1857.

Approved by the Mayor, April 11, 1857.

EIGHTH AVENUE RAILROAD.

Resolved, That the annexed form of agreement is approved as the form of agreement to be executed by the parties in whose favor resolutions were heretofore adopted by the Common Council, granting permission to lay or build the railroad known as the Eighth Avenue Railroad, and that the said parties be, and they are hereby, required to duly sign and execute said agreement within ten days after the same shall have been prepared for execution by the Counsel to the Corporation; and that any or either of the said parties, who shall neglect or refuse to sign and execute said agreement within the time aforesaid, shall be deemed to have waived and forfeited all and every right, benefit and advantage under the resolutions heretofore passed, granting said permission to and for the benefit of the persons named in the same, who duly execute said agreement in manner aforesaid, and the said permission shall take effect accordingly.

Resolved, That an agreement, in the like form as that

annexed, varied and adapted to the resolutions heretofore passed, granting permission to construct the Sixth Avenue Railroad, be prepared by the Counsel to the Corporation, and that the parties to whom such permission is granted be, and they are hereby, required to sign and execute said agreement within ten days after the same shall have been prepared for execution, as aforesaid, and that any or either of the said parties neglecting or refusing to execute said agreement, in manner aforesaid, shall be deemed to have waived and forfeited all and every right, benefit and advantage under said resolutions, to and for the benefit of those named in the said resolutions, who duly execute said agreement, and said permission shall take effect accordingly.

Adopted by the Board of Aldermen, Sept. 3, 1851.

Adopted by the Board of Assistants, Sept. 4, 1851.

Approved by the Mayor, Sept. 5, 1851.

AGREEMENT, made this sixth day of September, one thousand eight hundred and fifty-one, between the Mayor, Aldermen and Commonalty of the city of New York, parties of the first part, and the persons named in the resolutions hereinafter set forth, who shall duly sign and execute this agreement, and their successors, associates and assigns, duly becoming parties thereto, as hereinafter provided, of the second part:

Whereas, The said parties of the first part, in Common Council convened, did, on the fourth day of June, one thousand eight hundred and fifty-one, duly pass and adopt the following resolutions, which were afterwards and on the thirtieth day of July in said year duly signed and approved by the Mayor of said city, and became operative and binding in the words and figures following:

Resolved, That the persons to whom permission is granted by the following resolutions, and those who may hereafter become associated with them, have the authority and consent of the Common Council to lay a double track for a railroad in the following streets, viz.: from a point at the intersection of Chambers street and West Broadway, thence along West Broadway to Canal street, thence along and down Canal street to Hudson street, along Hudson street to Eighth avenue, to a point at or near 51st street and that said railroad be continued through the Eighth avenue to Harlem River, whenever required by the Common Council and as soon and as fast as said avenue is graded, upon the following stipulations and conditions, viz.:

Such track or tracks to be laid under the direction of the Street Commissioner and on such grades as are now established or may hereafter be established by the Common Council, the said parties to become bound in a sufficient penalty to keep in good repair the space between the track and the space outside the same on either side, of at least eight feet in width of each street in which the rails are laid, also that no motive power, excepting horses, be used below 51st street, and upon the further condition that said parties shall place new cars on said railroad, with all the modern improvements for the convenience and comfort of passengers, and that they run cars thereon each and every day, both ways, as often as the public convenience may require, under such directions as the Street Commissioner and Common Council may, from time to time, prescribe.

3. *And provided also*, that the said parties shall, in all respects, comply with the direction of the Street Commissioner and of the Common Council in the building of said railroad and in the running of the cars thereon, and in any other matter connected with the regulation of said railroad.

4. *And provided also*, that the said parties shall, before this permission takes effect, enter into a good and sufficient agreement with the Mayor, Aldermen and Commonalty of the city of New York, to be drawn and approved of by the Counsel to the Corporation, binding themselves to abide by and perform the stipulations and provisions herein contained and also all such other resolutions or ordinances as may be passed by the Common Council relating to the said road.

5. *And further*, that they run a car thereon each and every day, both ways, as often as every fifteen minutes from 5 to 6 o'clock A. M., and every four minutes from 6 o'clock A. M., to 8 o'clock P. M., every fifteen minutes from 8 o'clock P. M. to 12 o'clock P. M., and every thirty minutes from 12 o'clock P. M., to 5 o'clock A. M.; and as much oftener as public convenience may require, under such directions as the Common Council may, from time to time, prescribe.

6. *Also*, that the rate of passage on said railroad shall not exceed a greater sum than five cents for the entire length of said road, and also that the Common Council shall have

the power to cause the same, or any part thereof, to be taken up at any time they may see fit; and also that the said parties, or either of them, shall not assign their interest in the said road without first obtaining the consent of the Common Council thereto; also that such track or tracks shall be laid upon a foundation of concrete, with a grooved rail or such other rail as may be approved of by the Street Commissioner, even with the surface of the streets through which they may pass, and shall be commenced within three months and completed to 51st street within one year, and from 51st street to Harlem River within three years, from the passage of this resolution; also that the foundation on each side of the rails shall be paved with square grooved blocks of stone, similiar to the Russ pavement, as far up as 51st street; that the said parties are to keep an account of the receipts of each road monthly and report the same to the Comptroller monthly, under oath; that the said parties shall connect their road with such other roads as the Common Council may order to be connected therewith; that they shall file with the Comptroller a statement, under oath, of the cost of each mile of road completed, and agree to surrender, convey and transfer the said road to the Corporation of the city of New York, whenever required so to do, on payment, by the Corporation, of the cost of said road, as appears by said statement, with ten per cent. advance thereon; that said parties, on being required at any time by the Corporation, and to such extent as the Common Council shall determine, shall take up, at their own expense, said rails, or such part thereof as they shall be required, and on failure so to do, in ten days after such requirement, the same may be done at their expense by the Street Commissioner.

Resolved, That each of said passenger cars, to be used on said road, shall be annually licensed by the Mayor; and there shall be paid, annually, for such license, such sum as the Common Council may hereafter determine.

Resolved, That the permission granted to lay or build a railroad track in the following streets, viz: from a point at the intersection of West Broadway and Chambers street, thence through West Broadway to Canal street, down Canal street to Hudson street, along Hudson street and Eighth avenue to Harlem River, be granted and given to John Pettigrew, Edmund R. Sherman, Solomon Kipp, Abraham Brown, Washington Smith, Joseph N. Barnes, John O'Keefe, John J. Duryea, Jesse A. Marshall and Timothy Townsend.

And whereas, Said parties of the first part, on the said fourth day of June, one thousand eight hundred and fifty-one, in Common Council convened, did duly pass and adopt certain other resolutions, which were likewise duly signed and approved by the said Mayor, on the said thirtieth day of July, one thousand eight hundred and fifty-one, and became operative and binding, providing for the laying or building of another railroad, designated as the Sixth Avenue Railroad, provided for in said resolutions hereinbefore set forth; and further providing and directing that such parts of the Eighth Avenue Railroad as may be used by the Sixth Avenue Road, from the connection in Canal street and West Broadway to Chambers street, should be built at the joint expense of the said Sixth and Eighth Avenue Roads.

And whereas, It is deemed necessary by the said parties

of the first part, in order to preserve and duly effectuate the grants, objects and stipulations and intentions of the said resolutions, for the purpose of more specifically determining the interests of the said parties in the rights and privileges granted by said resolutions, that provision should be made for an organization or association between the said parties of the second part, their successors, associates and assigns, duly admitted, according to this agreement, defining the mode in which the necessary capital for building the said railroad shall be contributed, and the manner in which the construction and management of the said railroad shall be constructed and controlled. Now, it is hereby mutually declared that the separate or individual interest of any or either of the said parties of the second part, their successors, associates and assigns, in the said grant, and all licenses, rights, privileges and powers, conferred or provided for in the said resolutions, shall be conditioned and dependent upon the strict observance, performance and fulfilment by such person of the terms of said resolutions and of this agreement; and that, in case of failure to perform the same, and every part thereof, said grant shall be inoperative as to such person so failing, and his interest therein shall cease and determine; said grant remaining operative in every respect as to all others of said parties, their successors, associates and assigns. And it is hereby covenanted, agreed and declared, by and between the parties aforesaid, as follows, viz.:

FIRST. The said parties of the second part, for themselves and their successors, associates and assigns, do hereby covenant and agree with said parties of the first part, and with each other, that they will well and truly observe, perform, fulfill and keep the said resolutions hereinbefore particularly set forth, and all and every the provisions, stipulations, restrictions and conditions therein contained and thereby imposed, according to the true intent and meaning thereof, it being understood that the rate of passage on said road shall not exceed five cents for any distance; and, also, that the said road shall be completed at the times and in the manner stated in said resolutions.

SECOND. The said parties of the second part, to the end that the provisions and intentions of the said resolutions may be fully carried into effect, the interest of the respective parties definitely ascertained, and the manner in which the construction and management of said road shall be conducted and controlled effectually defined, do further covenant and agree with the said parties of the first part, and with each other, to associate and organize themselves in the manner and upon the terms and conditions following, viz.:

Within ten days after this agreement is duly executed the said parties of the second part, unless they, or a majority of them, shall have previously organized themselves to the same effect, as herein provided, shall and will organize themselves into an association or company, to be called the Eighth Avenue Railroad Company, for the purpose of constructing, operating and managing said railroad, the first meeting of said parties to be called by the Clerk of the Common Council, who shall, within three days after the due execution of this agreement, give, or cause to be given, a notice in writing, delivered to the persons composing the said parties of the second part, personally or left at their residences or places of business, specifying the time and place, when and where such meeting shall be held.

The said parties of the second part, or as many of them as shall meet in pursuance of said notice, shall thereupon proceed, as before provided, to organize themselves into the said company, and shall have power and authority, by the votes of a majority of the parties so assembled,

1. To estimate and declare the amount of capital requisite to construct the said railroad, provide cars, motive power, stations, buildings, fixtures, and for all other expenses requisite to put the said railroad into thorough practical operation.

2. To prescribe the mode in which said capital and all other sums that may thereafter be required for the business of said company, shall be subscribed for, and the time or times when the same shall be paid in, and the manner in which the shares and interests of the parties refusing or neglecting to subscribe or to pay, may be forfeited.

3. To adopt suitable resolutions, by-laws, rules and regulations for the organization of said company, the subscription and payment of its capital and all other sums that may thereafter be required for its construction, operation and future business, the execution of contracts, the liability of members, the term, compensation, accountability, election, removal and duties of its officers, the disbursement of moneys, the transfer or assignment of shares of its members, and the entire management, direction and control of its affairs, business, property and officers. Such by-laws may be altered, from time to time, in the manner prescribed therein.

THIRD. The said parties of the second part shall be entitled to subscribe equally for the amount proposed as the original capital stock of said company; and if any of them neglect to subscribe, or shall subscribe less than his proportion, the others may subscribe equally for the remainder, so as to make up a subscription for the whole amount. If, for any reason, it shall be requisite to make other subscriptions, the persons who shall then be members of said company shall be entitled to subscribe for the amount so required in proportion to the amount of capital stock then held by them, and if any shall neglect to subscribe, or shall subscribe for less than his proportion, the others may subscribe equally for the remainder.

FOURTH. Every person refusing or neglecting to subscribe to the capital stock of said company, as originally declared, or to any subsequent increase thereof, or to pay his subscription or any installment thereof, at the times prescribed at the first meeting of said company, as aforesaid, or by the resolutions or by-laws of the said company, all his rights, powers and privileges, under said grant of the parties of the first part, and all his interest therein, shall be deemed to be freely and voluntarily waived and abandoned, for the benefit of said company and its remaining members, and shall cease, determine and be utterly null and void, and he shall no longer be a member of said company, nor have any voice in the management of its affairs, nor any title or interest in its property; but such waiver and abandonment shall not be deemed to have taken place until twenty days shall have elapsed after such person shall have had written notice of the required subscription or payment. But such person may, by a resolution duly adopted by said company, be reinstated in any or all of the rights, privileges and advantages, &c., as aforesaid waived and lost, but upon such terms and conditions as may be thereby provided.

FIFTH. Every person who shall become a member of said company, shall thereby become a party to this agreement and all its conditions and stipulations, and the company may direct the mode by which future members shall become so obligated; and no person shall become a member except on condition of becoming so obligated by agreement in writing, duly executed.

SIXTH. The said railroad grant, property, rights and appurtenances shall belong to and be the property of the persons who, for the time being, shall compose the said Eighth Avenue Railroad Company, in proportions equivalent to their shares of said capital stock, subject, however, to the management of the same, in the manner herein provided.

SEVENTH. Any shareholder may transfer his shares or interest after he shall have paid one-third of his original subscription, on procuring the consent of a majority in interest of the stockholders, expressed by a resolution duly adopted, subject, however, to the provisions of this agreement, and on such terms and conditions as the by-laws may prescribe.

EIGHTH. This company shall not be dissolved by the death or insolvency of any of its members, nor by act or operation of law, but in such and the like cases shall continue, and the persons becoming lawfully entitled to the shares shall become members of the said company; and said company shall have authority to incorporate themselves under the general railroad act, whenever two-thirds in interest of the shareholders shall require the same.

In witness whereof, to one part of these presents, remaining with the said parties of the first part, the said parties of the second part have affixed their hands and seals; and to the other part thereof, remaining with the said parties of the second part, the said parties of the first part have caused the common seal of the city of New York to be affixed, the day and year first above written.

JOHN PETTIGREW, [L. S.]
E. R. SHERMAN, [L. S.]
JESSE A. MARSHALL, [L. S.]
TIMOTHY TOWNSEND, [L. S.]
JOHN O'KEEFE, [L. S.]
JOHN J. DURYEA, [L. S.]
WASHINGTON SMITH, [L. S.]
SOLOMON KIPP, [L. S.]
J. N. BARNES, [L. S.]
ABRAHAM BROWN, [L. S.]

Sealed and delivered in presence
of HENRY H. ANDERSON, as to
Sherman and Pettigrew, Marshall and Townsend and others.

CITY AND COUNTY OF NEW YORK, ss.—On the sixth day of September, one thousand eight hundred and fifty-one, before me personally came Edmund R.

Sherman; on the eighth day of said month, before me personally came John Pettigrew; on the tenth day of said month, before me personally came Jesse A. Marshall and Timothy Townsend; on the thirteenth day of said month, before me personally came Washington Smith, Solomon Kipp, Joseph N. Barnes and Abraham Brown, all of whom are known to me to be persons described in and who executed the foregoing agreement; and the said parties above named, severally upon the days above named, acknowledged that they executed said foregoing instrument.

HENRY H. ANDERSON,
Commissioner of Deeds.

Resolved, That the route of the Sixth Avenue Railroad be and the same is hereby changed from the present location so as to run as follows, viz.: commencing at the intersection of Chambers street and West Broadway, running thence with a double track through West Broadway to Canal street, through Canal street to Varick, through Varick to Carmine street, through Carmine street and the Sixth avenue to intersect with the original grant of the Sixth Avenue Railroad Company.

Resolved, That the portion of said railroad track to be laid down in West Broadway from Chambers street to Canal street shall be built jointly by the Sixth and Eighth Avenue Railroad Companies, and in the event of either party refusing or neglecting to unite in the construction of such portion of the road, or pay for their proportionate share of the expense therof, then it shall be competent for either of said parties to proceed with the work at their own expense and for their exclusive benefit until the other party shall actually pay their proportion of such expense; further, should any difficulty arise between said Sixth and Eighth Avenue Railroad Companies as to the cost and value of building said road and rights to run over the same, each party shall have the privilege to select a referee, not interested in any wise in either of said roads, to adjust all difficulties, but should said referees not be able to make a proper and amicable settlement of any dispute arising between the parties hereinbefore mentioned, then it shall be competent for the Common Council to select a third person as referee, who shall investigate the subject matter in dispute, and a decision from a majority of said referees shall be final and conclusive; nothing, however, contained in this resolution shall be construed to interfere with the power and authority of the Common Council to prescribe rules and regulations, from time to time, for the control and management of said railroad.

Adopted by the Board of Assistants, June 9, 1852.

Adopted by the Board of Aldermen, June 17, 1852.

Approved by the Mayor, June 23, 1852.

Resolved, That the Eighth Avenue Railroad Co. have authority, and the privilege is hereby granted to them, to extend their rail (which is to be constructed in like manner as their present) through Canal street to Broadway, and also from its present termination at Chambers street through College place to Barclay street, and through Barclay and Church streets, or across Barclay street through the buildings they have rented or procured, or may rent or procure, for the purpose, to and into Vesey street, through Vesey street to Broadway, and through Church street from Vesey street to Chambers street, and through Chambers street to its present termination aforesaid, and to run their cars over the same; and when they shall have made such extension, then and thereafter they shall be at liberty to charge every passenger, who may come to and ride any distance upon any part of their road below 51st street, 5 cents for riding on that part of their road. Anything in the resolutions or agreement under which the said Company are now acting, inconsistent with any of the privileges granted by this resolution, is hereby modified, so as to conform thereto. And also,

Resolved, That the Sixth Avenue Railroad Company, upon paying to the said Eighth Avenue Railroad Co. the half part of the cost of that portion of their road lying between Varick street and West Broadway, and of keeping it in repair from time to time hereafter, and also the half of the costs and of the repairs from time to time of the extensions above authorized, shall be at liberty to use and own half of the same, and run their cars thereon, and to charge every passenger, who may come to ride any distance upon any part of their road below 43d street, the like sum of 5 cents for riding on that part of the road, and anything in the resolutions or agreement under which they are now acting, inconsistent with the said privileges, is hereby modified, so as to conform to this resolution.

Adopted by the Board of Assistants, Nov. 11, 1852.

Adopted by the Board of Aldermen, Nov. 22, 1852.

Received from his Honor the Mayor, Dec. 13, 1852, without his approval or objections thereto; therefore, under the provisions of the amended charter, the same became adopted.

Whereas, A resolution has passed the Common Council, and which resolution was permitted to become a law by the non-action of the Mayor, authorizing the 6th and 8th Avenue Railroad Company to extend their road through College place to and across Barclay street, or through Barclay or Vesey street to Broadway, and to return through Chambers street to its present termination, and

Whereas, It was the understanding, although not specified in the resolution, that said extension should and was to be only with a single track, yet the said 8th Avenue Railroad Company is now engaged in constructing said road with a double track, which will have the effect to shut from said streets all other travel, and be a serious detriment to the interests of the citizens generally, and to the owners of property on the line especially; and as there seems to be a very serious misunderstanding as to whether there should be constructed a single or a double track, therefore, be it

Resolved, That the Street Commissioner be, and he is hereby, directed to cause all further proceedings of said Companies, in the construction of said roads through the streets mentioned in the preamble, to be stayed and suspended until the further action of the Common Council, except they build a single track only through said streets, and if that course be not adopted by said Companies, that then the said Street Commissioner be, and he is hereby, directed to have said streets restored to their former condition without delay.

Adopted by the Board of Aldermen, Dec. 18, 1852.

Adopted by the Board of Assistants, Dec. 20, 1852.

Approved by the Mayor, Dec. 21, 1852.

Resolved, That the President, Directors and Company of the 8th Avenue Railroad be and they are hereby directed, for the better accommodation of the public, to run their cars daily from and to 59th street and 8th avenue, the present terminus of the rails they have already laid, instead of, as they now run, from and to 51st street and 8th avenue.

Adopted by the Board of Aldermen, Nov. 21, 1853.

Adopted by the Board of Assistants, Nov. 29, 1853.

Approved by the Mayor, Nov. 30, 1853.

Resolved, That the 8th Avenue Railroad Company be and are hereby directed to run their accommodation cars from 52d to 59th street every 10 minutes, so as to start a car every 10 minutes from 52d street up to 59th street, and a car every 10 minutes from 59th street down to 52d street, daily from 5 o'clock, A. M., to 10 o'clock, P. M.

Adopted by the Board of Councilmen, July 6, 1854.

Adopted by the Board of Aldermen, July 10, 1854.

Approved by the Mayor, July 12, 1854.

Resolved, That the 8th Avenue Railroad Company be and they are hereby directed to relay the track of said railroad, and to run their cars from 51st street to the junction of 8th avenue and Broadway, and that said Company run their cars from 51st street to 59th street every five minutes, and the Street Commissioner is hereby authorized and directed to carry this resolution into effect.

Adopted by the Board of Aldermen, November 8, 1855.

Adopted by the Board of Councilmen, December 19, 1855.

Approved by the Mayor, December 20, 1855.

Resolved, That the Street Commissioner be and is hereby directed to give the 8th Avenue Railroad Company notice to repair the pavement on the 8th avenue, in accordance with their agreement with the Corporation.

Adopted by the Board of Councilmen, May 14, 1856.

Adopted by the Board of Aldermen, May 16, 1856.

Approved by the Mayor, May 17, 1856.

Resolved, That the curb and gutter-stones on the south side of Vesey street, between Church street and Broadway, be set in 5 feet 6 inches, under the direction of the Street Commissioner, provided the expense of the same is paid by the 8th Avenue Railroad Company, and that they be directed to lay their rails as near said curb as can be done with safety to the travel for other vehicles.

Adopted by the Board of Aldermen, May 21, 1857.

Adopted by the Board of Councilmen, June 15, 1857.

Approved by the Mayor, June 19, 1857.

The President of the Croton Aqueduct Board directed to notify the 8th Avenue Railroad Company to put in good repair, forthwith, all the pavements in and about their rails, and, in case of neglect or refusal, to have the same done at the expense of the 8th Avenue Railroad Company.

Adopted by the Board of Aldermen, September 10, 1857.

Adopted by the Board of Councilmen, September 14, 1857.

Approved by the Mayor, September 16, 1857.

Resolved, That the 8th Avenue Railroad Company be and they are hereby required to run all their cars to 59th street regularly.

Adopted by the Board of Councilmen, February 26, 1858.

Adopted by the Board of Aldermen, March 1, 1858.

Approved by the Mayor, March 2, 1858.

Resolved, That Hudson street, from the Eighth avenue to Canal street, be paved with Belgian pavement; the Eighth Avenue Railroad Company to pay their proportion of the expense, as compelled by their grant, under the direction of the Croton Aqueduct Department.

Adopted by the Board of Councilmen, June 26, 1859.

Adopted by the Board of Aldermen, July 7, 1859.

Board of Councilmen, July 18, 1859, received from his Honor the Mayor with his objections thereto.

Board of Councilmen, August 8, 1859, taken up and adopted, notwithstanding the objections of his Honor the Mayor, two-thirds of all the members elected having voted therefor.

Board of Aldermen, September 5, 1859, taken up and the above action of the Board of Councilmen concurred in, two-thirds of all the members elected having voted therefor; therefore, under the provisions of the amended charter, the same became adopted.

AN ORDINANCE

IN RELATION TO THE PAVEMENT WITHIN THE TRACKS OF THE EIGHTH AND NINTH AVENUE RAILROADS.

Be it ordained by the Mayor, Aldermen and Commonalty of the City of New York, in Common Council convened:

§ 1. The Eighth Avenue Railroad Company and the Ninth Avenue Railroad Company are hereby authorized to pave all the space within the outside rails of their respective tracks with small cobble-stone, and are hereby further required to keep the said space in repair and good traveling condition.

§ 2. All resolutions, ordinances or parts thereof, so far as they conflict herewith, are hereby repealed.

§ 3. This ordinance shall take effect immediately.

Adopted by the Board of Councilmen, Sept. 8, 1859.

Adopted by the Board of Aldermen, Sept. 8, 1859.

Approved by the Mayor, Sept. 10, 1859.

Resolved, That the Eighth Avenue Railroad Company be, and they are hereby permitted to lay a turnout or switch on the south side of their tracks in Canal street, at or near Broadway, and use the same for the accommodation of their cars or those of the Ninth Avenue Railroad Company.

Adopted by the Board of Aldermen, Sept. 8, 1859.

Adopted by the Board of Councilmen, Sept. 8, 1859.

Board of Aldermen, Sept. 19, 1859, received from his Honor the Mayor with his objections thereto.

Board of Aldermen, October 3, 1859, taken up and adopted, notwithstanding the objections of his Honor the Mayor, two-thirds of all the members elected having voted therefor.

Board of Councilmen, October 3, 1859, taken up and the above action of the Board of Aldermen concurred in, two-thirds of all the members elected having voted therefor; therefore, under the provisions of the amended charter, the same became adopted.

Resolved, That the Eighth Avenue Railroad Company and the Ninth Avenue Railroad Company be and are hereby authorized and permitted in hereafter relaying their track, and in extending the same, to lay down and use the "Hewitt Bridge patent rail" or such other form of rail as may be approved of by the Street Commissioner.

Resolved, That permission is hereby granted to the Ninth Avenue Railroad Company to lay a track from the Ninth

Avenue Railroad track at Greenwich street, through Canal street, to connect with the Eighth Avenue Railroad track at Hudson street, and also to lay a track from the Ninth avenue, through Fifty-fourth street, to connect with the Eighth Avenue Railroad; and that the Eighth and Ninth Avenue Railroad Companies are hereby permitted to agree to run their cars over each other's tracks during such times as they may be respectively relaying and repairing their tracks.

Adopted by the Board of Councilmen, September 8, 1859.

Adopted by the Board of Aldermen, September 19, 1859.

Approved by the Mayor, October 3, 1859.

Resolved, That the Eighth Avenue Railroad Company is hereby authorized and directed to pave the sidewalks on the streets in front of their depot buildings, car houses, stables and workshops with Belgian pavement, and to keep such pavement at all times hereafter in good repair.

Adopted by the Board of Councilmen, November 14, 1859.

Adopted by the Board of Aldermen, December 31, 1859.

Approved by the Mayor, December 31, 1859.

NINTH AVENUE RAILROAD.

Resolved, That the Common Council do hereby grant the right and privilege to James Murphy, William Radford and Miner C. Story and their respective assigns, and to those they may associate with them, to construct a railroad from 51st street to the Battery and back, in and through the following streets, viz.:

With a double track from 51st street through the 9th avenue to Gansevoort street, thence by a single track through Greenwich street to the Battery, and by a single track through Gansevoort street to Washington street and through Washington street to the Battery, and through Battery place, between Greenwich and Washington streets, to connect the said single tracks, and also to run cars for the conveyance of passengers, &c., upon said road each and every day, at such times as they may think proper, subject to provisions hereinafter named.

Provided, Said railroad shall be constructed in all respects after the manner of the construction of the Eighth Avenue Railroad.

Provided, That in no case steam power be used on any part of said railroad; and also

Provided, That the said grantees shall begin the construction of said railroad on or before the first day of May next, and shall complete the same and commence running cars thereon within 18 months thereafter; and also

Provided, That the said grantees shall run cars upon the road so constructed each way, between 51st street and the

Battery, every day, as often as 15 minutes from 5 to 6 A. M., and every 4 minutes from 6 A. M. to 12 M., every 15 minutes from 8 A. M. to 12 M., and as much oftener as public convenience may require, under such directions as the Common Council may, from time to time, prescribe; and

Provided, That no more than five cents be charged for each passenger riding over the whole or any portion of the distance of said road; and also

Provided, That said grantees shall keep the space, for two feet each side of the same, at all times in thorough repair, and also

Provided, That the said cars shall be licensed by the Mayor, and the grantees shall pay the annual fee of $20 per car for such license; and

Also, the said grantees and their associates and assigns, shall have the privilege to organize a joint-stock association, either with or without incorporation, to carry out the objects of this grant, and a majority in interest of the grantees, their assigns and associates, shall have the control, management and direction of the road and the business thereof; and should any or either of the grantees or their associates, or of the shareholders, neglect to pay their respective proportion of the money required for carrying into full effect the grant hereby made, when by such majority thereunto required, the others shall be at liberty to make such payment; and this grant shall enure to the benefit of those who pay in the proportion of their respective contributions.

These resolutions shall be certified by said grantees above named; and a copy thereof, signed by them, shall be deemed the agreement between the Mayor, Aldermen and Commonalty of the city of New York and said associates; and shall be sufficient in all respects to give and grant to the said grantees, their associates and assigns, aforesaid, the right and privilege above mentioned, and bind them to conform to the directions herein contained.

And also provided, that said railroad shall be continued from Fifty-first street along the Ninth avenue to the Bloomingdale road, to the Tenth avenue, thence along the Tenth avenue to the Harlem river, whenever required by the Common Council and as soon and as fast as said avenues are graded.

Adopted by the Board of Assistants, Dec. 20, 1852.

Adopted by the Board of Aldermen, Jan. 5, 1853.

Received from his Honor the Mayor, Jan. 12, 1853, with his objections thereto.

Board of Aldermen, November 14, 1853, taken up, reconsidered and adopted, notwithstanding the objections of his Honor the Mayor thereto, two-thirds of all the members elected voting in favor thereof.

Board of Assistants, December 28, 1853, taken up, reconsidered and adopted, notwithstanding the objections of his Honor the Mayor thereto, two-thirds of all the members elected voting in favor thereof; therefore, under the provisions of the amended charter the same became adopted.

        D. T. VALENTINE,
         Clerk of Common Council.

JAMES MURPHY,
WILLIAM RADFORD,
MINER C. STORY.

CITY AND COUNTY OF NEW YORK, ss.:—We, James Murphy, William Radford, and Miner C. Story the grantees in the foregoing resolutions do hereby certify as therein required that the said resolutions, and the conditions and provisions therein specified, contain the agreement between us and the Mayor, Aldermen and Commonalty of the city of New York, in relation to the right, privilege and grant made and conferred upon us and our associates and assigns, by said Mayor, Aldermen and Commonalty, in and by the same.

In witness whereof, we have hereunto subscribed our names at the city of New York, the thirtieth day of December, one thousand eight hundred and fifty-three.

JAMES MURPHY,
WILLIAM RADFORD
MINER C. STORY.

In the presence of
JOHN B. HASKIN.

Resolved, That Messrs. Story, Radford & Murphy, their associates and assigns, to whom was granted the right in 1853 to build a railroad in Ninth avenue, Gansevoort, Washington and Greenwich streets and Battery place, be and are hereby directed to proceed, immediately upon the removal of the injunction issued against them by the Supreme Court by which they have been prevented from completing their road, with the construction of said road and complete the same from Fifty-first street to Battery place within six months thereafter, in the manner set forth in said grant.

Resolved, That, until the said injunction be removed, the said grantees be directed to place and run cars upon such portion of said road as is completed and not affected by the said injunction, thereby granting to the public all the accommodation that the circumstances will allow, the said grantees being permitted, in consideration therefor, to make a charge of five cents as fare for each passenger carried by them over such portions of their road.

Adopted by the Board of Councilmen, April 29, 1858.

Adopted by the Board of Aldermen, May 13, 1858.

Approved by the Mayor, May 24, 1858.

Resolved, That the Street Commissioner be, and he is hereby, authorized and directed, forthwith, to cause the rails of the Ninth Avenue Railroad Company now laid at the intersection of Washington and Bethune streets, to be taken up, the bridges removed, the filth taken away, and the intersections repaved in such a manner that the surface water and filth will flow towards the North River without obstruction, and that the expense thereof be charged to the Ninth Avenue Railroad Company.

Adopted by the Board of Aldermen, Oct. 7, 1858.

Adopted by the Board of Councilmen, Oct. 11, 1858.

Approved by the Mayor, Oct. 21, 1858.

Whereas, The Corporation of the city of New York granted to James Murphy and others the right and privilege of constructing and operating a railroad in Ninth avenue and other streets, and inasmuch as the grantees have laid the rails of their said railroad from Fifty-fourth street to Canal street but have been prevented by legal difficulties, interposed by property-owners below Canal street, from completing their railroad, and

Whereas, The necessary accommodation of the public requires that the said grantees should be allowed an outlet or terminus for their road in the southern business portion of the city, and that they should be compelled to put their railroad into active operation ; therefore be it

Resolved, That James Murphy and others, the owners of the said railroad grant or license, and their assigns, are hereby authorized and directed to connect their railroad track with the tracks of the Hudson River Railroad and Sixth and Eighth Avenue Railroad Companies, in and below Canal street, and run their cars upon any portion of the tracks of the said other railroads, in and below Canal street, and to charge the rate of fare provided in their said grant or license.

Adopted by the Board of Councilmen, June 24, 1859.

Adopted by the Board of Aldermen, June 27, 1859.

Approved by the Mayor, July 2, 1859.

AN ORDINANCE

IN RELATION TO THE PAVEMENT WITHIN THE TRACKS OF THE EIGHTH AND NINTH AVENUE RAILROADS.

Be it ordained by the Mayor, Aldermen, and Commonalty of the City of New York, in Common Council convened:

§ 1. The Eighth Avenue Railroad Company and the Ninth Avenue Railroad Company are hereby authorized to pave all the space within the outside rails of their respective tracks with small cobble-stone, and are hereby further required to keep the said space in repair and good traveling condition.

§ 2. All resolutions, ordinances or parts thereof, so far as they conflict herewith, are hereby repealed.

§ 3. This ordinance shall take effect immediately.

Adopted by the Board of Councilmen, September 8, 1859.

Adopted by the Board of Aldermen, September 8, 1859.

Approved by the Mayor, September 10, 1859.

Resolved, That the Eighth Avenue Railroad Company and the Ninth Avenue Railroad Company be and are hereby authorized and permitted, in hereafter relaying their track and in extending the same, to lay down and use the " Hewitt Bridge Patent Rail, ' or such other form of rail, as may be approved of by the Street Commissioner.

Resolved, That permission is hereby granted to the Ninth

Avenue Railroad Company to lay a track from the Ninth Avenue Railroad track at Greenwich street, through Canal street, to connect with the Eighth Avenue Railroad track at Hudson street, and also to lay a track from the Ninth avenue, through Fifty-fourth street, to connect with the Eighth Avenue Railroad; and that the Eighth and Ninth Avenue Railroad Companies are hereby permitted to agree to run their cars over each other's tracks during such times as they may be respectively relaying and repairing their tracks.

Adopted by the Board of Councilmen, September 8, 1859.

Adopted by the Board of Aldermen, September 19, 1859.

Approved by the Mayor, October 3, 1859.

Resolved, That the Ninth Avenue Railroad Company is hereby authorized and directed to pave the sidewalks on the streets in front of their depot buildings, car houses, stables and work shops with Belgian pavement, and to keep such pavement, at all times hereafter, in good repair.

Adopted by the Board of Councilmen, November 14, 1859.

Adopted by the Board of Aldermen, December 31, 1859.

Approved by the Mayor, December 31, 1859.

HUDSON RIVER RAILROAD.

AN ORDINANCE.

The Mayor, Aldermen and Commonalty of the City of New York, in Common Council convened, do ordain as follows:

SECTION 1. Permission is hereby granted to the Hudson River Railroad Company to construct a double track of rails, with suitable turn-outs, along the line of the Hudson River, from Spuyten Devil Creek to near 68th street; occupying so much of the 12th avenue as lies along the shore, thence winding from the shore so as to intersect the 11th avenue at or near 60th street; thence through the middle of the 11th avenue to about 32d street; thence on a curve across to the 10th avenue, intersecting the 10th avenue at or near 30th street; thence through the middle of the 10th avenue to West street, and thence through the middle of West street to Canal street.

§ 2. The said Hudson River Railroad Company shall grade, pave, and keep in repair a space 25 feet in width, in and about the tracks, in all the avenues and streets through which the said track or tracks shall be laid, whenever the Common Council shall deem the interest of the public to require such pavement to be done. The said Company shall lay such rail track through the avenues and streets in conformity to such directions as to line and grade as shall be given by the Street Commissioner, and shall conform their said railroad to the grades of the avenues and streets through which it shall extend or cross, as shall be, from time to time, established by the Common Council, if the latter so require; and shall lay their rails or tracks in the streets or avenues in such manner as to cause no unnecessary impediment to the common or ordinary use of the street for all other purposes, and so as to leave all the water courses free and unobstructed. It shall be especially incumbent on the said Hudson River Railroad Company, at their own cost, to construct stone bridges across such of the streets intersected by the railroad as may, by the elevation of their grades above the surface of the said road, require to be arched or bridged, whenever, in the opinion of the Common Council, the same shall be necessary for public convenience; and also to make such embankments or excavations, as the Common Council may deem necessary to render the passage over the railroad and embarkments at the cross streets easy and convenient for all the purposes for which streets and roads are usually put to, and the said Company shall also make, at their own cost and charge, all such drains and sewers as their embankments or excavations may, in the opinion of the Common Council, render necessary; and said Company shall be at all times subject to such regulations, with reference to the convenience of public travel through such streets and avenues as are affected by the said railroad, as the Common Council shall, from time to time by resolution or ordinance, direct; and the Corporation hereby reserves the right to require said Company, at any time after the 11th avenue shall be made to 14th street, to take up their rails in the 10th avenue and lay them in the 11th avenue to said 14th street, and through 14th street to connect with West street.

§ 3. The said Company shall, within one year from the passage of this ordinance, and before entering upon any contracts for grading, file in the office of the Street Commissioner a map showing the location and intended grade of said railroad.

§ 4. Permission is hereby granted to the Hudson River Railroad Company to run their locomotives as far south as 30th street, and no further.

§ 5. The said Hudson Railroad Company shall be and are hereby prohibited from running a stated train between any points below 32d street for the carrying of passengers between those points, under the penalty of $25 for each passenger from whom fare shall be received therefor.

§ 6. This ordinance shall not be construed as binding upon the Corporation, nor shall it go into effect until the said Hudson River Railroad Company shall first duly execute, under their corporate seal, such an instrument in writing, covenanting and engaging, on their part and behalf, to stand to, abide by and perform all such conditions and requirements contained in the 2d and 3d sections of the ordinance, as the Mayor and the Counsel to the Corporation shall by their certificate approve, and not until such instrument shall be filed, so certified, in the office of the Comptroller of this city.

Adopted by the Board of Aldermen, April 30, 1847.

Adopted by the Board of Assistants, May 3, 1847.

Approved by the Mayor, May 6, 1847.

To ALL TO WHOM THESE PRESENTS SHALL COME, GREETING:

Whereas, The Mayor, Aldermen and Commonalty of the city of New York, by an ordinance approved on the sixth day of May, A. D. 1847, gave consent to the Hudson River Railroad Company to commence in the city of New York and construct therein a double track of rails, with suitable turnouts along the line therein mentioned, from Canal street to the Spuytenduyvel Creek, and did, in and by said ordinance, assent to the location by the directors of said company of said railroad on and over the streets and avenues mentioned in said ordinance and crossed by said line ; and

Whereas, Pursuant to said ordinances and the acts incorporating said company and amendatory thereof, the said directors have located the said railroad in the city of New York, according to the map prepared to be filed herewith, showing the location and intended grade of the Hudson River Railroad in the city of New York,

Now, know ye that the said the Hudson River Railroad Company, for themselves and their successors, do hereby, in the consideration of the premises, covenant and engage, to and with the Mayor, Aldermen and Commonalty of the city of New York, and their successors forever, to grade, regulate, pave and keep in repair a space twenty-five feet in width, in and about the tracks in all the avenues an ' streets through which the said track or tracks shall be laid, whenever the Common Council shall deem the interest of the public to require such pavement to be done.

And, that the said company will lay such rail track

through the avenues and streets in conformity to such direction, as to line and grade, as shall be given by the Street Commissioner, and shall conform their said railroad to the grades of the avenues and streets through which it shall extend or which it shall cross, as shall be, from time to time, established by the Common Council, if the latter so require.

And that said company will lay their rails, or tracks, in the streets or avenues in such manner as to cause no unnecessary impediment to the common and ordinary use of the streets for all other purposes, and so as to leave all the water courses free and unobstructed.

And further, that said company will at their own cost construct stone bridges across such of the streets, intersected by the said railroad, as may, by the elevation of their grades above the surface of said road, require to be arched or bridged, whenever, in the opinion of the Common Council, the same shall be necessary for public convenience.

And also, that the said company will make such embankments or excavations as the Common Council may deem necessary, to render the passage over the said railroad and embankments at the cross-streets easy and convenient for all purposes to which streets and roads are usually put.

And, that the said company will also make, at their own cost and charge, all such drains and sewers as their embankments or excavations may, in the opinion of the Common Council, render necessary.

And will at all times be subject to such regulations, with

reference to the convenience of public travel through such streets and avenues, as are affected by said railroad, as the Common Council shall, from time to time, by resolution or ordinance direct.

And further, that, if thereto required by the Corporation at any time after the Eleventh avenue shall be made to Fourteenth street, the said Company will take up their rails in the Tenth avenue and lay them in the Eleventh avenue to said Fourteenth street, and through Fourteenth street to connect with West street.

And, that the said company will, within one year from the passage of the said ordinance, and before entering upon any contracts for grading, file, in the office of the Street Commissioner, a map showing the location and intended grade of said railroad.

And, lastly, that said Company will stand to, abide by and perform, all and singular, the conditions and requirements contained in the second and third sections of the said ordinance.

In witness whereof, the said the Hudson River Railroad Company have hereunto affixed the corporate seal this 12th day of August, A. D. 1847.

WM. CHAMBERLAIN, [L. S.]
President.

I, William V. Brady, Mayor of the City of New York, do hereby certify that I approve of the preceding covenant as being in compliance with the ordinance of the Corporation approved May 6, 1847, referred to in said covenant.

WM. V. BRADY,
Mayor.

I, Willis Hall, Counsel to the Corporation of the city of New York, do hereby certify that I approve of the preceding covenant, as being in compliance with the ordinance referred to in the above certificate.

WILLIS HALL,
Counsel of Corporation.

City and County of New York: On this nineteenth day of August, A. D. 1847, before me personally appeared William Chamberlain, known to me to be the President of the Hudson River Railroad Company, and, being by me duly sworn, did depose and say that he resides in the city of New York, that the seal thereto affixed is the seal of the said company, and that the same was so affixed by their authority.

JOSEPH STRONG,
Commissioner of Deeds.

Resolved, That the Hudson River Railroad Company be authorized to lay down a double track of rails, with suitable curves and turn-out, from the northerly line of Canal street, at West street, through Canal and Hudson streets to Chambers street, under the direction of the Street Commissioner, and subject to all the restrictions, obligations, provisions and conditions of the ordinance authorizing said Company to lay down rails to Canal street.

Adopted by the Board of Aldermen, Aug. 1, 1849.

Adopted by the Board of Assistants, Sept. 24, 1849.

Approved by the Mayor, Sept. 25, 1849.

Resolved, That the Hudson River Railroad Company may extend one of their tracks around the country market (leased to them at foot of Canal street), with suitable curves and turn-outs, under the direction of the Street Commissioner, so as to connect with the track on West and Canal streets already constructed by them, subject to all the terms, conditions and restrictions of the annexed resolution passed and approved as stated below. (See resolution approved Sept. 25, 1849.)

Adopted by the Board of Aldermen, Dec. 24, 1849.

Adopted by the Board of Assistants, Dec. 28, 1849.

Approved by the Mayor, Jan. 7 (10 A. M.), 1850.

Resolved, That the market-house, and block of ground on which it stands, bounded by Washington and West streets, and Canal and Hoboken streets, be leased to the Hudson River Railroad Company for a passenger depot, for the term of ten years from the 1st of May, 1849, at the rent of $2,000 per annum, payable quarterly, subject to renewal for a further term of ten years at a rent to be determined by two appraisers mutually chosen, with power to select a third in case they cannot agree ; said appraisers to be duly sworn before entering upon their duties.

Adopted by the Board of Assistants, April 23, 1849.

Adopted by the Board of Aldermen, April 30, 1849.

Approved by the Mayor, May 3, 1849.

Resolved, That the Hudson River Railroad Company have permission to run their dumb engine to Chambers street, to test its power and probable safety for conducting their cars to Chambers street, under the direction of the Street Commissioner.

Adopted by the Board of Aldermen, July 6, 1850.

Adopted by the Board of Assistants, July 8, 1850

Approved by the Mayor, July 9, 1850.

Resolved, That the Hudson River Railroad Company be directed to build a substantial addition to the pier at Manhattanville, foot of 130th street, North River, by extending the same into the river for a distance equivalent to the portion of said pier cut off between the railway and the shore (the same being in length about 215 feet), the addition to consist of blocks and bridges, under such directions as shall be given by the Street Commissioner, and the work to be commenced on or before the 1st day of April, 1851, and completed within three months thereafter. And in case the Hudson River Railroad Company shall neglect to comply with this resolution and commence to build and complete the said pier at or before the periods herein mentioned, that then the said addition shall be built by the Street Commissioner, and legal measures taken by the Counsel to the Corporation to compel payment, by the Hudson River Railroad Company, of the expenses incurred : and the sum of $8,000 is hereby authorized to be taken from the appropriation for Docks and Slips, to carry this resolution into effect.

Resolved, That the Street Commissioner be directed to notify the Hudson River Railroad Company of the passage of the foregoing resolution.

Adopted by the Board of Assistants January 22, 1851.

Adopted by the Board of Aldermen, January 30, 1851.

Approved by the Mayor, February 10, 1851.

Resolved, That the Comptroller be and he is hereby directed to prepare and cause to be executed to the Hudson River Railroad Company, a lease of the piece of ground described in the annexed map, and bounded by 12th, Washington, Gansevoort, West street and Tenth avenue, for a term of fifteen years from the 1st of May, 1851, at a rent of $6,192 per annum, payable quarterly, subject, however, to the present existing leases to F. Depeyster, Foster & Van Nostrand, Patrick Noonan, and Edward W. Phelps; said lease to contain a covenant for two renewals for 15 years each, at a rent to be fixed by appraisement at the expiration of each term; also a covenant that the said Company pay all taxes imposed on said property during said terms; and also all assessments, ordinary or extraordinary, except the assessment that may be imposed for the continuation of Washington to 12th street; said ground to be occupied exclusively by said Company as a depot and other purposes connected with the said road.

Adopted by the Board of Aldermen, May 30, 1851.

Adopted by the Board of Assistants, June 2, 1851.

Approved by the Mayor, June 4, 1851.

Resolved, That the offer of the Hudson River Railroad Company, contained in the annexed petition, be accepted, and that the said sum of ten thousand dollars be paid by said Company on the contract for the bulkhead between the present pier, at 130th street, to the north line of 131st street, and upon said Company releasing all right to land under water conveyed to them by Schiefflin & Lawrence, south of the north line of 131st street, and upon such release being executed the Corporation to release the Company from the covenants in the grants to Schiefflin & Lawrence relating to the land so released.

Resolved, That the Street Commissioner be directed to proceed and build a bulkhead from the pier at the foot of 130th street to the north line of 131st street, on the North River, and a pier at the foot of 131st street, and that said Street Commissioner proceed forthwith to build and erect the same; and that the said sum of ten thousand dollars, to be received from the Hudson River Railroad Company, be appropriated and applied for that purpose; said bulkhead and pier to be completed within one year.

Resolved That a grant, confirming to said Railroad Company their roadway as now constructed, 78 feet in width, between 130th and 132d streets, and according to the map filed with the Clerk of the Common Council, and release the said Company from all claim upon them for building or extending any pier or bulkhead opposite the premises in question.

Resolved, That the resolution approved by the Mayor January 5, 1850, leasing to Francis R. Tillou the dock at the foot of 130th street for a public ferry, at the rent of $50 per annum, be repealed.

Adopted by the Board of Aldermen, June 4, 1851.

Adopted by the Board of Assistants, June 4, 1851.

Approved by the Mayor, June 5, 1851.

Resolved, That the Hudson River Railroad Company be,

and they are hereby, directed to take up their rails on the Tenth avenue, from Thirtieth street, fifty feet south, and relay them in a direct line until they reach Thirtieth street, before they commence making their curve towards the Eleventh avenue.

Adopted by the Board of Aldermen, May 29, 1851.

Adopted by the Board of Assistants, June 2, 1851.

Received from his Honor the Mayor, August 8, 1851, without his approval or objections thereto; therefore, under the provisions of the amended charter, the same became adopted.

Resolved, That the Hudson River Railroad Company be directed to take up their rails, and relay them so that at the southwest corner of Tenth avenue and Thirtieth street they shall be distant from the angle of the curb at least twelve feet.

Adopted by the Board of Assistants, August 6, 1851.

Adopted by the Board of Aldermen, August 7, 1851.

Approved by the Mayor, August 11, 1851

Whereas, By certain resolutions of the Common Council, approved by the Mayor, June 5, 1851, certain claims, existing between the Corporation and the Hudson River Railroad Company, in relation to the dock, &c., at Manhattanville were adjusted, by which adjustment the said Company were to pay $10,000, and assign certain water grants, owned by them, to the City; and whereas, said Company, on account of their large expenditure at the present time consequent upon the completion of their road, desire to substitute a bond of the Company, payable at a future day, with interest thereon, in lieu of the present payment of the said amount, therefore

Resolved, That the Comptroller be and he is hereby authorized to receive a bond of the Hudson River Railroad Company for $10,000, with interest, at six per cent. per annum, payable quarterly, and the principal sum payable in five years, in lieu of the present payment of said $10,000, as provided for in said resolutions.

Adopted by the Board of Aldermen, Nov. 11, 1851.

Adopted by the Board of Assistants, Nov. 17, 1851.

Approved by the Mayor, November 19, 1851.

Resolved, That the Hudson River Railroad Company be required to take up the present rails in Hudson street, as also in Canal and West streets, and put down a grooved rail, similar to the one in Park row put down by the Harlem Railroad Company, and that the Hudson River Railroad Company be required to complete the same in eight months from the passage of this resolution; and in case of their failing to comply herein, then the Street Commissioner be, and he is hereby required to take up the rails of said track, from Chambers to Thirty-first street, and repair said street in like manner as previous to the occupancy of said street by said Railroad Company.

Adopted by the Board of Assistants, Oct. 26, 1852.

Adopted by the Board of Aldermen, Nov. 8, 1852.

Received from his Honor the Mayor, December 4, 1852, without his approval or objection thereto; therefore, under the provisions of the amended charter, the same became adopted.

Resolved, That permission be, and is hereby, given to the Hudson River Railroad Company to lay grooved rails for a track on Pier No. 48, North River, foot of Clarkson street, for and during the continuance of the lease of said pier, the said track to connect with their railroad in West street.

Adopted by the Board of Aldermen, Dec. 27, 1853.

Adopted by the Board of Assistants, Dec. 29, 1852.

Approved by the Mayor December 30, 1852.

Resolved, That the Street Commissioner be, and he is hereby directed to notify the Hudson River Railroad Company to remove, and hereafter to refrain from standing the cars of their Company in Hudson street; and, further, if said Company refuse to comply therein, then the Street Commissioner is hereby directed to remove the same in accordance with the ordinances of the Corporation.

Adopted by the Board of Councilmen, March 13, 1854.

Adopted by the Board of Aldermen, June 10, 1854.

Approved by the Mayor, July 13, 1854.

Resolved, That the Hudson River Railroad Company be directed to cause Hudson street, from Canal to Chambers street, to be repaired, according to the terms of their grant.

Adopted by the Board of Councilmen, January 19, 1855.

Adopted by the Board of Aldermen, February 11, 1855

Approved by the Mayor, February 16, 1855.

Resolved, That the Hudson River Railroad Company be, and are hereby notified to fill in the low grounds adjoining their property, between 12th avenue and Hudson River, and 130th and 131st streets; and that unless the said Company forthwith comply with this resolution, that the Street Commissioner be, and is hereby directed to cause a notice to be sent to said Railroad Company, to the effect that, in their default, for one month after notice, he will cause the said filling to be done at the expense of said Railroad Company.

Adopted by the Board of Councilmen, October 22, 1855.

Adopted by the Board of Aldermen, August 11, 1856.

Approved by the Mayor, August 13, 1856.

The President of the Croton Aqueduct Board directed to notify the Hudson River Railroad Company to put in good repair, forthwith, all the pavements in and about their rails, and, in case of neglect or refusal, to have the same done at the expense of the Hudson River Railroad Company.

Adopted by the Board of Aldermen, September 10, 1857.

Adopted by the Board of Councilmen, September 14, 1857.

Approved by the Mayor, September 16, 1857.

Resolved, That the Hudson River Railroad Company be, and are hereby required to remove the present high rail in use upon their road, from the corner of Chambers street and West Broadway up to 53d street, and to lay down in the stead thereof the rail known as the grooved rail, and that the same be done within six months from the passage of this resolution by the Common Council.

Resolved, That the Hudson River Railroad Company be, and they are hereby, authorized and directed to place upon their road city passenger or small cars, to be run between the depot at Chambers street and 53d street; to take up and set down city passengers between those points; to be governed by the general rules regulating the Eighth Avenue Railroad; and, further, that they run a car thereon each and every day, both ways, as often as every 15 minutes from 5 to 6 o'clock, A. M., and every 5 minutes from 6 o'clock, A. M., to 8 o'clock, P. M.; every 15 minutes from 8 o'clock, P. M., to 12 o'clock, P. M., and every 30 minutes from 12 o'clock, P. M., to 5 o'clock, A. M., and as much oftener as public convenience may require, under the regulations of the Common Council; and that the said Company shall have the right to demand and receive from each passenger conveyed in said cars the sum of five (5) cents, and no more. The aforesaid cars to be placed and run upon said road within six months from the passage of this resolution by the Common Council. It being a special permission and understanding in making this grant to the Hudson River Railroad Company, that the said Company shall not, at any time, either directly or indirectly, in any way alienate from themselves, as a Company, or in any manner dispose of the right to run small cars upon their said road, hereby granted, unless by consent of the Common Council, under the penalty of the forfeiture of this grant immediately thereupon.

Resolved, That the Hudson River Railroad Company be, and they are hereby directed to cease the running of locomotives or steam engines below Fifty-third street immediately upon the small cars being placed upon their road, in accordance with the foregoing resolution.

Adopted by the Board of Aldermen, November 22, 1858.

Adopted by the Board of Councilmen, December 2, 1858.

Approved by the Mayor, December 13, 1858.

Resolved, That the Hudson River Railroad Company be, and they are hereby directed to have the grade of their railroad conform to the grade of Eleventh avenue, as heretofore put under contract, in order that the grading of said avenue may be completed, under the direction of the Street Commissioner.

Adopted by the Board of Councilmen, April 11th, 1859.

Adopted by the Board of Aldermen, June 30th, 1859.

Approved by the Mayor, July 2d, 1859.

Resolved, That at the expiration of the lease now held by the Hudson River Railroad Company, of the building on the plot of ground bounded by Canal, West and Hoboken streets, the said building be removed, under the direction of the Street Commissioner, and that the vacant space be appropriated as a country market.

Adopted by the Board of Aldermen, Dec. 19, 1859.

Adopted by the Board of Councilmen, Dec. 31, 1859.

Approved by the Mayor, Dec. 31, 1859.

RAILROAD IN FORTY-SECOND STREET.

Resolved, That permission be, and is hereby given to A. M. Allerton, Jr. and Company, to lay a track for a railroad on 42d street, to connect with the Hudson River Railroad at the 11th avenue and to extend to the Hudson River, to be used to convey stock, such as cattle, sheep and hogs; the said track to remain during the pleasure of the Common Council, the Common Council to give 60 days' notice for its removal.

Adopted by the Board of Councilmen, Dec. 20, 1858.

Adopted by the Board of Aldermen, Dec. 30, 1858.

Approved by the Mayor, Jan. 8, 1859.

ORDINANCES

AFFECTING THE

CITY RAILROADS,

OR

GENERAL IN THEIR APPLICATION.

AN ORDINANCE.

Be it ordained by the Mayor, Aldermen, and Commonalty of the City of New York, in Common Council convened:

That the grantees of all railroads within the city, their associates and successors, shall, in the construction, alteration and repairs of such railroads, at all times, furnish such new work, make such additions, and do all such repairs to man-hole heads and covers, receiving-basins, and stop-cocks and covers, and generally of all fixtures connected with sewers and the distribution of Croton Water, as may, in the process of laying down such rail tracks, be affected thereby; such additions, alterations and repairs to be done under the direction of, and to the satisfaction of the Croton Aqueduct Department, and that in no case shall such rail tracks be laid over the line of Croton water mains, stop-cocks or sewer man-holes.

Adopted by the Board of Aldermen, April 25, 1853.

Adopted by the Board of Assistants, May 13, 1853.

Approved by the Mayor, May 16, 1853.

Resolved, That the Common Council of the city of New York disapprove of the Legislature passing any law granting the privilege of railroads in the city of New York.

Resolved, That the above resolution be duly authenticated, and immediately sent to the Board of Councilmen, and if approved, that it be sent to the Legislature, through some of our Senators or Representatives, for their action.

Adopted by the Board of Aldermen, April 5, 1854.

Adopted by the Board of Councilmen, April 5, 1854.

Approved by the Mayor, April 6, 1854.

Resolved, That the President of the Croton Aqueduct Board be, and he is hereby, instructed to notify the several Railroad Companies to put in good repair, forthwith, all the pavements in and about their rails, in accordance with their agreements; and in case all or any of said Companies (viz., the Harlem, Hudson, Sixth, Eighth, Second, and Third Avenue Railroad Companies) refuse or neglect to comply with said notice, that the said President of the Croton Aqueduct Board cause the same to be done at the expense of the companies interested.

Adopted by the Board of Aldermen, Sept. 10, 1857.

Adopted by the Board of Councilmen, Sept. 14, 1857.

Approved by the Mayor, Sept. 16, 1857.

Resolved, That the Croton Aqueduct Board be, and they are hereby instructed to notify the several railroad companies, to wit: The New York and Harlem, Hudson River, Sixth Avenue, Eighth Avenue, Second Avenue, and Third Avenue Railroad Companies to put in good repair, within twenty days from the date of the service of a notice from said Board to that effect, all the pavements in and about their respective rail tracks, in accordance with the terms and conditions of their several grants from and agreements with the Mayor, Aldermen and Commonalty of this city, and in case said Companies, or either of them, shall neglect or refuse so to do, that said Board shall be, and they are hereby authorized and directed to cause the same to be done at the expense of the company or companies so neglecting or refusing to comply with said notice, and the expense incurred by said Board in so doing shall be certified to by them, and placed in the hands of the Corporation Counsel for immediate collection by process of law; and that the sum of $5,000 be, and it is hereby specially appropriated for the purpose of enabling said Board to carry this resolution into immediate effect.

Adopted by the Board of Councilmen, April 26, 1858.

Adopted by the Board of Aldermen, May 10, 1858.

Approved by the Mayor, May 11, 1858.

AN ORDINANCE

FOR THE LICENSING OF CITY RAILROAD PASSENGER CARS

The Mayor, Aldermen and Commonalty of the City of New York, in Common Council convened, do ordain as follows:

SECTION 1. Each and every passenger railroad car running in the city of New York below One Hundred and

Twenty-fifth street, shall pay into the city treasury the sum of 50 dollars, annually, for a license, a certificate of such payment to be procured from the Mayor, except the small one-horse passenger cars, which shall each pay the sum of 25 dollars, annually, for said license, as aforesaid.

§ 2. Each certificate of payment of license shall be affixed to some conspicuous place in the car, that it may be inspected by the proper officers.

§ 3. For every passenger car run upon any of the city railroads below One Hundred and Twenty-fifth street without the proper certificate of license, the proprietor or proprietors thereof shall be subject to a penalty of 50 dollars, to be recovered by the Corporation Attorney, as in the case of other penalties, and for the benefit of the city treasury.

§ 4. This ordinance shall go into effect immediately.

Adopted by the Board of Councilmen, Dec. 13, 1858.

Adopted by the Board of Aldermen, Dec. 22, 1858.

Approved by the Mayor, Dec. 31, 1858.

A message having been received from his Honor the Acting Mayor, in relation to sundry proposed railroad charters about to be granted by the Legislature, the following resolution was adopted:

Resolved, That the Counsel to the Corporation be, and he is hereby authorized and directed immediately to take all proper legal measures to restrain and prevent the use or occupation of any street, public place or highway in the city of New York, by any person or persons, company or com panies, corporation or corporations, claiming by any act or acts of the Legislature of this State, at its recent or any previous session, the right, exclusive or otherwise, of laying rails and running cars thereon in any such street, public place or highway in the said city of New York, without the consent of the Mayor, Aldermen and Commonalty of the said city being first had and obtained.

Adopted by the Board of Aldermen, April 20, 1860.

Adopted by the Board of Councilmen, April 20, 1860.

Approved by the Mayor, April 20, 1860.

STATE LAWS

RELATIVE TO THE

CITY RAILROADS.

AN ACT *relative to the construction of Railroads in Cities.*

Passed April 4, 1854.

The People of the State of New York, represented in Senate and Assembly, do enact as follows:

SECTION 1. The Common Councils of the several cities of this State shall not, hereafter, permit to be constructed, on either of the streets or avenues of said city, a railroad for the transportation of passengers, which commences and ends in said city, without the consent thereto of a majority in interest of the owners of property upon the streets in which said railroad is to be constructed, being first had and obtained. For the purpose of determining what constitutes said majority in interest, reference shall be had to the assessed value of the whole located upon such street or avenue.

§ 2. After such consent is obtained, it shall be lawful for the Common Council of the city, in which such street or avenue is located, to grant authority to construct and establish such railroad upon such terms, conditions and stipulations, in relation thereto, as such Common Council may see fit to prescribe. But no such grants shall be made except to such person or persons as shall give adequate security to comply in all respects with the terms, conditions, and stipulations, so to be prescribed by such Common Council, and will agree to carry and convey passengers upon such railroad at the lowest rates of fare. Nor shall such grants be made until after public notices of intention to make the same, and of the terms, conditions and stipulations, upon which it will be given, and inviting proposals therefor at a specified time and place, shall be published, under the direction of the Common Council, in one or more of the principal newspapers published in the city in which said railroad is proposed to be authorized and constructed.

§ 3. This act shall not be held to prevent the construction, extension or use of any railroad in any of the cities of this State which have already been constructed in part; but the respective parties and companies by whom such roads have been in part constructed, and their assigns, are hereby authorized to construct, complete, extend and use such roads, in and through the streets and avenues designated in the respective grants, licenses, resolutions or contracts, under which the same have been so in part constructed, and to that end the grants, licenses and resolutions aforesaid are hereby confirmed.

§ 4. This act shall take effect immediately.

CHAPTER 373.

AN ACT *in relation to the Second Avenue Railroad Company, of the city of New York.*

Passed April 12, 1855.

The People of the State of New York, represented in Senate and Assembly, do enact as follows:

§ 1. The Second Avenue Railroad Company of the city of New York, are hereby authorized to construct a bridge for the use of their road across the Harlem River, at and from the termination of the Second avenue in said city.

§ 2.   *   *   *   *   *   *   *

§ 3. The said bridge across the Harlem River shall be constructed with a draw of not less than sixty feet in width, in the clear, and with piers not less than sixty feet apart.   *   *   *   *

§ 4. The said bridges shall be constructed and maintained by said company, in such manner as not to unnecessarily impede or obstruct the navigation of said rivers.

§ 5. Said company shall keep some competent person stationed at each of the several draw-bridges constructed by them over said rivers, whose duty it shall be to swing the draws whenever any vessel is approaching and about to pass either of said bridges.

§ 6.   *   *   *   *   *   *   *

§ 7. This act shall take effect immediately.

CHAPTER 10.

AN ACT *relative to Railroads in the City of New York.*

Passed January 30th, 1860.

The People of the State of New York, represented in Senate and Assembly, do enact as follows :

§ 1. It shall not be lawful hereafter to lay, construct or operate any railroad in, upon or along any or either of the streets or avenues of the city of New York, wherever such railroad may commence, or end, except under the authority and subject to the regulations and restrictions which the Legislature may hereafter grant and provide. This section shall not be deemed to affect the operation, as far as laid, of any railroad now constructed and duly authorized. Nor shall it be held to impair in any manner any valid grant for or relating to any railroad in said city existing on the first day of January, eighteen hundred and sixty.

§ 2. All acts and parts of acts inconsistent with this act are hereby repealed.

§ 3. This act shall take effect immediately.

[NOTE.—The following five grants for railroads in the city of New York were passed by the last State Legislature, but have not, as yet, been acknowledged nor confirmed by the Common Council of the city.]

CHAPTER 511.

AN ACT *to authorize the construction of a railroad track on South, West, and certain other streets in the city of New York.*

Passed April 17, 1860; notwithstanding the objections of the Governor.

The People of the State of New York, represented in Senate and Assembly, do enact as follows:

SECTION 1. Charles W. Durant, Myron S. Clark, John Butler, Jr., Henry Rigley, Orson H. Sheldon, Warren E. Russel, Robert B. Van Valkenburgh, John Myers, John De La Montagnie, William R. Stewart, James S. Leach, James S. Sluyter, John A. Cooke, James C. Kennedy, Thomas C. Durant, Benjamin F. Bruce, Edward R. Phelps, Augustus L. Brown, and their assigns, are hereby authorized to lay, construct, operate, and use a railroad, with a double or single track, as hereinafter provided, and to convey passengers and freight thereon for compensation, through, upon, and along the following streets and avenues, route, or routes, in the city of New York, viz.: To commence at the intersection of Tenth avenue and Fifty-ninth street; thence through and along Tenth avenue, with a double track, into West Twelfth street; thence through and along West Twelfth street, with a single track, to Greenwich street; thence, from West Twelfth street, through and along both West and Greenwich streets, southerly, with a single or double track upon each of said streets, to Battery place; thence through and along Battery place to State street, with double track; thence through and along State street, with single track, to Whitehall street; thence through and along Whitehall street, with double track, to South Ferry; returning through and along Whitehall street, with single track, from its intersection with State street, to Bowling Green; thence along the southerly side of Bowling Green, with single track, to connect with the double track in Battery place, with the right to construct, maintain, and use a double track, from West street, through and along Chambers street, to its intersection with Hudson street; also from the intersection of Tenth avenue and Fifty-ninth street, with double track, through and along Fifty-ninth street, to First avenue; thence through and along First avenue, with double track, to Twenty-third street; thence through and along Twenty-third street, with double track, to avenue A; thence through and along avenue A, with double track, to Fourteenth street; thence through and along Fourteenth street, with double track, to avenue D; thence through and along avenue D, with double track, to Houston street; thence through and along Houston street, with double track, to Mangin street; thence through and along Mangin street, with single track, to Grand street: thence through and along Grand street to Corlears street, with single track; thence through Corlears street to South street, with single track; thence through and along South street to Montgomery street, with single track; thence through and along Montgomery street, with single track, to the junction of Front and South streets; thence through and along South street, with double track, to the junction of South and Front streets, at Roosevelt street; thence through and along South street to Old slip, with single track; thence through and along Old slip to Water street, with single track; thence through and along Water street to Whitehall street, with single track; thence through and along Whitehall street to South street, with double track; thence through and along South street to Coenties slip, with single track; thence through and along Coenties slip to Front street, with single track; and also with single track from Old slip, through and along Front street to Whitehall street; also a double track in Broad street, from Water street to South street; also through and along Houston street from its intersection with avenue D by the track already named, to Goerck street; thence through and along Goerck street to Grand street, with single track; thence through and along Grand street, with single track, to its intersection with Monroe street; thence through and along Monroe street to Jackson street, with single track; thence through and along Jackson street to Front street, with single track; thence through and along Front street, with single track, to its intersection with South street at Montgomery street; thence through and along South street, by the double track already named, to Front street, at the junction of South and Front streets, at Roosevelt street; thence through and along Front street to Old slip, and thence through and along Front street to Whitehall street, by the track already named; thence through and along Whitehall street, with single track, to South ferry, with the privilege of laying all necessary sidings, turnouts, connections, and switches for the proper working and accommodation of the said railroad, in any of the above-mentioned streets, and of connecting with, running on, or crossing all such other railroad tracks as may lie along or across any of said routes, streets, or avenues.

§ 2. Said railroad shall be constructed upon the most approved plan for the construction of city railroads, and the cars on the same shall run as often as the convenience of the public shall require, and shall be subject to such reasonable rules and regulations in respect thereto, in the transportation of passengers and freight in suitable cars, as the common council of the city of New York may, from time to time, by ordinance prescribe, and to the payment to the city of the same license fee annually, for each passenger car run thereon, as is now paid by other city railroads in said city; and no higher rate of fare shall be charged for the conveyance of passengers thereon than is now charged by the city railroads in said city, now chartered and constructed; and the said common council are hereby authorized and required to grant permission to the persons herein named, or their assigns, to construct, maintain, operate, and use said railroad in, upon, and along the several streets and avenues herein mentioned.

§ 3. In the construction, operation, and use of such railroad, should the said parties above named, or their assigns, deem it necessary or proper to run upon, intersect, or use any portion of any other railroad tracks now laid upon any of the streets or avenues above named, they are hereby authorized to run upon, intersect, and use the same; and in case they cannot agree with the owner or owners thereof respecting the compensation or payment to be made therefor, then the amount of such compensation or payment shall be ascertained and determined in the manner provided by subdivision six of the twenty-eighth section of the act entitled "An act to authorize the formation of rail road corporations and to regulate the same," passed April second, eighteen hundred and fifty ; and should any real estate or interest therein be required for the purpose of constructing said railroad on said route or routes, as above specified and authorized, for which the said persons above named, or their assigns, shall be unable to agree with the owner or owners for the use or purchase thereof, they may acquire the right to use, or title to the same, in the manner specified in the fourteenth, fifteenth, sixteenth, seventeenth, eighteenth, nineteenth, twentieth, and twenty-first sections of the said act of April second, eighteen hundred and fifty, except that, in any of the proceedings for any of the purposes authorized by this section, it shall not be necessary that the petition to the supreme court shall make any allegations of, or reference to any incorporation, capital, stock, surveys, or maps, or of the filing of any certificate of locations. But, in all cases, the use of said streets and avenues for the purposes of said railroad, as herein authorized, shall be considered one of the uses for which the mayor, aldermen, and commonalty of said city hold said streets and avenues.

§ 4. The mayor, common council, and the several officers of the corporation of the said city of New York, and the said corporation, are hereby prohibited from giving any assent to, or allowing any company claiming to derive authority, under the act entitled " An act to authorize the formation of railroad corporations and to regulate the same," passed April second, eighteen hundred and fifty, or act amendatory thereof, or in addition thereto, to construct any railroad in, or upon any or either of the said streets or avenues, and from doing any other act to hinder, delay, or obstruct the construction or operation of said rail road as herein authorized. And it is hereby made the duty of the said mayor, common council, and other officers, to do such acts, within their respective departments, as may be needful to promote the construction and protect the operation of the said railroad as provided in this law; any act or thing done in violation hereof shall be inoperative and void. All actions relating to, affecting, or arising under this act, or the authority herein given, shall be commenced in the supreme court of the first judicial district.

§ 5. All acts or parts of acts, inconsistent with the provision of this act, are hereby repealed, and declared to be inoperative so far as the same are applicable to this act.

§ 6. This act shall take effect immediately.

§ 7. The legislature may at any time modify, amend, or repeal this act.

CHAPTER 512.

AN ACT *to authorize the construction of a railroad in avenue D, East Broadway, and other streets and avenues of the City of New York.*

Passed April 17, 1860; notwithstanding the objections of the Governor.

The People of the State of New York, represented in Senate and Assembly, do enact as follows:

Section 1. John E. Devlin, William A. Hall, Cornelius Runkel, Bernard Smyth, Harry Clark, William A. Herring, William D. Marvin, John V. Coon, William P. Buckmaster, George L. Thomas, William N. Hays, James Murphy and their assigns, are hereby authorized to lay, construct, operate, and use a railroad with a double or single track, as hereinafter provided, and to convey passengers thereon for compensation, through, upon, and along the following streets and avenues, route or routes, in the city of New York, viz: Commencing on avenue D, at the northern extremity of the same; thence through and along avenue D with a double track to Eighth street; thence through and along Eighth street with a single track to Lewis street; thence through and along Lewis street with a single track to Grand street; thence through and along Grand street with a double track to East Broadway; thence through and along East Broadway, Chatham square, Chatham street, and Park row, with a double track to Broadway; also, from the corner of avenue D and Eighth street, through and along avenue D with a single track to Houston street; thence through and along Houston street with a single track to Goerck street; thence through and along Goerck street with a single track to connect with a double track in Grand street, hereinafter provided for; also connecting with the double track in East Broadway, through and along Canal street with a double track to the westerly side of Broadway; also connecting with the double track in Grand street at Lewis street, through and along Grand street with a double track to the Grand street ferry; also, commencing at the northern extremity of avenue B, through and along avenue B, with a double track, to Clinton street; thence through and along Clinton street, with a double track, to connect with the track in East Broadway; also connecting with the track in avenue B, through and along Tenth street and Eleventh street with single tracks to avenue D; also, connecting with the double track in Canal street at Broadway, with a single track across Broadway to Lispenard street; thence, with a single track, through and along Lispenard street, to and across West Broadway to Beach street; thence through and along Beach street, with a single track, to Washington street; thence through and along Washington street, with a single track, to Battery place; thence through and along Battery place, with a double track, to the Bowling Green at State street; also, connecting with the track in Battery place, through and along Greenwich street, with a double track, to the centre of Canal street; also, connecting with the track in Washington street at North Moore street, with a single track, through and along North Moore street and across West Broadway to Walker street, and thence through and along Walker street to, and to connect with, the double track in Canal street; also, connecting with the track in Washington street, through and along Washington street, with a single track, to the centre of Canal street; also, connecting with the double track in avenue D, through and along Fourteenth street, with a double track, to First avenue; thence through and along First avenue, with a double track, to Thirty-fourth street, thence through and along Thirty-fourth street, with a double track, to avenue A, and thence through and along avenue A, with a double track to, and to connect with, the double track in Fourteenth street, together with the necessary connections, turnouts, and switches for the proper working and accommodation of the road on the said route or routes.

§ 2. Said railroad shall be constructed on the most approved plan for the construction of city railroads, and shall be run as often as the convenience of passengers may require, and shall be subject to such reasonable rules and regulations in respect thereto as the common council of the city of New York may, from time to time, by ordinance prescribe; and to the payment to the city of the same license fee annually for each car run thereon, as is now paid by other city railroads in said city, and the said persons and their assigns are hereby authorized to charge the same rate of fare, for the conveyance of passengers on said railroad, as is now charged by other city railroads in said city.

§ 3. In the construction, operation, or use of such railroad, upon the route or routes above designated, should such persons above named, or their assigns, deem it necessary or proper to run upon, intersect, or use any portion of other railroad tracks now laid upon any of the streets or avenues above named, they are hereby authorized to run upon, intersect, and use the same, and in case they cannot agree with the owner or owners thereof respecting the compensation or payment to be made therefor, then the amount of such compensation or payment shall be ascertained and determined in the manner provided by subdivision six of the twenty-eighth section of the act entitled " An act to authorize the formation of railroad corporations, and to regulate the same," passed April second, eighteen hundred and fifty. And should any real estate or interest therein be required for the purpose of constructing said railroad on said route or routes, as above specified and authorized, for which the said persons above named, or their assigns, shall be unable to agree with the owner or owners for the use or purchase thereof, they may acquire the right to use, or title to the same, in the manner specified in the fourteenth, fifteenth, sixteenth, seventeenth, eighteenth, nineteenth, twentieth, and twenty-first sections of the said act of April second, eighteen hundred and fifty, except that, in any of the proceedings for any of the purposes authorized by this section, it shall not be necessary that the petition to the supreme court shall make any allegations of, or reference to any incorporation, capital stock, surveys, or maps, or of the filing of any certificate of location. But, in all cases, the use of said streets and avenues for the purposes of said railroad, as herein authorized, shall be considered a public use consistent with the uses for which the mayor, aldermen, and commonalty of said city hold said streets and avenues. The expense of constructing the tracks in Greenwich and Washington streets and Battery place, as herein provided, shall be borne equally by said persons or their assigns, and any company which is now or shall hereafter be authorized to construct tracks therein, and thereupon the said tracks shall be used in common by the said persons or their assigns and such company.

§ 4. The mayor, common council, and the several officers of the corporation of the said city of New York, and the said corporation are hereby prohibited from giving any assent to, or allowing any company claiming to derive authority under the act entitled "An act to authorize the formation of railroad corporations, and to regulate the same," passed April second, eighteen hundred and fifty, or act amendatory thereof, or in addition thereto, to construct any railroad in or upon any or either of the said streets or avenues, and from doing any other act to hinder, delay, or obstruct the construction or operation of said railroad as herein authorized. And it is hereby made the duty of the said mayor, common council, and other officers, to do such acts, within their respective departments, as may be needful to promote the construction and protect the operation of said railroad, as provided in this law. Any act or thing done, in violation hereof, shall be inoperative and void. All actions relating to, or affecting or arising under this act, or the authority herein given, shall be commenced in the supreme court of the first judicial district. Nothing in this section contained shall be deemed or held to impair the rights of any railroad now in operation in said city.

§ 5. All provisions of law, inconsistent with this act, are hereby repealed.

§ 6. This act shall take effect immediately.

CHAPTER 513.

An Act to authorize the construction of a railroad in Seventh avenue, and in certain other streets and avenues of the city of New York.

Passed April 17th, 1860, notwithstanding the objections of the Governor.

The People of the State of New York, represented in Senate and Assembly, do enact as follows:

SECTION 1. John Kerr, Edward P. Cowles, Anthony J. Hill, Hugh Smith, John S. Hunt, Jacob Sharp, Thomas H. Tower, Peter B. Sweeney, John B. Babcock, Robert Marshall, John Kelly, Jacob Hays, and their assigns, are hereby authorized and empowered to lay, construct, operate, and use a railroad with a double or single track, as hereinafter provided, and to convey passengers thereon for compensation, through, upon, and along the following streets and avenues, route or routes, in the city of New York, viz.: Commencing on the Seventh avenue at the southern extremity of the Central Park; thence through and along the Seventh avenue with a double track to the old Bloomingdale road or Broadway, thence through and along the old Bloomingdale road or Broadway and Union place, with a double track to University place; thence through and along University place with a double track to Clinton place or Eighth street; thence through and along University place and Wooster street with a single track to Canal street; thence through and along Canal street with a single track to West Broadway, thence through and along West Broadway and College place with a single track to Barclay street; thence through and along Barclay street with a single track to Church street; thence through and along Barclay street with a double track to Broadway, also, connecting with the double track in Barclay street, through and along Church street with a single track to Canal street, thence through and along Canal street with a single track to Greene street, thence through and along Greene street with a single track to Clinton place or Eighth street;

thence through and along Clinton place or Eighth street with a single track to connect with a double track in University place; thence to the place of beginning; also connecting with the double track in Seventh avenue at Broadway, through and along Seventh avenue with a double track to Greenwich avenue; thence through and along Greenwich avenue with a double track to and across the Sixth avenue to Clinton place or Eighth street; thence through and along Clinton place or Eighth street with a double track to Macdougal street; thence through and along Macdougal street with a double track to Fourth street, thence through and along Fourth street with a double track to Thompson street; thence through and along Thompson street with a double track to Canal street; thence through and along Canal street with a double track to West Broadway, thence through and along West Broadway with a double track to Chambers street; thence through and along West Broadway and College place with a single track to Barclay street; thence through and along Barclay street to Broadway; thence returning through Barclay street and Church street to Chambers street; thence through and along Chambers street to West Broadway, to connect with the track in said street, and by the aforesaid route to the place of beginning; also, connecting with the track in College place, through and along Park place with a double track to Broadway; also, connecting with the track in West Broadway, to and along Duane street with a single track to Church street, and thence through and along Duane street with a double track to Broadway; also, connecting with the track in Thompson street, through and along Broome street with a double track to Broadway; also, connecting with the track in

Union place at Fourteenth street, through and along Fourteenth street with a double track to Broadway, adjoining Union square; also connecting with the double track in Canal street at Thompson street, through and along Canal street with a double track to Varick street, and thence through and along Varick street with a double track to, and to connect with the track in West Broadway at Franklin street; together with the necessary connections, turnouts, and switches, for the proper working and accommodation of the said railroad, on the said route or routes.

§ 2. Said railroad shall be constructed on the most approved plan for the construction of city railroads, and shall be run as often as the convenience of passengers may require, and shall be subject to such reasonable rules and regulations in respect thereto as the Common Council of the city of New York may from time to time by ordinance prescribe; and to the payment to the city of the same license fee annually, for each car run thereon, as is now by other city railroads in said city; and the said persons and their assigns are hereby authorized to charge the same rate of fare, for the conveyance of passengers on said railroad, as is now charged by other city railroads in said city.

§ 3. In the construction, operation, or use of such railroad upon the route or routes above designated, should such persons above named, or their assigns, deem it necessary or proper to run upon, intersect, or use any portion of other railroad tracks now laid upon any of the streets or avenues above named, they are hereby authorized to run upon, intersect, and use the same, and in case they cannot agree with the owner or owners thereof respecting the compensation or payment to be made therefor, then the amount of such compensation or payment shall be ascertained and determined in the manner provided by subdivision six of the twenty-eighth section of the act entitled "An act to authorize the formation of railroad corporations, and to regulate the same," passed April second, eighteen hundred and fifty. And should any real estate or interest therein be required for the purpose of constructing said railroad on said route or routes, as above specified and authorized, for which the said persons above named, or their assigns, shall , unable to agree with the owner or owners for the use purchase thereof, they may acquire the right to use, or title to the same in the manner specified in the fourteenth, fifteenth, sixteenth, seventeenth, eighteenth, nineteenth, twentieth, and twenty-first sections of the said act of April second, eighteen hundred and fifty, except that, in any of the proceedings for any of the purposes authorized by this section, it shall not be necessary that the petition to the supreme court shall make any allegations of or reference to any incorporation, capital stock, surveys or maps, or of the filing of any certificate of location. But, in all cases, the use of said streets and avenues for the purposes of said railroad, as herein authorized, shall be considered a public use consistent with the uses for which the mayor, aldermen, and commonalty of said city hold said streets and avenues.

§ 4. The mayor, common council, and the several officers of the corporation of the said city of New York, and the said corporation, are hereby prohibited from giving any assent to, or allowing any company, claiming to derive authority under the act entitled "An act to authorize the formation of railroad corporations, and to regulate the same," passed April second, eighteen hundred and fifty, or act amendatory thereof, or in addition thereto, to construct any railroad in, or upon any or either of the said streets or avenues, and from doing any other act to hinder, delay, or obstruct the construction or operation of said railroad as herein authorized. And it is hereby made the duty of the said mayor, common council, and other officers, to do such acts within their respective departments, as may be needful to promote the construction and protect the operation of said railroad, as provided in this law. Any act or thing done, in violation hereof, shall be inoperative and void. All actions relating to, affecting, or arising under this act, or the authority herein given, shall be commenced in the supreme court of the first judicial district. Nothing in this section contained shall be deemed or held to impair the riphts of any railroad now in operation in said city.

§ 5. All provisions of law, inconsistent with this act, are hereby repealed.

§ 6. This act shall take effect immediately.

CHAPTER 514.

AN ACT *to authorize the construction of a railroad in Fourteenth street, and in other streets and avenues of the City of New York.*

Passed April 17, 1860; notwithstanding the objections of the Governor.

The People of the State of New York, represented in Senate and Assembly, do enact as follows·

SECTION 1. Stephen R. Roe, John Stewart, Charles W. Lawrence, John Kennedy, James S. Hunt, Charles C. Clarke, John Fox, William Ravensteyn, William H. Peck, John C. Thompson, Thomas Ryan, Joseph S. Craig, and their assigns, are hereby authorized and empowered to lay, construct, operate, and use a railroad with a double or single track, as hereinafter provided, and to convey passengers thereon, for compensation, through, upon, and along the following streets and avenues, route or routes, in the city of New York, viz.: Commencing at the intersection of Fourteenth street with the Eleventh avenue; thence through and along Fourteenth street, with a double track, to Hudson street; thence through and along Hudson street, with a double track, to Troy street; thence through and along Troy street, with a single track, to Fourth street; thence through and along Fourth street, with a single track, to Macdougal street; thence through and along Macdougal street, with a single track, to Bleecker street; thence through and along Bleecker street, with a double track, to Crosby street; thence through and along Crosby street, with a double track, to Howard street; thence through and along Howard street, with a double track, to Elm street; thence through and along Elm street, with a double track, to Leonard street; thence through and along Elm street, with a single track, to Reade street; thence through and along Reade street, with a single track, to Centre street; thence through and along Centre street, Chatham street and Park row, with a double track, to Broadway; also, connecting with the double track, in Centre street, at Reade street, through and along Centre street, with a single track, to Leonard street; thence through and along Leonard street, with a single track, to connect with the double track, in

Elm street; also, connecting with the double track, in Hudson street, at Troy street, through and along Hudson street, with a single track, to the southerly end of Abingdon square and Bleecker street; thence through and along Bleecker street, with a single track, to Macdougal street, there to connect with the double track in Bleecker street; also, connecting with the double track in Park row, through and along Beekman street, with a single track, to South street; thence through and along South street, with a single track, to Fulton street; thence through and along Fulton street, with a single track, to William street; thence through and along William street, with a single track, to Ann street, thence through and along Ann street, with a single track, to connect with the double track in Park row at Broadway; also, connecting with the double track in Elm street, through and along Canal street, with a double track, to Broadway; also, with a double track connecting with the double track in Fourteenth street, through and along the Eleventh and Twelfth avenues to Thirty-second street; also, connecting with the double track in Canal street at Elm street, through and along Canal street with a double track to the Bowery, thence through and along the Bowery and New Bowery, with a double track, to Pearl street; thence through and along Pearl street, with a double track, to Peck slip; thence through and along Peck slip, with a double track, to South street; thence through and along South street, with a double track, to the Fulton ferry; thence through and along Fulton street, with a double track, to Water street thence through and along Water street, with a double track, to connect with the said double track in Peck slip, together with the necessary connections, turnouts, and switches for the proper working and accommodation of the road on the said route or routes.

§ 2. Said railroad shall be constructed upon the most approved plan for the construction of city railroads, and shall be run as often as the covenience of passengers may require, and shall be subject to such reasonable rules and regulations in respect thereto as the common council of the city of New York may, from time to time, by ordinance prescribe; and to the payment to the city of the same license fee annually, for each car run thereon, as is now paid by other city railroads in said city; and the said persons and their assigns are hereby authorized to charge the same rate of fare, for the conveyance of passengers on said railroad, as is now charged by other city railroads in said city.

§ 3. In the construction, operation, or use of such railroad, upon the route or routes above designated, should such persons above named, or their assigns, deem it necessary or proper to run upon, intersect, or use any portion of other railroad tracks now laid upon any of the streets or avenues above named, they are hereby authorized to run upon, intersect, and use the same, and in case they cannot agree with the owner or owners thereof respecting the compensation or payment to be made therefor, then the amount of such compensation or payment shall be ascertained and determined in the manner provided by subdivision six of the twenty-eighth section of the act entitled "An act to authorize the formation of railroad corporations and to regulate the same," passed April second, eighteen hundred and fifty. And should any real estate or interest therein be required for the purpose of constructing said railroad on said route or routes, as above specified and authorized, for which the said persons above named, or their assigns, shall be unable to agree with the owner or owners for the use or purchase thereof, they may acquire the right to use, or title to the same, in the manner specified in the fourteenth, fifteenth, sixteenth, seventeenth, eighteenth, nineteenth, twentieth, and twenty-first sections of the said act of April second, eighteen hundred and fifty, except that, in any of the proceedings for any of the purposes authorized by this section, it shall not be necessary that the petition to the supreme court shall make any allegations of, or reference to any incorporation, capital stock, surveys, or maps, or of the filing of any certificate of location. But, in all cases the use of said streets and avenues for the purposes of said railroad, as herein authorized, shall be considered a public use consistent with the uses for which the mayor, aldermen, and commonalty of said city hold said streets and avenues.

§ 4. The mayor, common council, and the several officers of the corporation of the said city of New York, and the said corporation, are hereby prohibited from giving any assent to, or allowing any company, claiming to derive authority under the act entitled "An act to authorize the formation of railroad corporations, and to regulate the same," passed April second, eighteen hundred and fifty, or act amendatory thereof, or in addition thereto, to construct any railroad in, or upon any or either of the said streets or avenues, and from doing any other act to hinder, delay, or obstruct the construction or operation of said railroad as herein authorized. And it is hereby made the duty of the said mayor, common council, and other officers to do such acts, within their respective departments, as may be needful to promote the construction and protect the operation of said railroad, as provided in this law. Any act or thing done, in violation hereof, shall be inoperative and void. All actions relating to, affecting, or arising under this act, or the authority herein given, shall be commenced in the supreme court of the first judicial district. Nothing in this section contained shall be deemed or held to impair the rights of any railroad now in operation in said city.

§ 5. All provisions of law, inconsistent with this act, are hereby repealed.

§ 6. This act shall take effect immediately.

CHAPTER 515.

AN ACT to authorize the construction of a railroad in Tenth avenue, Forty-second street, and certain other avenues and streets of the city of New York.

Passed April 17, 1860; notwithstanding the objection of the Governor.

The People of the State of New York, represented in Senate and Assembly, do enact as follows:

SECTION 1. John T. Conover, Moses Ely, Matthew T. Brennan, Truman Smith, Rufus F. Andrews, Bloomfield Usher, Justin D. White, John M. Miller, Elijah B. Holmes, Leonard W. Brainard, Junior, Delos De Wolf, Thomas Black, and their assigns, are hereby authorized and empowered to lay, construct, operate, and use a railroad with a double or single track, as hereinafter provided, and to convey passengers thereon for compensation, through, upon, and along the following streets and avenues in the city of New York, viz.: Commencing at the ferry, at the western extremity of Forty-second street; thence through and along Forty-second street, with a double track, to Tenth avenue; thence through and along Tenth avenue, with a double track, to Thirty-fourth street, thence through and along Thirty-fourth street, with a double track, to Broadway, thence through and along Broadway, with a double track, to Twenty-third street; thence through and along Twenty-third street, with a double track, to Fourth avenue; thence through and along Fourth avenue and Union place, with a double track, to Fourteenth street; thence through and along Fourteenth street, with a double track, to avenue A; thence through and along avenue A, with a double track, to Second street; thence through and along avenue A, with a single track, to First street; thence through and along First street and Houston street, with a single track, to Cannon street; thence through and along Cannon street, with a single track, to Grand street; thence through and along Grand street, with a single track, to Goerck street; thence through and along Grand street, with a double track, to Grand street ferry, at the foot of Grand street, East river; thence returning through and along Grand street to Goerck street; thence through and along Goerck street, with a single track, to Houston street; thence through and along Houston street and Second street, with a single track, to, and to connect with, the double track in avenue A, and thence along the aforesaid route to the place of beginning; together with the necessary connections, turnouts and switches, for the proper working and accommodation of the road on the said route.

§ 2. Said railroad shall be constructed on the most approved plan for the construction of city railroads, and shall be run as often as the convenience of passengers may require, and shall be subject to such reasonable rules and regulations in respect thereto as the common council of the city of New York may from time to time by ordinance prescribe; and to the payment to the city of the same license fee annually, for each car run thereon, as is now paid by other city railroads in said city; and the said persons and their assigns are hereby authorized to charge the same rate of fare for the conveyance of passengers on said railroad as is now charged by other city railroads in said city.

§ 3. In the construction, operation, or use of such railroad upon the route or routes above designated, should such persons above named, or their assigns, deem it necessary or proper to run upon, intersect, or use any portion of other railroad tracks now laid upon any of the streets or avenues above named, they are hereby authorized to run upon, intersect, and use the same, and in case they cannot agree with the owner or owners thereof respecting the compensation or payment to be made therefor, then the amount of such compensation or payment shall be ascertained and determined in the manner provided by subdivision six of the twenty-eighth section of the act entitled "An act to authorize the formation of railroad corporations, and to regulate the same," passed April second, eighteen hundred and fifty. And should any real estate or interest therein be required for the purpose of constructing the said railroad on the said route or routes, as above specified and authorized, for which the said persons above named, or their assigns, shall be unable to agree with the owner or owners for the use or purchase thereof, they may acquire the right to use, or title to the same, in the manner specified in the fourteenth, fifteenth, sixteenth, seventeenth, eighteenth, nineteenth, twentieth, and twenty-first sections of the said act of April second, eighteen hundred and fifty, except that, in any of the proceedings for any of the purposes authorized by this section, it shall not be necessary that the petition to the supreme court shall make any allegations of, or reference to any incorporation, capital stock, surveys or maps, or of the filing of any certificate of location. But, in all cases, the use of said streets and avenues for the purposes of the said railroad, as herein authorized, shall be considered a public use consistent with the uses for which the mayor, aldermen, and commonalty of said city hold said streets and avenues.

§ 4. The mayor, common council, and the several officers of the corporation of the said city of New York, and the said corporation, are hereby prohibited from giving any assent to, or allowing any company, claiming to derive authority under the act entitled " An act to authorize the formation of railroad corporations, and to regulate the same," passed April second, eighteen hundred and fifty, or act amendatory thereof, or in addition thereto, to construct any railroad in, or upon any or either of the said streets or avenues, and from doing any other act to hinder, delay, or obstruct the construction or operation of said railroad, as herein authorized. And it is hereby made the duty of the said mayor, common council, and other officers, to do such acts, within their respective departments, as may be needful to promote the construction and protect the operation of said railroad, as provided in this law. Any act or thing done, in violation hereof, shall be inoperative and void. All actions relating to, affecting, or arising under this act, or the authority herein given, shall be commenced in the supreme court of the first judicial district. Nothing in this section contained shall be deemed or held to impair the rights of any railroad now in operation in said city.

§ 6. All provisions of law, inconsistent with this act, are hereby repealed.

§ 7. This act shall take effect immediately.

INDEX TO FERRY RIGHTS.

(A)

ASTORIA FERRY :

   vide "HORNE'S HOOK FERRY."

(B)

BARCLAY STREET FERRY—TO HOBOKEN, N. J. :

   Lease of ....148 to 152

      term of... 148

      reservations in.....................................148, 151

      not to be transferred or underlet without the written consent of the city authorities.................... 151

      penalty for non-compliance with the conditions of...... 149

   Premises leased... 148

   Termini defined....... 148

   Lessees of... 148

      obligations of..................................149 to 151

   Rent to be paid for... 149

      how and when to be paid............................. 149

      penalty for default in payment of.................... 149

   Boats, description and number of, to be employed......... ... 150

      additional, to be put on when required by the Common Council... 150

BARCLAY STREET FERRY—TO HOBOKEN, N. J.—CONTINUED:

 to be properly manned, &c........................... 150

 Ferriage to be charged................................. 151

 Management of, to be subject to the ordinances, resolutions, &c.,
  of the Common Council......................... 151

 Provisions in relation to the claim of the heirs of Wm. Rhinelander to the bulkhead at the foot of Barclay street. 148, 151

BERRY, ABRAHAM J., & JOHN J. HICKS:

 Lease of a ferry to, from pier No. 35 to Williamsburgh.. 74

 transfer of lease of ferry to Williamsburgh to Brooklyn Ferry Company, by............................ 82

BLISS, NEZEIAH, & HEZEKIAH BRADFORD:

 lease of ferry from foot of Sixteenth street, E. R., to Greenpoint, L. I., to........................... 117

 assignment of lease of ferry from foot of Sixteenth street, to Greenpoint, L. I., to Alex. H. Shultz, by...... 109, 124

BROOKLYN FERRY COMPANY:

 authorized to agree with the lessees of the Peck Slip ferry for the purchase of that ferry and fixtures.... 44

 authorized to change Brooklyn terminus of the Peck Slip ferry... 44

 authorized to occupy the slip between piers Nos. 31 and 32, E. R., as the New York terminus of their ferry to South Seventh street, Williamsburgh.......... 50, 82

 authorized to change the Brooklyn terminus of the "James Slip ferry" to Hunter's Point, L. I....... 51, 82

 authorized to agree with the Union Ferry Company for the purchase of the lease, fixtures, &c., of the

BROOKLYN FERRY COMPANY—Continued:

 "Roosevelt Street ferry," and to change the Brooklyn terminus thereof.................................. 51

 transfer to, of lease of ferry to Williamsburgh, by A. J. Berry & John J. Hicks......................... 82

 authorized to run boats from slip north of Grand street to South Seventh street, Williamsburgh, until a lease of such ferry shall be sold...................... 99

BULLS FERRY—Ferry to:

 from Thirty-ninth street, N. R.,

  vide "Thirty-ninth Street Ferry."

 from Eighty-sixth street, N. R.,

  vide "Eighty-sixth Street Ferry."

(C)

CAMPBELL, FREEMAN, & RUTHERFORD MOODY:

 consent given to the transfer of an undivided half interest in the ferry from foot of Wall street to Brooklyn, to.................................... 33

CANAL STREET FERRY—to Jersey City:

 New Jersey Railroad and Transportation Company directed to establish, in accordance with the terms of their agreement with the city.................... 169

CATHARINE STREET FERRY—to Brooklyn:

 Lease of .... 52 to 59

 preambles and resolutions in relation to selling the, in connection with the Hamilton avenue, South, Wall street, and Fulton ferries........................ 61 to 63

CATHARINE STREET FERRY—TO BROOKLYN—CONTINUED:

    in connection with the Hamilton avenue, South, Wall street, and Fulton ferries..................... .63 to 71

    term of...................................... 52, 53, 62, 64

    agreement as to the determination of, on May 1st, 1861. 61, 63

    reservations in........................... 55, 58, 68, 69, 70

    not to be assigned or underlet, &c., without the written consent of the city authorities................... 55, 68

    not to affect nor interfere with the establishing of other ferries... 58

    penalty for non-compliance with the conditions of...... 54, 65

    bond for the faithful performance of the covenants of.. 72

    consent given to the transfer of, to C. S. Woodhull..... 59

    consent given to the transfer of, to C. P. Smith & W. F. Bulkley..................................... 59

Premises leased..53, 60, 62, 63

    to be kept in good order by the lessees................ 55, 67

    to be peaceably surrendered, in good condition, upon the termination of the lease...... .... 56, 70

    city not to be responsible in damages in consequence of any suit in relation to its rights, to any of the..... 69

Termini defined..53, 62, 69

    certain, may be changed............................. 69

Lessees of..52, 59, 63

    obligations of......................53, 54, 58, 62, 65 to 71

    to take ferry property of former lessees.............. 68

    to erect, maintain, and keep in good repair, the necessary fixtures, &c..................................... 60, 67

    directed to erect new ferry houses, &c................ 60

Rent to be paid..52, 53, 64

CATHARINE STREET FERRY—TO BROOKLYN—CONTINUED:

how, and when to be paid.................................53, 64
penalty for default in payment of...................54, 65
Boats, description, and number to be employed 55, 66
    extra, to be kept on hand 66
    to be approved by the Comptroller................... 66
    to be kept in repair and properly manned, &c......... 66
    to have fire apparatus attached to engine............. 71
    relative to time of running the...................55, 60
    relative to persons employed upon the................58, 66
Ferriage to be charged...................................55, 62, 68
Compensation to be allowed for the use of the fire apparatus on board boats for the extinguishing of fires.......... 71
Management of, to be subject to the ordinances, resolutions, &c., of the Common Council........................56, 67
Discontinuance of any one of the ferries included in this lease, to be a forfeiture of all............................62, 65
Ferry property of former lessees to be taken by present lessees.. 68
    to be taken by the city upon the termination of lease..57, 71
    how the value of, shall be determined................57, 71

CHAMBERS STREET FERRY—TO PAVONIA, N. J.:

Lease of..152 to 161
term of..152, 154
reservations in..............................155, 157, 160
not to be transferred or underlet without the written consent of the Comptroller...................... 157
not to affect or interfere with the establishing of other ferries... 160
penalty for non-compliance with the conditions of...... 155

CHAMBERS STREET FERRY—to Pavonia, N. J.—Continued:

Premises leased 153, 154
    to be kept in good repair by the lessees 15
    to be surrendered upon termination of lease 158
    used by the Erie Railroad Company 161
Termini defined 152, 153
    New Jersey terminus to be approved by the Comptroller 152, 153
Lessees of 152
    obligations of .... 155 to 160
    to erect, maintain and keep in good repair the necessary bridges, fixtures, &c., for 157
    extent and position of fixtures to be put up by, designated 157
    not to permit or cause to be erected any obstruction on the south side of Pier No. 30, E. R., nor any blocks to be sunk in the slip leased 156, 157
Rent to be paid for 154
    how and when to be paid 154
    penalty for default in the payment of 155
    paid by the Erie Railroad Company 161
Boats, description and number to be employed on 156, 159
    additional to be put on when required by the Common Council 159
    to be kept in repair and properly manned, &c. 156
    to be approved by the Mayor or Comptroller 159
    relative to time of running the 158
    relative to persons employed upon the 160
Ferriage to be charged .... 156, 161 to 163
Management of the, to be subject to the ordinances, resolutions, &c., of the Common Council 158

INDEX. 375

CHAMBERS STREET FERRY—TO PAVONIA, N. J.—CONTINUED:

Time when the ferry shall be put into operation.............. 156

Ferry property shall be taken by parties obtaining lease of the ferry subsequent to the termination of the present lease... 159

    how valuation shall be made of the................... 158

CHRISTOPHER STREET FERRY—TO HOBOKEN, N. J. :

Lease of...169 to 174

    term of... 170

    reservations in................................... 173

    not to be transferred or underlet without the written consent of City authorities......................... 172

    penalty for non-compliance with the conditions of..... 174

Premises leased... 170

    to be surrendered peaceably upon the termination of lease 172

Termini defined... 170

Lessees of.. 170

    obligations of............................... .171 to 173

    to set back ferry-houses and gates from West street..... 173

Rent to be paid for...................................... 170

    how and when to be paid........................... 171

    penalty for default in payment of.................... 173

    note in relation to................................ 175

Boats, description and number of, to be employed on....... 171, 173

    additional, to be placed on when required by the Common Council................................. 173

    to be kept in good repair and properly manned, &c...171, 172

    to be approved by Committees on Ferries.............. 171

    relative to time of running the...................... 172

CHRISTOPHER STREET FERRY—TO HOBOKEN, N. J.—CONTINUED:

 Ferriage to be charged.................................... 172, 173

 Management of, to be subject to the ordinances, resolutions, &c.,
  of the Common Council.......................... 172

COCKROFT, WILLIAM, & GEORGE G. TAYLOR :

 Lease of ferry from Catharine street to Brooklyn to..... 52

 consent given to transfer of lease of ferry from Catharine
  street to Brooklyn, to Caleb S. Woodhull, by....... 59

COMMITTEES ON FERRIES :

 to approve of boats employed on the Christopher Street
  Ferry to Hoboken............................. 171

 to approve of boats employed on the Fulton Ferry..... 21

 to approve of boats employed on the Hamilton Avenue
  Ferry... 21

 to approve of boats employed on the Hoboken Street
  Ferry to Hoboken............................. 165

 to approve of boats employed on the Houston Street
  Ferry.....................................102, 103

 to approve of boats employed on the South Ferry....... 21

 Chairmen of, to be ex-officio members of the Board of Managers of the Hamilton Avenue, South and Fulton
  Ferries.. 23

COMMISSIONERS OF THE SINKING FUND :

 to approve of boats employed on the Staten Island Ferry. 15

COMMUTATION :

 to be charged on Fourteenth Street Ferry to Greenpoint...113, 115

INDEX. 377

COMMUTATION—Continued:

 to be charged on Grand Street Ferry to Williamsburgh...94, 98

 to be charged on Hamilton Avenue, South and Fulton Ferries 26

 not to be increased on Hamilton Avenue, South and Fulton Ferries.. 22

 Union Ferry Company directed to comply with rates of, on the Hamilton Avenue, South and Fulton Ferries. 25

 on Jersey City Ferry to be enjoyed by the citizens of New York on same terms, &c., as by citizens of Jersey City.. 147

 to be charged on Peck Slip Ferry to Williamsburgh.... 42

 to be charged on Sixteenth Street Ferry to Greenpoint...120, 123

COMPTROLLER:

 consent of, to be obtained before making any transfer, &c., of lease of Chambers Street Ferry............. 157

 consent of, to be obtained before making any transfer, &c., of lease of Hamilton Avenue, South, Wall Street, Fulton and Catharine Streets Ferries........ 68

 consent of, to be obtained before making any transfer, &c., of lease of Thirty-fourth Street Ferry......... 137

 to approve of boats to be employed on the Chambers Street Ferry.... 159

 to approve of boats to be employed on Hamilton Avenue, South, Wall Street, Fulton and Catharine Street Ferries.................................... 66

 to approve of boats to be employed on Grand Street Ferry. 93

 to approve of boats to be employed on Peck Slip Ferry.. 37

 to approve of boats to be employed on Thirty-fourth Street Ferry.... ....136. 140

COMPTROLLER—Continued:

    to approve of the selection to be made of a terminus in New Jersey for the Chambers Street Ferry 152, 153

    Sale of Grand Street and Peck Slip Ferries by, declared void... 43

    directed to advertise and sell leases of Grand Street and Peck Slip Ferries............................... 43

    directed to advertise and sell a lease of a ferry from the north side of foot of Grand street, New York, to South Seventh street, Williamsburgh 99

CONKLIN, HENRY :

    Lease to, of a ferry from Eighty-sixth street (N. R.) to Bull's Ferry.. 189

    permission given to, to transfer lease of ferry from Eighty-sixth street to Bull's Ferry, to Horace P. Russ and others................................. 195

CORTLANDT STREET FERRY—TO JERSEY CITY :

    Lease of .... 143 to 147

        term of.. 145

        reservations in..................................... 145

    Premises leased... 145

    Termini defined.. 144

    Lessees of 143, 145

        obligations of.................................... 145, 146

        to establish a ferry to Jersey City from some point in the vicinity of Canal Street, when required so to do by the Common Council........................... 146

        directed to establish a ferry to Jersey City from the foot Canal Street, or vicinity, in accordance with their agreement...................................... 169

CORTLANDT STREET FERRY—TO JERSEY CITY—CONTINUED:

 Rent to be paid... 146
  how and when to be paid............................. 146
 Boats, relative to the time of running the, upon............. 146
 Ferriage to be charged...................................... 147

COUNSEL TO THE CORPORATION:

 directed to take measures to prevent the use of or interference with the Grand Street and Peck Slip ferries.   43

(E)

EIGHTY-SIXTH STREET FERRY—TO ASTORIA, L. I:

 Permission given to — Halsey to run....................... 142

EIGHTY-SIXTH STREET FERRY—TO BULL'S FERRY:

 Lease of.......................................189 to 195
  term of... 190
  reservations in..............................191, 194
  not to be transferred or underlet without the written consent of City authorities....................... 194
  not to affect or interfere with the establishing of any other ferries...................................... 194
  penalty for non-compliance with the conditions of....... 191
  consent given to transfer of, to H. P. Russ, G. W. Reed, and E. Griffin... 195

EIGHTY-SIXTH STREET FERRY—to BULL'S FERRY—CONTINUED :

Premises leased.. 190

    to be kept in good repair, &c., by lessee............... 193

    to be peaceably surrendered in good condition upon termination of lease.............................. 193

Termini defined..189, 190

Lessee of...189, 195

    obligations of..............................189, 191 to 193

    to erect, maintain, and keep in good repair all the necessary bridges, fixtures, &c., for.................189, 193

Rent to be paid for.......................................199, 191

    how and when to be paid..........................189, 191

    penalty for default in payment of.................... 189

Boats, description and number of, to be employed upon......190, 192

    additional, to be put on when required by the Common Council.. 192

    to be kept in repair and properly manned, &c.......... 192

    to be approved by the Street Commissioner............ 192

    relative to time of running the......................190, 193

Ferriage to be charged subject to regulation by the Common Council....................................... 193

Management of the, to be subject to the ordinances, resolutions, &c., of the Common Council.......... 193

City to have the right to extend the piers at foot of Eighty-sixth street without prejudice to lease, or being liable to claim for damage by lessee..................... 194

ERIE RAILROAD COMPANY:

    Occupation of premises leased to the Pavonia Ferry Company, by... 161

(F)

FERRIAGE:

on *Barclay street ferry to Hoboken*, rates of, to be charged, 151

on *Catharine street ferry*, rates of, to be charged.......... 55, 68

on *Chambers street ferry, to Pavonia*, rates of, to be charged,
159, 161 to 163

on *Christopher street ferry*, rates of, to be charged....... 172, 173

on *Eighty-sixth street ferry, to Bull's ferry*, to be subject to regulation by the Common Council............... 193

on *Forty-second street ferry to Weehawken*, to be subject to regulation by the Common Council............... 186

on *Fourteenth street ferry to Greenpoint*, rates of, to be charged..................................... 113, 115

on *Grand street ferry*, rates of, to be charged............ 94, 98

on *Hamilton avenue, South and Fulton ferries*, rates of, by commutation.... .... 26, 68

    not to be raised during term of lease............... 22

    Union Ferry Company directed to commute for..... 25

on *Hamilton avenue, South, Wall street, Fulton, and Catharine street ferries*, rates of, to be uniform.............. . 62, 68

on *Hoboken street ferry*, rates of, to be charged........... 167

on *Houston street ferry*, to be regulated by the Common Council... 103

on *James slip ferry*, rates of, to be charged.............. 78

on *Jersey City ferry*, to be commuted for with citizens of New York on same terms as with citizens of Jersey City.. 147

on *Peck slip ferry*, rates of, to be charged.. .... 37, 41

on *Roosevelt street ferry*, rates of, to be charged.. 48

FERRIAGE—Continued :

 on *Sixteenth street ferry to Greenpoint*, rates of, to be
   charged..120, 123
 on *Thirty-ninth street ferry to Bull's ferry*, to be subject to
   regulation by the Common Council............... 179
 on *Wall street ferry*, to be subject to regulation by the
   Common Council................................ 30, 68

FORTY-SECOND STREET:

 Lessee of ferry from foot of, to Weehawken, to keep the street
   in repair for twenty-five feet from the bulkhead.... 186

FORTY-SECOND STREET FERRY—TO WEEHAWKEN, N. J. :

 Lease of...181 to 188
  term of........................... ....182, 183, 184
  reservations in...................................184, 187
  not to affect or interfere with the establishing of other
   ferries... 187
  penalty for non-compliance with conditions of......... 184
  consent given to the transfer of, to the Weehawken
   Ferry Company................................ .. 189
 Security for the faithful performance of covenants of lease..... 189
 Premises leased.. 183
  to be kept in good repair by lessee............. 186
  to be peaceably surrendered, in good condition, upon the
   termination of lease........................... 187
 Termini defined...182, 183
 Lessee of..181, 183, 188
  obligations of..................................184 to 187
  to erect, maintain, and keep in good repair the necessary bridges, fixtures......................... 186

FORTY-SECOND STREET FERRY—TO WEEHAWKEN, N. J.—CONTINUED:

  to keep in good repair the docks, &c., hereafter to be constructed.................................... 186

  to keep in good repair Forty-second street for twenty-five feet from bulkhead.......................... 186

 Rent to be paid for.. 184

  how and when to be paid............................ 184

  penalty for default in payment of................... 184

 Boats, description and number of, to be employed on......... 185

  additional, to be put on when required by the Common Council..................................... 185

  to be kept in repair and properly manned, &c.......... 185

  to be approved...................................... 185

  relative to time of running the..................... 185, 186

 Ferriage to be subject to regulation by the Common Council..... 186

 Management of, to be subject to the ordinances, resolutions, &c., of the Common Council............................ 186

 Corporation may extend piers at the foot of Forty-second street, without prejudice to lease, or being liable to the lessee in a claim for damages.................... 187

FOURTEENTH STREET FERRY—TO GREENPOINT, L. I.:

 Lease of..108 to 116

  term of..109, 110

  reservations in...................................114, 115

  not to be transferred or underlet without the written consent of the City authorities................... 114

  not to affect or interfere with the establishing of other ferries... 115

  penalty for non-compliance with the conditions of...... 111

  consent given to the transfer of, to Gideon Lee Knapp.. 116

FOURTEENTH STREET FERRY—TO GREENPOINT, L. I.—CONTINUED :

 Premises leased.. 110

  to be kept in good repair by lessee..................... 113

  to be peaceably surrendered, in good condition, upon the
   termination of lease............................. 114

 Termini defined..109, 110

 Lessee of...108, 116

  obligations of..............................109, 111 to 114

  to erect, maintain, and keep in good repair the necessary
   bridges, &c...................................... 113

  to keep in repair piers hereafter to be built............. 113

  assignment of lease of Sixteenth street ferry to.......109, 124

  to put ferry into operation by or before September 26th,
   1853 ....110, 113, 125

 Rent, to be paid for................................109, 110, 125

  how and when to be paid............................... 110

  penalty for default in payment of..................... 111

 Boats, description and number to be employed............. 112

  additional to be placed on when required by the Common Council... 112

  to be kept in repair and properly manned, &c.......... 112

  to be approved by the Street Commissioner............ 112

  relative to the time of running the..................112, 113

 Ferriage to be charged..................................113, 115

 Management of, to be subject to the ordinances, resolutions, &c.,
   of the Common Council 113

  Corporation to have the right to extend the piers at the
   foot of Fourteenth street, without prejudice to lease,
   or being liable to lessees in a claim for damages.... 114

INDEX. 285

FULTON FERRY—to Brooklyn:

 Lease of, in connection with the Hamilton avenue and South ferries..18 to 24

 preamble and resolutions in relation to selling the, in connection with the Hamilton avenue, South, Wall street, and Catharine street ferries...............61 to 63

 in connection with the Hamilton avenue, South, Wall street, and Catharine street ferries...............63 to 71

 term of...19, 62, 64

 reservations in.........................20, 22, 24, 68, 69, 70

 not to be assigned or underlet, &c., without the written consent of the city authorities....................22, 68

 not to affect nor interfere with the establishing of other ferries... 22

 penalty for non-compliance with the conditions of...... 20, 65

 bond for the faithful performance of the covenants of... 72

 consent given to transfer of, to the Union Ferry Company.. 25

Premises leased......................................18, 19, 62, 63

 to be kept in good order by the lessees................ 22, 67

 to be peaceably surrendered, in good condition, upon the termination of lease............................. 23, 70

 city not to be responsible in damages in consequence of any suit in relation to its rights to any of the...... 69

Termini defined...19, 62, 69

 certain, may be changed............................. 69

 New York terminus of, to be changed if required by the Common Council................................... 24

Lessees of..18, 24, 25, 63

 obligations of..................18, 20 to 22, 23, 62, 65 to 71

25

FULTON FERRY—TO BROOKLYN—CONTINUED :

    to take ferry property of former lessees................ 68

    to erect, maintain, and keep in good repair the necessary
        fixtures..22, 67

    to remove or extend ferry-houses or fixtures, if required
        by the Common Council......................... 24

    not to run any ferry or ferries under any State law, during
        the term of this lease, under penalty of forfeiture.. 24

    directed to commute with passengers.................. 25

Rent to be paid... 20, 64

    how and when to be paid........................... 20, 64

    penalty for default in payment of............ .... 20, 65

Boats, description and number to be employed............... 21, 66

    Extra, to be kept on hand.......................... 66

    to be approved by Committees on Ferries and Mayor.... 21

    to be approved by the Comptroller................. 66

    to be kept in repair and properly manned, &c.......... 21, 66

    to have fire apparatus attached to engine............. 71

    relative to the time of running the.................. 21, 67

Ferriage to be charged..............................22, 26, 62, 68

    commutation rates to be charged..................... 22

    commutation rates not to be raised during the term of
        the lease....................................... 26

Compensation to be allowed for the use of the fire apparatus on
        oard boats for the extinguishing of fires........... 71

Management of, to be subject to the ordinances, resolutions, &c.,
        of the Common Council........................ 21, 67

    Mayor and Chairmen of Committees on Ferries to be ex-
        officio members of the Board of Managers.......... 23

INDEX. 387

FULTON FERRY—TO BROOKLYN—CONTINUED:

 Discontinuance of any one of the ferries included in this lease to
  be a forfeiture of all 62, 65
 Ferry property of former lessees to be taken by present lessees..   68
  to be taken by the City upon the termination of lease.. 22, 71
  how a valuation of, shall be determined............... 23, 71

(G)

GRAND STREET FERRY—TO SOUTH SEVENTH STREET, WILLIAMSBURGH:

 Comptroller directed to advertise and sell a lease of.....   99
 Termini and premises, proposed to be leased, defined....   99
 Brooklyn Ferry Company authorized to run boats for
  the accommodation of the public, until sale of lease
  shall be made.................................   99

GRAND STREET FERRY—TO GRAND STREET, WILLIAMSBURGH:

 Lease of ....91 to 97
  term of...   92
  not to be assigned nor underlet, &c., without the written
   consent of the City authorities...................   95
  penalty for non-compliance with the conditions of......   96
  sureties for faithful performance of covenants of.......   97
  declared void......................................   43
  Comptroller directed to advertise and sell.............   43
 Premises leased   92
  to be kept in good repair by lessees...................   95
 Termini defined...   92

GRAND STREET FERRY—TO GRAND STREET, WILLIAMSBURGH—CONTINUED:

   Lessees of.. 91

      obligations of.................................... 93 to 96

         to construct, maintain, and keep in good repair the necessary bridges and fixtures.................... 94

   Rent to be paid... 91

      how and when to be paid........................... 92

      penalty for default in payment of.................... 96

   Ferriage to be charged...............................94, 96, 98

   Boats, description and number to be employed................ 92, 93

      extra, to be kept on hand........................... 93

      to be approved by the Comptroller 93

      to be kept in repair and properly manned, &c.......... 94

      to have fire apparatus attached to engine............ 93

      relative to time of running the..................... 94

   Compensation to be allowed for the use of fire apparatus on board boats for the extinguishing of fires............... 93

   Management of, to be subject to the ordinances, resolutions, &c., of the Common Council....................... 96

   Preamble and resolutions relative to the sale of lease of, by the Comptroller, without the sanction of the Common Council..................................42 to 44

   Counsel to the Corporation directed to take measures to prevent the use of, or interference with the........... 43

GREENPOINT FERRY :

   from foot of Fourteenth street:
      vide " FOURTEENTH STREET FERRY."

   from foot of Sixteenth street:
      vide " SIXTEENTH STREET FERRY."

GREENPOINT FERRY—Continued:

   from foot of Tenth street:
      vide "Tenth Street Ferry."
   from foot of Twenty-third street:
      vide "Twenty-third Street Ferry."

. (H)

HALSEY, —:

   permission given to, to run a ferry from the foot of Eighty-sixth street, E. R., to Astoria, L. I.............. 142

HAMILTON AVENUE FERRY—from Whitehall Street:

   Lease of, in connection with South and Fulton Ferries........18 to 24
      Preamble and resolutions in relation to selling the, in connection with the South, Wall street, Fulton and Catharine street Ferries........................61 to 63
      in connection with the South, Wall street, Fulton and Catharine street Ferries........................63 to 71
      term of..... ....19, 62, 64
      reservations in.......................20, 22, 24, 68, 69, 70
      not to be assigned, underlet, &c., without the written consent of the City authorities.................... 22, 68
      not to affect nor interfere with the establishing of other ferries... 22
      penalty for non-compliance with the conditions of...... 20, 65
      Bond for the faithful performance of covenants of...... 72
      consent given to the transfer of, to the Union Ferry Company.. 25

HAMILTON AVENUE FERRY—from Whitehall Street—Continued :

Premises leased..19, 62, 63

    to be kept in good repair by lessees................... 22, 67

    to be peaceably surrendered, in good order, upon the
        termination of lease............................ 23, 70

    City not to be responsible in damages in consequence of
        any suit in relation to its rights to any of the...... 69

Termini defined..19, 62, 69

    Brooklyn terminus may be changed.................. 62, 69

Lessees of..18, 24, 25, 63

    obligations of...................18, 20 to 22, 23, 62, 65 to 71

    to take fixtures, &c., of former lessees................ 68

    to erect, maintain and keep in good repair the necessary
        bridges, floats, fixtures, &c....................... 22, 67

    to remove or extend ferry houses and fixtures if required
        by the Common Council......................... 24

    not to run any ferry or ferries under any State law during
        the term of this lease, under penalty of forfeiture... 24

    directed to commute with passengers.................. 25

Rent to be paid.. 20, 64

    how and when to be paid............................ 20, 64

    penalty for default in payment of.................... 20, 65

Boats, description and number to be employed............... 21, 66

    spare or extra, to be kept on hand.................... 66

    to be approved by the Committees on Ferries and the
        Mayor.. 21

    to be approved by the Comptroller.................... 66

    to be kept in repair and properly manned, &c.......... 21, 66

    to have fire apparatus attached to engine.............. 71

    relative to the time of running the................... 21, 67

HAMILTON AVENUE FERRY—from Whitehall Street—Continued:

   Ferriage to be charged.............................22, 26, 62, 68

      commutation rates to be charged.................... 22

      commutation rates not to be raised during term of lease   26

   Management of, to be subject to the future ordinances, resolutions, &c., of the Common Council.................... 21, 67

      Mayor and Chairmen of Committees on Ferries to be ex-officio members of Board of Managers............. 23

   Discontinuance of any one ferry under this lease to be a forfeiture of all rights under the general lease.............. 62, 65

   Compensation to be allowed for the use of the fire apparatus on board the boats for the extinguishing of fires....... 71

   Ferry property to be taken by the City upon termination of lease 22, 71

      how a valuation of, shall be determined.............. 23, 71

HOBOKEN FERRY:

   from the foot of Barclay street:
      vide "Barclay Street Ferry."

   from the foot of Christopher street:
      vide "Christopher Street Ferry."

   from the foot of Hoboken street:
      vide "Hoboken Street Ferry."

HOBOKEN STREET FERRY—to Hoboken, N. J.:

   Lease of.. 164 to 168

      term of.. 164

      reservations in..................................... 166, 167

      not to be transferred or underlet without the written consent of City authorities...................... 166

      not to affect or interfere with the establishing of other ferries... 167

HOBOKEN STREET FERRY—TO HOBOKEN, N. J.—CONTINUED :

    penalty for non-compliance with the conditions of 167

Premises leased 164

    to be peaceably surrendered upon termination of lease .. 166

Termini defined 164

Lessees of 164, 168

    obligations of............................... 165 to 167

Rent to be paid 164

    how and when to be paid........................... 164

    penalty for default in payment of................... 167

Boats, description and number of, to be employed upon..... 165, 167

    additional, to be placed on when required by the Common Council................................... 167

    to be kept in repair and properly manned, &c........ 165, 166

    to be approved of by Committees on Ferries............ 165

    relative to time of running the..................... 165, 156

Ferriage to be charged 167

Management of, to be subject to future ordinances, resolutions, &c., of the Common Council 166

HORNE'S HOOK FERRY—TO ASTORIA, L. I. :

Proprietor of.. .. 142

Rent paid for 142

Remarks relative to.. 142

HOUSTON STREET :

    Lessees of ferry from the foot of, to keep the street in repair for 25 feet from the bulkhead............................ 104

HOUSTON STREET FERRY—TO WILLIAMSBURGH:

Lease of .... 100 to 106
    term of 101
    reservations in 104, 105
    not to be transferred or underlet without the written consent of the City authorities 104
    not to affect or interfere with the establishing of other ferries 105
    penalty for non-compliance with the conditions of 101

Premises leased 100
    to be kept in good repair by lessees 103
    to be peaceably surrendered, in good order, upon the termination of the lease 104

Termini defined 100

Lessees of 100, 106
    obligations of .... 102 to 105, 107
    to erect, maintain and keep in good repair the necessary bridges, fixtures, &c 103
    to remove ferry-houses, &c., whenever Tompkins street may be extended 104
    to keep Houston street, for twenty-five feet from the bulkhead, in good repair during term of lease 104
    directed to have a suitable lamp placed at the entrance of the ferry-house 107

Rent to be paid 101
    how and when to be paid 101
    penalty for default in payment of 101

Boats, description and number to be employed upon 102, 103
    additional, to be placed on when required by the Common Council 103

HOUSTON STREET FERRY—to Williamsburgh—Continued:

  to be kept in repair and properly manned, &c.......... 103

  to be approved by Committees on Ferries........... 102, 103

  relative to time of running the 102, 103

  Ferriage to be regulated by the ordinances, &c., of the Common
    Council and laws of the State.................... 103

  management of, to be subject to ordinances, &c., of the
    Common Council and laws of the State.......... 103

  ferry to be established and in operation by May 1st, 1853.. 102

  provisions in relation to building and completing piers at
    the foot of Houston street..................... 101

  in relation to docking out and building Tompkins
    street...................................... 104, 105

HUNTER'S POINT FERRY :

 from James Slip:
  vide "James Slip Ferry."
 from foot of Thirty-fourth street:
  vide "Thirty-fourth Street Ferry."

(J)

JACKSON STREET FERRY—to Brooklyn :

 Lease of... 83 to 89

  term of...................................... 83, 84, 85

  reservations in..................................... 88, 89

  not to be transferred or underlet without the written con-
    sent of the City authorities..................... 88

  not to affect or interfere with the establishing of other
    ferries.. 89

JACKSON STREET FERRY—to Brooklyn—Continued:

  penalty for non-compliance with the conditions of..... 85
Bond for faithful performance of covenants of lease........... 90
Premises leased 83, 84
  to be kept in good repair by lessee................... 87
  to be peaceably surrendered, in good order, upon the termination of lease............................... 88
Termini defined.. 83, 84
Lessee of... 83, 84, 89
  obligations of..................................... 86 to 89
  to erect, maintain, and keep in good order the necessary bridges, fixtures, &c............................. 87
Rent to be paid.. 85
  how and when to be paid............................. 85
  penalty for default in payment of..................... 85
Boats, description and number to be employed on............. 86
  additional, to be placed on when required by the Common Council... 86
  to be kept in repair and properly manned, &c.......... 87
  to be approved by the Common Council............... 87
  relative to the time of running the................... 86
  relative to persons employed upon the................ 86, 87
Management of, subject to the ordinances, resolutions, &c., of the Common Council................................ 87
Corporation to have the right to extend piers at the foot of Jackson street, without prejudice to lease, or being liable in damages to lessee....................... 88

JAMES SLIP FERRY—TO HUNTER'S POINT, L. I. :

 Lease of, to A. J. Berry & John J. Hicks.................. 74 to 82

  term of.. 74, 76

  reservations in..................................... 78, 81

  not to be transferred or underlet without written consent of City authorities............................ 78

  not to affect or interfere with the establishment of other ferries.. 81

  penalty for non-compliance with the conditions of...... 76

  transfer of, to Brooklyn Ferry Company............... 82

 Premises leased... 76

  to be kept in good repair by lessees 78

  to be peaceably surrendered upon termination of lease.. 75, 79

 Termini defined.. 74, 76, 82

  New York terminus authorized to be changed...... 50, 51, 82

  Williamsburgh terminus authorized to be changed..... 82

  Williamsburgh terminus authorized to be changed to Hunter's Point.............................. 51, 82

 Lessees of, to erect, maintain, and keep in good repair the necessary bridges, fixtures, &c....................... 75, 78

  obligations of............................. 75, 77 to 79, 80

 Rent to be paid... 75, 76, 82

  how and when to be paid........................... 75, 76

  penalty for default in payment of.................... 76

 Boats, description and number to be employed upon........... 77

  relative to time of running the..................... 75, 78

  relative to persons employed upon the.............. 80

 Ferriage to be charged................................... 78

 Management of, to be subject to the ordinances, resolutions, &c., of the Common Council....................... 79

JAMES SLIP FERRY—to Hunter's Point, L. I.—Continued:

Ferry property to be taken by lessors, upon the termination of the
lease 79, 80
how valuation of, shall be made..................... 79

(K)

KNAPP, GIDEON LEE:

transfer of lease of Fourteenth street ferry to........... 116
consent given to transfer of lease of Twenty-third street
ferry to.. 130

(L)

LAING, SOPHIA V. D.:

Lease to, of a ferry from the foot of Thirty-ninth street
(N. R.), to Bull's Ferry, or vicinity....... 175

LAMP:

Lessees of Houston street ferry directed to place a, at the
entrance to the ferry-house 107

LEROY, JACOB R., & HENRY E. PIERREPONT:

Lease of Hamilton avenue, South and Fulton ferries, to   18
consent given to the transfer by, of the lease to Hamilton avenue, South and Fulton ferries to the Union
Ferry Company of Brooklyn...................   25
consent given to transfer of lease of ferry from Roosevelt street to Brooklyn to......... .   50

(M)

MARTINE, JOHN H.:

    Lease to, of ferry from Roosevelt street to Brooklyn... 45

    consent given to transfer of lease of ferry from Roosevelt street to Brooklyn, to Jacob R. Leroy & Henry E. Pierrepoint, by.......................... 50

MAYOR:

    to be ex-officio member of the Board of Managers of the Hamilton avenue, South and Fulton ferries........ 23

    to approve boats to be employed on Chambers street ferry... 159

    to approve boats to be employed on Hamilton avenue, South and Fulton ferries.......... 21

    to approve boats to be employed on Thirty-fourth street ferry..136, 140

MESEROLE, J. V., AND OTHERS:

    Lease to, of ferry from Peck slip to Williamsburgh..... 34

    Lease to, of ferry from Peck slip to Williamsburgh, declared void............................... 42

    consent given to transfer by, of lease of Peck slip ferry to the Brooklyn Ferry Company.................... 44

    Lease to, of ferry from foot of Grand street to Williamsburgh...................................... 91

    Lease to, of ferry from foot of Grand street to Williamsburgh, declared void. 42, 98

(N)

NEW JERSEY RAILROAD AND TRANSPORTATION COMPANY:

    Lease of ferry to, from foot of Cortlandt street to Jersey City...... 143

    to establish a ferry from the vicinity of the foot of Canal street to Jersey City, when required so to do by the Common Council of New York.................. 146

    directed to establish a ferry from the vicinity of the foot of Canal street to Jersey City, in accordance with their agreement............................. 169

(P)

PAVONIA FERRY:

    Vide "CHAMBERS STREET FERRY."

PAVONIA FERRY COMPANY:

    Lease to, of a ferry from the foot of Chambers street to Pavonia avenue, N. J., or vicinity............ 152

PECK SLIP FERRY—TO WILLIAMSBURGH:

    Lease of..34 to 41

    term of... 35

    reservations in.. 38, 39, 40

    not to be transferred nor underlet without the written consent of the City authorities.................. 39

PECK SLIP FERRY—TO WILLIAMSBURGH—CONTINUED:

  penalty for non-compliance with the conditions of 40
  declared void.. 43
  Comptroller directed to advertise and sell 43
  authorized to be transferred to the Brooklyn Ferry Company... 44
Premises leased.. 35, 38
  to be surrendered, in good order, upon the termination of the lease.................................... 38
Termini defined... 35
  Brooklyn terminus authorized to be changed........... 44
Lessees of... 34, 40
  obligations of............................... 35, 36, 37, 39
  to erect, maintain, and keep in good repair the necessary bridges, fixtures, &c......... 37
  authorized to transfer lease of to the Brooklyn Ferry Company... 44
  ferry-houses, &c,, constructed at certain points, to remain the property of................................. 39
  to have the privilege of removing any ferry-houses or fixtures erected by them upon the northerly basin of Peck slip 39
Rent to be paid... 35
  how and when to be paid............................. 35
  penalty for default in payment of..................... 40
Boats, description and number to be employed.............. 36
  to be approved by the Comptroller 37
  to be kept in repair and properly manned, &c.......... 37
  to have fire apparatus and hose attached to engine...... 36
  relative to the time of running the................... 37

PECK SLIP FERRY—to Williamsburgh—Continued :

 Ferriage to be charged...................................... 37, 41

 Management of, to be subject to the ordinances, resolutions, &c., of the Common Council......................... 39

 Compensation to be paid by the City for the use of the fire apparatus on board the boats, in cases of fires............ 36

 Preambles and resolutions in relation to sale of lease of, by the Comptroller without the sanction of the Common Council... 42 to 44

 Counsel to the Corporation directed to take measures to prevent the use of or interference with the................ 43

PIER :

 No. 30, North River, Pavonia Ferry lessees not to permit any obstruction to be erected on the south side of.. 156

PIERS :

 at *foot of Eighty-sixth street, North River,* Corporation may extend without prejudice to lease of ferry from, or being liable to a claim for damages by lessee....... 194

 at *foot of Forty-second street, North River,* Corporation may extend without prejudice to lease of ferry from, or being liable to a claim for damages by lessee....... 187

 at *foot of Fourteenth street, East River,* Corporation may extend without prejudice to lease of ferry from, or being liable to a claim for damages by lessee....... 114

 at *foot of Houston street, East River,* Corporation may extend without prejudice to lease of ferry from, or being liable to a claim for damages by lessee............ 101

 at *foot of Jackson street, East River,* Corporation may extend without prejudice to lease of ferry from, or being liable to a claim for damages by lessee............ 88

PIERS—Continued:

    at foot of *Sixteenth street, East River*, Corporation may extend without prejudice to lease of ferry from, or being liable to a claim for damages by lessee............ 122

    at foot of *Thirty-ninth street, North River*, Corporation may extend without prejudice to lease of ferry from, or being liable to a claim for damages by lessee....... 180

PRICE, FRANCIS:

    lease to, of a ferry from the foot of Forty-second street (N. R.) to Weehawken, N. J...................... 181

    consent given to transfer of lease of ferry from foot of Forty-second street (N. R.) to the Weehawken Ferry Company, by................................. 189

(R)

RHINELANDER, ESTATE OF WILLIAM:

    provisions in lease of ferry from the foot of Barclay street to Hoboken, New Jersey, in relation to claim of, to the bulkhead at the foot of Barclay street..... 148, 151

ROOSEVELT STREET FERRY—to Williamsburgh:

    Lease of ....45 to 49

    term of 45

    reservations in....................................... 46, 48

    not to be assigned, underlet, &c., without the written consent of the City authorities.................. 49

    not to affect or interfere with the establishing of other ferries 49

ROOSEVELT STREET FERRY—to Williamsburgh—Continued:

    penalty for non-compliance with the conditions of...... 46

    consent given to the transfer of, to Jacob R. Leroy and Henry E. Pierrepoint............................ 50

    consent given to the sale of, to the Brooklyn Ferry Company 51

Premises leased... 45

    to be kept in good repair by lessee.................... 48

    to be peaceably surrendered, in good order, upon the termination of the lease............................ 48

Termini defined... 45, 51

    Brooklyn terminus authorized to be changed........... 51

Lessee of.. 45, 49

    obligations of....................................46 to 49

    to construct, maintain and keep in good repair the necessary bridges, fixtures, &c......................... 48, 50

Rent to be paid... 46

    when to commence................................... 50

    how and when to be paid............................. 46

    penalty for default in payment of..................... 46

Boats, description and number to be employed.............. 47

    additional, to be placed on when required by the Common Council... 47

    to be approved by the Common Council............... 47

    to be kept in good repair, and properly manned, &c..... 47

    relative to the time of running the.................... 47

Ferriage to be charged..................................... 48

To be put into operation by or before 1st May, 1853............ 47, 49

Penalty for failure to put into operation by May 1st, 1853..... 49

Management of, to be subject to ordinances, &c., of the Common Council, and laws of State Legislature 48

RUSS, HORACE P., AND OTHERS:

    Consent given to the transfer to, of a ferry lease from the foot of Eighty-sixth street, North River, to Bull's Ferry.. 195

(S)

SCHEDULE:

    of ferries... 7, 8

    of ferry rates to be charged on Chambers Street Ferry.161 to 163

    of ferry rates to be charged on Fourteenth Street Ferry. 115

    of ferry rates to be charged on Grand Street Ferry...... 98

    of ferry rates to be charged on Hamilton Avenue, South and Fulton Ferries............................ 26

    of ferry rates to be charged on Peck Slip Ferry........ 41

    of ferry rates to be charged on Sixteenth Street Ferry .120, 123

SCHULTZ, ALEXANDER H.:

    Lease to, of ferry from the foot of Fourteenth street, to Greenpoint, L. I............................. 108

    transfer to, of lease of ferry from the foot of Sixteenth street, to Greenpoint, L. I.....................109, 124

SHARP, JACOB:

    Lease of ferry from Wall street to Brooklyn, to........ 26

    permission given to, to transfer one undivided half interest in the Wall Street Ferry to Freeman Campbell and Rutherford Moody......................... 33

SIXTEENTH STREET FERRY—TO GREENPOINT, L. I. :

   Lease of... 117 to 124
      term of... 117, 118
      reservations in... 121, 122
      not to be transferred or underlet without the written consent of the City authorities....................... 121
      not to affect or interfere with the establishing of other ferries... 122
      penalty for non-compliance with the conditions of...... 119
      transfer of, to Alexander H. Schultz................ 109, 124
   Premises leased... 118
      to be kept in good repair by lessees................... 121
      to be peaceably surrendered in good condition upon termination of lease............................. 121
   Termini defined.. 117, 118
      N. Y. terminus changed to foot of Fourteenth street.. 109, 124
   Lessees of.. 117, 124
      obligations of.. 119 to 121
      to erect, maintain, and keep in good repair the necessary bridges, fixtures, &c........................ 121
   Rent to be paid.. 117, 118
      when and how to be paid............................ 118
      penalty for default in payment of..................... 119
   Boats, description and number to be employed upon......... 117, 120
      additional, to be placed on when required by Common Council... 120
      to be approved by the Street Commissioner............ 120
      to be kept in repair and properly manned, &c.......... 120
      relative to time of running the...................... 120

SIXTEENTH STREET FERRY—TO GREENPOINT, L. I.—CONTINUED :

 Ferriage to be charged................................... 120, 123

 Management of, to be subject to future ordinances, resolutions,
  &c., of the Common Council...................... 120

 Corporation may extend piers at foot of Sixteenth street without prejudice to lease, or being liable to lessees in a claim for damage.............................. 122

SLIP :

 at foot of Wall street, rent to be paid for by ferry company until their ferry shall be in operation......... 20

 between piers Nos. 31 and 32, East River, New York terminus of ferry leased to Berry & Hicks authorized to be changed to.................................... 50, 82

 between piers Nos. 34 and 35, East River, resolution to sink a bulkhead, to be used for ferry purposes in......... 60

 between piers Nos. 30 and 31, North River, lessees of Chambers Street Ferry not to permit any block or blocks to be sunk in.................................. 157

SMITH, JACOB L.:

 Lease to, of ferry from Whitehall street to Staten Island. 9

SMITH, CYRUS P. & W. F. BULKLEY :

 permission given to transfer to, lease of ferry from foot of Catharine street to Brooklyn................. 59

SOUTH FERRY—TO ATLANTIC STREET, BROOKLYN :

 Lease of, in connection with Hamilton Avenue and Fulton Ferries..18 to 24

 Preamble and resolutions in relation to selling the, in connection with the Hamilton Avenue, Wall Street, Fulton and Catharine Street Ferries.............61 to 63

SOUTH FERRY—TO ATLANTIC STREET, BROOKLYN—CONTINUED :

    in connection with the Hamilton Avenue, Wall Street,
Fulton and Catharine Street Ferries .... 63 to 71

    term of... 19, 62, 64

    reservations in........................ 20, 22, 24, 68, 69, 70

    not to be assigned, underlet, &c., without the written consent of the City authorities................... 22, 68

    not to affect nor interfere with the establishing of other ferries... 22

    penalty for non-compliance with the conditions of....... 20, 65

    Bond for the faithful performance of the covenants of.. 72

    consent given to the transfer of, to the Union Ferry Company.. 25

Premises leased....................................... 19, 62, 63

    to be kept in good repair by the lessees................ 22, 67

    to be peaceably surrendered, in good order, upon the termination of the lease........................... 23, 70

    City not to be reponsible in damages, in consequence of any suit in relation to its rights to any of the...... 69

Termini defined....................................... 19, 62, 69

    certain, may be changed............................. 69

Lessees of... 18, 24, 25, 63

    obligations of........................ 18, 20 to 22, 23, 62, 65 to 71

    to take ferry property of former lessees............... 68

    to erect, maintain and keep in good repair the necessary bridges, fixtures, &c........................... 22, 67

    to remove or extend ferry-houses and fixtures if required by the Common Council......................... 24

    not to run any ferry or ferries under any State law during the term of this lease, under penalty of forfeiture.. 24

    directed to commute with passengers................. 25

SOUTH FERRY—TO ATLANTIC STREET, BROOKLYN—CONTINUED :

 Rent to be paid... 20, 64

  how and when to be paid........................... 20, 64

  penalty for default in payment of..................... 20, 65

 Boats, description and number to be employed............... 21, 66

  extra, to be kept on hand........................... 66

  to be approved by Committees on Ferries and Mayor.... 21

  to be approved by Comptroller....................... 66

  to be kept in repair and properly manned, &c.......... 21, 66

  to have fire apparatus attached to engine.............. 71

  relative to the time of running the................... 21, 67

 Ferriage to be charged.............................22, 26, 62, 68

  commutation rates to be charged..................... 22

  commutation rates not to be raised during the term of lease.. 26

 Compensation to be allowed for the use of the fire apparatus on board the boats in cases of fires.................. 71

 Management of, to be subject to the ordinances, resolutions, &c., of the Common Council.......................... 21, 67

  Mayor and Chairmen of Committees on ferries to be ex-officio members of the Board of Managers......... 23

 Discontinuance of any one of the ferries included in this lease to be a forfeiture of all............................. 62, 65

 Ferry property of former lessees to be taken by present lessees.. 68

  to be taken by the City upon the termination of lease.. 22, 71

  how a valuation of, shall be determined............... 23, 71

STATEN ISLAND FERRY—FROM WHITEHALL STREET :

 Lease of..9 to 17

  term of... 9, 13

STATEN ISLAND FERRY—FROM WHITEHALL STREET—CONTINUED:

 reservations in.......................... 10, 11, 12, 16, 17
 not to affect or interfere with the establishing of other
  ferries..11, 17
 penalty for non-compliance with the conditions of...... 13
 bond for the faithful performance of the covenants of... 11, 17

Premises leased..10, 11
 to be kept in good repair by lessee............... 11, 14, 15
 to be peaceably surrendered, in good condition, upon
  the termination of the lease...................... 16

Termini defined..10, 12

Lessee of.. 9, 17
 obligations of.............................. 10, 11, 13 to 16
 to erect, maintain and keep in good repair the necessary bridges, fixtures, &c........................ 11, 14

Rent to be paid.. 9, 13
 how and when to be paid........................... 13, 14
 penalty for default in payment of.................... 13

Boats, description and number to be employed.......... 10, 11, 15
 to be approved by the Commissioners of the Sinking
  Fund... 15
 to be kept in repair and properly manned, &c.......... 11, 15
 relative to the time of running the................... 15

Management of, to be subject to future ordinances, laws, &c.,
 of the Common Council or State Legislature.......... 11, 16

FROM PIER NO. 2, NORTH RIVER—

 relative to... 142

STEAMBOATS:

 on *Barclay Street Ferry*, description and number of, to be employed.. 150

STEAMBOATS—Continued :

    additional, to be put on when required by the Common
        Council... 150

    on *Catharine Street Ferry*, description and number of, to be em-
        ployed....................................... 55, 66

        extra, to be kept on hand........................ 66

        to be approved by the Comptroller............... 66
        to have fire apparatus attached to engine........ 71

        relative to the time of running the............. 55, 60

    on *Chambers Street Ferry*, description and number of, to be em-
        ployed..................................... 156, 159

        additional, to be put on when required by the Common
            Council.. 159

        to be approved by the Mayor or Comptroller.......... 159

        relative to the time of running the.................. 158

    on *Christopher Street Ferry*, description and number of, to be em-
        ployed..................................... 171, 173

        additional, to be placed on when required by the Com-
            mon Council................................... 173

        to be approved by Committees on Ferries............ 171

        relative to the time of running the.................. 172

    on *Cortlandt Street Ferry*, relative to the time of running the..... 146

    on *Eighty-sixth Street Ferry*, description and number of, to be em-
        ployed..................................... 190, 192

        additional, to be put on when required by the Common
            Council.. 192

        to be approved by the Street Commissioner........... 192

        relative to the time of running the................ 190, 193

    on *Forty-second Street Ferry*, description and number of, to be em-
        ployed... 185

STEAMBOATS—Continued:

  additional, to be put on when required by the Common Council.. 185

  to be approved.................................. 185

  relative to the time of running the.............. 185, 186

 on *Fourteenth Street Ferry*, description and number of, to be employed... 112

  additional, to be put on when required by the Common Council.. 112

  to be approved by the Street Commissioner........ 112

  relative to the time of running the.............. 112, 113

 on *Fulton Ferry*, description and number of, to be employed. 21, 66

  extra, to be kept on hand........................ 66

  to be approved by Committees on Ferries and Mayor... 21

  to be approved by the Comptroller................ 66

  to have fire apparatus attached to engine........ 71

  relative to the time of running the.............. 21, 67

 on *Grand Street Ferry*, description and number of, to be employed... 92, 93

  extra, to be kept on hand........................ 93

  to be approved by the Comptroller................ 93

  to have fire apparatus attached to engine........ 93

  relative to time of running the.................. 94

 on *Hamilton Avenue Ferry*, description and number of, to be employed... 21, 66

  extra, to be kept on hand........................ 66

  to be approved by Committees on Ferries and Mayor... 21

  to be approved by Comptroller.................... 66

  to have fire apparatus attached to engine........ 71

  relative to the time of running the.............. 21, 67

STEAMBOATS—Continued:

   on Hoboken Street Ferry, description and number of, to be employed................................. 165, 167

      additional, to be put on when required by the Common Council.. 167

      to be approved by Committees on Ferries.............. 165

      relative to the time of running the................. 165, 166

   on Houston Street Ferry, description and number of, to be employed..................................... 102, 103

      additional, to be placed on when required by the Common Council................................ 103

      to be approved by Committees on Ferries........... 102, 103

      relative to the time of running the................. 102, 103

   on Jackson Street Ferry, description and number of, to be employed on.. 86

      additional, to be placed on when required by the Common Council................................. 86

      to be approved by the Common Council.............. 87

      relative to the time of running the.................. 86

   on James Slip Ferry, description and number of, to be employed... 77

      relative to the time of running the................... 75, 78

   on Peck Slip Ferry, description and number of, to be employed.. 36

      to be approved by the Comptroller.................. 37

      to have fire apparatus attached to engine............. 36

      relative to the time of running the.................. 37

   on Roosevelt Street Ferry, description and number of, to be employed... 47

      additional, to be placed on when required by the Common Council................................. 47

INDEX. 413

STEAMBOATS—Continued:

 to be approved by the Common Council............ 47
 relative to the time of running the... 47
 on *Sixteenth Street Ferry*, description and number of, to be employed................................. 117, 120
  additional, to be placed on when required by the Common Council................... 120
  to be approved by the Street Commissioner............ 120
  relative to the time of running the......... 120
 on *South Ferry*, description and number of, to be employed. 21, 66
  extra, to be kept on hand........................... 66
  to be approved by Committees on Ferries and Mayor.... 21
  to be approved by the Comptroller................... 66
  to have fire apparatus attached to engine............. 71
  relative to the time of running the.................. 21, 67
 on *Staten Island Ferry*, description and number of, to be employed..................................... 10, 11, 15
  to be approved by the Commissioners of the Sinking Fund 15
  relative to the time of running the................... 15
 on *Thirty-fourth Street Ferry*, description and number of, to be employed................................. 136, 137, 139
  additional, to be placed on when required by the Common Council.. 136
  to be approved by the Mayor or Comptroller......... 136, 140
  relative to the time of running the.............. .. 136, 137
 on *Thirty-ninth Street Ferry*, description and number of, to be employed.....................................176, 178
  additional, to be placed on when required by the Common Council... 178
  to be approved by the Street Commissioner............ 178

STEAMBOATS—Continued:

    relative to the time of running the.................... 179

    on Twenty-third Street Ferry, description and number of, to be
        employed..128, 132

    additional, to be placed on when required by the Common
        Council.. 132

    to be approved by the Street Commissioner............ 128

    relative to the time of running the.................. 128, 132

    on Wall Street Ferry, description and number of, to be employed... 30, 66

    additional, to be provided if required................ 30

    extra, to be kept on hand........................... 66

    to be approved by the Street Commissioner............ 30

    to be approved by the Comptroller................... 66

    to have fire apparatus attached to engine............. 71

    relative to the time of running the.................... 30, 67

STEVENS, JOHN C., ROBERT L., AND EDWIN A.:

    lease to, of ferry from foot of Barclay street to Hoboken   148

    lease to, of ferry from foot of Christopher street to Hoboken.. 169

    lease to, of ferry from foot of Hoboken street to Hoboken.. 164

STREET COMMISSIONER:

    to approve boats to be employed on Eighty-sixth street ferry... 192

    to approve boats to be employed on Fourteenth street ferry... 112

    to approve boats to be employed on Sixteenth street ferry... 120

STREET COMMISSIONER—Continued :

    to approve boats to be employed on Thirty-ninth street ferry... 178

    to approve boats to be employed on Twenty-third street ferry... 128

    to approve boats to be employed on Wall street ferry... 30

STUYVESANT, GERARD, and OTHERS :

    lease to, of ferry, from foot of Houston street to Williamsburgh... 100

(T)

TENTH STREET FERRY—to Greenpoint, L. I. :

    remarks relative to.................................. 108

THIRTY-FOURTH STREET FERRY—to Hunter's Point, L. I. :

    Lease of...132 to 140

    term of.. 135

    reservations in.............................133, 137, 140

    not to be transferred, underlet, &c., without the written consent of the Comptroller......................... 137

    not to affect or interfere with the establishing of other ferries.. 140

    penalty for non-compliance with the conditions of...... 135

    bond for faithful performance of the covenants of...... 141

    Premises leased.......................................133, 134

    to be kept in good repair by the lessee................ 137

THIRTY-FOURTH STREET FERRY—TO HUNTER'S POINT, L. I.—CONTINUED :

 t : peaceably surrendered upon the termination of
lease.. 138
Termini defined.. 133, 134
Lessee of... 132, 140
 obligations of........................... 133, 136 to 138, 139
 to erect, maintain and keep in good repair the necessary
  bridges, fixtures, &c............................ 137
 land and water front to be used for the L. I. terminus,
  to be conveyed by, to the city in fee............. 133
Rent to be paid... 135
 how and when to be paid............................. 135
 penalty for default in the payment of............... 135
Boats, description and number to be employed....... 136, 137, 139
 additional, to be placed on when required by the Common
  Council... 136
 to be approved by the Mayor or Comptroller........ 136, 140
 to be kept in repair and properly manned, &c........ 136
 relative to time of running the..................... 136, 137
Management of, to be subject to the ordinances, resolutions, &c.,
 of the Common Council............................... 137
Date when the ferry shall be put into operation............... 136
Ferry property to be purchased by parties obtaining the lease
 subsequently to expiration of the present............ 139
 valuation of, how to be made........................ 138

THIRTY-NINTH STREET FERRY—TO BULL'S FERRY :

Lease of... 175 to 181
 term of.. 177
 reservations in...................................... 177, 180

INDEX. 417

THIRTY-NINTH STREET FERRY—TO BULL'S FERRY—CONTINUED:

    not to be transferred or underlet without the written consent of City authorities.................... 180

    not to affect or interfere with the establishing of other ferries.. 181

    penalty for non-compliance with the conditions of...... 177

Premises leased... 176

    to be kept in good repair by lessee.................... 179

    to be peaceably surrendered, in good order, upon the termination of lease............................ 179

Termini defined..175, 176

Lessee of..175, 181

    obligations of....................................176, 178 to 180

    to erect, maintain and keep in good repair the necessary bridges, fixtures, &c........................176, 179

    to keep in repair piers, &c., to be constructed........ 179

Rent to be paid for...................................... 175, 177

    date of commencement of......................... 181

    how and when to be paid......................... 177, 181

    penalty for default in payment of.................. 177

Boats, description and number to be employed on 176, 178

    additional, to be placed on when required by the Common Council............................... 178

    to be kept in repair and properly manned, &c......... 178

    to be approved by the Street Commissioner............ 178

    relative to the time of running the................... 179

Ferriage to be subject to regulation by the Common Council.... 179

Management of, to be subject to the ordinances, resolutions, &c., of the Common Council........................ 179

418   INDEX.

THIRTY-NINTH STREET FERRY—To Bull's Ferry—Continued:

 Corporation to have the right to extend piers at the foot of Thirty-ninth street, without prejudice to lease, or being liable to lessee in a claim for damage........ 180

TOMPKINS STREET:

 Provisions in lease of ferry from the foot of Houston street to Williamsburgh, in relation to docking out and building......................................104, 105

TRUSTEES OF ST. PATRICK'S CATHEDRAL:

 Lease to, of ferry from foot of Twenty-third street to Penny Bridge, L. I.................................. 125

  permission granted to, to transfer lease of the ferry from the foot of Twenty-third street to Gideon Lee Knapp................................. 130

TWENTY-THIRD STREET FERRY—To Greenpoint, L. I.:

 Lease of..125 to 130

  term of..125, 127

  reservations in........................... 127, 129, 130

  not to be transferred or underlet without the written consent of the City authorities 129

  not to affect or interfere with the establishing of other ferries 130

  consent given to the transfer of, to Gideon Lee Knapp.. 130

 Premises leased 126

  to be kept in good repair by lessees 129

  to be peaceably surrendered, in good condition, upon termination of lease 129

 Termini defined..................................125, 126

  portion of water front of bulkhead to be used for, on the New York side, designated 127

TWENTY-THIRD STREET FERRY—TO GREEN POINT, L. I.—CONTINUED:

 change of Long Island terminus authorized............ 130
Lessees of...125, 130
 obligations of......... ....127 to 129
 to erect, maintain and keep in good repair the necessary
  bridges, &c...................................... 129
 position of fixtures to be erected by, specially designated 126
 directed to run their boats to Penny Bridge while the
  ferry slips at Greenpoint are being completed...... 131
 directed to run boats more frequently and regularly.... 132
Rent to be paid for.. 127
 how and when to be paid........................... 127
Boats, description and number to be employed..............128, 132
 additional, to be run on when required by the Common
  Council....................................... 132
 to be kept in repair, and properly manned, &c.......... 128
 to be approved by the Street Commissioner........... 128
 directed to be run more frequently and regularly....... 132
 relative to time of running the....... ....128, 132
Management of, to be subject to the ordinances, resolutions, &c.,
 of the Common Council........................ 128
Relative to a ferry run by the lessees of, from the foot of Tenth
 street, E. R., to Greenpoint, L. I.................. 108

(U)

UNION FERRY COMPANY:

 consent given to transfer of lease of Hamilton avenue
  South and Fulton ferries to.................... 25

420   INDEX.

UNION FERRY COMPANY—Continued:

    directed to commute with passengers by the Hamilton
        avenue, South, and Fulton Ferries.............. 25

    authorized to agree with the Brooklyn Ferry Company
        for the sale of the lease, fixtures, &c., of the Roose-
        velt street Ferry............................. 51

    directed to run boats at certain times on the Catharine
        street Ferry................................. 60

    lease of Hamilton avenue, South, Wall street, Fulton,
        and Catharine street Ferries to.................. 63

UNITED STATES GOVERNMENT:

    not to be interfered within the use of pier No. 1, E. R., by
        the lessee of Staten Island Ferry................ 10, 12

    to have the use of part of the pier west of pier No. 1, E.R.   10

(W)

WALL STREET FERRY—to Brooklyn:

Lease of... 26 to 33

    Preamble and resolutions in relation to selling, in connec-
        tion with the Hamilton avenue, South, Fulton, and
        Catharine street Ferries .... 61 to 63

    in connection with the Hamilton avenue, South, Fulton,
        and Catharine street Ferries.. .... 63 to 71

    term of...................................... 27, 28, 62, 64

    agreement as to the determination of, on May 1st, 1861..61, 63

    Reservations in............................ 32, 68, 69, 70

    not to be transferred or underlet, &c., without the written
        consent of the city authorities 31, 68

WALL STREET FERRY—TO BROOKLYN—CONTINUED:

  not to affect nor interfere with the establishing of other
    ferries   32

  penalty for non-compliance with the conditions of......
     27, 28, 32, 65

  bond for the faithful performance of the covenants of..   72

  consent given to transfer of, to F. Campbell and R. Moody   33

Premises leased 26, 27, 62, 63

  to be kept in good repair by the lessees 31, 67

  to be peaceably surrendered, in good order, upon the termination of the lease........................... 31, 70

  City not to be responsible in damages, in consequence of
    any suit in relation to its rights to any of the   69

Termini defined 27, 30, 62, 69

  certain, may be changed   69

Lessees of 26, 33, 63

  obligations of .... 29 to 32, 62, 65 to 71

  to take ferry property of former lessees.............   68

  to erect, maintain, and keep in good repair the necessary
    bridges, fixtures, &c. 31, 67

  to put the ferry into operation within fifteen months after
    the execution of the lease 27, 32

Rent to be paid...................................27, 28, 33, 64

  of slip only to be paid until ferry shall be established..   29

  when to commence................................ 27, 28

  how and when to be paid 27, 28, 64

  penalty for default in payment of 28, 64

Ferriage to be charged........... ....30, 62, 68

Boats, description and number of, to be employed........... 30, 66

WALL STREET FERRY—TO BROOKLYN—CONTINUED:

    additional, to be provided if required................ 30

    extra, to be kept on hand.. 66

    to be approved by the Street Commissioner............ 30

    to be approved by the Comptroller 66

    to be kept in repair and properly manned, &c.......... 30, 66

    to have fire apparatus attached to engine 71

    relative to the time of running the............. ..... 30, 67

    Compensation to be allowed for the use of fire apparatus on board boats for the extinguishing of fires.............. 71

    Penalty for default in putting the ferry into operation by the period specified in lease........................ 27, 32

    Management of, to be subject to the ordinances, resolutions, &c., of the Common Council......................... 30, 67

    Discontinuance of any one of the ferries included in the lease to be a forfeiture of all............................ 62, 65

    Ferry property of former lessees to be taken by present lessees. 68

    to be taken by the city upon the termination of lease... 71

    how the value of, shall be determined............... 71

WEEHAWKEN FERRY:

    from foot of Forty-second street:

        vide "FORTY-SECOND STREET FERRY."

WEEHAWKEN FERRY COMPANY:

    consent given to transfer of lease of ferry from the foot of Forty-second street, North River, to............. 189

WILLIAMSBURGH FERRY:

    from foot of Grand street:

        vide "GRAND STREET FERRY."

WILLIAMSBURGH FERRY—Continued:

   from north of foot of Grand street:

      vide "GRAND STREET FERRY."

   from foot of Houston street:

      vide "HOUSTON STREET FERRY."

   from Peck Slip:

      vide "PECK SLIP FERRY."

   from foot of Roosevelt streeet:

      vide "ROOSEVELT STREET FERRY."

WILSON, JAMES:

   Lease to, of ferry from foot of Jackson street to Brooklyn,   83

WINANS, ANTHONY W.:

   Lease to, of ferry from foot of Thirty-fourth street, East River, to Hunter's Point, Long Island............   132

WOODHULL, CALEB S.:

   permission given to transfer lease of ferry from Catharine street to Brooklyn to...........................   59

   consent given to transfer of lease of ferry from Catharine street to Brooklyn to Cyrus P. Smith and William F. Bulkley by.................................   59

INDEX TO RAILROAD GRANTS.

(A)

ALLERTON, A. M., JR., & COMPANY :

    privilege granted to, to lay a rail track in Forty-second street, from the Hudson River, to connect with the track of the Hudson River Railroad at Eleventh avenue.. 334

ARCH :

    New York and Harlem Railroad Company directed to build an, over their track from Thirty-fourth to Thirty-ninth street............................... 237

AVENUE :

    First, Second Avenue Railroad Company authorized to lay a rail track in..................................... 199

    Second, Second Avenue Railroad Company authorized to lay a rail track in.................................199, 200

    from Forty-eighth to Sixty-first street, one-third of the expense of paving, with Belgian pavement, to be paid by the Railroad Company.................... 206

    from Forty-ninth to Fifty-third street, rails in, directed to be removed..................................... 204

    from Forty-ninth to Sixty-first street, rails in, directed to be removed to centre of avenue.................... 205

(425)

AVENUE—Continued :

> *Third*, Third Avenue Railroad Company authorized to lay rail-
> tracks in.. 207
>> from Fifty-sixth to Eigthy-sixth street, a portion of the
>> expense of paving, with Belgian pavement, to be paid
>> by the Railroad Company....................... 219
>
> *Madison*, from Forty-second to Seventy-ninth street, New York
> and Harlem Railroad Company authorized to lay rail
> tracks in.. 251
>
> *Fourth*, New York and Harlem Railroad Company authorized to
> lay rail tracks in........................220, 224, 226
>> between Twenty-eighth and Thirty-second streets, New
>> York and Harlem Railroad Company directed to
>> regulate and grade............................. 234
>> between Thirty-second and Thirty-fourth streets, New
>> York and Harlem Railroad Company authorized to
>> reduce the grade on the east side of, and to lay a
>> turn-out track in.............................. 244
>> between Thirty-second and Forty-second streets, New
>> York and Harlem Railroad Company directed to
>> build a wall on each side and arch over a portion of
>> their track in, &c............................. 236
>> at intersection with Thirty-fourth street, New York and
>> Harlem Railroad Company directed to reduce the
>> grade of....................................... 253
>> at intersection with Thirty-fourth street, New York and
>> Harlem Railroad Company directed to construct a
>> bridge... 233
>> at intersection with Thirty-eighth street, New York and
>> Harlem Railroad Company directed to construct a
>> bridge... 233

INDEX. 427

AVENUE—Continued :

    between Forty-second and Fiftieth streets, New York and Harlem Railroad Company authorized to lay down additional tracks in.................................. 252

    Fourth, at intersection with Fiftieth street, New York and Harlem Railroad Company directed to restore the bridge on... 233

    at intersection with Seventieth street, New York and Harlem Railroad Company directed to construct a bridge... 253

    at intersection with Seventy-ninth street, New York and Harlem Railroad Company directed to construct a bridge... 233

    at intersection with Eighty-third street, New York and Harlem Railroad Company directed to construct a bridge... 243

    at intersection with Eighty-fourth street, New York and Harlem Railroad Company directed to construct a bridge... 243

    at intersection with Eighty-fifth street, New York and Harlem Railroad Company directed to construct a bridge... 233, 235

    at intersection with Eighty-eighth street, New York and Harlem Railroad Company directed to construct a bridge... 243

    at intersection with Ninetieth street, New York and Harlem Railroad Company directed to construct a bridge... 246

    at intersection with One Hundred and Fourth street, New York and Harlem Railroad Company directed to construct a bridge............................... 245

AVENUE—Continued:

 between One Hundred and Twenty-fifth and One Hundred and Twenty-seventh streets, petition that the New York and Harlem Railroad Company be permitted to lay a side track in........................... 236

 Sixth, from Fourth street to Harlem, Sixth Avenue Railroad Company authorized to lay rail tracks in.... 270, 271, 279

 Space between outside rails of tracks in, authorized to be paved with small cobble stone................... 285

 to Forty-fourth street, petition that the gas pipes may be extended in............................... 280

 Seventh, remonstrance against the passage of a bill by the Legislature granting a franchise for a railroad in......... 286

 Eighth, Eighth Avenue Railroad Company authorized to lay rail tracks in.............................. 267, 289, 292

 Street Commissioner directed to notify the Railroad Company to repair the pavements in.............. 304

 from Fifty-first to Fifty-ninth street, track directed to be relaid in....................................... 303

 Ninth, from Gansevoort to Fifty-first street, Ninth Avenue Railroad Company authorized to lay rail tracks in... 309, 312

 from Fifty-first street to Bloomingdale road, Ninth Avenue Railroad Company authorized to lay rail tracks in....................................... 311

 Tenth, from West to Thirtieth street, Hudson River Railroad Company authorized to lay rail tracks in.......... 317

 track in, directed to be taken up and relaid with the grooved rail..................................... 331

 from Fourteenth to Thirtieth street, Railroad Company to take up rail tracks in, and to lay them in Eleventh avenue, when required by the Common Council 318, 322

AVENUE—Continued:

 near Thirtieth street, rail track in, directed to be taken up and to be relaid in a different manner...327, 328

 from Bloomingdale road to Harlem, Ninth Avenue Railroad Company authorized to lay rail tracks in...... 311

 Eleventh, from Fourteenth to Thirty-second street, Hudson River Railroad Company to lay their tracks in, when required by the Common Council..........318, 322

 from Thirty-second to Fifty-third street, Hudson River Railroad Company directed to take up their track and relay the same with the grooved rail.......... 331

 from Thirty-second to Sixtieth street, Hudson River Railroad Company authorized to lay rail tracks in.. 317

 Hudson River Railroad Company directed to make the grade of their road in, conform to the grade of the avenue.. 333

 Twelfth, Hudson River Railroad Company authorized to lay rail tracks in...................................... 317

(B)

BRIDGE:

 New York and Harlem Railroad Company directed to construct a, at each of the intersections of Fourth avenue with Thirty-fourth and Thirty-eighth streets 233

 New York and Harlem Railroad Company directed to have the iron railing on the, at Thirty-fourth street, properly secured............................. 245

 New York and Harlem Railroad Company directed to restore the, at the intersection of Fourth avenue and Fiftieth street.................................. 233

BRIDGE—Continued:

 New York and Harlem Railroad Company directed to construct a, at the intersection of Fourth avenue and Seventieth street............................ 253

 New York and Harlem Railroad Company directed to construct a, at each of the intersections of Fourth avenue with Seventy-ninth and Eighty-fifth streets. 233, 235

 New York and Harlem Railroad Company directed to construct a, at each of the intersections of Fourth avenue with Eighty-third, Eighty-fourth, and Eighty-eighth streets... 243

 New York and Harlem Railroad Company directed to construct a, at the intersection of Fourth avenue and Ninetieth street................................. 246

 New York and Harlem Railroad Company directed to construct a, at the intersection of Fourth avenue and One Hundred and Fourth street................. 245

BRIDGES:

 to be constructed by the New York and Harlem Railroad Company at such intersections of their road with the streets, as their embankments or excavations may render necessary................................ 221

 to be constructed by the Hudson River Railroad Company, at such intersections of their road with the streets, as their embankments or excavations may render necessary............................318, 321

BROADWAY RAILROAD:

 Grant of franchise...................................... 261
 Grantees.. 261
  to keep attendants at stopping points................ 264

BROADWAY RAILROAD—Continued:

 to keep sleighs for accommodation of passengers when cars cannot be run in Winter 264

 to cause Broadway to be swept and cleaned 264

 provision in case of refusal by, to pay license fees for the cars 265

 to form themselves into a joint-stock association 265

 powers of such association 265

 association to be formed not to be deemed dissolved by the death or act of any associate 265

 provisions in case of the death or default of any member of the association 265

 association to be formed may be incorporated under the general railroad act 266

 relative to the admission of new associates. 266

 to file with the Clerk of the Common Council their written acceptance of and agreement to fulfill the terms and conditions of this grant 266

Route defined 261, 263

Tracks to be laid under the direction of the Street Commissioner   262

 not to be over twelve and a half feet between outside rails 262

 to be laid on such grades as may be established by the Common Council 262

 may be divided at the Bowling Green 263

 may be carried around public squares 263

 description of rails to be used 262

 how rails shall be laid 262

Cars, description of, to be used 262, 263

 a portion of, not to be run below the Park 263

BROADWAY RAILROAD—Continued :

<blockquote>

provisions in relation to the stopping of the, for passengers... 263

provision regulating the number of passengers to be carried by the................................. 263

to be licensed.. 265

relative to the time of running the................. 262

Depot to be established at the lower end of the route.......... 263

Fare to be charged.. 264

Management of, to be subject to regulation by the Common Council... 262

</blockquote>

BULKHEAD :

<blockquote>

between One Hundred and Thirtieth and One Hundred and Thirty-first streets, resolutions relative to the offer of the Hudson River Railroad Company in relation to constructing............................... 326

Street Commissioner directed to have constructed....... 327

between One Hundred and Thirtieth and One Hundred and Thirty-second streets, Hudson River Railroad Company released from all claim for building or extending... 327

</blockquote>

(C)

CITY RAILROADS :

<blockquote>

vide " RAILROADS IN CITIES."

</blockquote>

Charters for :

<blockquote>

vide " RAILROAD CHARTERS GRANTED BY THE LEGISLATURE."

</blockquote>

COMPTROLLER—DIRECTED TO :

    cause a lease to be made to the New York and Harlem Railroad Company, of a lot on Centre street....... 231

    cause a lease to be executed to the New York and New Haven Railroad Company, of the property bounded by Centre, Franklin, Elm, and White streets...... 254

    cause a lease to be executed to the Hudson River Railroad Company, of the property bounded by Twelfth, Washington, Gansevoort, and West streets, and Tenth avenue.............................. 326

    receive a bond from the Hudson River Railroad Company, instead of a cash payment, in the matter of certain claims existing between the Corporation and that Company................................. 329

CONOVER, JOHN T., AND OTHERS :

    Act of the Legislature, granting a charter to, for a Railroad from the foot of Forty-second street, at the North River, to Grand street ferry........................... 364

COUNSEL TO THE CORPORATION—DIRECTED TO :

    restrain the Second Avenue Railroad Company, by injunction, from laying rails in any of the streets under authority conferred by the Legislature....... 205

    take legal measures to prevent the use of steam by the New York and Harlem Railroad Company below Thirty-second street............................ 232

    take legal measures to compel the New York and Harlem Railroad Company to construct a bridge at the intersection of Fourth avenue with Eighty-fifth street, and to enclose their road with a protection wall from Eighty-fourth to Ninety-second street... 235

COUNSEL TO THE CORPORATION—DIRECTED TO—CONTINUED:

    prepare a remonstrance against the passage of any bill by the Legislature, giving to the New York and Harlem Railroad Company, the privilege of continuing the use of steam below Forty-second street.... 249

    take legal measures to compel the Sixth Avenue Railroad Company to complete their road to Fifty-fourth street................................. 284

    take all proper legal measures to prevent the use or occupation of any of the streets of the city by any one claiming the right, under any act of the Legislature of 1860, of laying rails, &c................. 338

CROTON AQUEDUCT BOARD—DIRECTED TO:

    notify the Second Avenue Railroad Company to put the pavements in and about their rails in good repair. 205, 336

    notify the Third Avenue Railroad Company to put the pavements in and about their rails in good repair. 218, 336

    notify the New York and Harlem Railroad Company to put the pavements in and about their rails in good repair....................................... 248, 336

    notify the Sixth Avenue Railroad Company to put the pavements in and about their rails in good repair. 284, 336

    notify the Eighth Avenue Railroad Company to put the pavements in and about their rails in good repair. 304, 336

    notify the Hudson River Railroad Company to put the pavements in and about their rails in good repair... 331

    remove the rail track in Broome street, between Elizabeth and Baxter streets, and restore the street to its original condition, in case of neglect or refusal on the part of the New York and Harlem Railroad Company to obey the order of the Common Council in relation thereto............................. 250

CROTON AQUEDUCT BOARD—DIRECTED TO—CONTINUED:

 cause the track of the Sixth Avenue Railroad to be put in good order, if the Company refuse or neglect to do it.. 285

 cause certain resolutions in relation to the paving of Sixth avenue to Forty-second street to be carried into effect. 285

(D)

DEVLIN, JOHN E., AND OTHERS:

 Act of the Legislature, granting a charter to, for a railroad from the northern extremity of avenue D to the Bowling Green, &c....................................... 349

DURANT, CHARLES W., AND OTHERS:

 Act of the Legislature, granting a charter to, for a railroad from the intersection of Tenth avenue and Fifty-ninth street to the southern extremity of the city....... 344

(E)

EIGHTH AVENUE RAILROAD:

 Grant of franchise...................................... 288
 Grantees.. 292
  obligations of........... 268 to 270, 287, 289 to 291, 293, 294
  to enter into an agreement with the Mayor, Aldermen, and Commonalty before the grant shall take effect 268, 287, 290

EIGHTH AVENUE RAILROAD—Continued:

 not to transfer nor assign any interest in the grant without first obtaining the consent of the Common Council... 291

 to comply in all matters in relation to the road with the directions of the Common Council...............269, 290

 to become bound, under penalty, to to keep certain portions of the streets in repair....................268, 289

 to keep an account of the receipts of the road, and to report the same monthly to the Comptroller.......269, 291

 to file with the Comptroller an account of the cost of each mile of road completed....................269, 291

 to transfer the road to the city, whenever required, upon certain conditions............................270, 291

 penalty for the non-fulfillment of the conditions of the grant...291, 293

 penalty for not signing the agreement within a given time.. 287

 to form themselves into an association................ 293

 rights, powers, and obligations of association to be formed..............................293, 294 to 297

 association to be formed to be styled the "Eighth Avenue Railroad Company"...................... 294

Route defined...267, 289

 extended through College place, &c., to the corner of Broadway and Vesey street............281, 282, 300, 302

 extended to the corner of Broadway and Canal street..281, 300

Track, when to be commenced.........................269, 291

 when to be completed........................269, 291, 294

 to be laid under the direction of the Street Commissioner...267, 289

INDEX. 437

EIGHTH AVENUE RAILROAD—Continued :

 to be laid on such grades as may be established by the
  Common Council............................268, 289
 how to be laid.....................................269, 291
 rail to be used for..........................269, 291, 307, 315
 rail to be used to be approved by the Street Commissioner...........................269, 291, 307, 315
 to be taken up whenever so directed by the Common
  Council............................269, 270, 290, 291
 to be connected with such other roads as may be directed
  by the Common Council.....................269, 291
 Statement of cost of each mile of, to be filed with the
  Comptroller................................269, 291
 that portion of, used in common with the Sixth Avenue
  Railroad Company to be constructed at the joint expense of the two companies. 271, 272, 280, 282, 292, 299, 301
 the space between the outside rails of, authorized to be
  paved with small cobble stones..................306, 315
 authorized to be laid in Canal street to the corner of
  Broadway...................................281, 300
 authorized to be laid in College place, &c., to corner of
  Broadway and Vesey street....................281, 300
 in Vesey street, to be laid as near as possible to the
  curb... 304
 relative to the track being laid in Chambers and other
  streets.....................................282, 302
 a turn-out, authorized to be laid in Canal street, near
  Broadway.................................... 307
 between Fifty-first and Fifty-ninth streets, directed to be
  relaid....................................... 303

EIGHTH AVENUE RAILROAD—Continued:

 Ninth Avenue Railroad Company authorized to connect their track with the, at corner of Hudson and Canal streets, and of Fifty-fourth street and Eighth avenue....................................308, 315

 Cars, description of to be used............................268, 289

  to be licensed....................................... 292

  directed to be run to Fifty-ninth streets.........303, 304, 305

  time for running the.....................268, 290, 303, 304

  time for running the, to be subject to regulation by the Common Council....................268, 269, 289, 290

 Motive power to be used..................................268, 289

 Fare to be charged...........................269, 290, 294, 301

 Management of, to be subject to the regulation of the Common Council................................268, 290, 300

EIGHTH AVENUE RAILROAD COMPANY :

 of whom to be constituted 293, 294

 relative to the time and mode of the organization of the, 294, 295

 may be incorporated under the general railroad act..... 298

 not to be dissolved by the death or act of any associate. 297

 Title 294

 Capital, relative to estimating and requiring the amount of, required 295

  relative to the mode of subscribing, and paying in subscriptions for................................. 295

  how original, may be subscribed for.................. 296

  how additional, may be subscribed................... 296

 Individual rights and interests of members, conditioned upon the strict observance of the provisions, &c., of the agreement with the Mayor, Aldermen and Commonalty.. 293

EIGHTH AVENUE RAILROAD COMPANY—Continued:

    to be forfeited upon refusal or neglect to subscribe or pay   296

    to be forfeited upon failure to fulfill conditions of the agreement with the Mayor, Aldermen and Commonalty.................... 293

    to be forfeited upon failure to sign the agreement within a certain time................................. 287

    how to be reinstated in case of forfeiture.............. 297

    how to be proportioned............................. 297

  Transfers of shares or interests, how and when to be made........ 297

  Rules and by-laws, how and by whom to be made............. 295

    how to be altered................................. 295

  Persons becoming associates, to become parties to the agreement with the Mayor, Aldermen and Commonalty....... 297

  Provisions in case of the death or insolvency of a member... 293, 297

    in case of difficulty in relation to such portions of their roads as are to be constructed jointly with the Sixth Avenue Railroad Company.....................280, 300

  To pay one half of the cost of such portions of the road as as shall be used in common with the Sixth Avenue Railroad Company.......271, 272, 280, 282, 292, 299, 301

    for setting back the curb and gutter stones in Vesey street... 304

    a portion of the expense of laying Belgian pavement in Hudson street, from Canal street to Eighth avenue... 305

  Directed to repair pavement in Eighth avenue................. 304

    repair the pavements in and about their rail tracks..... 305

    pave the sidewalks in front of their buildings with Belgian pavement................................. 308

EIGHTH AVENUE RAILROAD COMPANY—Continued :

    lay but a single track in Barclay and certain other streets.................................... 282, 302

    lay their track in Vesey street as near as possible to the curb... 304

    relay their track from Fifty-first to Fifty-ninth street   303

    run their cars to Fifty-ninth street............ 303, 304, 305

    Authorized to construct an extension of their road in Canal street to Broadway................................. 281, 300

    construct a turn-out track in Canal street, near Broadway   307

    construct an extension of their road to the corner of Vesey street and Broadway............281, 282, 300, 302

    pave the space between the outside rails of their track with small cobble stone....................... 306, 315

    use "Hewitt Bridge patent rail" for their tracks..... 308, 315

    agree with the Ninth Avenue Railroad Company, in relation to running cars over their respective tracks....................................... 308, 316

(F)

FARE :

    To be charged on the Second Avenue Railroad................. 200

    on the Third Avenue Railroad..................... 208, 212

    on the New York and Harlem Railroad............... 227

    on the Sixth Avenue Railroad................. 269, 273, 282

    on the Eighth Avenue Railroad....... 269, 281, 290, 294, 301

    on the Ninth Avenue Railroad....................... 310

    on the Hudson River Railroad, in city passenger-cars.... 332

FLAGMAN:

    New York and Harlem Railroad Company, directed to station a, at the corner of Grand street and the Bowery........ 246

    directed to station a, at the corner of Broome street and the Bowery................................... 247

    directed to station a, at the corner of Pearl and Centre streets.. 248

(H)

HAMILTON SQUARE:

    New York and Harlem Railroad Company authorized to lay a temporary track at........................ 246

HARLEM RAILROAD:

    vide "NEW YORK AND HARLEM RAILROAD."

HARLEM RAILROAD COMPANY:

    vide "NEW YORK AND HARLEM RAILROAD COMPANY."

HEWITT PATENT RAIL BRIDGE:

    Eighth and Ninth Avenue Railroad Companies authorized to make use of.......................... 307, 315

HUDSON RIVER RAILROAD:

    Grant of franchise of the, from Spuyten Devil Creek to Canal street................................... 317, 320

    reservations in................................. 318, 319

    Grantees, obligations of.............. 317 to 319, 320 to 322

    prohibited from running stated trains below Thirty-second street for carrying passengers, under penalty 319

HUDSON RIVER RAILROAD—Continued:

to execute an instrument in writing before the grant
shall take effect............................... 319

Route defined.. 317

a portion of the, to be changed whenever required by the
Common Council............................318, 322

authorized to be extended through Canal and Hudson
streets to Chambers street....:.................. 323

Map of the location and intended grade of the road to be filed
with the Street Commissioner....................318, 322

Bridges to be constructed at such intersections as, in the opinion
of the Common Council, may require it............318, 321

Track, how to be laid..................................317, 320

to be laid on such grades as may be established by the
Common Council............................317, 321

to cause no unnecessary impediment to the ordinary use
of the streets in which to be laid................318, 321

not to obstruct the water courses of the streets.......318, 321

authorized to be extended around the country market at
foot of Canal street........................... 324

authorized to be laid on pier No. 48, North River...... 330

in Hudson, Canal, and West streets, ordered to be taken
up, and relaid with the grooved rail.... 329

from Chambers to Fifty-third street, ordered to be taken
up, and laid with the grooved rail............... 331

in Tenth avenue, near Thirtieth street, directed to be
taken up, and relaid in a different manner.......327, 328

in Eleventh avenue, ordered to be made to conform to
the grade of the avenue...................... . 333

Ninth Avenue Railroad Company authorized to make a
connection with, in Canal street................. 314

INDEX. 443

HUDSON RIVER RAILROAD—Continued :

 A. M. Allerton, Jr., & Co. authorized to make a connection with, in Eleventh avenue, at Forty-second street   334

 Depot, lease of building and lot of ground, bounded by Washington, West, Canal, and Hoboken streets, for the purposes of a passenger, directed to be made to the Company...   324

  at foot of Canal street, directed to be removed upon the expiration of lease.............................   333

  lot of ground, bounded by Twelfth, Washington, Gansevoort, and West streets, and Tenth avenue, directed to be leased to the Company for the purpose of a...   326

 Cars prohibited to be left standing in Hudson street..........   330

 City passenger, directed to be run from Chambers street to Fifty-third street.....................................   332

  time of running the, specified.......................   332

  regulations to be observed relative to................   332

  to be placed upon the road within a given time.   332

  the right to run, not to be alienated without the consent of the Common Council........................   332

 Motive power to be used.....................................   319

  the use of steam directed to be discontinued below Fifty-third street.....................................   333

 Fare to be charged in the city passenger-cars................   332

HUDSON RIVER RAILROAD COMPANY :

 Grant of right to construct a railroad from Spuyten Devil Creek to Canal street......................... 317, 320

 Obligations contained in grant............... 317 to 319, 320 to 322

  to pave a space of twenty-five feet in width of those streets in which their tracks shall be laid........ 317, 320

HUDSON RIVER RAILROAD COMPANY—Continued:

    to construct bridges at such intersections as, in the opinion of the Common Council, their road shall render necessary.................................. 318, 321

    to make such embankments and excavations on the line of the road as the Common Council may deem necessary................................... 318, 321

    to make such drains and sewers as their embankments and excavations may render necessary........... 318, 321

    to file a map with the Street Commissioner, showing the location and intended grade of the road......... 318, 322

    to run no stated train for carrying passengers below Thirty-second street under penalty................ 319

    to comply with the regulations of the Common Council in reference to the convenience of public travel through the streets in which their track shall be laid....................................... 318, 322

    to execute an instrument in writing to fulfill the conditions, &c., of the grant before the same shall take effect.. 319

    Authorized to extend their track through Canal and Hudson streets to Chambers street..................... 323

    lay a track around the Country Market at foot of Canal street.. 324

    lay rails on pier No. 48, North River................. 330

    run a dumb engine to Chambers street............... 324

    to substitute a bond in the place of a cash payment to the Corporation, in the matter of certain claims existing between the Corporation and the Company........ 328

    Directed to build an addition to the pier at the foot of One Hundred and Thirtieth street....................... 325

HUDSON RIVER RAILROAD COMPANY—Continued:

 fill in the low grounds between Twelfth avenue and Hudson River, and One Hundred and Thirtieth and One Hundred and Thirty-first streets.............. 331

 make the grade of their road conform to the grade of Eleventh avenue............................... 333

 take up the rails in Tenth avenue, near Thirtieth street, and to relay the same with a different curve......327, 328

 take up the track in Hudson, Canal, and West streets, and to put down the grooved rail in its stead...... 329

 take up the track from Chambers street to Fifty-third street, and to relay the same with the grooved rail. 331

 remove their cars from Hudson street, and to refrain from leaving them standing in the street.......... 330

 cause Hudson street, from Chambers to Canal street, to be repaired..................................... 330

 put in good repair the pavements in and about their track... 331

 cease running locomotives below Fifty-third street..... 333

 run city passenger cars from Chambers to Fifty-third street.. 332

Lease to, directed to be made of the building and lot of ground bounded by Washington, West, Canal, and Hoboken streets, for the purpose of a passenger depot.. 324

  term of... 324

  conditions of........................... 324

 directed to be made of lot of ground, bounded by Twelfth, Washington, Gansevoort, and West streets and Tenth avenue, for a depot and other railroad purposes.. 326

HUDSON RIVER RAILROAD COMPANY—Continued:

    term of... 326

    conditions of..................................... 326

    Relative to the offer of the, in relation to the construction of a bulkhead between One Hundred and Thirtieth and One Hundred and Thirty-first streets, &c......... 326, 328

    To release to the city all right to land under water south of north line of One Hundred and Thirty-first street, conveyed to them by certain parties..................... 326, 328

    To be released from covenants in grants relating to land under water, to be conveyed to the city................ 327

    Grant confirming roadway between One Hundred and Thirtieth and One Hundred and Thirty-second streets, and releasing the Company from all claim for building piers or bulkheads opposite the same 327

(K)

KENNEDY, JOHN A., AND OTHERS:

    Remonstrance against the passage of a bill by the Legislature granting to, the franchise for a railroad in Seventh avenue.. 286

KERR, JOHN, AND OTHERS:

    Act of the Legislature, granting a charter to, for a railroad from the intersection of Seventh avenue and Fifty-ninth street, to corner of Broadway and Barclay street.... 354

(L)

LEASE OF:

    a lot on Centre street, directed to be made to the New York and Harlem Railroad Company............. 231

    property bounded by Centre, Franklin, Elm, and White streets, made to the New York and New Haven Railroad Company............................ 254

    property bounded by Canal, Hoboken, Washington, and West streets, directed to be made to the Hudson River Railroad Company............................ 324

    property bounded by Twelfth, Washington, Gansevoort, and West streets, and Tenth avenue, directed to be made to the Hudson River Railroad Company...... 326

LIBBY, JAMES S., AND OTHERS:

    grant of a franchise to, for a railroad in Sixth avenue and other streets................................... 267

LICENSES TO BE PAID:

    ordinance in relation to, by city railroads............. 337

    by the Third Avenue Railroad Company............... 210

    by the Broadway Railway Company.................. 265

    by the Sixth and Eighth Avenue Railroad Companies... 292

    by the Ninth Avenue Railroad Company.............. 310

(M)

MURPHY, JAMES W., AND OTHERS:

    grant of franchise to, for a railroad in Ninth avenue and other streets.................................. 309

(N)

NEW YORK AND HARLEM RAILROAD:

    Grants of franchise................................. 220, 225, 239

    Grantees.. 220, 225, 240

        obligations of.................... 221 to 223, 226, 227, 241

        to enter into an agreement with the Mayor, Aldermen and Commonalty before the grant shall take effect 223, 227

        to suffer penalty of forfeiture of grant for non-compliance with terms of agreements......... 221, 222, 225, 241, 252

    Route defined... 220

        Map of, from Twenty-third street to Harlem River, confirmed...................................... 220, 224

        permission given to extend, South to Prince street...... 226

        permission given to extend, South to Walker street..... 229

        permission given to extend, through Broome and Centre streets from the Bowery to Chatham street........ 229

        South of Broome street, in Bowery, to be discontinued.. 229

        permission given to extend, up Canal street to near Broadway...................................... 234

INDEX. 449

NEW YORK AND HARLEM RAILROAD—Continued :

 permission given to extend, through Sixth street to rear of Tompkins market............................ 235
 permission given to extend, down Bowery to Grand street, and through Grand street to Centre street.... 238
 permission given to extend to southerly end of City Hall Park.. 238, 240
 through Chambers street to Broadway, to be discontinued 243
Road, construction and management of, to be subject to the directions of the Common Council................ 221
 when to be commenced........................... 222
 when to be completed........................ 222, 227
 penalty for non-completion of, within the specified time.. 222, 225
 width of not to exceed twenty-four feet.............. 220
 to conform to such grades as may be established by the Common Council............................... 222
 stone arches and bridges to be constructed for the streets intersected by the embankments or excavations made for the..................................... 221
 such drains and sewers to be constructed as may be rendered necessary by the embankments and excavations for the............................... 222
 provisions in case of discontinuance, &c., of the, in regard to the strip of land taken therefor................ 222
 no buildings to be erected on the strip of land taken for the..................................... 223
 railings or fences to be placed on edges of embankments and excavations for the......................... 223
 land lying on the line of, and belonging to the city, authorized to be taken............................ 225

NEW YORK AND HARLEM RAILROAD—Continued:

Bridges to be constructed at streets intersected by the embankments or excavations for the road................ 221

a bridge directed to be constructed at Thirty-fourth street   233

iron railing on bridge at Thirty-fourth street directed to be secured.................................... 245

a bridge directed to be constructed at Thirty-eighth street   233

the bridge directed to be restored at Fiftieth street..... 233

a bridge directed to be constructed at Seventieth street..   253

a bridge directed to be constructed at Seventy-ninth street... 233

directed to be constructed at Eighty-third, Eighty-fourth and Eighty-eighth streets.................. 243

a bridge to be constructed at Eighty-fifth street...... 233, 235

sides of bridge at Eighty-seventh street directed to be enclosed.. 233

a bridge directed to be constructed at Ninetieth street..   247

a bridge directed to be constructed at One Hundred and Fourth street................................ 245

Track, how the, shall be laid.............................. 226

to be laid on such grades as may be established by the Common Council....................... 222

to be laid under the direction of the Street Commissioner.................................... 226, 239, 240

not to obstruct the water courses of the streets......... 227

not to interfere with the travel on any of the streets.. 221, 225

to be removed in case of forming an impediment to the ordinary use of the streets...................... 221

to be removed when required by the Common Council. 221, 226, 227, 239, 240

NEW YORK AND HARLEM RAILROAD—Continued:

 to be kept in good repair.................................... 227

 rail to be used for............................ 238, 240, 245

 permission given to lay a, through Fourth avenue, Union place, Bloomingdale road, Broadway, and the Bowery, to Prince street............................. 226

 permission given to lay a, in the Bowery from Prince to Walker street.. 229

 in Bowery, south of Broome street, ordered to be removed.. 229

 permission given to lay a, in the Bowery between Grand and Broome streets.............................. 238

 permission given to lay a, in Broome and Centre streets. 229

 in Broome street directed to be taken up and relaid according to original grade........................ 250

Track, permission given to lay a, in Grand and Centre streets.. 238

 permission given to lay a, in Centre street and Park row, 238, 240

 laid in Park row not to be within twenty feet of crosswalk at Broadway............................ 239, 240

 permission given to lay a, in Canal street, with turnouts.. 234, 245

 plans for curves for, at Bowery, Broome, and Canal streets, referred to Street Commissioner................ 236

 in Canal street directed to be relaid with the grooved rail.. 245

 in Chambers street directed to be removed............. 243

 permission given to lay a, in Sixth street.............. 235

 permission given to lay a, temporarily in Twenty-sixth street.. 242

NEW YORK AND HARLEM RAILROAD—Continued :

    to be lowered from Twenty-eighth to Thirty-second street.. 234

    to be lowered at Thirty-fourth street................. 253

    walls to be built on each side of, from Thirty-second to Forty-second street, and to be arched over from Thirty-fourth to Thirty-ninth street.............. 236

    turn-out, to be laid between Thirty-second and Thirty-fourth streets................................ 244

    turn-out, to be laid at Forty-second street............ 251

    permission given to lay a, in Forty-second street and Madison avenue................................ 251

    permission given to lay additional, between Forty-second and Fiftieth streets.......................... 252

    a temporary, authorized to be laid at Hamilton square.. 246

    from Eighty-fourth to Ninety-second street directed to be enclosed with protection walls.............. 233, 235

    petition for a turn-out, in Fourth avenue, between One Hundred and Twenty-fifth and One Hundred and Twenty-seventh streets........................ 236

    directed to be put into thorough repair, under penalty.. 248

Plan, of curves at corner of Bowery and Broome street, Broome and Centre streets, and Canal and Centre streets, relative to.................................... 236

    of walls and arch between Thirty-second and Forty-second streets, to be conformed to............... 237

    of extension from corner of Centre and Chatham streets to the southerly end of the City Hall Park, to be conformed to.................................... 239

    for lowering grade of Fourth avenue between Thirty-second and Thirty-fourth streets, and for a turn-out, &c., to be conformed to............................ 244

NEW YORK AND HARLEM RAILROAD—Continued:

Cars to be used upon............................... 239, 240, 250

    City passenger, directed to be run regularly to Forty-second street................................... 250

    relative to the time of running the................... 250

Motive power and speed to be used to be subject to regulation by the Common Council........................... 221

    Steam directed to be discontinued below Thirty-second street.. 232

    extension of time granted for the use of steam below Thirty-second street............................ 232

    Steam directed to be discontinued below Forty-second street...................................... 247, 249

    Ordinance authorizing the use of steam to Forty-second street for a period of thirty years from 31st December, 1858....................................... 251

    Locomotives allowed to be run to Thirty-second street, for repairs, until new machine shops may be finished.. 251

Fare to be charged, relative to............................ 227

NEW YORK AND HARLEM RAILROAD COMPANY:

Grant to, of right to construct a railroad from Twenty-third street to Harlem River, with a branch at One Hundred and Twenty-fifth street..................... 220

To enter into an agreement with the Mayor, Aldermen and Commonalty before grant shall take effect............. 223

    227, 239

To construct stone arches and bridges for streets intersected by the embankments or excavations of their road........ 221

To make all such drains and sewers as may be rendered necessary by the embankments and excavations of their road 221

NEW YORK AND HARLEM RAILROAD COMPANY—Continued:

Not to erect any building on the strip of land to be taken for their road.. 223

To erect railings and fences on edges of embankments and excavations... 223

To grade and pave certain portions of the streets in which their rails shall be laid, and keep same in repair... 221, 222, 227, 230, 239, 241

To restore the streets and avenues to proper condition in case of removing the rails...................... 221, 227, 241

To pay for setting back curb in Centre street................. 230

To pave space in Centre street, opposite the market, with wooden blocks, between the rails and the curb stones... 230

To widen Fourth avenue, between Thirty-second and Thirty-fourth streets, on the west side.................. 244

To complete title to the Corporation of strip of land on the west side of Fourth avenue, between Thirty-second and Thirty-fourth streets.. 252

To remove engine-houses situated between Thirty-second and Thirty-third streets................................ 252

Tax of, for 1840, in Sixth ward remitted.................... 231

Penalty for not commencing or completing their road within the time prescribed............................. 222, 225

for not putting track in condition according to the direction of the Common Council................... 248

for not removing rails when directed so to do by the Common Council........................... 221

for non-compliance with terms of agreement........ 241, 252

Authorized to take possession of the property of the city lying on the line of their proposed road............... 225

continue their railroad south to Prince street.......... 225

NEW YORK AND HARLEM RAILROAD COMPANY—Continued:

continue their railroad through the Bowery to Walker street	229
continue their railroad through Broome and Centre streets to Chatham street	229
continue their railroad to the southerly end of City Hall park	238
lay rails in Canal street	234
lay rails in Sixth street	235
take up the double track, from the corner of Grand street through Centre and Broome streets to the Bowery, and to lay a single track through the Bowery, Centre, Grand, and Broome streets	238
lay a temporary track to depot in Twenty-sixth street	242
lay a turn-out track in Fourth avenue, between Thirty-second and Thirty-fourth streets	244
lay a temporary track at Hamilton square	246
lay tracks in Forty-second street and Madison avenue	251
lay two additional tracks in Fourth avenue, between Forty-second and Fiftieth streets	252
construct a roof over the additional tracks in Fourth avenue, from Forty-second to Forty-fourth street	252
construct a sewer from Tryon row to Chatham street	238
reduce the grade on the east side of Fourth avenue, between Thirty-second and Thirty-fourth streets	244
use steam below Thirty-second street until expiration of additional time granted for completion of buildings at Thirty-second street	232
use steam to Forty-second street, for thirty years, from 31st December, 1858	251

NEW YORK AND HARLEM RAILROAD COMPANY—Continued :

 run their locomotives to Thirty-second street, for repairs,
  until their new machine shops can be completed... 251

Petition of residents of Harlem for permission for the, to construct a turn-out track in Fourth avenue, between One Hundred and Twenty-fifth and One Hundred and Twenty-seventh streets...................... 236

Directed to take up the track in the Bowery, south of Broome street, and to repair the street.................... 229

 take up tracks in Canal street, and relay the same with the grooved rail............................. 245

 take up track and pavement in Broome street, and to relay the same according to the original grade....... 250

 put their track into thorough order.................. 248

 put into good repair the pavements in and about their rails.. 248

 pay the cost of paving twenty feet in width in Centre street, from Walker to Chatham street............ 231

 grade and regulate Fourth avenue from Twenty-eighth to Thirty-second street......................... 234

 regulate Fourth avenue from Thirty-fourth to Thirty-ninth street.................................. 237

 reduce the grade in Fourth avenue at Thirty-fourth street, 253

 construct a bridge at intersection of Thirty-fourth street and Fourth avenue.............................. 233

 secure iron railing on bridge at Thirty-fourth street..... 245

 construct a bridge at intersection of Thirty-eighth street and Fourth avenue.............................. 233

 restore the bridge at intersection of Fiftieth street and Fourth avenue................................. 233

 construct a bridge at intersection of Seventieth street and Fourth avenue................................. 253

NEW YORK AND HARLEM RAILROAD COMPANY—Continued:

    construct a bridge at intersection of Seventy-ninth street and Fourth avenue............................... 233

    construct bridges at intersections of Eighty-third, Eighty-fourth, and Eighty-eighth streets, with Fourth avenue................................. 243

    construct a bridge at intersection of Eighty-fifth street and Fourth avenue........................... 233, 235

    enclose the sides of the bridge at Eighty-seventh street.. 233

    construct a bridge at intersection of Ninetieth street and Fourth avenue................................. 247

    construct a bridge at intersection of One Hundred and Fourth street and Fourth avenue................... 245

    build a wall on each side of their track from Thirty-second to Forty-second street, and to arch over their track from Thirty-fourth to Thirty-ninth street..... 236

    enclose their road from Eighty-fourth to Ninety-second street.. 233, 235

    station a flagman at the corner of Grand street and the Bowery.. 246

    station a flagman at the corner of Broome street and the Bowery.. 247

    station a flagman at the corner of Centre and Pearl streets.. 248

    discontinue the use of steam below Thirty-second street. 232

    discontinue the use of steam below Forty-second street. 247, 249, 251

    run small passenger-cars to Forty-second street......... 250

    Comptroller directed to lease a lot on Centre street to......... 231

    Corporation Counsel directed to adopt legal measures to prevent the use of steam by, on Fourth avenue, below Thirty-second street................................. 232

NEW YORK AND HARLEM RAILROAD COMPANY—Continued:

    directed to prepare a memorial to the Legislature against the passage of any bill authorizing the use of steam by, below Forty-second street.................... 249

    directed to adopt legal measures to compel the, to inclose their road from Eighty-fourth to Ninety-second street, &c.. 235

    Street Commissioner directed to take up track of, in Chambers street... 243

NEW YORK AND NEW HAVEN RAILROAD COMPANY:

    Lease to, of premises between Franklin and White, and Centre and Elm streets................................ 254

    covenant for a renewal of......................... 254, 258

    term of... 254, 255

    penalty for non-compliance with the conditions of.... 256, 259

    to become forfeited if any portion of the premises leased be assigned or transferred without the consent of the City authorities................................. 259

    not to be construed into consent by the City authorities to the use of any of the avenues, &c., for the purpose of running cars thereon, by virtue of any agreement with the New York and Harlem Railroad Company, &c. 254, 258

    Rent to be paid..................................... 254, 256

        to be paid under renewal, how to be fixed............ 258

        how and when to be paid......................... 256

        penalty for default in payment of.................. 256

    Premises leased to be improved within one year............ 254, 258

        use to which to be put........................... 254, 258

NEW YORK AND NEW HAVEN RAILROAD COMPANY—Continued:

    arsenal buildings to remain on, until May 1st, 1851...254, 259

    taxes and assessments on, to be paid by lessees.......254, 257

    to be delivered up on expiration of lease, in case of no renewal of lease................................. 259

NINTH AVENUE RAILROAD:

    Grant of franchise... 309

    Grantees.. 309

        obligations of................................309 to 311

        to keep certain portions of the streets in repair......... 310

        may form themselves into a joint-stock association..... 310

        rights, powers and obligations of association to be formed 310

    Route defined 309, 311

    Road how to be constructed, &c............................. 309

        when to be commenced............................... 309

        when to be completed..............................309, 313

        authorized to be connected with the track of the Hudson River and of the Sixth and Eighth Avenue Railroads at Canal street............................. 314

        authorized to be connected with the Eighth Avenue Railroad at Canal street, and at Fifty-fourth street...308, 315

        to be continued northerly when required by the Common Council... 311

    Track directed to be taken up at intersection of Bethune and Washington streets............................ 313

        space between the outer rails of, authorized to be paved with small cobble stones......................306, 315

        "Hewitt Bridge patent rail" authorized to be used for..307, 315

NINTH AVENUE RAILROAD—Continued:

rail to be used for, to be approved by the Street Commissioner 307, 315

Cars, time of running... 309

 time of running to be subject to regulation by the Common Council 310

 to be licensed 310

 directed to be run on the portion of the road completed. 313

Motive power to be used... 309

Fare to be charged................................... 310, 313, 314

NINTH AVENUE RAILROAD COMPANY:

of whom to be constituted 309, 310

Organization of, relative to.................................. 310

Directed to proceed and complete their road as soon as the legal impediments thereto shall be removed............. 312

 run cars on the portion of the road completed.......... 313

 pay expense of removing filth accumulated at the intersection of Washington and Bethune streets, &c.,... 313

 pave the sidewalks, in front of their depot buildings, with Belgian pavement.................................. 316

Authorized to connect their road with the Hudson River and Sixth and Eighth avenue Railroads, at Canal street.. 314

 connect their road with the Eighth avenue Railroad, at Canal street and at Fifty-fourth street.......... 308, 315

 pave the space between the outer rails of their track with small cobble stones................................. 306, 315

 use the "Hewitt Bridge patent rail" for their track.. 308, 315

 to agree with the Eighth Avenue Railroad Company in relation to running cars upon one another's tracks 308, 316

(O)

ORDINANCE:

    authorizing the New York and Harlem Railroad Company to construct their railway........................ 220

    authorizing the New York and Harlem Railroad Company to use steam power on their railroad to Forty-second street, for thirty years, &c.................. 251

    authorizing the Hudson River Railroad Company to lay down rail tracks in the city...................... 317

    in relation to the pavements between the tracks of the Eighth and Ninth Avenue Railroads............ 306, 315

    in relation to sewer fixtures affected by the laying down of rail tracks............................. 335

    providing for the licensing of city railroad cars........ 337

ORDINANCES:

    affecting city railroads and general in their application.. 335

(P)

PEARSALL, DENTON, AND OTHERS:

    grant of franchise to, for a railroad in Second avenue and other streets................................ 199

PECK SLIP:

    Second Avenue Railroad Company authorized to lay a rail track in...................................... 200

PETITION OF :

    Citizens of Harlem, that the New York and Harlem Railroad Company be permitted to lay down a side track in Fourth avenue, between One Hundred and Twenty-fifth and One Hundred and Twenty-seventh streets.. 236

    New York and Harlem Railroad Company, for permission to continue the use of steam power below Thirty-second street for three months......................... 232

        for permission to construct a sewer from Tryon row to Chatham street............................ 238

    Sixth Avenue Railroad Company, that the gas pipes in Sixth avenue may be extended to Forty-fourth street....... 280

PETTIGREW, JOHN, AND OTHERS :

    Grant of franchise to, for a railroad in Eighth avenue and other streets............................... 288

PIER

    No. 48, North River, Hudson River Railroad Company authorized to lay a track upon.................. 330

    at foot of One Hundred and Thirtieth street, Hudson River Railroad Company directed to build an addition to... 325

    between One Hundred and Thirtieth and One Hundred and Thirty-second streets, Hudson River Railroad Company released from all claim for constructing any 327

    at foot of One Hundred and Thirty-first street, Street Commissioner directed to construct............... 327

(R)

RAILROAD CHARTERS GRANTED BY THE LEGISLATURE—

not confirmed by the Common Council:

Act authorizing the construction of a railroad track from the corner of Tenth avenue and Fifty-ninth street to the southern extremity of the city..................	344
Act authorizing the construction of a railroad from the northern extremity of avenue D to the Bowling Green......	349
Act authorizing the construction of a railroad from the corner of Seventh avenue and Fifty-ninth street to the corner of Broadway and Barclay street..................	354
Act authorizing the construction of a railroad from the corner of Twelfth avenue and Thirty-second street to the Fulton Ferry.................................	359
Act authorizing the construction of a railroad from the foot of Forty-second street, at the North River, to Grand Street Ferry..................................	364
Counsel to the Corporation directed to take legal measures to prevent the use or occupancy of any of the streets, under or by virtue of.................................	338

RAILROAD IN FORTY-SECOND STREET:

A. M. Allerton, Jr., & Co. authorized to construct a, from the Hudson River to connect with the Hudson River Railroad at Eleventh avenue...............	834
purpose for which to be used.......................	834
to be removed, upon sixty days' notice by the Common Council.....................................	834

RAILROADS IN CITIES:

 not to be authorized to be constructed without the consent of a majority in interest of the property-owners on the streets through which the same shall pass... 340

 majority in interest of the property-owners, how to be determined............ 340

 Common Council may authorize to be constructed, upon such consent being obtained............ 340

 Grants for, to be made only to such parties as shall give security to comply with conditions, &c............ 341

 notice to be given of intention to make, &c............ 341

 proposals for, to be invited............ 341

 Roads already constructed in part not to be affected by the act..... 341

IN THE CITY OF NEW YORK—

 prohibited to be constructed except under authority from the Legislature............ 343

 Roads constructed and duly authorized, not affected by the act..... 343

 Grants for, valid and existing on 1st January, 1860, not to be impaired by the act............ 343

REAL ESTATE:

 New York and Harlem Railroad Company authorized to take possession of such property belonging to the City as may lay on and be required for the line of their road............ 225

 to cede to the city a strip of land on the west side of Fourth Avenue between Thirty-second and Thirty-fourth streets............ 252

 Hudson River Railroad Company to release all right to land under water, south of north line of One Hundred and Thirty-first street, conveyed to them by Schieffelin and Lawrence............ 326

REAL ESTATE—Continued :

    Lease of a lot on Centre street directed to be made to the New York and Harlem Railroad Company.............. 231

    property bounded by Centre, Franklin, Elm and White streets made to the New York and New Haven Railroad Company................................. 254

    Property bounded by Canal, Hoboken, Washington and West streets directed to be made to the Hudson River Railroad Company......................... 324

    property bounded by Twelfth, Washington, Gansevoort and West streets and Tenth avenue, directed to be made to the Hudson River Railroad Company...... 326

    property bounded by Canal, Hoboken, Washington and West streets to be used for a country market upon expiration of lease to the Hudson River Railroad Company 333

REMONSTRANCE :

    against the passage of any bill by the Legislature authorizing the New York and Harlem River Railroad Company to use steam below Forty-second street.... 249

    against the passage of a bill authorizing John A. Kennedy and others to construct a railroad in Seventh avenue and other streets................ 286

    against the passage of any law granting railroad privileges in the city of New York.................. 336, 338

ROE, STEPHEN R., AND OTHERS :

    act of the Legislature granting a charter to, for a railroad from the intersection of Thirty-second street and Twelfth avenue to Fulton Ferry.................. 359

(S)

SECOND AVENUE RAILROAD:

Grant of franchise 199

    dependent upon the strict observance of the conditions,
        &c., therein contained......................... 201

Grantees.. 199

    obligations of.............................. 200, 201, 202

        to pave the streets in and about the rails, and to keep the
            same in repair................................. 200

        to comply, in all matters in relation to the road, with the
            directions of the Street Commissioner and of the
            Common Council............................... 201

        to enter into an agreement with the Mayor, Aldermen
            and Commonalty, before the grant shall take effect. 201

Route defined.. 199

    portion of, changed.............................. 203

Track, when to be commenced to be laid 201

    when to be completed............................ 201

    not to impede the ordinary use of the streets........... 200

    not to obstruct the water courses of the streets......... 200

    rails for, to be laid in such manner and in such part of
        the streets as shall be approved by the Street Com-
        missioner....................................... 200

    pavement in and about the, to be laid and kept in good
        repair by grantees............................. 200

    Third Avenue Railroad Company authorized to make a
        connection with the, at the junction of the Bowery
        and Grand street 200

SECOND AVENUE RAILROAD—Continued:

 in Bowery and Chatham street, from Grand to Pearl street, to be used in common with the Third Avenue Railroad Company.. 209

 to be used in common with the Third Avenue Railroad Company, to be constructed and kept in repair at the joint expense of the two companies 209

 between Forty-ninth and Fifty-third streets, directed to be removed 204

 between Forty-ninth and Sixty-first streets, directed to be removed to the centre of the avenue 205

Cars, time of running the, designated 200

Motive power to be used.. 200

Fare to be charged... 200

Act of the Legislature, in relation to........................... 342

SECOND AVENUE RAILROAD COMPANY:

 to have free use, in common with the Third Avenue Railroad Company, of the track to be laid in the Bowery and Chatham street, from Grand to Pearl street.... 209

 to pay one half the expense of constructing and keeping in repair the track used in common with the Third Avenue Railroad Company........................ 209

 to pay one third of the expense of paving Second avenue with Belgian pavement, from Forty-eighth to Sixty-first street.. 206

 Preamble and Resolution, in relation to the passage of an act by the Legislature to permit the, to lay rails for a railroad track in certain streets in the city 204

 Directed to cause Grand street, from the Bowery to Allen street, to be repaired, according to the terms of their grant 203

SECOND AVENUE RAILROAD COMPANY—Continued :

    pay for a certain portion of the pavement laid in Grand
and Allen streets............................... 204

    repair the pavements in and about their rails........... 205

    remove that portion of their track lying between Forty-
ninth and Fifty-third streets..................... 204

    have that portion of their track lying between Forty-
ninth and Sixty-first streets removed to the centre of
the Second avenue............................. 205

    Authorized to construct a bridge across Harlem River.......... 342

SEVENTH AVENUE RAILROAD :

    Preamble and Resolution, remonstrating against the passage of any
law by the Legislature granting a charter for...... 286

SEWERS :

    To be constructed by the New York and Harlem Railroad Company   222

    by the Hudson River Railroad Company............ 318, 321

    Ordinance in relation to fixtures of, affected by the laying down
of rail tracks................................. 335

    Petition of the New York and Harlem Railroad Company, for per-
mission to construct a sewer from Tryon row to
Chatham street............................... 238

SHARP, JACOB, AND OTHERS :

    grant of a franchise to, for a railroad in Broadway..... 261

SIXTH AVENUE RAILROAD :

    Grant of franchise....................................... 267

    Grantees... 271

    obligations of..................... 268 to 270, 272 to 274

INDEX. 469

SIXTH AVENUE RAILROAD—Continued:

 to enter into an agreement with the Mayor, Aldermen and Commonalty, before this grant shall go into effect.. 268

 not to assign any interest without first obtaining the consent of the Common Council................... 269

 to comply in all matters with the directions of the Common Council................................... 268, 280

 to become bound, under penalty, to keep certain portions of the streets in good repair...................... 268

 to keep an account of the receipts of the road, and to report the same monthly to the Comptroller....... 269

 to file with the Comptroller an account of the cost of each mile of the road completed................. 269

 to transfer the road to the city, whenever required by the Common Council, upon certain conditions......... 270

 penalty for non-fulfillment of the conditions of the grant 273

 penalty for not signing agreement without a certain time.. 288

 to form themselves into an association............... 272, 274

 rights, powers and obligations of the association to be formed.................................. 272, 274 to 277

 association to be formed to be styled the "Sixth Avenue Railroad Company"............................. 274

Route defined... 270

 a portion of, to be changed........................ 279, 299

 extended to the corner of Broadway and Canal street. 281, 300

 extended to the corner of Broadway and Vesey street
              281, 282, 300, 302

Track, when to be commenced............................. 271

 when to be completed........................... 271, 273

SIXTH AVENUE RAILROAD—Continued:

    to be laid under the direction of the Street Commissioner   268

    to be laid on such grades as may be established by the Common Council.............................. 268

    how to be laid.................................... 271

    rail to be used for 269

    rail to be used to be approved by the Street Commissioner 269

    to be taken up whenever ordered by the Common Council..269, 270

    to be connected with that of such other roads as may be directed by the Common Council................ 269

    statement of cost of each mile of, to be filed with the Comptroller.................................. 269

    that portion of, used in common with the Eighth Avenue Railroad, to be constructed at joint expense of the two Companies........ 271, 272, 280, 282, 292, 299, 301

    space between outside rails of, permitted to be paved with small cobble stones......................... 285

    authorized to be laid in Canal street to Broadway,....281, 300

    authorized to be laid in Chambers and other streets to corner of Broadway and Vesey street............281, 300

    directed to be completed to Fifty-fourth street........ 284

    directed to be put in good repair..................... 284

    relative to, being laid in College place, Church street, &c. 282, 302

Cars to be used upon the................................. 268

    to be licensed 271

    time specified for running the....................... 268

    time of running the, subject to regulation by the Common Council 268, 269

INDEX. 471

SIXTH AVENUE RAILROAD—Continued:

 Motive power to be used.................................... 270
 Fare to be charged.............................275, 278, 282
 Management of, to be subject to regulation by the Common
  Council....................................268, 280

SIXTH AVENUE RAILROAD COMPANY:

 of whom to be constituted...............271, 272, 274
 relative to the time and mode of the organization of the 274
 may be incorporated under the general railroad act.... 277
 not to be dissolved by the death or act of any member.. 277
 Title.. 274
 Capital, relative to estimating and declaring the amount of, required... 274
 relative to the mode of subscribing for, and of paying in
  subscriptions... 275
 how original, may be subscribed for.................... 275
 how additional, may be subscribed for................. 275
 Individual rights and interests of members conditioned upon the strict
  observance of the provisions, &c., contained in the
  agreement with the Mayor, Aldermen and Commonalty... 272
 to be forfeited upon refusal or neglect to subscribe or
  pay..275, 276
 to be forfeited in case of failure to fulfill the conditions
  of the agreement with the Mayor, Aldermen and
  Commonalty... 273
 how to be reinstated in case of forfeiture............. 276
 how to be proportioned................................... 277
 Transfers of shares or interests, how and when to be made........ 277
 Rules and by-laws, how and by whom to be made..........274, 275

SIXTH AVENUE RAILROAD COMPANY—Continued:

    how to be altered...... 275

    Persons becoming associates to become parties to the agreement with the Mayor, Aldermen and Commonalty............ 276

    Provisions in case of the insolvency or death of any member..273, 277

    in case of difficulty in relation to portions of the road to be build jointly with the Eighth Avenue Railroad Company..................................280, 300

    Petition of, that the gas-pipes may be extended in the Sixth avenue, granted................................. 281

    Directed to have gates put to the railroad alley between Barclay and Vesey streets............................. 283

    complete their track to Fifty-fourth street............. 284

    have the pavements in and about their rails put in good repair 284

    repair their track............ 284

    Authorized to construct an extension of their road, in connection with the Eighth avenue road, through College place and other streets, to the corner of Broadway and Vesey street........................281, 282, 300, 302

    extend the track in Canal street to the corner of Broadway 281, 300

    pave the space between their rails with small cobble stones... 285

    pay one-half the cost of constructing such portions of the road as shall be used in common with the Eighth Avenue Railroad Company...................... 271, 272, 280, 282, 292, 299, 301

SLEIGHS :

    to be run by the Broadway Railroad Company when their cars are prevented by the snow.................. 264

INDEX. 473

STATE LAWS :

    In relation to the City Railroads .... 340 to 364

STEAM POWER :

    On the Second Avenue Railroad, not to be used below Forty-second street.. 200

    On the Third Avenue Railroad, not to be used on any portion... 207

    On the New York and Harlem Railroad, directed to be discontinued south of Thirty-second street................ 231

        Counsel to the Corporation directed to take measures to compel the discontinuance of, south of Thirty-second street 232

        petition of Company for permission to continue the use of, south of Thirty-second street, for three months. 232

        directed to be discontinued south of Forty-second street.247, 249

        ordinance authorizing the use of, to Forty-second street for thirty years............................... 251

    On the Sixth Avenue Railroad, not to be used below Forty-second street.. 270

    On the Eighth Avenue Railroad, not to be used below Fifty-first street 268, 289

    On the Ninth Avenue Railroad, not to be used on any portion 309

    On the Hudson River Railroad, not to be used below Thirtieth street.. 319

        directed to be discontinued south of Fifty-third street.. 333

STREET COMMISSIONER—DIRECTED TO :

    have the track in the Second avenue, from Forty-ninth to Fifty-third street, removed, in case of neglect or refusal by the Railroad Company to remove the same................. 204

    request the New York and Harlem Railroad Company to pay him the cost of paving a certain portion of Centre street, from Walker to Chatham street 231

STREET COMMISSIONER—DIRECTED TO—CONTINUED:

have the railroad track in Chambers street, between Centre
    street and Broadway, removed 243

construct a bridge for the New York and Harlem Railroad at
    One Hundred and Fourth street, in case of failure of the
    Company to construct same 245

cause the New York and Harlem Railroad Company to put
    their track in thorough condition forthwith............ 248

construct a bridge over the New York and Harlem Railroad, at
    Seventieth street, in case of failure by the Company to con-
    struct the same....................................... 253

cause the work of laying down rail tracks by the Sixth and
    Eighth Avenue Railroad Companies, in College place and
    certain other streets, to be stayed unless but a single track
    be laid 283, 302

notify the Sixth Avenue Railroad Company to have the rail-
    road alley, between Vesey and Barclay streets, closed up
    with gates 283

notify the Eighth Avenue Railroad Company to repair the pave-
    ment in Eighth avenue................................. 304

have the rails in Washington street, at the corner of Bethune
    street, taken up, and the filth removed, &c............. 313

notify the Hudson River Railroad Company of passage of reso-
    lution directing them to build an addition to the pier at
    foot of One Hundred and Thirtieth street, North River... 325

construct a bulkhead from One Hundred and Thirtieth to
    One Hundred and Thirty-first street, North River, and also
    a pier at the foot of One Hundred and Thirty-first street.. 327

notify the Hudson River Railroad Company to remove and to
    refrain from leaving their cars standing in Hudson street.. 330

INDEX.

STREET COMMISSIONER—DIRECTED TO—CONTINUED:

 notify the Hudson River Railroad Company to fill in the low ground between Twelfth avenue and Hudson River, and One Hundred and Thirtieth and One Hundred and Thirty-first streets, or that he will do it at their expense.. 331

STREETS:

 Allen street, from Grand to Houston street, Second Avenue Railroad Company authorized to lay a rail track in..... 199

 from Grand to Broome street, Second Avenue Railroad Company directed to pay for a portion of the pavement laid in.................................. 204

 Barclay street, from College place to Broadway, Eighth Avenue Railroad Company authorized to lay a rail track in 281, 282, 300, 302

 Battery place, from Greenwich to Washington street, Ninth Avenue Railroad Company authorized to lay a rail track in 309, 312

 Bloomingdale road, New York and Harlem Railroad Company authorized to lay a rail track in................. 226

 to Manhattanville, Broadway Railroad Company authorized to lay a rail track in...................... 262

 from Ninth to Tenth avenue, Ninth Avenue Railroad Company authorized to lay a track in 311

 Bowery, Second Avenue Railroad Company authorized to lay rail tracks in................... ....199, 200

 Third Avenue Railroad Company authorized to lay rail tracks in...........................207, 209, 217, 248

 New York and Harlem Railroad Company authorized to lay rail tracks in.......................226, 229, 238

 from Broome to Walker street, rails laid in, by the New York and Harlem Railroad Company, directed to be removed.. 229

STREETS—Continued :

Broadway, New York and Harlem Railroad Company authorized to lay rail tracks in 226

 from Battery place to Fifty-ninth street, Broadway Railroad Company authorized to lay rail tracks in...... 261

 to be swept and kept clean by the Broadway Railroad Company 264

Broome street, from Bowery to Centre street, New York and Harlem Railroad Company authorized to lay rail tracks in.................................... 229

 New York and Harlem Railroad Company authorized to take up the double and lay a single track in....... 238

 New York and Harlem Railroad Company directed to take up the pavement and track in and relay same on the original grade........................... 250

Canal street, from Centre street to near Broadway, New York and Harlem Railroad Company authorized to lay rail tracks in................................ 234

 rail track in, directed to be taken up and relaid with grooved rail.................................. 245

from Broadway to West Broadway, Eighth Avenue Railroad Company authorized to lay rail tracks in. 281, 300, 307

from Church to Wooster street, Sixth Avenue Railroad Company authorized to lay rail tracks in.... 270, 271, 279

from West Broadway to Varick street, Sixth Avenue Railroad Company authorized to lay rail tracks in.. 279

from West Broadway to Hudson street, Eighth Avenue Railroad Company authorized to lay rail tracks in.. 267, 289, 292

from Hudson to Greenwich street, Ninth Avenue Railroad Company authorized to lay rail tracks in. 307, 314, 316

STREETS—Continued :

    from Hudson to West street, Hudson River Railroad Company authorized to lay rail tracks in 323

    track in, directed to be taken up and relaid with grooved rail 329, 331

    Carmine street, from Varick to Fourth street, Sixth Avenue Railroad Company authorized to lay rail tracks in 279

    Centre street, New York and Harlem Railroad Company authorized to lay rail tracks in........................ 229

    New York and Harlem Railroad Company to pave a certain portion of, with blocks of wood.............. 230

    from Chatham to Walker street, New York and Harlem Railroad Company directed to pay a portion of the expense of paving 231

    between Grand and Broome streets, curb stone in, opposite to the market, directed to be set back......... 230

    double track in, authorized to be taken up and a single track to be laid in its stead 238

    Chambers street, from Centre street to Broadway, track in, directed to be removed................................ 243

    from Church street to West Broadway, Sixth Avenue Railroad Company authorized to lay a rail track in . 270, 271, 279

    Eighth Avenue Railroad Company authorized to lay a rail track in 281, 282, 300, 302

    Chatham street, Second Avenue Railroad Company authorized to lay rail tracks in 199, 200

    Third Avenue Railroad Company authorized to lay rail tracks in 207, 209, 217

    New York and Harlem Railroad Company authorized to lay rail tracks in 238, 240

    Third Avenue Railroad Company authorized to lay iron pavement between the rails on the up grades of.... 219

STREETS—Continued:

between Chambers and Pearl streets, Third Avenue Railroad Company directed to repair.................. 218

Chrystie street, from Grand to Houston street, Second Avenue Railroad Company authorized to lay a rail track in. 200

Church street, from Vesey to Chambers street, Eighth Avenue Railroad Company authorized to lay a rail track in. 281, 282, 300, 302

from Chambers to Canal street, Sixth Avenue Railroad Company authorized to lay a rail track in... 270, 271, 279

College place, Eighth Avenue Railroad Company authorized to lay a rail track in...................... 281, 282, 300, 302

Front street, from Peck slip to Roosevelt street, Second Avenue Railroad Company authorized to lay a rail track in. 200, 203

route of Second Avenue Railroad in, changed to South street 203

Gansevoort street, from Greenwich to Washington street, Ninth Avenue Railroad Company authorized to lay a rail track in.................................. 309, 312

Grand street, from Allen street to Bowery, Second Avenue Railroad Company authorized to lay rail tracks in ... 199, 200

Second Avenue Railroad Company directed to repair.. 203

Second Avenue Railroad Company directed to pay for a portion of pavement laid in 204

from Bowery to Centre street, New York and Harlem Railroad Company authorized to lay a rail track in. 238

Greenwich street, from Battery place to Gansevoort street, Ninth Avenue Railroad Company authorized to lay a rail track in.................................. 309, 312

Hoboken street, from Canal to West street, Hudson River Railroad Company authorized to lay a rail track in......... 324

STREETS—Continued :

    Hudson street, from Chambers to Canal street, Hudson River Railroad Company authorized to lay a rail track in 323

        track in, directed to be taken up and relaid with grooved rails 329, 331

        cars prohibited to be left standing in 330

        Hudson River Railroad Company directed to repair 330

        from Canal street to Eighth avenue, Eighth Avenue Railroad Company authorized to lay rail tracks in 267, 289, 292

        Eighth Avenue Railroad Company to pay a portion of the expense of paving, with Belgian pavement .. 305, 306, 315

    Oliver street, Second Avenue Railroad Company authorized to lay a rail track in 199

    Park row, Third Avenue Railroad Company authorized to lay rail tracks in 207, 217

        New York and Harlem Railroad Company authorized to lay rail tracks in 238, 240

    Pearl street, from Peck slip to Chatham street, Second Avenue Railroad Company authorized to lay a rail track in.. 200

    Roosevelt street, at South street, Second Avenue Railroad Company authorized to lay a rail track across 200

    South street, Second Avenue Railroad Company authorized to lay a rail track in 199, 203

    State street, Broadway, Second Avenue Railroad Company authorized to lay a rail track in 261, 263

    Thompson street, Sixth Avenue Railroad Company authorized to lay a rail track in 270, 271, 279

    Union place, New York and Harlem Railroad Company authorized to lay a rail track in 226

    Varick street, Sixth Avenue Railroad Company authorized to lay rail tracks in 279

STREETS—Continued:

Vesey street, from Broadway to College place, Eighth Avenue Railroad Company authorized to lay rail tracks in....... 281
282, 301, 302

from Broadway to Church street, resolution to set back curb and gutter stones in ...., 304

Eighth Avenue Railroad Company directed to place their rails in, as near to the curb as possible....... 304

Washington street, Ninth Avenue Railroad Company authorized to lay a rail track in............................ 309, 312

at the corner of Bethune street, track in, directed to be taken up, the filth cleared away, &c.............. 313

West street, Hudson River Railroad Company authorized to lay tracks in.................................. 317, 324

track in, directed to be taken up and relaid with grooved rails.. 329, 331

West Broadway, Sixth Avenue Railroad Company authorized to lay rail tracks in.............................. 279

Eighth Avenue Railroad Company authorized to lay rail tracks in............................... 267, 289, 292

Whitehall street, Broadway Railroad Company authorized to lay a rail track in................................ 261, 263

Wooster street, from Canal to Fourth street, Sixth Avenue Railroad Company authorized to lay a rail track in... 270, 271, 279

Fourth street, from Wooster street to Sixth avenue, Sixth Avenue Railroad Company authorized to lay a rail track in. 270, 271, 279

Sixth street, east of Bowery, New York and Harlem Railroad Company authorized to lay a rail track in............. 235

Fourteenth street, from West street to Eleventh avenue, Hudson River Railroad tracks to be laid in, when required by the Common Council....................... 318, 322

STREETS—Continued :

 Twenty-third street, between First and Second avenues, Second Avenue Railroad Company authorized to lay a rail track in.................................... 199

 Twenty-sixth street, from Fourth avenue 300 feet west, New York and Harlem Railroad Company authorized to lay a temporary track in............................. 242

 Thirty-fourth street, at intersection of Fourth avenue, New York and Harlem Railroad Company directed to construct a bridge.. 233

 Thirty-eighth street, at intersection of Fourth avenue, New York and Harlem Railroad Company directed to construct a bridge.. 233

 Forty-second street, between Fourth and Madison avenues, New York and Harlem Railroad Company authorized to lay rail tracks in 251

 from Eleventh avenue to North River, A. M. Allerton, Jr., & Co. authorized to lay a rail track in......... 334

 Fiftieth street, at intersection of Fourth avenue, New York and Harlem Railroad Company directed to restore the bridge.. 233

 Fifty-fourth street, between Eighth and Ninth avenues, Ninth Avenue Railroad Company authorized to lay rail tracks in...308, 316

 Seventieth street, at intersection of Fourth avenue, New York and Harlem Railroad Company directed to construct a bridge.. 253

 Seventy-ninth street, at intersection of Fourth avenue, New York and Harlem Railroad Company directed to construct a bridge.. 233

 Eighty-third street, at intersection of Fourth avenue, New York and Harlem Railroad Company directed to construct a bridge.. 243

STREETS—Continued:

Eighty-fourth street, at intersection of Fourth avenue, New York and Harlem Railroad Company directed to construct a bridge.. 243

Eighty-fifth street, at intersection of Fourth avenue, New York and Harlem Railroad Company directed to construct a bridge................................... 233, 255

Eighty-eighth street, at intersection of Fourth avenue, New York and Harlem Railroad Company directed to construct a bridge.. 243

Ninetieth street, at intersection of Fourth avenue, New York and Harlem Railroad Company directed to construct a bridge.. 246

One Hundred and Fourth street, at intersection of Fourth avenue, New York and Harlem Railroad Company directed to construct a bridge.......................... 245

One Hundred and Twenty-fifth street, from Fourth avenue to North River, New York and Harlem Railroad Company authorized to lay rail tracks in................ 220, 224

Arches and bridges to be constructed by the New York and Harlem Railroad Company at such intersections of, with their road as may in the opinion of the Common Council require it............................. 221

by the Hudson River Railroad Company at such intersections of, with their road as may in the opinion of the Common Council require it............... 318

that portion of the, lying between the outside rails of the Sixth Avenue Railroad authorized to be paved with small cobble stones.................................. 285

that portion of the, lying between the outside rails of the Eighth and Ninth Avenue Railroads authorized to be paved with small cobble stones...................306, 315

SUNKEN LOTS:

lying between Twelfth avenue and Hudson River and One Hundred and Thirtieth and One Hundred and Thirty-first streets, directed to be filled in by the Hudson River Railroad Company.................. 331

(T)

THIRD AVENUE RAILROAD:

Grant of franchise... 206
Grantees... 207
    obligations of................................207 to 212
        to comply in all matters relating to the road with the directions of the Common Council............... 208
        to enter into an agreement with the Mayor, Aldermen and Commonalty before the grant shall take effect. 208
        to become bound, under penalty, to keep a certain portion of the streets in good repair................ 207
        to place on the road new cars with the modern improvements.. 207
        to have free use in common with the Second Avenue Railroad Company of the tracks to be laid in the Bowery and Chatham street, from Grand to Pearl street.................................... 209
        to pay one-half of the expense of keeping the track used in common with the Second Avenue Railroad Company in repair................................. 209
    to form themselves into an association............. 210, 212
    rights, powers, and obligations of the association to be formed by....................................210 to 215

THIRD AVENUE RAILROAD—Continued :

    association to be formed by, to be styled the "Third Avenue Railroad Company".................... 212

Route defined... 207

Track, when to be commenced........................... 209

    when to be completed.............................209, 212

    additional time granted for the completion of, to Forty-second street................................... 217

    to be laid under the direction of the Street Commissioner....................................... 207

    to be laid on such grades as may be established by the Common Council............................. 207

    how the, shall be laid............................. 209

    rail used for, to be approved by the Street Commissioner....................................... 209

    authorized to be connected with that of the Second Avenue Railroad at the junction of the Bowery and Grand street................................ 209

    relative to the construction of the, from Pearl and Chatham streets to Bowery and Grand street........... 206

Cars to be used upon the............................... 207

    to be licensed....................................... 210

    time of running the, specified...................... 208

Motive power to be used................................. 207

Fare to be charged.................................208, 212

THIRD AVENUE RAILROAD COMPANY :

    of whom to be constituted............ ..210, 212, 213, 215

    relative to the time and mode of organization........212, 213

    to have power to make contracts for the purchase of property for the use or benefit of their road.......... 210

THIRD AVENUE RAILROAD COMPANY—Continued:

  may be incorporated under the general railroad act..210, 216

  not to be dissolved by the death or act of any of the associates..210, 215

Title.. 212

Capital, relative to estimating and declaring the amount required... 213

  relative to the mode of subscribing for, and the time of paying in subscriptions........................... 213

  how original, may be subscribed for................ 214

  how additional, may be subscribed for.............. 214

Individual rights and interests of members, conditioned upon the strict observance of the provisions, &c., contained in the agreement with the Mayor, Aldermen and Commonalty..210, 211

  to be forfeited upon refusal or neglect to subscribe or pay..213, 214

  to be forfeited in case of failure to fulfill the conditions of the agreement with the City, or of the by-laws of the Company..................................210, 211

  how to be reinstated in case of forfeiture.............. 215

  how to be proportioned............................. 215

Transfers of shares or interests, how and when to be made....... 215

Rules and by-laws, how and by whom to be made............210, 213

  how to be altered.................................. 214

Persons becoming associates to become parties to the agreement with the Mayor, Aldermen and Commonalty...... 215

Provisions in case of the death or insolvency of any member of the company....................................210, 215

Granted additional time for the completion of their road below Forty-second street............................. 217

THIRD AVENUE RAILROAD COMPANY—Continued :

    Petition of, for permission to build a portico and balcony to their new depot, granted................................. 218

    Directed to cause Chatham street, from Pearl to Chambers street, to be repaired according to the terms of their agreement.. 218

    put in good repair all the pavements in and about their rails, under penalty............................ 218

    Permitted to lay iron pavement on the up grades in Chatham street... 219

    To pay a proportion of the expense of laying Belgian pavement in Third avenue, from Fifty-sixth to Eighty-sixth street.. 219

(V)

VAN SCHAICK, MYNDERT, AND OTHERS :

    grant of a franchise to, for a railroad through Third avenue and other streets........................ 206

(W)

WALL :

    directed to be built on each side of the New York and Harlem Railroad, from Thirty-second to Forty-second street.. 236

    directed to be built on each side of the New York and Harlem Railroad, from Eighty-fourth to Ninety-second street..233, 235

www.ingramcontent.com/pod-product-compliance
Lightning Source LLC
Chambersburg PA
CBHW051232300426
44114CB00011B/711